Also by Mark Hyman

Washington Babylon: From George Washington to Donald Trump,
Scandals that Rocked the Nation

PARDONGATE

How Bill & Hillary Clinton and Their Brothers Profited from Pardons

MARK HYMAN

Post Hill PRESS

A POST HILL PRESS BOOK
ISBN: 978-1-64293-628-5
ISBN (eBook): 978-1-64293-629-2

Pardongate:
How Bill & Hillary Clinton and Their Brothers Profited from Pardons
© 2020 by Mark Hyman
All Rights Reserved

Post Hill Press
New York • Nashville
posthillpress.com

Published in the United States of America

*This book is dedicated to Julie, Chris, Jenn, Kelly, and Kyle,
whose love makes each day special.*

TABLE OF CONTENTS

A NOTE TO THE READER

THE PUBLIC IS skeptical. And it should be. There is so much information that is available nowadays and separating fact from fiction can be challenging. Previously well-respected newspapers have become propagandists for one cause or another. Some network and cable news outlets have been caught selectively editing or even doctoring videos. Other news outlets have been guilty of misstating or ignoring inconvenient facts, and citing non-credible, and perhaps even non-existent, anonymous sources in order to support their narratives.

Some news outlets have been victimized by false reporting. Others have been complicit in it. The public has every right to be jaded about who or what to trust.

You may notice that I have used what some may consider an excessive number of endnotes. An endnote (or footnote) is generally used to provide amplifying information or to attribute the use of another's material. I have used endnotes to do just that. In addition, I have added endnotes to aid the reader to easily find many of the facts and sources I have used in this book. I want the reader to be confident in the truthfulness and accuracy of what is written in these pages.

You have every right to be skeptical. Skepticism is healthy and helps build a better, more accurate narrative of historical events, especially if the author is accountable.

While I have strived to make this book completely accurate, I realize mistakes do occur. If you find a mistake, I ask you to bring it to my attention using the "Contact" page on my personal website: http://www. markhyman.tv. Please include a citation with the correct information. You can also find a complete index for this book at the same website.

FOREWORD

GEORGE WASHINGTON, WE are told, could not tell a lie. Hillary Clinton, who has repeatedly sought the office Washington once held, cannot seem to tell the truth. I have followed her dishonesty for decades—yes, decades. Her mendacity and cavalier attitude toward what we call the rule of law make her unfit for the presidency, the vice presidency, or dogcatcher in a town without dogs.

Modern-day politicians tell two types of lies. The first we can call BS-ing. That is to say, lies that are exaggerations, lies that cover up a temporary memory lapse, and, of course, lies about loving everyone in whatever state you happen to be campaigning in. Other lies are more serious. Hillary tells both kinds of lies. For instance, lying about her landing in Bosnia under enemy fire back in the 1990s. As for the more serious lies, consider a sampling of the lies that were found on her private email server and exposed to the public.

Thanks to Hillary's private server we know that the night of the September 2012 Benghazi attack when she was secretary of state she told her daughter the truth about the attack. To Chelsea she wrote, "Two of our officers were killed in Benghazi by an Al Queda-like [sic] group." Afterward, she told the American people a boldfaced lie, which she kept repeating. She said the deaths were caused by a video containing "inflammatory material posted on the Internet." Moreover, days later when the bodies of the murdered American diplomats and security personnel were returned to Andrews Air Force Base Hillary repeated her lie, first to Patricia Smith, the mother of Sean Smith whose coffin lay nearby on the tarmac. Then to Charles Woods whose son, Tyrone, was also one of the fallen.

There is no debate about this. These are just a few of the lies Hillary has told in pursuit of high office. She has not only told an abundance of lies, but thanks to her server, which she thought her IT people had wiped clean, the lies have been preserved—like the DNA on Monica Lewinsky's dress.

Hillary served up an illuminating concatenation of such lies in the summer of 2016 when she lied in her interview with the FBI. She repeated the lies she uttered months before in testimony before Congress and that she would repeat to the American public subsequently. All these lies were discovered thanks to her modern, high-tech server. Hillary's server proved to be for Hillary what Monica Lewinsky's DNA bespattered dress was for Bill Clinton, to wit: high-tech evidence that the Clintons are inveterate liars. The Clintons lie when they don't have to, and they tell an enormous rococo whopper when a little white lie would be perfectly satisfactory. Their lies about the pardons and commutations are nothing new.

Hillary's demonstrated lies to the FBI and to the Congress could make her the first candidate for high office to be ineligible to hold a security clearance. All major polls in recent years confirm that the American people consider her "untrustworthy." Consider her concatenation of lies in the summer of 2016 when she was running for the presidency.

Hillary told the FBI on July 2, 2016—as she had previously testified to Congress on October 22, 2015—that she had never sent nor received information that was "classified" on her private server.

In subsequent testimony before Congress on July 7, 2016, FBI Director James Comey said her statements were untrue.

She lied again when she told Fox News that Comey had agreed with her that her testimony was "truthful." He did not.

Also on July 2nd, Hillary told the FBI—as she had earlier testified to Congress—that she had belatedly returned all her work-related emails to the government after her lawyers had gone "through every single email." Director Comey said this statement, too, was not truthful.

Incidentally, we now have tens of thousands of documents discovered by Freedom of Information Act requests proving that she lied about their nature and with her staff's help attempted to hide many of these emails from discovery.

Hillary's earliest statement to the American people about her server was in March 2015, and it was a lie. She said she had used a home server so she would not have to suffer the inconvenience of carrying more than one digital device. Comey said she used multiple devices. Every time she has trotted out this statement she has been lying. She repeated the lies in her testimony before Congress in October 2015 and in her statements to the FBI the following July.

For nearly thirty years, Hillary has complained she has been the victim of a vast right-wing conspiracy, but that does not explain her ordeals with the FBI. She has had run-ins with them for decades, and few would call the FBI partisan. It began in Arkansas in the 1980s with FBI Special Agent I. C. Smith questioning her role in fund-raising for her husband. It continued in the 1990s, coming to a boil in 1997 when FBI Director Louis Freeh, responded to a question in a Congressional hearing if he had ever experienced anything like the FBI's interactions with the Clintons. He responded, "Actually I have." And he likened his dealing with the Clintons to his "16 years doing organized crime cases in New York City." I am not the first to liken Hillary to a career criminal. There's also FBI Director Freeh.

Perhaps Hillary's trials reached a climax the summer of 2016 with Director Comey. Comey may not have recommended her indictment as many observers thought he would, but he most emphatically told Congress she had lied to the Bureau during her interview.

From her server we now know that she mishandled intelligence documents and co-mingled her Clinton Foundation work with State Department responsibilities—and concealed it. Director Comey said she lacked the sophistication to discern "classified" from "unclassified" documents. He called her behavior "extremely careless." With the Clinton Foundation, her term as a senator, and her tenure as secretary of state, Hillary and Bill built a vast personal fortune in a very short time using pay-to-play tactics. They personally amassed an estimated $240 million since leaving the White House and you will see how they have accomplished it in the following pages. No first family has ever accumulated so much money so fast from so many donors, foreign, domestic, and often common criminals.

As editor-in-chief of *The American Spectator*, I am uniquely familiar with Hillary's record of concealing evidence. It did not start with her server. It started at least forty years earlier.

Today's vanishing emails were preceded in the 1980s and 1990s by the vanishing papers documenting the Clintons' Whitewater real estate dealings and the disappearance of Hillary's Rose Law Firm billing records in the White House family quarters.

After White House Deputy Counsel Vince Foster, a former Rose Law Firm partner, committed suicide in northern Virginia's Fort Marcy Park there was a race for the papers stored in his office. It was believed by Congress and by the Office of Independent Counsel that these documents would have implicated Hillary deeply in Whitewater, for which her real estate partners, James and Susan McDougal, went to federal prison. By the time Congress and the Independent Counsel subpoenaed the documents they had vanished. Two years later, the documents miraculously turned up laying out in the open in the Clintons' family quarters. And this is rich. They had Hillary's fingerprints on them.

The mystery of the Rose Law Firm billing records was not as strange to me as it apparently was to other reporters. Down in Little Rock we witnessed a lot of documents disappear. One of our sleuths actually went drinking with a fellow who, when not drinking with him, was spending his nights at the Rose Law Firm destroying records.

Nor is Hillary's co-mingling of her Clinton Foundation affairs with her State Department work without precedent. Recall if you will the Clintons' renting out the Lincoln Bedroom for fundraising purposes, occasionally to representatives of foreign governments—the Riady family of Indonesia comes to mind—and donations from the Chinese military. Or for that matter the Clintons selling pardons and commutations as they left the White House. You will read about that in the pages ahead. I wrote about it years ago, but now in this book, *Pardongate: How Bill & Hillary and Their Brothers Profited from Pardons*, Mark has done a masterful job bringing us all up to speed with new revelations.

Has America ever seen an operation like the Clintons before? Well, FBI Director Freeh answered that question when he compared them to an organized crime family. No one sued Director Freeh.

—R. Emmett "Bob" Tyrrell Jr.

PREFACE

"They were about pardons—desperate pleas from thieves and embezzlers and liars, some still in jail and some who'd never served time but who nonetheless wanted their good names cleared and their beloved rights restored. All claimed to be friends, or friends of friends, or die-hard supporters, though only a few had ever gotten the chance to proclaim their support before the eleventh hour.... Which thieves should be allowed to steal again? That was the momentous question facing the President as the hours crept by."[1]

JUSTICE HAD A price. The politically connected and the financially well-off were able to buy executive clemency from President William Jefferson Clinton. Although only Bill Clinton held the power to actually grant pardons and commutations, the adult members of his family were major participants in Pardongate. The entire Clinton clan—Bill, Hillary, First Brother Roger and First Brothers-in-Law Hugh and Tony Rodham—got into the act. Everyone profited financially or politically from Bill Clinton dishing out pardons and commutations. The most influential figure behind the most shocking clemency decisions was Hillary.

There was also more-than-ample involvement from the entire Clinton network. The sheer number of Clinton friends, fundraisers, campaign officials, business associates, cronies, appointees, political insiders, and current and former staffers who were directly involved in the scandalous clemencies is beyond words. "Chicanery is a genetic strain in that enormous extended family called Friends of

Bill," observed a Durham, North Carolina *Herald-Sun* editorial. The pardons of the Bill and Hillary Clinton era certainly underscored the chicanery at play. By making pardons and commutations a profit-sharing business for his wife and their three brothers, Bill Clinton stood the entire clemency process on its head.

Preferential treatment was given to friends and "friends of friends." Clinton family considerations also took center stage. Conflicts of interest and ethical shortfalls were the hallmark of a dizzying number of the Clinton clemency decisions. Overall, the Clintons knew no shame when it came to dishing out pardons to anyone who had the right connections. In the end, most connections were those that directly and indirectly benefited the Clintons. Because Bill was leaving elected office, the chief beneficiary of the pardon peddling was Hillary, who was only just launching her political career.

Major Clinton supporters who were involved in egregious pardon decisions included political activist Jesse Jackson, Boston fundraiser Thomas Dwyer, William Cunningham, who served as campaign treasurer for Hillary's first Senate race, and Democrat Party fundraising chair Beth Dozoretz. Denise Rich, a particularly close insider of Bill and Hillary who funneled more than three million dollars to the Clintons and their causes, was key to one of the most atrocious pardons in American history. Bank of America CEO Hugh McColl had a close friend pardoned only days after McColl announced a $500,000 contribution to the William J. Clinton Presidential Library and Museum.

Giving absolutely no consideration to the obvious conflicts of interest, current and former Clinton staffers were active in the lobbying for pardons. Among them were David Dreyer, former White House communications deputy, longtime Clinton operative Harold Ickes, former White House counsels Bernard Nussbaum and Jack Quinn, and White House Chief of Staff John Podesta. Justice Department officials including Deputy Attorney General Eric Holder and US Attorney Alejandro Mayorkas were complicit in shameful pardon decisions.

A steady stream of influential Democrat politicians also played prominent roles in springing free countless felons or in wiping clean their criminal records. Some of the more widely known were Senator Christopher Dodd (Connecticut), former New York governor Mario Cuomo, Congressman Jerrold Nadler of New York, Clinton Education Secretary Richard Riley, and Antonio Villaraigosa, the former California Assembly speaker who was elected Los Angeles mayor.

There were lesser known but equally influential Democrats whose support would be sought as Hillary Clinton made her run for the presidency in 2008 that were also accomplices in the pardon factory. They were Gloria Molina, who served as vice chair of the 2000 Democrat National Convention, Salt Lake City Mayor "Rocky" Anderson, New York City Councilman Jose Rivera, California Senator Richard Polanco, US Representative Xavier Becerra (California) and Congressman Sam Gejdenson (Connecticut), just to name a few. Philip Grandmaison, the former chairman of the New Hampshire Democrat Party and an eight-year Clinton appointee as the Director of the US Trade and Development Agency, was a key supporter for Hillary to have when she participated in New Hampshire's first-in-the nation presidential primary. Grandmaison's brother received a Clinton pardon.

There were plenty of politically active lawyers who participated in various Clinton political activities including fundraising, campaign support, legal representation, or had worked alongside the Clintons at some point during their careers. Among them were James Lyons, who was behind the infamous Lyons Report, an unsuccessful attempt to exonerate the Clintons in the Whitewater scandal that was released during the 1992 campaign, Reid Weingarten, who represented countless Clinton associates in several fundraising scandals, James Hamilton who served alongside Hillary in 1974 during the Watergate hearings, Kendall Coffey, the former US attorney in

Clinton's Justice Department who was fired for biting a stripper in a Miami strip club, and the scandal-plagued William Kennedy, who was Hillary's longtime partner at the Rose Law Firm.

Close Clinton friends inextricably involved in clemencies or with clemency recipients underscored the sheer amount of cronyism at play. Douglas Eakeley was Bill's roommate at Yale and Oxford. He parlayed that relationship into a pardon for a client. Harry Thomason was the Hollywood executive who (along with his wife) virtually lived at the White House during the Clintons' first year. He made successful pardon arrangements for friends. Dan Lasater was one of the closest and most loyal of the Clintons' Arkansas supporters. He also happened to have been a convicted drug felon. Some of his cocaine chums, including First Brother Roger Clinton, received pardons. Simply by asking Clinton, Jesse Jackson got clemency for three colleagues, including one who had a sexual relationship with a fifteen-year-old. The recipients did not even bother submitting clemency petitions to the Justice Department.

Still, there were other well-known Clinton supporters who wanted felons freed from prison or completely pardoned. Some of these people were Walter Cronkite, Lady Bird Johnson, and Abraham Foxman of the Anti-Defamation League. Perhaps the most notorious were Hillary's brothers, Hugh and Tony Rodham, and Bill's half-brother, Roger. All three brothers made hundreds of thousands of dollars from both successful and unsuccessful pardon efforts. They cashed in handsomely on Bill's constitutional prerogative.

The pardon scandal that erupted as Bill and Hillary packed up government-owned furnishings for their move to Chappaqua, New York should not have been a surprise to anyone who had been paying attention. The eight-year White House tenure of Bill and Hillary Clinton was marked by influence peddling from the very beginning to the very end. On Bill's very first day in office, Hugh and Tony Rodham attempted to shake down lobbyists, corporations, and organizations seeking to curry favor with the forty-second president by asking them to underwrite a lavish inaugural party at the Renaissance Mayflower Hotel in downtown Washington, DC. The Rodham boys threw a for-profit party, although the brothers fell short in the financial arrangements and the Democratic National Committee was stuck with paying off the event's debts.

On Clinton's very last day in office, Hugh and Tony were still at it, benefiting from the largesse of Bill handing out pardons to those felons who generously paid the Rodham brothers to have their prison records wiped clean. In the very middle of the entire fiasco was Hillary Rodham Clinton, the family matriarch who, at times, turned a blind eye to it, and, at other times, was complicit in the Rodhams' equivalent of launching a pardon yard sale.

Pardons and commutations are universally recognized as being given in truly exceptional situations. They denote official forgiveness by the government toward certain deserving individuals convicted of committing crimes. Clemency removes some of the stigma of being a convicted felon. A pardon can also restore certain rights, such as voting or gun ownership, and allows convicts to obtain certain professional or recreational licenses. In the instances in which a pardon recipient is convicted yet again, the pardon will allow a sympathetic courtroom to view the recidivist criminal as a first-time offender. This very set of circumstances occurred with more than one lucky Clinton pardon recipient.

There are established Justice Department guidelines to be followed for every application to ensure a basic level of qualification before an individual receives serious consideration for clemency. There are five major issues to be considered by the Justice Department's pardon attorney before forwarding a favorable recommendation to the president. These include the applicant's post-conviction conduct, character, and reputation. First, has the applicant "demonstrated [an] ability to lead a responsible and productive life"? Second, the seriousness and recentness of the offense are to be considered in order to "avoid denigrating the seriousness of the offense or undermining the deterrent effect of the conviction." Third, the applicant must accept "responsibility, remorse and atonement" for committing the offense. Clemency is "[official] forgiveness rather than vindication." Fourth, does the applicant have a demonstrated need for relief? Pardon attorney guidelines note that a compelling need to restore employment licenses or bonding may make the difference in an otherwise marginal case. Lastly, input from "concerned and knowledgeable officials" is required. This is to allow prosecutors, trial judges, prison officials, parole officers, and victims to comment and/or make recommendations, either favorable or unfavorable.

Justice Department reviews also include a rigorous criminal background check. This is to ensure an intended recipient has been forthright and honest in the clemency application and has led a law-abiding life since the commission of earlier crimes.

The Clinton family, staff, and friends of Bill skipped the due diligence and circumvented the established DOJ procedures by appealing directly to Bill to issue clemency *without any* legal and criminal review. In dozens of cases, Clinton awarded pardons and commutations to individuals who did not even seek them and had therefore never submitted an application that would have undergone scrutiny to ascertain the facts. Others refused to accept responsibility for their crimes, a key component before gaining consideration.

One pardon recipient engaged in illegal conduct only days after receiving his pardon. In another case, Clinton gave a pardon to a felon, represented by Hillary's brother Hugh Rodham, who was the subject of an ongoing federal investigation of further criminal wrongdoing. Rodham's client later pleaded guilty to crimes related to those for which Clinton gave him a pardon.

Most of the attention regarding presidential pardons and commutations handed out by Clinton toward the end of his presidency was focused on the 176 he doled out literally in the dead of night only hours before George W. Bush was sworn in as the forty-third president. Forty-seven recipients, or nearly one in three, did not have a current application filed with the Department of Justice at the time Clinton pardoned them or issued commutations. Thirty recipients had not submitted a clemency application at all. Another fourteen had previously filed applications, but Clinton had denied clemency. Two more lucky recipients had filed applications with the Justice Department, but they were deemed ineligible because they did not meet the bare minimum requirement of having waited five years since their release from imprisonment. Inexplicably, they all received executive clemency from Clinton.

The process became so absurd during the final hours that the pardon attorney had to resort to conducting internet searches, looking for news stories of criminal involvement, to determine an applicant's fitness for clemency. Dozens of the last-minute pardons and commutations were clearly undeserving. Some of those inappropriate clemency decisions were more scandalous than others.

The Clinton White House executed a sharp break from the Justice Department standards and historical precedent and began issuing pardons and commutations to individuals who were defiant rather than contrite and remorseful. Several refused to acknowledge, let alone accept, responsibility for their crimes, a key component of DOJ guidelines in order to be considered for pardons or commutations.

Executive clemency was bestowed upon those who did not ask for it and for whom Clinton's White House lawyers, the pardon attorney, Clinton's Justice Department, prosecuting attorneys, trial judges, and victims of the crimes (including crimes of violence) felt were unworthy of being pardoned or in having their sentences commuted. In every known instance, victims were never given the opportunity to voice their opinions or enter into the deliberative process the impact the crimes had on their lives.

Not surprisingly, Clinton doled out pardons and commutations to dozens who had inside connections with the Clintons, or had showered the Clinton family with money, gifts and political influence.

Time and time again, the Clintons and Rodhams enriched themselves by abusing the presidential clemency process.

Countless questions that arose regarding the flurry of last-minute pardons went unanswered. Information trickled out slowly in the months after Bill and Hillary left Washington, DC with Clinton and Rodham family members expressing shock and surprise with each new revelation. Each time they were questioned, answers from William Jefferson and Hillary Rodham Clinton did not square with the facts.

There were other executive clemency actions in addition to those handed down on January 20, 2001, that were equally appalling. Executive clemency that Clinton irresponsibly gave away started with his commutations of the sentences of a dozen Puerto Rican terrorists who were guilty of a decade's worth of murder and domestic terrorism.

Bill Clinton received nearly four thousand petitions for executive clemency from the day he took office until January 1999. Compared with every president since George Washington, Clinton was stingy in approving clemency requests. Of the 3,923 requests received during his first six years in office, every petitioner was left empty-handed except for seventy-seven. The fifty-six Clinton approved during his first term were the fewest of any president since Thomas Jefferson, the nation's third commander-in-chief when the US had a population of only five million.

Clinton's rejection rate was a stunning 98 percent. That is, until Hillary Rodham Clinton decided she wanted to run for the seat of New York's retiring US Senator Daniel Patrick Moynihan. Then, everything changed.

When it was clear Hillary would run for the US Senate, Bill dished out clemency to the dozen domestic terrorists and he gave them the luxury of a month to decide to accept his offer of freedom in return for the simple agreement of not returning to a life of committing terrorism. The terrorists were conflicted and took the entire month before electing to accept the proffered clemency.

Another purely political clemency opportunity went to the spectacularly undeserving Carlos Vignali. The Los Angeleno was a major drug kingpin whose drug operation conspired to ship eight hundred pounds of powder cocaine from Los Angeles to Minneapolis to be processed into crack cocaine.

Clinton commuted Vignali's sentence after he served just five years in prison. What apparently turned the clemency request in Vignali's favor was the more than $200,000 that was paid to Hillary's brother, Hugh Rodham, for Hugh to lobby Bill for the commutation.

Although a lawyer, Hugh Rodham did not prepare Vignali's clemency petition. That was someone else's job. Rodham's sole assignment was to ensure Vignali had his sentence cut short. On this task, he succeeded quite nicely. Both Bill and Hillary avoided directly addressing the extent of their knowledge of Hugh's selling White House access to clemency applicants.

Rodham also successfully represented A. Glenn Braswell Sr., an unrehabilitated direct mail con artist who was under scrutiny by the Food and Drug Administration, the Federal Trade Commission, and the US Postal Service, and who was actively being investigated by the US Attorney's Office and the Internal Revenue Service at the time he applied for clemency. He, too, paid Rodham a $200,000 "success fee" to arrange for a pardon. Clinton gave him one.

Is one to believe that Bill and Hillary thought that Hugh just happened to work on behalf of a convicted drug kingpin who lived on the opposite coast, or that he represented a multimillion-dollar swindler who was under ongoing criminal and regulatory scrutiny, and that Rodham did so without receiving any financial remuneration? Observers have long claimed that both Bill and Hillary are exceptionally intelligent individuals, yet America's premier power couple wanted the public to believe they blindly accepted, without asking any questions whatsoever, the premise that Hugh was simply doing good deeds for people he didn't even know.

Perhaps what Bill and Hillary Clinton needed was a $29.95 bottle of Memory Caps that Braswell's company was pushing on unsuspecting consumers. According to the supplement magnate's website, "With Memory Caps, you can hold onto your memory once and for all."[2]

If the Clintons had taken Memory Caps, then perhaps they would not have forgotten conversations they had with Hugh, Tony, and Roger regarding their pardon-brokering shenanigans. In addition, Bill and Hillary might have remembered to add their Whitewater investment to their required financial disclosure after Bill declared his candidacy. Somehow, they inadvertently, and conveniently, omitted any mention of the failed multimillion-dollar venture. Hillary could have also remembered where she squirreled away the subpoenaed Rose Law Firm billing records, which remained "lost" in the White House residential quarters for more than two years after they were subpoenaed and more than four years after it was apparent that Whitewater was going to become an epic political scandal.

Hillary's youngest brother, Tony Rodham, told Bill that he worked for Edgar and Vonna Jo Gregory, bank fraud convicts, while he was aggressively advocating for pardons on their behalf. Yet, the genius Clinton never stopped Tony in mid-sentence and asked him to explain in what capacity Rodham worked for the Gregorys. The fact alone that Rodham was receiving money from the Gregorys should have set off alarm bells and caused Clinton to untangle himself from the obvious ethical dilemma of passing out pardons to the clients of Hillary's brother.

The good news for Bill and Hillary was they did not have to concern themselves with ethical dilemmas as they had long ago freed themselves from the restraint of conscience. Bill Clinton asked no questions of his wife's youngest brother regarding his financial relationship with the Gregorys and allowed Tony to plow ahead with pushing for pardons. The younger Rodham's pardon-seeking effort was a successful one at that.

There have been other presidents who had embarrassing relatives. Lyndon Johnson's younger brother Sam Johnson was a notorious alcoholic who was virtually kept under house arrest by the Secret Service on the orders of LBJ. Richard Nixon's brother Donald was a failed fast-food restaurateur caught up in a loan fiasco. Jimmy Carter had his beer-swigging brother, Billy, who tried to lobby US officials while on the payroll of the Libyan government. Ronald Reagan had son, Ron, and daughter, Patti, who were open about their break with their parents and demonstrated it with embarrassing antics. Even in death, John Kennedy has endured more than four decades of embarrassment from brother, Ted Kennedy, the town drunk of Capitol Hill. Then there were Bill and Hillary Clinton.

Bill and Hillary's siblings were three of life's losers: a Clinton and two Rodhams. There was the hapless Roger Clinton, a college dropout, cocaine-dealing addict, part-time no-talent singer and full-time freeloader, who successfully marketed his ties to half-brother Bill. His career highlights include roles in several B-movies such as *Pumpkinhead II: Blood Wings*, in which he played the role of Mayor Bubba and he had a stint as a "gofer" on a Hollywood TV set. Competing for the title of First Freeloader were Hillary's two brothers, Hugh and Tony Rodham.

The eldest of the two Rodham boys was Hugh, known affectionately as "Hughie" by those close to him. He was an obese, slovenly dressed lout who appeared to fail at nearly everything in his life, from Peace Corps volunteer work to radio talk show hosting to assistant public defending to entrepreneurship. Hugh became a political punch line for his embarrassing run for the Senate in 1994 when he lost in a landslide to Florida's Connie Mack.

Similarly, younger brother Tony eked out a living bouncing from job to job. A college dropout and sometimes marijuana user, Rodham was at various times in the metal equipment manufacturing business, in insurance sales, a prison guard, a private detective, a process server, a Democrat National Committee staffer, and he worked a stint as a repo man. He even failed at his attempt at a "power marriage" to the daughter of California Senator Barbara Boxer. His estranged wife accused him of being a deadbeat dad for not meeting timely child support obligations, claiming he fell behind in payments by as much as six months.[3]

Their failings aside, Hugh and Tony Rodham still had one tremendous business asset: Hillary Rodham Clinton. "You're not doing enough for your brothers," was the constant refrain Hillary received from her mother right up through the White House years.[4] In spite of her mother's harping on the topic, the fact of the matter was that Hillary was continually supporting her brothers in their wild and wacky business ventures through both tacit and explicit approval.

To suggest Hillary is embarrassed by her brothers' antics is an understatement. In her 562-page autobiography *Living History*, Hillary wrote more references about the long-deceased Eleanor Roosevelt (died in 1962) whom Hillary *never* met than she wrote of either of her brothers. Often, her only references to the Rodham boys were fleeting mentions of "my brothers."

Hillary did everything she could to distance herself from one egregious clemency decision to the next after each became public. She claimed she had no role in her husband's pardon of fugitive billionaire Marc Rich, whose ex-wife Denise had generously contributed to several of Hillary's causes, including giving $10,000 to her legal defense fund and $120,000 to her political campaign and then showering Hillary with gifts. Rich and business partner Pincus Green fled the US ahead of a fifty-one-count federal indictment for tax evasion and other crimes, including trading with the enemy that could have led to a sentence of 325 years in prison.

Five days after Clinton pardoned Rich, he was at it again. Rich's company was buying oil from worldwide pariah Saddam Hussein as part of Iraq's corrupt Oil-for-Food program.[5]

For her part, the "copresident" was miraculously ignorant of any aspect or detail of dozens of undeserving pardons including those that directly benefited her. (There is no doubt Hillary thought of herself as the copresident. During the 1992 campaign, Bill told a New Hampshire crowd that by electing him they would "buy one, get one free." Hillary later wrote, "It was a good line, and *my* campaign staff adopted it" [emphasis added].[6] Bill was the declared the presidential candidate, but in Hillary's mind it was *her* campaign staff.)

Hillary claimed "she had passed 'many, many' pardon requests to the president's staff without inspecting them."[7] That statement alone defies credulity. It was Hillary who said, "[Bill] and I *always talk about everything*. I'm not going to talk about the process. Anyone who knows us knows that *we work together on everything*" [emphasis added].[8]

The most-involved First Lady in the day-to-day affairs of the presidency in American history was suddenly and completely uninvolved in her husband's most crucial, final-hour decisions, she claimed. Yet Hillary never made a complete, unqualified, and unequivocal denial of having any knowledge of her two brothers' pardon activities or her husband's clemency decisions. She cleverly couched her words and offered carefully nuanced statements. As the *New York Times* editorial board observed following her remarks distancing herself from Hugh's pardons involvement, "Mrs. Clinton's press conference yesterday was smoothly performed but evaded the key issues.... [S]he expressed her disappointment about the way events have 'unfolded,' as if she were talking about the weather."[9]

Hillary acted surprised when her husband freed from prison Linda Sue Evans and Susan Lisa Rosenberg, a pair of domestic terrorists who were embroiled in a trail of murders, bombings, and robberies in the 1970s and 1980s. These terrorists supported a particularly violent offshoot of the Black Panthers, an organization that Hillary personally supported in 1971 when she directed groups of supporters during the trial of eight Black Panthers who gruesomely tortured and killed one of their own.

It goes without saying that few were surprised when Clinton issued pardons to figures from the Whitewater scandal that nearly dragged down the Clintons shortly after they took office. A strong criminal case was never made against the Clintons, yet there is little doubt the entire story was never told. The fact that the Clintons did not include any mention of their financial stake in Whitewater in their mandatory financial disclosures after entering the presidential race underscores that they believed *something* was seriously wrong with the failed venture and that explains their reason for trying to hide their involvement. The Clinton campaign chalked up the blatant omission to a mere oversight by amending the disclosure when word leaked about their Whitewater involvement.

Even critics can easily understand Clinton's pardon of his half-brother for a 1980s conviction for cocaine dealing. "If you can't give your brother a pardon," wrote Steve Dunleavy of the *New York Post*, "who can you pardon?" As in the case of Glenn Braswell, Roger Clinton was under active investigation by the Federal Bureau of Investigation and that fact alone should have immediately disqualified him from any consideration of a pardon for dealing drugs. Nevertheless, Bill Clinton pardoned him.

Yet the real scandalous aspect of Roger Clinton's involvement in the pardon fiasco may not have been his own pardon, but of his willingness to brazenly hustle several felons, promising to deliver pardons and commutations in return for steep payments.

Roger fell short in freeing all his "close" friends from prison or in getting pardons for them, even in the cases in which he was paid to arrange favorable clemency decisions. His failure to deliver results was a continuation of his life: he was the hapless Roger Clinton. And he didn't have Hillary Rodham Clinton as his sister to ensure he got what he wanted. Bill Clinton only had to weather Roger's disappointment in not fulfilling Roger's pardon requests. On the other hand, Bill would have had to deal with the anger and wrath of Hillary if he didn't acquiesce to *her* brothers' demands. Roger did not get his clients pardoned; Hugh and Tony Rodham's clients got the freedom for which the Rodham boys were handsomely paid.

Everyone in the Clinton-Rodham family profited in one manner or another from the sale of pardons, but none profited more than Hillary Rodham Clinton. Bill Clinton had nothing to gain. After all, he did not have any elections ahead of him. He was on his way out of the most powerful office in the world and into retirement where he would no doubt make millions of dollars giving speeches and possibly sitting on a few corporate boards. Giving away undeserved pardons did not personally benefit him in any meaningful way. In fact, he stood to damage his legacy by issuing inappropriate pardons and commutations.

In the year 2000, Bill Clinton's career in electoral politics was drawing to an end. This was not the case for Hillary. She was finally launching her own long-delayed political career and she desperately needed financial and political capital. She no longer aspired to be an unelected "copresident." She wanted to become *the* president. However, she had to first win her New York Senate race and the election outcome was far from a foregone conclusion. Pardons to wealthy or influential New Yorkers were just the elixir.

Those close to Hillary also profited handsomely. William Cunningham III, Hillary's Senate campaign treasurer, made more than $4,000 when he filed expedited pardon applications on behalf of two men from Arkansas less than one week before Clinton left office. Not surprisingly, the Cunningham-prepared pardon applications got head-of-the-line privileges despite being filed only a few days before Clinton left office. Yet, only Hillary Clinton could claim with a straight face that Cunningham's clients were treated no differently than the thousands of other clemency applications that were filed ahead of his, but were never favorably acted upon or even reviewed by Clinton.

Jim Manning and Robert Clinton Fain, who were referred to Cunningham by Harold Ickes, a longtime confidant and political operative of Hillary, received pardons from Clinton. In contrast, 7,032 clemency petitioners who did not have close ties to the Clintons and had properly filed their applications months or years in advance did not receive pardons or commutations.

Felons who had deep political ties to Bill and Hillary also benefited from Clinton's executive clemency largesse. Disgraced Chicago former congressman Mel Reynolds, who committed bank fraud, wire fraud, conspiracy to defraud the Federal Election Commission, making false statements to federal investigators, and was also convicted in Illinois state court for the criminal sexual assault of a fifteen-year-old campaign worker and various related charges, was freed. Jesse Jackson not only asked Clinton to free Reynolds from prison, but he also hired Reynolds to work for him at the Operation PUSH/Rainbow Coalition.

One month after he left office, Bill Clinton attempted to defend his clemency decisions in a rambling 1600-word *New York Times* op-ed filled with half-truths, distortions, and outright lies.

He claimed he made his decisions based "on the merits as I saw them." Yet nearly one-third of the eleventh-hour pardons and commutations he gave out as he left office did not even have petitions properly filed. On what "merits" did he decide to issue the pardons and commutations when no merits, details, or facts were even put forward? Some of the recipients were surprised at receiving clemency since they did not even request it.

Clinton wrote, "I regret that Mr. [Eric] Holder [deputy attorney general] did not have more time to review the case [of Marc Rich]." However, Clinton failed to acknowledge that it was Holder who purposely withheld the pardon application from receiving timely and appropriate Justice Department scrutiny. He also claimed he "required them [Marc Rich and Pincus Green] to waive any and all defenses, including their statute of limitations defenses" before issuing their pardons. That claim, if true, was entirely meaningless since Clinton gave both fugitives unconditional pardons for their crimes. It would be impossible for any criminal prosecutor to override an unconditional pardon for their crimes.

In the matter of Rich and Green, Clinton went so far as to falsely claim "the case for the pardons was reviewed and advocated...by three distinguished Republican lawyers." America learned that nothing was further from the truth. In fact, none of the lawyers Clinton mentioned by name worked on Rich's pardon request. All three lawyers worked on various Rich legal difficulties in their normal course of duties as his attorneys at various times, but none of them were involved in the pardon review and application process.

The Clinton-Rodhams' many pardons and commutations were so indefensible that longtime Clinton apologist and former adviser Lanny Davis, could not bring himself to write even a single paragraph of spirited defense of the clemency decisions in his book. Davis' *Scandal: How "Gotcha" Politics is Destroying America* was a noble effort to excuse and explain away Clinton scandals, but when it came to the pardons, Davis took a pass. For that matter, Hillary, too, skipped the topic entirely in her *Living History*.

For his part, Bill Clinton made a meager effort to explain away his scandalous pardons. He devoted barely three pages out of his nearly one thousand-page autobiography *My Life* to the matter. Not surprisingly, his comments were replete with one lie after another.

Clinton wrote that his policy was "liberal in granting pardons for nonviolent offenses once people had served their sentences and spent a reasonable amount of time afterward as law-abiding citizens."[10] He claimed, "[M]ost...served their time."[11] Not only did Clinton not come close to fulfilling his own policy, but he lied about the circumstances surrounding dozens of recipients. Clinton gave away pardons to cronies who served *little* or *no* time for their crimes. For others, the bare minimum of five years had not elapsed since the completion of their sentence in order to be even considered for clemency. Some were suspected of or were proven to have engaged in further criminal activities. Dozens of pardon recipients engaged in major narcotics activities yet, Clinton wanted his readers to believe that trafficking in millions of dollars in cocaine, crack, and heroin did not include any violent offenses whatsoever.

Clinton blamed others for his own actions and he implied worthy recipients were difficult to find due to inaction on the part of Justice Department officials. He claimed DOJ staffers dragged their feet in sending clemency petitions to him. He wrote he "had been pushing Justice [Department] hard to send us more files."[12] This claim was a complete lie. Clinton left office not having bothered reviewing 1,512 pardon and commutation applications that the Justice Department had forwarded to him.

Bill Clinton even recycled a lie that he used—and was criticized for using—in the weeks after the scandalous Marc Rich pardon. His claim that I. Lewis "Scooter" Libby, who later served as chief of staff to Vice President Dick Cheney, worked for the Rich pardon. That assertion was a complete falsehood in 2001 when Clinton first made it and it was a falsehood in 2004 when he reused it.

Clinton wrote of denying one pardon request because the felon "had not been out of jail for the usual period [of time] before being considered for a pardon."[13] Yet Clinton pardoned dozens for whom the customary waiting period had not yet elapsed including Marc Rich, whom he mentioned in the previous paragraph, who did not serve any time, was a fugitive abroad from justice, had renounced his citizenship, and had engaged in further illegal conduct when Clinton pardoned him.

Joan Walsh, writing for Salon.com, perhaps best summed up the various Clinton and Rodham activities that comprised what eventually became known as Pardongate. "The sleaziness and recklessness of the pardons reeks of Clinton's worst excesses: grandiosity, self-indulgence, sentimentality; and...a sense that he was beyond rebuke, somehow beyond punishment, and the normal rules just didn't apply to him."[14]

To this, one can only add: it was Hillary Rodham Clinton who was the key influence behind the worst of the worst pardons and commutations that disgraced the office of the President, undermined the legal system and demonstrated that justice could be sold. Imagine to what extent a President Hillary Rodham would thoroughly abuse the legal system to turn loose unrepentant, hardened criminals; reward wealthy donors; enrich her family and friends; and turn the executive clemency process into a glorified eBay get-out-of-jail-free card.

CHAPTER 1

History, Process, and Controversies

"When one evaluates Bill Clinton's incessantly arrogant presidency...we are seeing are the echoes of a pervasive elitism, from people who were taught when young that the laws that applied to their countrymen did not necessarily apply to them."[1]

THE HISTORY

The roots of the US pardon system were in England where the act of granting clemency to criminals is believed to have begun during the late sixth century. King Æthelberht (560–616 AD) is the first monarch who may have granted relief to certain individuals accused or convicted of crimes. It would not be for another four centuries before the legal precedent of granting pardon powers to the monarch was firmly established. It was during the reign of William the Conqueror (1028–1087) that English law first contained references to executive clemency.[2]

For several hundred years, the king was not the only individual in England to have issued pardons. The Church of England, Parliament, and other English nobility contended they had right to issue or approve clemency and oftentimes they exercised that authority. The power of the king as the sole entity to issue pardons was not solidified until July 1, 1536, when Parliament enacted legislation stipulating that "the king's highness, his heirs and successors, kings of his realm, shall have the whole and sole power and authority" to pardon.[3]

The colonies in North America, as a de facto extension of England, adopted much of English law. However, pardon policies were not uniform throughout the individual colonies. As the colonies moved away from England and toward independence, there was also a movement to adopt laws that divested power from the colonial governors and instead invested it in elected legislatures. Some states allowed governors to exercise wide-sweeping pardon powers while other states concentrated the power in the hands of legislators.

Such was not the case with the formation of a national government. Executive clemency powers were not included in the colonies' Articles of Confederation, but that changed when the Constitution was drawn up. When representatives convened the Constitutional Convention at the Philadelphia State House in 1787, most agreed that the executive branch should be able to grant clemency. However, there was considerable back and forth discussion over the extent of the pardon powers to be granted to the president. Much of the disagreement focused on precluding the president from granting clemency in cases of treason and impeachment.

Critics of near limitless pardon powers were concerned that those guilty of treason could be accomplices of the president and granting the president the right to pardon them would be self-serving. Others pointed out that the ability to offer clemency to treasonous individuals would provide a tool for the president to coerce conspirators to turn on one another.

The final draft of the Constitution contained a mere twenty words that spelled out the president's power to grant executive clemency. Article II, Section 2 of the United States Constitution states, in part, "he shall have Power to grant Reprieves and Pardons for Offenses against the United States, except in Cases of Impeachment." It would be nearly a century and a half before the boundaries of executive clemency would be spelled out in greater detail.

A pair of Supreme Court rulings during the next 140 years formed the basis of law regarding presidential clemency. In 1833, Supreme Court Chief Justice John Marshall wrote that

> *"a pardon is an act of grace, proceeding from the power entrusted with the execution of laws, which exempts the individual, on whom it is bestowed, from punishment the law inflicts for a crime he has committed. It is the private, though official act of the executive magistrate.... A pardon is a deed, to the validity of which delivery is essential, and delivery is not complete without acceptance. It may then be rejected by the person to whom it is tendered; and if it be rejected, we have discovered no power in a court to force it on him."*[4]

Nearly a century later, Supreme Court Justice Oliver Wendell Holmes Jr., delivered an opinion that made the president's power to grant clemency absolute, even in the face of rejection by the intended recipient. Vuco Perovich was convicted of murder and was sentenced to death in 1905. There were numerous delays in carrying out the execution and in June 1909, President William Howard Taft commuted Perovich's sentence to life imprisonment in a penitentiary. Perovich did not consent to the commutation; nonetheless, prison officials ended plans for execution.

Perovich twice petitioned the president for a pardon and was denied each time. He then filed suit in US District Court arguing the president's commutation significantly altered rather than reduced his sentence, a change he argued the president did not have the authority to make and was beyond what the Constitution granted the president. Perovich further argued that he should instead be given a full pardon and released from prison. The District Court agreed with Perovich and ordered his release. The case was eventually appealed all the way to the Supreme Court, which ruled against Perovich.

In the decision, Holmes wrote "A pardon in our days is not a private act of grace from an individual happening to possess power. It is a part of the Constitutional scheme. When granted it is the determination of the ultimate authority that the public welfare will be better served by inflicting less than what the judgment fixed.... and that the convict's consent is not required."[5]

THE PROCESS

The US Code of Federal Regulations details the procedures to be followed in determining eligibility for clemency, the application process, the consideration of the application, notification of victims, the Justice Department review process, and the notification procedures.

Application for clemency shall be addressed to the president and submitted to the pardon attorney of the US Department of Justice. No application shall be submitted until at least five years after the completion of confinement, or in the cases in which there was no incarceration, at least five years after the conviction. Federal regulations state "no petition should be submitted by a person who is on probation, parole, or supervised release." Additionally, petitions should not be submitted for commutation of a sentence or remission of a fine until all other forms of judicial or administrative relief have been exhausted.

An important element of the clemency process is that there is no question of the petitioner's guilt. The petitioner must accept responsibility and show remorse and atonement for their crime(s). It is required that a petitioner be "genuinely desirous of forgiveness rather than vindication.... Persons seeking a pardon on grounds of innocence or miscarriage of justice bear a formidable burden of persuasion."

The Department of Justice is to ensure appropriate investigations are conducted by pertinent agencies to include the Federal Bureau of

Investigation. In addition, the attorney general has the responsibility to ensure those cases in which there were victims

"shall cause reasonable effort to be made to notify the victim or victims of the crime for which the clemency is sought:

> (i) That a clemency petition has been filed:

> (ii) That the victim may submit comments regarding clemency; and

> (iii)Whether the clemency request ultimately is granted or denied by the President."

Solicitation of victim impact statements is amplified by Title 42 § 10607 "Services to Victims." This federal law requires officials to notify a victim of the earliest possible notice of "the escape, work release, furlough, or *any other form of release from custody* of the offender [emphasis added]."

Recommendations and reports from officials knowledgeable of the felon and the offense, such as the prosecuting attorney and the sentencing judge, are important in ascertaining fitness for clemency. "The likely impact of favorable action in the district or nationally, particularly on current law enforcement priorities, will always be relevant to the President's decision."

The US pardon attorney is to request the US attorney in the district of conviction to provide comments and recommendations on petitions that have merit for consideration. The US attorney is also requested to address issues of fact that might arise in a petition. The guidelines note "the United States Attorney's prosecutive perspective lends valuable insights to the clemency process."

In addition, the guidelines state "the views of the United States Attorney are given considerable weight in determining what recommendations the Department [of Justice] should make to the President." The US attorney significantly aids the review process by providing facts and perspectives on events surrounding the crime that may not be available in court's presentence report or in a law enforcement agency's background investigation.

The US attorney is expected to comment on the extent of the petitioner's involvement in the crime, the amount of money or the scope of the losses sustained, the criminal background of the petitioner, the petitioner's standing in the community, and all victim impact statements.

The pardon attorney must also obtain from the US Probation Office a copy of the petitioner's presentence report and the judgment of conviction. In addition, the pardon attorney must review the petitioner's compliance with any supervised release and inputs from the petitioner's probation officer.[6]

The pardon attorney may also be required to solicit inputs from other government agencies such as the Bureau of Immigration and the Internal Revenue Service. Importantly, the pardon attorney must notify the prosecutor's office to ensure victims are informed of the clemency petition and are advised they may submit comments.[7]

The guidelines lay out widely accepted standards for the favorable consideration of pardon petitions. First and foremost, the petitioner must have "demonstrated good conduct for a substantial period of time after conviction and service of sentence." Included for consideration is the question of whether the petitioner has led a "responsible and productive life for a significant period after conviction or release from confinement." This is one aspect in which the FBI's investigation contributes significantly to the review and recommendation process.

Does the petitioner demonstrate financial and employment stability? Will the petitioner demonstrate responsibility toward their family? Has the petitioner performed community service or charitable or meritorious activities?

Another consideration is the seriousness and recentness of the criminal offense. Guidelines note that a very serious offense such as a violent crime, major drug trafficking, breach of the public trust, or fraud involving substantial sums of money require a suitably long period of time to elapse before favorable consideration for clemency is given. This is to "avoid denigrating the seriousness of the offense or undermining the deterrent effect of the conviction."

The pardon attorney can take into consideration the reason for clemency in reaching a recommendation. For example, a felony conviction that results in the loss of licensure or bonding that affects employment may make a marginal case more compelling for favorable consideration.

Finally, the Justice Department serves as the messenger when resolution is reached on an executive clemency decision. If approved, then the Justice Department issues the warrant of pardon or commutation to the petitioner. The Justice Department must also notify the petitioner when clemency is denied; it then closes the case.

In addition to the DOJ guidelines were other factors Clinton insisted be taken into consideration when reviewing an executive clemency application. A January 26, 1996, memo to the Justice Department from then White House Counsel Jack Quinn outlined additional restrictions Clinton had placed on favorable clemency consideration. Adoption of these restrictions would have made it *more difficult* for an applicant to get a pardon or commutation from Clinton than from previous presidents. The memo stated there were "certain categories of crimes which are so serious that the President will not consider granting a pardon for them under almost any circumstances." Among the included crimes was "large scale drug trafficking" and "offenses involving central involvement in political corruption."[8]

Presidential pardons have not been without controversy, oftentimes with the public and sometimes with Congress. There have a number of instances of executive clemency that raised concerns, generally over the limits of the president's power to pardon and to grant amnesty and the circumstances surrounding such clemency.

THE CONTROVERSIES

George Washington and the Whiskey Rebellion

In 1791, as an effort to raise revenue in order to pay off war debts from the American Revolution, the newly formed US government levied a tax on whiskey. Distilling and selling whiskey was a lucrative business for farmers who seized on a profitable method to utilize their grain. Farmers had been constrained in marketing opportunities for their grain as trading routes to Europe were limited when the Spanish closed the Mississippi River to American farmers. Instead, they turned their grain into alcohol to sell locally.

Farmers in western Pennsylvania's Monongahela Valley were unhappy with the federal government-imposed excise tax. They refused to pay the tax and they forced government tax collectors to flee the area. Scores of whiskey tax protesters threatened to attack federal institutions in the major cities of Pittsburgh and Philadelphia as a sign of protest. In response, President George Washington raised an army of thirteen thousand federal troops to put down the "whiskey rebellion" and deal with the "treasonous" rebels.

The army marched on western Pennsylvania but found only a small number of insurrectionists. Less than two dozen suspects were apprehended, charged, and eventually went to trial. Two were found guilty. Washington issued the first ever pardons when it was determined that the pair were incapable of acting responsibly. One was deemed insane and the other feebleminded.

On July 10, 1795, President Washington pardoned the remaining "insurrectionists" who agreed to sign a loyalty oath to the United States. At the time, Washington said the

"misled have abandoned their errors, and pay the respect to our
Constitution and laws which is due.... though I shall always think it
a sacred duty to exercise with firmness and energy the constitutional
powers with which I am vested, yet it appears to me no less consistent

with the public good... to mingle in the operations of Government every degree of moderation and tenderness which the national justice, dignity, and safety may permit."

John Adams and the Fries Rebellion

The US government levied its first ever direct tax on US property in July 1798 to defray costs in an anticipated war with France that would eventually be known as the Quasi War. The state of Pennsylvania's share of the two million dollars that was needed to be raised was about a quarter of a million dollars. The tax was to be levied primarily on homes. However, the predominately German-descended farmers in southeastern Pennsylvania were not enthusiastic about paying the tax and they were suspicious of the tax assessors who were gathering information on private homes in order to levy tax rates.

John Fries was a local auctioneer who was known to many of the farmers in the region, and he took it upon himself to organize a resistance to the tax. In March 1799, he assembled a group of several hundred men who chased tax assessors from the area. The group then freed a handful of tax resisters from the Bethlehem, Pennsylvania jail.

Fries and his followers were labeled as being guilty of sedition and treason. The Pennsylvania militia was called upon to put down the resisters. The militia never found the band of rebels because they had dispersed, but it did apprehend Fries and two other leaders. All three were charged with treason and were tried and convicted. They were then sentenced to death.

Learning of the sentence, President John Adams elected to show compassion toward Fries and the other two. In April 1800, Adams pardoned all three. He followed up their pardons on May 21, 1800, with a "full, free and absolute pardon" to the rest of the tax resisters. Adam's pardon was opposed by most of his cabinet and is deemed to have contributed to his reelection defeat by Thomas Jefferson.

James Madison and the Barataria Pirates

In the late 18th and early 19th centuries, Barataria Bay along Louisiana's Gulf Coast was home to Captain Jean Lafitte and his fleet of more than four dozen sloops, schooners, and brigantines. Pirates by trade, Lafitte and his men made their home among the bay's three islands, Grande Terre, Grande Isle, and Cheniere Caminada. The barrier islands were a strategic location as they formed a choke point for any vessel sailing into or out of the Mississippi River.

Jean and his brother, Pierre, lived the good life, pampered with the spoils of their ill-gotten goods. Politically astute, Lafitte ordered his men to not rob any American ships, thereby ensuring there would be little effort to evict him and his men from their makeshift pirate colony. This de facto truce allowed Lafitte and US officials to live in peaceful coexistence even after the area was sold by France to the US in what became known as the Louisiana Purchase.

This relationship changed when the War of 1812 broke out between the US and England. British forces captured strategic forts along the Great Lakes and much of the upper Mississippi River. US officials were fearful the British would strike a deal with Lafitte and together would capture the lower Mississippi River. For this reason, Louisiana's governor took preemptive action to neutralize Lafitte and his men by issuing an arrest order.

For nearly two years, a cat-and-mouse game played out between Lafitte and the authorities as they attempted to apprehend him, but he managed to escape each time. Then in September 1814, representatives of the British Army and Navy met with Lafitte, offering him a Royal Navy commission and money if he and his men aided the British in an attack on New Orleans. Lafitte sent them on their way, promising to consider the offer. Instead, Lafitte immediately dispatched a letter to the Louisiana governor, offering his loyalty to the United States.

The governor and his advisers were suspicious of Lafitte's proffered loyalty and instead agreed to pursue his capture. Lafitte's island colony was only accessible by sea. A small flotilla of US Navy ships and barges sailed into Barataria Bay. Lafitte anticipated the American forces were there to establish an alliance. Instead, cannon fire rained onto the unsuspecting pirates. Lafitte's colony fell and about eight hundred pirates fled to sanctuary miles away.

Lafitte made a personal appeal to General Andrew Jackson, who commanded all American forces in the defense of New Orleans. As many as twelve thousand British troops were en route to New Orleans. Jackson had fewer than four thousand. Lafitte promised one thousand men and flint and gunpowder, which were desperately needed by Jackson's forces, in return for a pardon for himself and his men. Jackson agreed.

The Battle of New Orleans took place on the morning of January 1815. When it was over, the British suffered 2,600 deaths. The Americans lost just over a dozen men. Jackson kept his end of the bargain and requested a pardon for Lafitte and his men. President James Madison granted it on February 6, 1815.

Abraham Lincoln and the Confederate Rebels

Civil War clemency was notable because the granting of pardons and amnesty proved to be complex and very political. Numerous clemency proclamations were issued before final resolution was reached regarding official forgiveness for Confederate citizens, soldiers, and government officials. The final clemency regarding the Civil War was not issued until 1898, some thirty-four years after the war ended. Between Presidents Abraham Lincoln and Andrew Johnson, the two issued six pardons that dealt with the Civil War and its aftermath.

Midway through the Civil War most of Louisiana, North Carolina, and Tennessee fell to Union forces. Lincoln, who had been consistent in his statements that the purpose of the war was to preserve the Union, appointed military governors to immediately begin the process of readmitting the fallen secessionist states as members of the Union.

Lincoln issued a Proclamation of Amnesty and Reconstruction on December 8, 1863, that permitted Southerners who swore an oath of allegiance to the US Constitution and swore to abide by Union proclamations regarding slavery would be granted "a full pardon...with restoration of all rights of property, except as to slaves." Excluded from the proclamation were senior military officers and civilian leaders of the states or the Confederacy. The readmission into the Union began once a threshold of 10 percent of a state's population complied with the provisions of the proclamation.

Congressional Republicans were dissatisfied with Lincoln's "10 Percent Plan" and attempted to make the requirements for the readmission into the Union by Southern states more stringent. Congress passed the Wade-Davis Bill, which increased the allegiance requirement from 10 percent to a majority of a state's voters. It also placed further limits on the participation in the political process by many former Confederates. Lincoln refused to sign the bill, keeping it from becoming law.

Andrew Johnson and Readmission of the Confederates

In May 1865, President Johnson (who assumed the presidency after Lincoln's assassination the previous month) announced a general amnesty as part of his Presidential Reconstruction plan. Southerners who swore an oath to the Union would be granted amnesty and would have property (but not including slaves) that was confiscated during the war returned to them. Large landowners and Confederacy officials were excluded from the general amnesty, and they would instead have to petition the president individually.

Members of Congress were predominately Republicans and President Johnson was a Democrat. Most of Congress believed Johnson had assumed too liberal of a stance in readmitting Southerners that many Northerners believed had been disloyal and treasonous. Most of Congress viewed a pardon as an absolute necessity in restoring the South as part of the union. However, they also believed it was critical that Southerners take positive and concrete steps to assure their loyalty to the Constitution and that key Confederate figures be excluded from readmission.

The Senate Judiciary Committee took issue with Johnson's universal amnesty announced on December 25, 1968. That amnesty included the provision that Southerners were entitled to the return of captured and abandoned property without having to demonstrate their loyalty to the Union. On February 17, 1969, the Judiciary Committee issued a report stating the president lacked the authority to issue amnesty. It was the legislative branch, the committee asserted, and not the executive branch that held the power to grant amnesty. This legislative rebuttal to the president was rendered moot when then US Supreme Court ruled in *Armstrong v. United States*, 80 US 154, that the president had the authority to offer amnesty without the approval of Congress.[9]

It was not until June 6, 1898, that Congress passed a universal and unconditional amnesty bill that included all remaining South-erners previously excluded from earlier amnesties. This closed the final chapter on the status of former Confederates four decades after the Civil War ended.

Warren G. Harding and Eugene Debs

Eugene V. Debs began working for the railroad as a young teenager in the 1870s. In 1875, he became the founder of the local Broth-erhood of Locomotive Firemen. About the same time, he became active in the Democrat Party and was elected to the Indiana General Assembly in 1884.

Debs was instrumental in forming the American Railway Union in 1893 and was arrested for his participation in Chicago's Pullman Strike of 1894. The Pullman boycott and strike began on May 11, 1894 and effectively ended all railroad traffic in the western half of the US. Pullman Palace Car Company workers went on strike to protest wage cuts after Pullman railcar sales fell off. A month later,

American Railway Union members boycotted the railroad industry and more than 125,000 workers walked off the job. On July 23, Debs and other American Railway Union leaders were jailed after refusing to comply with a federal injunction ordering the strikers to return to work. The following year, Debs and other strike organizers were again jailed for contempt of court charges relating to the strike.

While serving a brief sentence in prison, Debs became devoted to the writings of Karl Marx and converted to socialism. After his release from prison, he cofounded the Social Democratic Party of America in 1897, the Socialist Party in 1901, and the Industrial Workers of the World in 1905.

Debs ran as the Social Democratic Party nominee for president in 1900, finishing with less than one hundred thousand votes. He again ran for president in 1904, 1908, and 1912, not representing the Social Democratic Party but instead as the nominee of the Socialist Party. He polled just over four hundred thousand votes in 1904 and 1908 and doubled his votes to more than eight hundred thousand in 1912.

As with many other Socialists of the day, such as American Civil Liberties Union founder Roger Baldwin, Debs was very critical of the US and he opposed America's entry into World War I. He became an outspoken critic of US policies and he blamed all of World War I on imperialism. He was arrested under the Espionage Act after one infamous speech in Canton, Ohio in 1918 in which he spoke passionately in favor of Socialism in America. He was tried and convicted and then sentenced to ten years in prison.

While still incarcerated, Debs was the Socialist Party's standard-bearer for the 1920 presidential race. He received just under one million votes. The Socialist Party launched a campaign to gain his release from prison. President Woodrow Wilson denied pardon requests for Deb. Wilson remarked, "This man was a traitor to his country and he will never be pardoned during my administration."

The Socialist Party launched a nationwide petition drive requesting Debs be released from prison. The party threatened to begin picketing the White House unless Debs was freed. By August 1921, Warren G. Harding, who had followed Wilson into the White House, had conferred with the US attorney general about possibly issuing pardons or a general amnesty to wartime protestors. However, Harding believed such action would be inappropriate until after a final peace agreement was signed with Germany. On Christmas Day 1921, Harding pardoned two dozen war protestors, including Debs.

Richard Nixon and Jimmy Hoffa

Born in 1913, James R. Hoffa grew up during the tough times of the Depression. His father died when Hoffa was a youngster. While living in the Detroit area, young Hoffa dropped out of high school and began working as a stock boy at a Kroger supermarket.

When he was just seventeen years old, Hoffa organized his first labor strike. He and other workers walked off the job at Kroger just after a fresh fruit delivery arrived. Concerned that a large shipment of strawberries would perish, Kroger's management negotiated a new wage deal with the workers. Hoffa and his fellow workers became known as the "Strawberry Boys."

Hoffa eventually joined Teamsters Local 299 and he quickly rose through its ranks. Once he became the local's business manager, he quickly transformed the union shop of a few dozen members to one of more than five thousand. By 1940, Hoffa was the president of the Michigan Conference of Teamsters. He rose to the position of international vice president of the Teamsters union in 1952 and became the president in 1957 when his predecessor, David Beck, was sentenced to prison for criminal activity.

During the 1950s, the Teamsters were investigated by the US Senate Select Committee on Labor and its young chairman, Massachusetts Senator John F. Kennedy. Robert Kennedy was counsel to his brother's committee. The younger Kennedy pursued allegations of mob connections among the Teamsters and Jimmy Hoffa.

Robert Kennedy's pursuit of Hoffa continued through the Kennedy and Lyndon Johnson presidential administrations when he was a US attorney general. Hoffa was eventually indicted for allegedly accepting illegal payments from a trucking company and for raiding the Teamsters' pension fund.

The jury in Hoffa's trial declared it was hung, but the trial judge suspected Hoffa may have bribed jurors. In a second trial in 1964, Hoffa was convicted of jury tampering and of stealing pension funds. After exhausting all his appeals, Hoffa reported to prison in 1967 to serve a thirteen-year sentence.

In 1971, after serving less than five years, Hoffa received a conditional pardon from President Richard Nixon. He was to refrain from participating in any union activities until at least 1980. It was widely believed Hoffa was planning his return to Teamster affairs when he mysteriously disappeared in July 1975.

Gerald Ford and Richard Nixon

It is generally believed that Gerald Ford's fate to lose the 1976 presidential election was sealed when he pardoned Richard Nixon for "for all offenses against the United States which he, Richard Nixon, has committed or may have committed or taken part in during the period from January 20, 1969 through August 9, 1974." Ford granted clemency to Nixon a mere month after Ford assumed the presidency upon Nixon's resignation.

At the time, conspiracy theorists were convinced there was a secret deal between Nixon and Ford. The record showed otherwise. In retrospect, it has been accepted that Ford's act of compassion was the proper course of action to close the final chapter on Watergate. The pardon ended what Ford referred to as "our long national nightmare."

Nixon's apparent involvement in the cover-up of the Watergate break-in was rivaled by the actions of another president a mere generation later when he perjured himself by lying under oath regarding his sexual peccadilloes.

At his acceptance of the Republican nomination for president in 1976 Ford observed how Nixon's critics had poisoned the political discourse and had coarsened public debate. Ford remarked, "It was an hour in our history that troubled our minds and tore at our hearts. Anger and hatred had risen to dangerous levels, dividing friends and families. The polarization of our political order had aroused unworthy passions of reprisal and revenge. Our governmental system was closer to stalemate than at any time since Abraham Lincoln took that same oath of office."

In its cover story, *Time* magazine asked, "The real question is whether justice—and the country—is served by giving Nixon a pardon."[10]

Emblematic of the critics' anger and hatred was the *New York Times*, which editorialized that Ford's pardon of Nixon was "a profoundly unwise, divisive and unjust act."[11] More reasonable minds at the time and history has shown the *New York Times* to have been dead wrong in its assessment.

In his pardon proclamation, Ford noted the "trial of Richard Nixon, if it became necessary, could not fairly begin until a year or more has elapsed. In the meantime, the tranquility to which this nation has been restored by the events of recent weeks could be irreparably lost by the prospects of bringing to trial a former President of the United States."

Jimmy Carter and the Draft Dodgers

In his first full day as President, Jimmy Carter issued an unconditional pardon of all draft dodgers from the Vietnam War. Those who refused to register and others who chose to flee the country rather than serve or even register were permitted to return to the US without any conditions whatsoever. More than one hundred thousand draft dodgers fled the US with about nine in ten choosing Canada as their destination.

The Baby Boomer generation had an inordinate share of self-indulgent people who practiced "self above service." As President Lyndon Johnson quickly escalated US troop presence in Vietnam after he was safely reelected from fifteen thousand in 1964 to more than one-half million by late 1967, some draft-age men refused their call to service. This stood in stark contrast to the more than six million servicemen and women who served in Vietnam.

Most of the country was in an uproar over Carter's amnesty. It was publicly opposed by a thirteen-to-one margin. Millions of former servicemen including World War II and Korean War veterans were angered that Carter issued a blanket amnesty to draft dodgers who willingly broke the law while millions proudly served and more than fifty-eight thousand lost their lives in the Vietnam War. A generation later, James Webb, a future Democrat US Senator from Virginia, wrote "Mr. Carter's gesture had the symbolic effect of elevating everyone who had opposed the Vietnam War to the level of moral purist, and by implication insulting those who often had struggled just as deeply with the moral dimensions of the war and had decided, often at great sacrifice, to honor the laws of their country and serve."[12]

George H. W. Bush and Caspar Weinberger

Lawrence E. Walsh was the independent counsel who investigated the Iran-Contra affair. He engineered an "October surprise" by announcing a highly politicized indictment of former Defense secretary Caspar Weinberger only four days before the November 1992 election. Walsh's previous indictment of Weinberger on June 16, 1992, had been dismissed in court. Walsh responded to the court's ruling striking down his first indictment by indicting Weinberger again on October 30, 1992. The second indictment undoubtedly contributed to President George H. W. Bush's 1992 reelection defeat.

Prior to the Weinberger indictments, Walsh suffered one setback after another. Felony convictions of National Security Adviser Vice Admiral John Poindexter of the US Navy and National Security Council staffer Lieutenant Colonel Oliver North of the US Marine Corps were overturned. Other Iran-Contra figures were convicted of or pled guilty to relatively minor charges that resulted in modest fines and did not yield any prison time. Considering all of the time, effort, money and hype, the Iran-Contra investigation was a legal bust until late in its waning months when Walsh decided to pursue Weinberger and exact political revenge on his targets of Ronald Reagan and Bush.

After the November election, the court dismissed one of Walsh's charges from the second indictment, leaving in place an allegation that Weinberger withheld documents from the independent counsel. In fact, the documents Walsh sought had already been turned over to the Library of Congress by Weinberger. Looking in the wrong area of the library and unable to locate the documents, Walsh pressed his claim that Weinberger had lied. The documents were in the library exactly where Weinberger's attorneys had informed Walsh could find them.

Because Walsh had been playing politics with indictments, Bush returned the favor on Christmas Eve 1992. With only a matter of weeks left in his presidency, Bush pardoned Weinberger and five others from the Iran-Contra affair. Joining the former defense secretary was former national security adviser Robert "Bud" McFarlane, former assistant secretary of state Elliott Abrams, and Central Intelligence Agency employees Duane Clarridge, Clair George, and Alan Fiers.

In his pardon declaration, Bush underscored his ire at Walsh's abuse of the independent counsel process for political means. Bush stated, "The prosecutions of the individuals I am pardoning represent what I believe is a profoundly troubling development in the political and legal climate of our country: the criminalization of policy differences. These differences should be addressed in the political arena, without the Damocles sword of criminality hanging over the heads of some of the combatants. The proper target is the president, not his subordinates; the proper forum is the voting booth, not the courtroom…. It is my hope that the action I am taking today will begin to restore these disputes to the battleground where they properly belong."

George W. Bush and I. Lewis Libby

Syndicated columnist Robert Novak reported the identity of Valerie Plame in a July 14, 2003 column. Novak wrote that Plame was a CIA analyst as well as the wife of former ambassador Joseph C. Wilson IV. At the urging of his wife, Wilson was sent on a junket to Niger in 2002, ostensibly to ascertain any information regarding a British intelligence report that representatives of Saddam Hussein's Iraq sought yellowcake uranium. The Novak column began an odyssey that landed a senior White House official in court.

Eighteen months after his trip, Wilson wrote a July 6, 2003, *New York Times* op-ed claiming he proved a negative. Wilson wrote that Iraq had not sought yellowcake uranium from Niger, contrary to one sixteen-word sentence in President Bush's 2003 State of the Union address. In his State of the Union remarks, Bush said, "The British Government has learned that Saddam Hussein recently sought significant quantities of uranium from Africa."

As one of the poorest countries in the world, the landlocked nation of Niger has little to sell to foreigners other than uranium ore since it has one of the largest uranium deposits on the planet. Aside from uranium ore, Niger's other exports are misery, despair, and refugees. Iraqi officials had purchased large quantities of uranium ore from Niger since the 1970s.

British intelligence confirmed Iraqi officials had visited Niger and other West African countries in 1999. It was this and other intelligence that led to the British conclusion that Saddam Hussein sought uranium ore from Niger. The Review of Intelligence on Weapons of Mass Destruction, chaired by The Right Honorable Lord Butler of Brockwell (the "Butler Report"), was Britain's own "9/11 Commission Report." The Butler Report concluded that the original British report of Iraq seeking uranium ore from Niger, which led to the 16-word sentence used in the 2003 State of the Union address, was "well-founded."

Wilson was a diplomat whose career apparently ended prematurely. He was a poor choice for the fact-finding trip as he did not possess the necessary skills to clandestinely find the evidence to prove or disprove the British uranium report. Moreover, Wilson did not have any expertise in weapons grade uranium or in nuclear weapons systems, making him completely unqualified for the trip. Perhaps this explains why Wilson admitted in his *New York Times* op-ed that he spent "eight days drinking sweet mint tea" while in Niger.

The political left was insistent that I. Lewis "Scooter" Libby and other senior officials in the Bush Administration leaked Plame's identity to Novak to discredit Wilson. An exhaustive investigation by a special prosecutor revealed that Plame's name was casually mentioned to Novak in a conversation with the gossiping diplomat Richard Armitage. Early in his investigation, Special Prosecutor Patrick Fitzgerald reached the conclusion there was no underlying crime regarding the revelation of Plame's identity. No one "leaked" Plame's name to the media despite wishful thinking by the political left.

Moreover, even if her name had been leaked there was no crime as Plame's identity did not fall within the scope of the Intelligence Identities Protection Act, a law that was intended to protect US intelligence officials working undercover while abroad. More than a decade earlier, Plame was working overseas as a classified employee of the CIA, typically known as a "case officer." As such, she may have been among the most incompetent in performing her job.

A commercially available database showed that Plame's official mailing address in the early 1990s was "American Embassy, New York, NY 09255." This, it turns out, was the APO address for the US Embassy in Athens, Greece. Additionally, she claimed to have been a consultant living and working in Europe for a company named Brewster-Jennings & Associates.

Further database research revealed that Brewster-Jennings reported annual sales revenues of $60,000 and a work force of only a single employee (presumably, Plame). Foreign intelligence services use databases, the internet, and credit reports to uncover the real identity of suspected US case officers. There can be little doubt that interested foreign intelligence services knew almost immediately that Plame was a CIA or other US government agency case officer and not a business consultant, as she had claimed. While Plame's identity may not have been widely known in the US, there is little doubt it was known by the foreign intelligence services of the countries in which she traveled.

Fitzgerald acknowledged there was no "leaking" of Plame's name and, therefore, no underlying crime. Nonetheless, Fitzgerald alleged Libby lied to cover up information that was never "leaked." Libby claimed a poor memory was the reason why he gave incorrect dates regarding his conversations with journalists during the investigation. Nonetheless, Fitzgerald indicted Libby.

Jurors in the trial of *United States of America v. I. Lewis Libby* found Libby guilty of committing perjury and of making false statements to FBI agents and had thereby obstructed justice regarding what he said to reporters concerning the identity of Valerie Plame. Libby lost an attempt to appeal his case.

On July 2, 2007, Bush commuted the sentence of Lewis Libby shortly before he was to report to prison to serve a thirty-month sentence. Bush kept in place Libby's $250,000 fine and two-year probationary period.

On April 13, 2018, President Donald Trump gave Libby a full pardon.

CHAPTER 2

Cronies

"The president's willingness to consider pardons was not communicated through the legal grapevine, but through the loose Clinton network of longtime friends, campaign contributors and insiders with access to the White House."[1]

MOST OF THE attention following the dozens of pardons and commutations handed out by Bill Clinton during his last day office focused on the big-name recipients and the reasons why they received clemency.

The crooked billionaire Marc Rich, whose ex-wife was responsible for more than three million dollars in fundraising events and personal contributions to Bill and Hillary Clinton and related causes, garnered the most news. The motive behind pardoning Symbionese Liberation Army captive-turned-accomplice Patty Hearst was quickly understood. She was an heiress to the Hearst Corporation, a media giant that included a dozen newspapers, twenty magazines, interests in several popular cable TV channels, and nearly thirty television stations that reach almost one in five households in America. Currying favor with the Hearst media empire was a smart political move that would benefit Hillary and her political career.

Pardons that went to complete strangers who paid hundreds of thousands of dollars to Hillary's brothers, Hugh and Tony, simply represented yet another chapter in the continuing saga America came to know as the Clinton presidency. The Rodhams shamelessly peddled their influence and access to friends and strangers alike. And they got away with it.

The press reported on some of those clemency decisions in which members of the Clinton clan—Bill, Hillary, Roger, and Hugh and Tony Rodham—profited, either financially or politically, or both. Yet, many other egregious cases were overlooked by the media, such as those that pacified the political leanings of Bill and Hillary. Domestic terrorists, cold-hearted killers, major drug traffickers, a drug cartel money launderer, multimillion-dollar swindlers, and other undeserving dregs of American society got pardons and commutations. Thousands of other clemency petitioners, including hundreds of anonymous citizens convicted of minor felonies and misdemeanors, who had neither cash to contribute nor the important political and personal ties of value to the Clintons, never received cursory, let alone serious, consideration of their requests.

Upon close inspection, it is painfully obvious that the one group that was significantly underrepresented on Clinton's late-term pardon lists were the people for whom executive clemency was most needed. The little people who were victims of circumstances, those who received harsh sentences that were disproportionate for the crimes committed, the people who actually redeemed themselves by performing good deeds after completing their sentences, the plain folk who needed a professional license reinstated, and those whose pardons would hasten national healing were virtually absent from Clinton's list of recipients. Clinton ignored nearly two thousand clemency petitions during his final months in office.[2] More than one thousand of these petitions arrived in just the last month.[3] Bill Clinton cherry-picked those recipients that directly benefited him, Hillary, and their brothers.

Those who were politically connected, had close ties to Bill and Hillary and their brothers, were friends of friends, or to whom the

Clintons were indebted, those who could later pay back the Clintons, or had paid the Rodham brothers for their access and influence, were the ones who received nearly all of the pardons and commutations Clinton gave away.

JOHN H. BUSTAMANTE

John H. Bustamante was a longtime friend and associate of Jesse Jackson. He was Jackson's personal attorney and he served as general counsel to Jackson's organization, Operation PUSH. Bustamante was with PUSH when the organization was at the center of a controversy regarding the group's misuse of nearly $5 million in federal grants.[4]

Operation PUSH had received from the Commerce and Education Departments and other federal agencies millions of dollars in taxpayer money during the last three years of the Jimmy Carter administration. Most of the funds went to a program named Push for Excellence that claimed to aid students in inner city schools. However, suspicions arose that grant money was not being properly spent.

An initial audit of Push for Excellence conducted by the Commerce Department in 1980 found irregularities in the bookkeeping.[5] Three successive federal government studies of the Push for Excellence operation found the organization failed to fulfill its promised performance levels. At least $1.4 million in federal grant money was spent improperly.[6] The early "report card" was not well-received by Jackson and his associates. In 1981, Operation PUSH officials refused access by federal auditors to further audit the group's financial records in order to confirm taxpayer money was being spent in accordance with the grant guidelines.

Even after PUSH refused access by federal auditors, that did not end the organization's insatiable appetite for more taxpayer dollars or diminish the gall of PUSH officials who asked for more federal money. In 1981, Bustamante sent a letter to the Education

Department demanding another $825,000 in grant monies. Rather than doling out additional grants as Bustamante had requested, the Reagan administration instead cut off Operation PUSH from further receiving taxpayer money.

By 1983, Push for Excellence had its license as a charitable organization revoked by the Illinois secretary of state for failing to file mandatory disclosure forms with the state.[7] Complicating matters was that Operation PUSH had not filed a single financial statement certified by an independent auditor as required by state law during the group's first fifteen years of operation.

Succumbing to intense outside pressure, PUSH finally hired an outside auditor to check the group's books. The independent audit firm found Operation PUSH had "[i]nadequate working capital, [and] substantial liabilities and obligations." The organization's immense debt "cause[d the auditors]…to question the viability of Operation PUSH Inc., as a going concern."[8]

Bustamante had other interests besides his close ties to Jackson and Operation PUSH. Bustamante was a partner of the Cleveland law firm, Bustamante, Donohue and Palmisano. He was also the chairman and chief executive officer of First Intercity Banc Corporation. He served in similar capacities with the corporation's principal subsidiary, First Bank National Association. Additionally, he was chairman and editor of the Cincinnati, Cleveland and Columbus *Call & Post*, a trio of black-focused weekly newspapers.

The financial irregularities of Operation PUSH were not the only setback for Bustamante. By 1991, his business empire was crumbling. The Internal Revenue Service filed six liens against P. W. Publishing, the parent company of the *Call & Post*, to recover a tax liability that was nearly $350,000. Several creditors reported P. W. Publishing had outstanding debts totaling several hundred thousand dollars and many creditors had successful judgments levied against the company. Principles in P. W. Publishing were Bustamante, as chairman, and his two sons, J. W. Andre Bustamante, who served as president, and Michael Tuan Bustamante, who was the company attorney.[9]

A few years earlier, Bustamante's First Bank National Association was in a financial death spiral. Senior bank officials were guilty of approving insider loans, and they made several poor management and investment decisions. In 1988, the US Office of the Comptroller of the Currency, the federal banking regulator, took the unusual step of ordering the bank to cease making loans. In a matter of months, the financial situation of First Bank had deteriorated so badly that the Federal Deposit Insurance Corporation ordered the bank's closing. First Bank went out of business in 1990.

About the same time, the fiscal health of Bustamante's newspapers was plummeting. The building that housed the *Call & Post* publishing operations was sold in a foreclosure sale in mid-1995. Then in December 1995, agents of the Internal Revenue Service raided the newspapers and seized publishing equipment in order to satisfy an outstanding tax bill that climbed to more than $500,000. This forced the company to file for Chapter 11 bankruptcy reorganization. After a couple of years, the newspapers remained insolvent. A court appointed bankruptcy trustee auctioned off the papers in 1998.

Bustamante's legal predicament worsened with the revelation he defrauded an insurance company. In April 1993, Bustamante pleaded guilty to wire fraud perpetrated against the Consumer's United Insurance Co. Bustamante borrowed $275,000 from the insurance company in 1986 under the false pretense the funds were part of a business investment. Instead, Bustamante used the money for personal expenses. Criminal charges against his son Andre were dropped as part of a plea deal. John Bustamante also faced criminal charges for misappropriating nearly $30,000 from the banking account of a deceased client whose affairs he was managing.[10]

Bustamante was convicted by a federal jury in January 1991 of five charges stemming from the Consumer's United Insurance fraud case. However, US District Court Judge John M. Manos threw out all five convictions, asserting his jury instructions may have confused the jurors. A frontpage editorial in Bustamante's Cincinnati *Call &*

Post newspaper claimed the publisher was railroaded by "an almost all-white jury."[11]

Rather than face a new trial, Bustamante pleaded guilty in April 1993 to one charge of wire fraud in the insurance fraud case. Bustamante faced five years in prison from his guilty plea, but Judge Manos, even in light of the allegation Bustamante stole funds from a dead client, spared Jackson's friend from any prison time at a June 1993 sentencing. Citing Bustamante's promise to "do good," Manos sentenced him to only five years of probation.[12] Manos also ordered Bustamante to make restitution on the $275,000 he took from the insurance company, but the judge neglected to identify a specific restitution amount and the judge failed to specify the consequences if Bustamante did not make restitution. As part of the plea deal, allegations that Bustamante stole $30,000 from a client were referred to the local prosecutor who promptly dismissed the charges.

By 1998, Bustamante was nearing the end of his probation, but he had little to look forward to regarding his business life. His newspapers had fallen into bankruptcy and were auctioned off. His bank had failed nearly a decade earlier.

Then, a little more than two years after he finished his probation, things started looking up for Bustamante. His criminal record was wiped clean as Bill Clinton pardoned him at the request of Jesse Jackson. Bustamante received Clinton's pardon gift even though an executive clemency petition was never filed with the Justice Department. Moreover, Bustamante did not meet the Justice Department guidelines of having completed his sentence at least five years earlier.

MEL REYNOLDS

First elected in 1980, six-term Congressman Augustus "Gus" Savage was as disgusting an individual as one could imagine. He was a bigot and a bona fide racist, claiming, "Racism is white. There ain't no black racism."[13] He frequently made anti-Semitic remarks and he

denounced campaign contributions made by Jews to a primary opponent. He cited his political opposition as coming from the "suburban
Zionist lobby."[14] He called his critics "faggots," "Oreos," and "white
racists."[15] In 1990, the House Ethics Committee found that Savage
made unwanted sexual advances toward a Peace Corps volunteer
during an overseas junket, but the committee virtually dismissed the
matter and only issued Savage a mild rebuke.[16]

In 1992, during his third attempt to unseat Savage, Mel Reynolds defeated the incumbent in the Democrat primary for Illinois's
2nd Congressional District. Reynolds was popular with his constituents during his freshman term even after news broke in August
1994 that he had carried on a sexual relationship with a fifteen-
year-old campaign volunteer from June 1992 to September 1993.
Reynolds faced nearly two dozen felony counts, including criminal
sexual assault, aggravated criminal sexual abuse, child pornography,
solicitation of child pornography, obstruction of justice, and commu-
nicating with a witness.

In spite of the seriousness of the charges filed against him only
three months earlier, Reynolds was safely reelected to Congress in
November 1994. He even ran unopposed. However, his second term
in Congress ended prematurely when he was convicted in August
1995 on multiple counts of criminal sexual assault, criminal sexual
abuse, obstruction of justice and child pornography. The prosecution asked for a fifteen-year sentence. The judged handed down only
five years in a decision announced September 28, 1995. Reynolds
resigned his congressional seat three days later.

The situation for Reynolds only worsened after his conviction
on a variety of sex offenses in Illinois state court. While he was
preoccupied with his legal difficulties in the Illinois criminal justice
system, authorities uncovered numerous irregularities with his
campaign finances. This time Reynolds was indicted in federal court.
In April 1997, Reynolds was convicted of fifteen counts including
bank fraud, wire fraud, conspiracy to defraud the Federal Election
Commission, and making false statements to federal investigators.

Reynolds remained defiant throughout his Illinois state and federal court trials. He denied any wrongdoing. However, during his sentencing following his federal convictions, Reynolds became contrite and admitted he broke the law. He was sentenced to six and one-half years in prison and was to begin serving his federal sentence once he completed his Illinois prison sentence in January 1998.

In early 2001, with more than three years remaining in Reynolds's prison term Bill Clinton commuted Reynold's federal sentence at the request of Jesse Jackson. Once freed from prison, Reynolds went to work for Jackson at Operation PUSH.

In 2014, Reynolds ran into legal difficulties in Zimbabwe, including allegations that he overstayed his visa and was in possession of pornographic videos. He was deported to South Africa. The following year, Reynolds was indicted in the US on four counts of failing to file income tax returns for 2009–2012. After he was released from custody on bond, court officials pursued efforts to have Reynolds fitted with an electronic monitoring device. He lashed out, saying, "In 2015, they want to treat a black man like he's a slave."[17]

DOROTHY RIVERS

Chicago's Dorothy Rivers was known for her lavish parties, profligate spending, and generous gift-giving. The invitations to one New Year's Eve party were hand-delivered by a limousine-driven Santa Claus who also handed out glasses of champagne with each invitation. Rivers literally had herself chauffeured to upscale stores such as Neiman Marcus. One clothing shop owner called her "the Duchess" because of her expensive spending habits. River's spending did not end with just her needs and wants. She spread good cheer when she bought her son a new Mercedes-Benz.

Rivers had a couple of business interests. One was running the Chicago Mental Health Foundation, a facility for pregnant teens and mentally disabled young girls. However, Rivers was best known for her other business activity. She had a key management role in Jesse Jackson's Operation PUSH/Rainbow Coalition.

Because neither the foundation nor PUSH paid her the salary she needed to finance her opulent activities, Rivers got the money the old-fashioned way. She stole it from the taxpayers. The status quo unraveled for Rivers when suspicions arose with federal investigators at the Department of Housing and Urban Development regarding how she was spending government grants intended to fund the Chicago Mental Health Foundation. Rivers stole much of the money and used it to support her lavish lifestyle. An investigation uncovered Rivers' fraud.

After she was caught and charged, Rivers admitted that federal investigators had overwhelming evidence she misappropriated at least five million dollars from various government grants. In April 1997, she entered an Alford guilty plea, a specific type of plea agreement meaning that Rivers agreed there was more than enough evidence to convict her and she was not contesting the charges. The following November, she was sentenced to five years and ten months in federal prison. However, three years later, she was freed from prison when Bill Clinton commuted her sentence at the request of Jesse Jackson. Rivers did not even trouble herself with submitting to the Justice Department an executive clemency request.

Henry G. Cisneros

At the age of thirty-three years, Henry G. Cisneros was elected mayor of San Antonio, Texas, in 1981, making him the first Mexican-American to lead a major American city. A dozen years later, Bill Clinton nominated Cisneros be his first secretary of Housing and Urban Development.

While he was mayor, Cisneros engaged in an extramarital affair with Linda D. Medlar, a two-time divorcee whose third husband was a local jewelry store owner. Medlar had been a volunteer for

Cisneros over the course of several campaigns. Their affair was the worst-kept secret in the city. Everyone talked openly about it, but it was not until one local newspaper published an exposé that the rest of the media began reporting it.

Cisneros was already in the middle of a proactive damage-control effort in anticipation of a run for statewide office when the exposé was published. Cisneros had been holding a series of one-on-one, off-the-record meetings with area reporters. He informed them of his extramarital affair in an elaborate plan to co-opt the media and gain their support if the affair was to become widely known by the public.

Legal difficulties ensued for Cisneros when he lied to FBI agents during the routine background check and interview that was conducted as part of his 1993 nomination to be HUD secretary. He was untruthful about the amount of money he paid to Medlar following their affair, claiming he gave her about $60,000 on human-itarian grounds because she had fallen on hard times after their tryst became public. In fact, Cisneros paid Medlar more than $250,000, a dizzying amount that smacked of hush money. The evidence against Cisneros was so overwhelming that in March 1995 US Attorney General Janet Reno was forced to appoint David M. Barrett as an independent counsel to investigate the wrongdoing.

Two years later, Cisneros was indicted on eighteen counts of conspiracy, giving false statements to federal investigators, and obstruction of justice. In September 1999, Cisneros worked out a plea deal with prosecutors and he pleaded guilty to lying to FBI agents. A deal was quickly negotiated when Cisneros learned Medlar had taped dozens of telephone conversations in which Cisneros admitted he lied to the FBI. Cisneros was given neither jail time nor probation, but he was fined $10,000. Less than eighteen months later, Bill Clinton pardoned him, although Cisneros had not submitted a clemency request to the Justice Department.

After receiving his presidential pardon, Cisneros became a prolific contributor to Democratic candidates and political action committees. Between 2000 and 2019, he contributed more than $105,000 to various Democratic candidates and PACs, including nearly $30,000 to political committees and campaign organizations in support of Hillary Clinton.[18]

Linda Medlar

The other woman in the married Cisneros's life was Linda Medlar. The pair brazenly carried on a relatively open romance for years. When Cisneros began plotting a run for higher office, he ended the relationship. After the first press report made the affair completely public, Cisneros began paying Medlar large sums of money in a likely attempt to impede investigations into the details of their affair.

While Cisneros was fighting his legal battles, Medlar had to contend with her own legal difficulties. Like Cisneros, Medlar lied to investigators about the money she received from Cisneros. She also lied on bank documents when she applied for a mortgage to purchase a home in Lubbock, Texas.

Medlar was indicted on twenty-eight counts, including bank fraud and money laundering. In September 1997, Medlar struck a plea deal with prosecutors and she pleaded guilty to several charges. She was sentenced to three and one-half years in prison, but she was released after eighteen months for cooperating in the investigation against Cisneros. Linda Medlar, divorced for the third time following the revelation of her affair with Cisneros, was pardoned by Bill Clinton without ever having filed a formal clemency petition.

John M. Deutch

John M. Deutch served as the director of Central Intelligence for Clinton between May 1995 and December 1996. He began his tenure by launching a massive political correctness campaign aimed at fast-tracking the hiring and promotion of women and minorities as part of a strategic diversity plan. However, the action he undertook to handcuff the ability of "case officers"—those CIA employees that work clandestinely—to meet with bad actors on the world stage seriously undermined human intelligence collection efforts and had widespread repercussions, especially regarding the growing threat of terrorism. CIA case officers and "agents"—foreigners in the employ of or who are working with US intelligence officers—must sometimes associate with undesirable elements if they are to gather valuable intelligence.

After Deutch left the CIA, classified information was discovered on the government-owned laptop he was using at home. He stored large amounts of sensitive intelligence on the laptop designated for the storage of only unclassified information. Moreover, the laptop was connected to a modem, which made all of the information vulnerable for exploitation by hostile governments. Mishandling of classified information is a serious breach of security for persons working with such information. Of all people, the CIA director should know better.

CIA security specialists immediately commenced an investigation of Deutch's mishandling of the classified material. Upon conclusion of the eighteen-month investigation, the CIA's Office of General Counsel declined to refer the matter to the Justice Department as was standard protocol in such matters. The CIA also decided to not disclose the matter to the Intelligence Oversight Committees of the Congress or the Intelligence Oversight Board of the president's Foreign Intelligence Advisory Board.[19]

The CIA's Inspector General picked up the matter where the agency's general counsel office left-off by opening a formal investigation in March 1998. Shortly thereafter, the Inspector General's office referred the matter to DOJ.

A Justice Department investigation confirmed that Deutch knowingly mishandled classified information. Yet, in April 1999, Attorney General Janet Reno declined to pursue criminal charges against him. Instead, she directed an investigation to determine the fitness of Deutch to retain his security clearances.

Simultaneously, the Defense Department launched its own investigation regarding Deutch's handling of classified information while he served as under secretary of defense for acquisition and technology from April 1993 to March 1994 and as deputy secretary of defense from March 1994 to May 1995.

Forensic analysis of the information technology equipment Deutch used revealed he had 675 pages of text stored on unclassified computers and related media that "contain[ed] many entries that include[d] collaterally classified material and should, therefore, have been marked and treated as classified when written."[20] A further review found that an additional fourteen entries contained references to special access programs—information that is classified at the absolute highest levels. A fifteenth entry also referred to a special access program when Deutch entered the information, but the entry was no longer classified when the review was conducted.

Nearly another two years elapsed before Deutch finally admitted his guilt in improperly safeguarding classified material. He was negotiating a plea agreement with Justice Department officials when Clinton preempted the entire matter by pardoning Deutch on January 20, 2001.

According to Federal Election Commission disclosures, Deutch gave $7,500 in political contributions in the twenty years prior to the year 2000. However, between 2001 and 2019, Deutch contributed almost $47,000 in political contributions. Nearly all were given to Democratic candidates and causes. Deutch gave $4,300 of that money to Hillary Clinton.

CHARLES D. RAVENEL

Charles D. Ravenel was already a seasoned veteran of electoral politics before he turned forty years old. He unsuccessfully ran for governor of South Carolina in 1974 at the age of thirty-five. Four years later, he ran against and lost to Strom Thurmond for a US Senate seat. His Senate candidacy was likely doomed when it was learned he told a New York audience he was embarrassed to have been from South Carolina and, if elected, he would essentially become New York's third US Senator.

In January 1980, President Jimmy Carter named Ravenel the Associate Deputy Secretary of Commerce. Ravenel left the post a few months later to run for the US House of Representatives, a race he lost in November 1980.

Fifteen years later, Ravenel pleaded guilty to conspiring to defraud the US government in a scheme that resulted in the one of the largest bank frauds in South Carolina history. Ravenel and a partner owned nearly 25 percent of Citadel Federal Savings Bank in Charleston, South Carolina. As an insider, Ravenel had limits in borrowing money from Citadel. Board members and federal regulators were to be notified when Ravenel did borrow money from the bank.

Prosecutors accused Ravenel and his partner of using Citadel as their "personal piggy bank."[21] When Ravenel got into a financial squeeze over some poor investments he conspired to have as many as eight people apply for and receive straw loans, that is, money that was really intended for Ravenel and not the loan recipients on record.

Ravenel pleaded guilty on October 5, 1995, for his role in conspiring to have accomplices secretly borrow $70,000 on his behalf. That specific loan was never repaid.[22] Ravenel also admitted taking part in a check-kiting scheme in which he wrote three bad checks in the total amount of $155,000.[23] The Citadel Federal Savings Bank was seized by federal regulators after it posted a loss of more than $1.3 million in 1991. The bank failed the following year at a cost of $8 million to taxpayers.[24] Investors lost nearly $11 million that was attributable to Ravenel.[25]

In December 1996, US District Judge Sol Blatt Jr. sentenced Ravenel to eleven months in federal prison and ordered him to pay $65,000 in restitution for his role in the bank fraud. Ravenel got off lightly considering one accomplice received a sentence of two and a half years and Ravenel accepted a plea agreement sentencing range of fifteen to twenty-one months in prison without parole that was well short of the sentencing guidelines of twenty-four to thirty months.[26] In addition, at his sentencing, Ravenel disputed the very facts he agreed to when he pleaded guilty. He even submitted a bogus letter of support that misstated the facts and his responsibility in the fraud.[27]

Ravenel was originally to have been sentenced in October 1996, but he asked for probation instead of the prison time he agreed to in his plea agreement. Judge Blatt postponed the sentencing hearing one month to give Ravenel and the prosecution time to restate their cases. In spite of Ravenel's backpedaling and reneging on his plea agreement, Judge Blatt looked kindly upon Ravenel and gave him a much lighter sentence than he could have received.

Clinton pardoned Ravenel in 2001 for his crimes, even though Ravenel did not bother to submit a clemency petition to the Justice Department.

ARNOLD PROSPERI

Bill Clinton and Palm Beach, Florida real estate lawyer Arnold Prosperi had a friendship that was more than three decades old. The two attended Georgetown University together and Prosperi managed Clinton's 1967 campaign for student council president. According to press reports, Prosperi also rescued Clinton from the water during a summer boating accident.

Prosperi was an active campaigner on behalf of Clinton when he ran for president in 1992. Prosperi engaged in fundraising activities throughout the state of Florida and he was a special guest at the Clintons' post-election reception for Florida campaign participants.

In 1993, Prosperi cochaired a nearly $500,000 fundraising effort alongside Susan Thomases to raise money for the White House Historical Association to remodel the White House. Unfortunately,

Hillary's choice of decorators was fellow Arkansan and her good friend Katherine "Kaki" Hockersmith, whose refurbishment of the White House was garish. It was a combination of white trash sophisticate and redneck chic and the end result was described as befitting a "Hot Springs bawdy house."[28] Banana yellow curtains, "peachy-pink" drapes, candy stripe upholstery, gold silk-gilded high-back chairs, and a royal blue rug were just a few of Hockersmith's tasteless choices for the president's official residence and office. It was no surprise other decorators referred to her as "Tacky Kaki."[29]

Prosperi contributed $10,000 to the fund in 1993 and another $25,000 in 1994. According to federal prosecutors, the $25,000 contribution came from funds Prosperi embezzled from a client.[30]

On November 6, 1997, a federal jury convicted Prosperi on five of the fifteen counts he faced. US District Judge Kenneth L. Ryskamp threw out Prosperi's three convictions for counterfeiting bank documents. Ryskamp also tossed out several mail fraud and money laundering charges just before the jury was to begin deliberations.

Prosperi was found guilty on two counts of filing false tax returns in an effort to hide millions of dollars he embezzled from a client. Prosperi failed to report $1.4 million of the $7.9 million he stole from eighty-four-year-old client Patrick Donovan and his wife, Christine.[31] Nearly $1 million of Donovan's money was deposited into Prosperi's bank account. Prosperi also misused Donovan's funds to pay mortgages on a pair of ocean-front homes Prosperi owned.

In March 1998, Judge Ryskamp sentenced Prosperi to three years' imprisonment and one year of probation and fined him $25,000. He was also ordered to pay off a $700,000 tax bill owed to the IRS.

Prosperi resigned from the Florida Bar Association in 1998 on the eve of disciplinary hearings before the Florida Supreme Court over his tax fraud convictions.

In January 2001, Clinton commuted Prosperi's sentence to home detention.

According to Federal Election Commission records, Prosperi made about $53,000 in political contributions to Democratic candidates and committees following his $1,000 contribution to Bill Clinton in 1991. This included $3,000 to Hugh Rodham's failed 1994 Senate candidacy and $2,300 to Hillary Clinton's 2008 presidential campaign.[32]

DAVID C. OWEN

Washington, DC lawyer James Hamilton was a longtime acquaintance of Hillary Clinton. The pair worked on the congressional Watergate proceedings targeting President Richard Nixon in 1974. A partisan political operative, Hamilton was deeply involved in the Democrat investigation of Ronald Reagan's 1980 presidential campaign. The politically inspired investigation uncovered no improprieties whatsoever.

In private practice, Hamilton represented three US Senators embroiled in ethics investigations. The three were Dennis DeConcini, David Durenberger, and Herman Talmadge. DeConcini was one of the infamous Keating Five. Durenberger violated congressional limits on honoraria in raking in more than $100,000. He also devised a scheme to defraud the Senate of more than $40,000 in travel reimbursements. Talmadge filed more than $43,000 in bogus expense reimbursement claims.

Hamilton was the chief counsel of the Clinton-Gore transition team and he made recommendations on political appointee nominations. He also advised Clinton on Supreme Court nominations. Hamilton represented David C. Owen, a former lieutenant governor in Kansas from 1973 to 1975. Owen was sentenced on May 10, 1993, to one year and one day in federal prison and fined more than $6,000 for failing to report $100,000 in income. Hamilton pressed Clinton for a pardon for Owen. Clinton gave him one.

Between 2000 and 2018, James Hamilton donated more than $15,000 to Hillary Clinton's various campaign organizations.

CHAPTER 3

Crooks and Other Miscreants

"It was clear it was a last-minute decision," said a lawyer who represented one of the people pardoned in the [Espy] case. "And there were no applications for these guys. It was clear that it was coming from the White House."[1]

BILL CLINTON REWARDED with executive clemency a staggering number of no-doubt-about-it political crooks. These were not average Americans who mistakenly got swept up in a questionable business deal. Nearly all these people were political operatives who cheated the system to get ahead, to make more money, to exert improper influence or take advantage of some unsuspecting and trusting souls. Not surprisingly, nearly every crook was a friend of Bill and Hillary Clinton or was a "friend of a friend."

ALPHONSO M. ESPY

Alphonso Michael "Mike" Espy was the proverbial flypaper when it came to influence peddling, making and accepting illegal gratuities, and the improper solicitation of gifts during his tenure as secretary of agriculture. Espy served as Bill Clinton's agriculture secretary from 1993–1994.

During Espy's short service as ag secretary, businesses with significant financial interests before the Agriculture Department began plying Espy with countless gifts. Espy received tens of thousands of dollars in improper gifts including airline tickets, hotel lodging, limousine rides, crystal ware, cash, and illegal campaign contributions directed to his brother in a likely attempt to influence Espy's decision-making.

In September 1994, Attorney General Janet Reno reluctantly appointed Donald Smaltz as independent counsel to investigate the allegations of rampant graft involving and related to Mike Espy. Espy resigned three months after the investigation began. After an exhaustive investigation, Espy was indicted on thirty-nine counts of illegally soliciting and accepting gifts and gratuities valued at more than $35,000.

During the criminal trial, the prosecution never attempted to prove a link between the improper gratuities and any official act by Espy. Bribery requires a quid pro quo, whereas the federal statute prohibiting illegal gratuities does not require proof there was a payback. It only stipulates that receiving gratuities by government officials is illegal. The jury did not see it that way. They accepted the defense argument that Espy merely accepted gifts without strings attached from various corporate interests and the jury acquitted him.

Although Espy ultimately was not convicted of soliciting and accepting illegal gifts and gratuities, the various lobbyists and corporate executives who provided the largesse were not so lucky. A dozen entities and individuals pleaded guilty or were convicted in federal trials of involvement in illegal gift-giving to and/or influence peddling of Espy while he was a cabinet officer, or in engaging in related illegal activities during Espy's stewardship of the Agriculture Department.

Independent counsel Donald Smaltz had remarkable success for a man labeled as "a nickel-and-dime guy with nickel-and-dime charges" by longtime Clinton adviser and confidante James Carville.[2] Nearly all of those convicted as a result of the Espy scandal were pardoned by Bill Clinton. One was pardoned on December 22, 2000. Seven more were pardoned on January 20, 2001. None of the January recipients submitted pardon petitions to the Department of Justice.

JOHN J. HEMMINGSON

John J. Hemmingson was the chairman and chief executive officer of Crop Growers, a Kansas-based crop insurance firm. Hemmingson was convicted in December 1996 on three charges of making illegal campaign contributions to Espy's brother, Henry W. Espy Jr., during his failed run for a Mississippi seat in the US House of Representatives. A money laundering conviction stemmed from Hemmingson providing $20,000 in illegal campaign cash to a colleague to pass on to Henry Espy. The company, Crop Growers, was fined $2 million for making $46,000 in illegal contributions to Henry Espy's campaign.

Hemmingson was sentenced to one year in federal prison, fined $30,000, and ordered to pay $20,000 in restitution. He was pardoned by Bill Clinton even though he never submitted a clemency petition to the Justice Department.

In 2008, Hemmingson was appointed to the Board of Regents for Gonzaga University and four years later became a trustee of the Spokane, Washington-based school.

ALVAREZ T. FERROUILLET

Alvarez T. Ferrouillet Jr. was a codefendant at the Hemmingson trial. He chaired a committee that was formed to retire the campaign debt after Henry Espy's failed run for a US House seat. Ferrouillet was convicted of ten counts, including interstate transportation of stolen property and making false statements to government agents. He was the middleman of the illegal $20,000 campaign contribution made by Hemmingson.

Ferrouillet pleaded guilty in February 1997 to six additional charges related to bank fraud regarding a $75,000 loan to Henry Espy's political campaign. His law firm, Ferrouillet & Ferrouillet, pleaded guilty to one count of conspiracy regarding the same bank fraud allegation. Ferrouillet was sentenced to one year in prison and fined $10,000. His law firm was fined $10,000. Ferrouillet, too, was pardoned by Clinton despite never having filed a Justice Department clemency petition.

RICHARD DOUGLAS

Sun-Diamond Growers of California was the country's largest grower of nuts and dried fruit, such as raisins. In the mid-1990s, the company had millions of dollars in contracts with the Defense and Agriculture Departments to provide various food products to military commissaries and subsidized school lunch programs. Sun-Diamond was found guilty on eight counts and fined $1.5 million stemming from illegal gifts and campaign contributions the company gave to Mike and Henry Espy. One guilty conviction was later overturned on appeal.

Richard Douglas was senior vice president for corporate affairs for Sun-Diamond when he gave Mike Espy various illegal gifts including luggage, meals and tickets valued at more than $7,600. A jury convicted Douglas in November 1997 of one count of giving illegal gratuities. Douglas was acquitted of a second felony count of providing a $3,100 airline ticket for Mike Espy to fly to Europe on vacation with his girlfriend, Patricia Dempsey.

JAMES H. LAKE

A prominent lobbyist for Sun-Diamond Growers, James H. Lake admitted guilt regarding illegal activities related to Mike Espy. In October 1995, Lake pleaded guilty to one count of making illegal corporate campaign contributions and committing wire fraud when fundraising for Henry Espy. He gave a $5,000 contribution to Espy's campaign and was improperly reimbursed by Sun-Diamond. He also confessed to two counts of violating the Federal Election Campaign Act for making an additional $4,000 in illegal contributions to Henry Espy's campaign. He was given two years of probation and fined $150,000.

Both Lake and Richard Douglas were pardoned by Clinton. Neither man submitted a clemency request to the Justice Department.

DON TYSON

The Arkansas-based poultry giant Tyson Foods, Inc., headed by longtime Clinton supporter Don Tyson, paid $6 million in fines and investigation reimbursement fees for giving $12,000 in illegal gifts to Espy. Influence peddling of Espy by Tyson Foods employees violated the *Meat Inspection Act of 1907*, which prohibited the agriculture secretary from receiving anything of value from any "[a]ny person, firm, or corporation, or any agent or employee of any person, firm, or corporation" he regulated. Don Tyson referred to the illegal gifts the company gave to Espy, including four tickets to Clinton's 1993 inauguration dinner valued at $6,000 and a weekend trip to watch a Dallas Cowboys football game, as "common hospitality."

Espy wasn't the only one who received special attention from Tyson Foods, the world's largest poultry processing facility. Don Tyson and Bill and Hillary Clinton were inextricably tied. As Arkansas governor, Clinton engineered the awarding of millions of dollars in tax breaks to Tyson Foods. Coincidentally, of course, Tyson's executives generously donated to Clinton's political campaigns.

Bestowing state largesse on Arkansas's biggest corporate firms was a policy that served the Clintons well. In one four-year period, Arkansas business interests paid for more than two hundred trips taken by Bill and Hillary Clinton, and nearly half of those were paid for by Tyson Foods.[3] On at least nine occasions, the Clintons were treated to free trips on Don Tyson's executive jet.[4]

Tyson's ties to the Clintons ran deep. Rose Law Firm partner Hillary Clinton represented Tyson Foods, and the Clintons frequently vacationed at the summer home of the poultry firm's general counsel and his wife, James and Diane Blair. Diane Blair also happened to be a Clinton campaign adviser.[5] Environmentalists claim the Clinton administration ran roughshod over the environment when it studiously ignored the pollution of Arkansas waterways by poultry waste from Tyson Foods.[6]

When Clinton launched his 1992 presidential run, Tyson said he and his family "maxed-out" in political contributions to Clinton's campaign.

Such deep political ties no doubt heavily influenced Clinton to pardon Tyson Foods' senior executives Jack Williams and Archibald Schaffer (see Chapter 6). Williams and Schaffer were convicted in the bribery and illegal gratuities scandal involving Espy.

Don Tyson continued his generosity by contributing $1,000 to Hillary's 2000 Senate campaign and $4,600 to her 2008 presidential run.

JACK L. WILLIAMS

Jack L. Williams was a senior lobbyist for Tyson Foods when he was convicted of making false statements to federal agents regarding having given illegal gifts to Mike Espy, having given a cash "scholarship" to Espy's girlfriend, Patricia Dempsey, and having lied about his relationship to Espy. Williams did not bother submitting a petition to the Justice Department requesting a pardon. Clinton gave him a pardon anyway.

RONALD H. BLACKLEY

Ronald H. Blackley was the longtime chief of staff for Espy. Blackley first worked for Espy when he was elected to Congress and later, when Espy became Clinton's Agriculture Secretary.

Attention was focused on Blackley during the Espy scandal, when it was learned that while he worked for Espy in the House of Representatives, Blackley was paid by farmers seeking government subsidy payments. Blackley operated Ron Blackley & Associates, a consulting business, concurrent with his House employment. He told Senate Agriculture Committee staff during Espy's confirmation process that he ended the consulting business before he became an employee of the Agriculture Department. That statement was untrue.

Shortly after Espy began receiving gifts and gratuities from Tyson Foods, Blackley ordered Agriculture Department employees to cease working on tougher inspection standards for the poultry industry.[7] Only ten agricultural businesses nationwide had appeals requesting increased subsidy levels that reached the highest level of USDA review during Blackley's first year as chief of staff. Five of those were former Blackley clients, and all five had favorable appeal outcomes after Blackley intervened in the appeal process.[8]

A federal grand jury indicted Blackley on April 22, 1997, on three counts of failing to properly disclose in mandatory ethics filings that he and his wife had received $22,025 in outside income from two farmers in 1993 only weeks after he became an Agriculture Department employee.[9] Blackley received $21,025 from Charles Fuller and $1,000 from Charles Cochran, a pair of farmers from Espy's home state of Mississippi. Fuller and Cochran received $63,000 and $284,000, respectively, in Agriculture Department subsidies in 1993 after they paid Blackley for his consulting work.[10]

On multiple occasions from 1993 to 1996 Blackley told federal officials and investigators, both verbally and in writing, that he did not have any income outside of his government job. He also claimed he had received "absolutely no money" from outside entities, including former clients. Those statements were complete lies. Moreover, Blackley came under the Ethics in Government Act of 1978 that required him to report all outside income and gifts.

On December 7, 1997, a federal jury convicted Blackley of all three counts of making false statements to government agencies. He faced a maximum sentence of five years in prison and a fine of $750,000 for all three counts.

US District Judge Royce Lamberth imposed sentence on Blackley on March 18, 1998. Blackley received a sentence of twenty-seven months in prison and three years of probation. Blackley appealed his conviction all the way to the US Supreme Court, arguing in *Blackley v. U.S.*, 99-15, that the independent counsel did not have the authority to prosecute his criminal actions. The Supreme Court rejected his appeal without comment, allowing the conviction and the sentence to stand.

Blackley was pardoned in 2001 despite of not having submitted a pardon application to the Justice Department.

BROOK K. MITCHELL

One of Blackley's former clients who were among the five agriculture companies that received a favorable appeal review was Brook K. Mitchell Sr., and his company, Five M Farming Enterprises. Mitchell and Five M Farming pleaded guilty in November 1996 to four counts of illegally obtaining $776,860 in crop subsidy payments from 1992 to 1995. The limit in crop subsidies was set at $50,000 per company.

Mitchell fraudulently applied for multiple subsidies, claiming various companies were the recipients. USDA officials turned down Mitchell's subsidy request, but he later received the payments when Blackley interceded and had the earlier decision overturned. Mitchell pleaded guilty to the fraud after he was caught and was sentenced to three years of probation and ordered to make restitution to the government. Despite not having submitted a clemency petition, Mitchell was pardoned by Clinton as he left office.

STUART COHN

Stuart Cohn of New Haven, Connecticut sold commodity options from his business, Cohn Precious Metals, Inc., in direct violation of a 1979 law banning such sales. Cohn Precious Metals eventually went bankrupt when it was unable to deliver the millions of dollars of deferred delivery contracts it sold to unsuspecting customers. Cohn pled guilty and was sentenced in 1983.

Cohn received a pardon at the end of Clinton's presidency in 2001. A key figure who helped him get the pardon was Congressman Sam Gejdenson of Connecticut, who just happened to be married to Cohn's sister. Cohn remarked, "This is nothing. I'm just an average person who has a brother-in-law who's prominent."[11]

Gejdenson was a very liberal Congressman who was a staunch supporter of Bill and Hillary Clinton and their politics. In addition, Gejdenson and Clinton had a friendship that went back over thirty years. As college students, they worked together on the 1970 Senate campaign of Americans for Democratic Action chairman Reverend Joseph Duffey, an antiwar activist who ran against incumbent Democrat Senator Thomas Dodd.[12] As president, Clinton appointed Duffey to head the US Information Agency.

WILLIAM D. FUGAZY

William D. Fugazy was a prominent New Yorker who owned Fugazy International, a city limousine service. His company operated a private car-and-driver service that served Manhattan, Westchester County, and parts of western Connecticut. Fugazy was a close friend of New York Governor Mario Cuomo and political supporter of New York City Mayor Rudolph Guiliani.

By the mid-1980s, Fugazy's businesses faced tax and legal difficulties. By the end of the 1980s, Fugazy personally owed $1.7 million in back taxes to the Internal Revenue Service and New York state. In 1990, he lost a $46 million judgment stemming from a suit filed by a company regarding a business transaction that soured.

Fugazy filed for personal bankruptcy in 1990 and proceeded to hide approximately $2.4 million in money and assets. After he was caught, he struck a plea deal with federal prosecutors. In 1997, Fugazy pleaded guilty to a single count of perjury in bankruptcy proceedings in return for an agreement by prosecutors to not pursue criminal charges against members of his family. He was sentenced to two years' probation and fined $2,400.

Fugazy's criminal record was wiped clean by Clinton even though he was not eligible for consideration of clemency according to Justice Department guidelines. A minimum five-year period had not elapsed since the completion of Fugazy's sentence.

Bernard Nussbaum, a close Hillary friend since their days together on the Watergate committee, lobbied for the pardon.[13] However, what likely put the pardon request over the top was the lobbying by billionaire John Catsimatidis, who was chief executive officer of Gristede's Foods, Manhattan's largest grocery store chain. Catsimatidis, who went straight to Clinton Chief of Staff John Podesta with his pardon request, also promised to raise one million dollars for the Clinton library.[14]

Catsimatidis was also very generous to Hillary's political campaigns following the pardon of Fugazy. According to Federal Election Commission records, between 2003 and 2016, Catsimatidis gave nearly $100,000 to political campaigns in support of Hillary Clinton.

WILLIAM A. BORDERS

US District Court Judge Alcee Hastings was appointed to the federal bench by President Jimmy Carter in 1979. It did not take him long to become crooked. Hastings accepted a $150,000 bribe in a 1981 racketeering trial in return for giving a lenient sentence and for ordering the return of seized assets to the two criminal defendants who were convicted on twenty counts. When the bribery was discovered, Hastings perjured himself during the criminal investigation. Unfortunately, the criminal trial of Hastings fell apart when Hastings' accomplice, attorney William A. Borders Jr., refused to testify against the judge. Hastings was acquitted, but the criminal matter did not end there.

In 1988, the Democrat-controlled US House of Representatives impeached Hastings by a stunning vote of 413-3 and the Senate convicted him sixty-nine-to-twenty-six, leading to his removal from the federal bench. Regrettably, the Senate failed to bar Hastings from seeking federal elective office, opening the door for his successful run for the House in 1992.

Hastings' accomplice, William Borders, was convicted in a separate criminal trial on numerous counts related to Hastings' bribery case. He was convicted of conspiring with Hastings to solicit bribes from defendants, and other related charges. Borders was disbarred and sent to prison, his third trip to jail related to the Hastings case. Borders was found in contempt of court and was sent to jail when he refused to testify during the criminal trial of Hastings. Borders was sent to jail a second time for contempt when he refused to testify during Hastings' impeachment.

Borders did not meet the Justice Department's basic clemency criteria of having demonstrated an upstanding character following his own conviction because he refused to cooperate in Hastings' criminal trial and impeachment proceeding. Nonetheless, Clinton pardoned Borders as Clinton left the White House.

Despite the pardon, Borders was unsuccessful in having his law license restored despite the support of the *Washington Post*.[15]

EDWARD R. DOWNE

Edward Reynolds Downe Jr. committed insider trading. During the summer of 1992 he pleaded guilty to conspiracy to commit wire fraud and filing false tax returns.[16] He also admitted he failed to disclose he owned stock in Bear, Stearns & Company while he was a serving on that firm's board of directors.

Throughout the latter half of the 1980s, Downe traded stock using insider information. For example, an executive at Kidde International, Inc. gave confidential information to Downe, which he used in his trading activities to enrich himself and as many as fifty-three friends and family members. The scope of Downe's illegal trading activities was said to rival that of "the Ivan Boesky and Michael Milken scandals."[17]

Downe, whose company, Downe Communications, owned *Ladies' Home Journal*, *American Home*, and *Family Weekly* magazines among others, admitted he hid his trading activities and concealed his ill-gotten profits from the Internal Revenue Service in Broadsword Ltd, a company he set up in Bermuda. All totaled, Downe and his pals made more than $23 million in illegal profits, alleged the Securities and Exchange Commission.

Downe was a member of New York's social elite. When arrested, he was married to Charlotte Ford, heiress to the Ford Motor Company, and he counted among his friends Martin Revson, cofounder of makeup giant Revlon; Leonard Lauder, the head of Estee Lauder; and the chairman and CEO of Warner Music, Robert Morgado.

Revson was implicated with Downe and five others—public relations guru Steven A. Greenberg; London businessman David Salamone; Kidde International Chairman Fred R. Sullivan; California real-estate investor Thomas Warde; and stockbroker Milton Weinger—in the illegal trading ring that became known as "the Southampton Seven."

The Long Island socialites would trade inside information during poker card games or while on Caribbean yachting trips. Some of the seven sat on corporate boards or had business relationships with companies that allowed them access to sensitive, nonpublic information that they passed to one another.

In September 1993, Downe was sentenced to only three years' probation and was ordered to perform three thousand hours of community service. In order to settle a separate civil suit filed by the Securities and Exchange Commission, Downe agreed to sell two residential properties and his art collection and forfeit the proceeds to the SEC.

In the three decades before he was pardoned, Downe became an active fundraiser and contributor to numerous politicians, nearly all of them Democrats. These included New York Governors Hugh Carey and Mario Cuomo, and New York City Mayors John Lindsay, Ed Koch, and David Dinkins. He gave money to Hillary Rodham Clinton for her 2000 Senate election, Vice President Al Gore in his presidential run, and he contributed money to New York Congressman Eliot Engel.

A close friend of Downe's was Connecticut Senator Christopher Dodd who wrote a letter to Clinton urging him to pardon Downe.[18] Perhaps only coincidentally, Downe helped Dodd buy a vacation home in Ireland at the time the Connecticut senator was lobbying for Downe's pardon. Clinton came through and pardoned Downe. Downe returned the favor by donating nearly $3,500 to Hillary's election campaigns between 2006 and 2016.

In 2016, Downe was again involved in a legal scandal. Downe was sued by an investor who alleged Downe failed to repay a $100,000 loan.[19]

SANDY LEWIS

"I recognize my conduct was wrong. For this I am deeply sorry," said Salim B. "Sandy" Lewis in December 1989 as he admitted his guilt in a stock price manipulation scheme from three years earlier. In May 1986, Lewis, the head of the broker-dealer firm S. B. Lewis & Co., requested two other brokers purchase more than four hundred thousand shares of Fireman's Fund stock.

Lewis wanted to drive up the price of the stock the day before American Express announced it would sell a new stock offering. Lewis promised to reward the brokers for any losses they might have suffered and for hiding his role in the scheme. American Express made $88 million from the new stock sale. Notorious stock cheat Ivan F. Boesky had ties to Lewis.[20]

Lewis was given three years' probation and fined $250,000. The sentencing judge ordered him to work in a drug rehabilitation clinic as terms of his probation. The attorney who prepared Lewis' pardon application was Douglas Eakeley, who just so happened to have been Clinton's roommate at Yale Law School and Oxford University.[21] Not surprisingly, Lewis received a presidential pardon.

RICHARD H. PEZZOPANE

By the time Richard H. Pezzopane was sentenced in November 1988, more than eighty judges, prosecutors, defense attorneys, court personnel, and police officers had been convicted. Like Pezzopane, they were nabbed in Operation Greylord, a joint federal investigation by the Federal Bureau of Investigation and the Internal Revenue Service Criminal Investigation Division into corruption in the judicial system of Cook County, Illinois.

Pezzopane was one of many conspirators involved in a scheme in which corrupt judges struck deals with various defense attorneys to pay cash bribes in exchange for favorable court treatment. Two of the judges involved had received "not recommended" ratings from the Chicago Bar Association in 1983 after questions arose regarding their integrity. One was voted off the bench by full Circuit Court of judges while the other was retained.

Dozens of judges, lawyers, law enforcement officers, and other officials participated in a widespread bribery scheme where verdicts, sentences, and other judicial decisions were purchased for as little as one hundred dollars. Alleged crimes in the bribery scheme ranged from drunk driving to narcotics possession charges.

Court charging documents described the scheme as a "successful, long-lasting, and thriving criminal enterprise in the midst of the court system."[22] One judge began collecting bribes from defense attorneys to recoup the bribe money he paid out when he was a defense attorney.

Pezzopane was a defense lawyer when he was caught in the "verdicts for sale" dragnet. He was sentenced to six months in prison and six months in a work release program.

Denver, Colorado attorney James M. Lyons joined Pezzopane's cause and requested Clinton pardon Pezzopane. This was another example of a convict in one state selecting an attorney who had a legal practice located several states and more than one thousand miles away who just so happened to be a close friend and supporter of the Clintons.

Lyons was a contributor of both hard and soft money exclusively to Democrats and Democratic causes having given tens of thousands of dollars since 2000. Lyons gave more than $14,000 to Hillary Rodham Clinton for her senate and presidential campaigns.

Lyons had been a longtime supporter of the Clintons, even before Bill was elected to the White House. The Clintons commissioned Lyons in early 1992 to create a report of Bill and Hillary's involvement in Whitewater Development Corporation when questions arose during the presidential campaign. The Whitewater scandal came to symbolize the excesses and cover-ups of the Clintons.

The independent counsel investigation into the Whitewater scandal resulted in the convictions of fourteen prominent Arkansans including Clinton's lieutenant governor, Jim Guy Tucker, several Clinton aides, friends and business associates, and the Clintons' 50 percent Whitewater investment partners, James B. and Susan H. McDougal.

The Lyons Report, as it came to be known, was a hastily prepared document that claimed the Clintons lost $68,000 in the

Whitewater deal and there were no improprieties committed by the Clintons. The irony of the Lyons Report was that although the Clintons claimed there was nothing scandalous about Whitewater, they had "inadvertently" neglected to mention Whitewater in mandatory financial disclosures required during the presidential race. The omission of Whitewater was a mere "oversight," according to the Clinton campaign.

It was later learned that Lyons' figure of $68,000 was wildly inaccurate. The Lyons Report had tens of thousands of dollars in incorrect Clinton expenses listed, according to the final report from the Whitewater independent counsel. Income tax filings by the Clintons revealed the actual figure was less than $22,000, and there were some questions regarding whether all that money was Whitewater related or if it involved other real estate investments the Clintons made and instead claimed were related to Whitewater.

At the time it was issued in March 1992, the Lyons Report served its purpose. It ended press inquiries regarding Whitewater during the 1992 presidential race.[23]

Still, there was more to the Clinton-Lyons relationship. Lyons was an accomplice in one of the sleaziest chapters of Clinton politics that was managed by Hillary. Bill's womanizing and trail of broken romances and one-night stands is what delayed Clinton from running for president in 1988, as he had originally planned. In the 1992 race, Hillary was better prepared to deal with what the Clinton campaign referred to as "bimbo eruptions" by going on the offensive. The campaign hired Jack Palladino of the investigative firm Palladino and Sutherland.

By reputation, Palladino would stoop to any level and use any means to achieve his clients' goals. For Hillary, his assignment was to eliminate as many of the potential bimbo eruptions as possible. Palladino sought affidavits from women denying they had a sexual tryst with Bill. Hillary confidante Betsey Wright managed Palladino's efforts on behalf of Hillary. Wright let on to the *Washington Post* that Palladino was used to ferret out bimbo eruptions. The money to first hire Palladino was funneled through the Clintons' friend, Jim Lyons.[24]

Jim Lyons' client, Richard Pezzopane, received a pardon without even submitting a clemency petition to the Department of Justice.

RUBEN JOHNSON

Texas state banking regulators closed Austin's United Bank of Texas on June 4, 1987, just six years after it opened and after four straight years of losses. United Bank was declared insolvent after posting a loss of $6 million in 1986 and it was on track to posting a similar loss for 1987. About $2 million in depositors' money was lost when the bank was ordered closed.[25]

United Bank suffered through a series of bad loans and high operating costs. The bank's chairman, Ruben Johnson, lavishly decorated the bank with opulent furnishings and artwork. A liquidator working for the Federal Deposit Insurance Corporation (FDIC) estimated the bank had enough furnishings—including mahogany desks, Karastan rugs, grandfather clocks, statues, sculptures, figurines and paintings—to fill twenty-one tractor trailers.[26]

In 1988, Johnson, who was a successful real estate developer prior to entering the banking business, was indicted on thirteen counts of misapplying $731,609 in bank funds in 1983 and 1984. He was charged with bilking tenants of surcharges he received in order to complete new construction of office spaces in the United Bank Tower. Federal prosecutors allege he received $131,000 in kickbacks from contractors performing work on United Business Tower and he received an additional $1 million in kickbacks from other construction projects.

Johnson was convicted in April 1989 and he faced up to sixty years in prison and a $65,000 fine. Instead, he was sentenced to eight years in prison and ordered to pay $4.5 million in restitution to the

FDIC. Johnson was released in July 1994 after serving just fifty-nine months.

On March 1, 1995, Johnson filed for Chapter 7 bankruptcy to stave off an auction of his multimillion-dollar estate in an exclusive West Austin neighborhood. The IRS claimed Johnson owed $214,000 in back taxes and penalties. The estate included a 6,319-square-foot main house and 2,448-square-foot guest house.[27]

Although Johnson dodged the IRS bullet, the FDIC in October 1995 requested permission from a federal judge to foreclose on the estate in order to recover funds toward satisfying the $4.5 million restitution bill. As of the date of the court filing, Johnson had paid less than $1,600 toward the restitution. A US bankruptcy judge ruled in September 1995 that the IRS could not foreclose on Johnson's property. Bankruptcy proceedings kept federal officials at bay. However, Johnson faced other financial difficulties as he lost a $900,000 civil judgment in a 1986 lawsuit brought by businessmen who lost money in the bank's closing. Compounding Johnson's difficulties was Travis County, which sought payment for back taxes on the property.

Johnson was a longtime major contributor to Democratic candidates and party organizations. Among his Democratic supporters lobbying Clinton for a pardon on his behalf were Lady Bird Johnson (a former First Lady), and retired CBS News anchor Walter Cronkite.[28] Ruben Johnson allowed Democratic politicians to use his private jet.[29] He contributed more than $100,000 to Democratic candidates in just one year, 1982. His bank lent more than $1 million to various Democratic candidates, including $228,000 to Gerry Mauro, who was elected Texas Land Commissioner in 1982.[30] Mauro eventually lost his gubernatorial challenge by a landslide to then Governor George W. Bush in 1998. Years after he was released from prison, Johnson was hired by Mauro at an annual salary of more than $61,000 to work for the Land Commission in July 1997 to help oversee a $52 million construction project.

Clinton's pardon of Johnson was not a surprise considering the personal relationship between Gerry Mauro and Bill Clinton. The two politicians had known each other since working together on the George McGovern campaign in Texas in 1972. Their friendship blossomed over the years. In 1992, Mauro violated Texas state ethics rules by placing more than two hundred telephone calls from his state office on behalf of Clinton's presidential run.[31] Clinton returned the political favor by pardoning Mauro's close friend and wealthy campaign contributor, Ruben Johnson.

JOHN F. McCORMICK

Detective John F. McCormick was one of seven detectives caught in the most extensive corruption scandal in the history of the Boston Police Department. In the fall 1988, the seven police detectives were convicted by a federal jury on fifty-six of the fifty-seven counts they faced including charges of conspiracy, extortion, and bribery. The evidence against them was overwhelming. Federal prosecutors presented over seventy witnesses and three hundred exhibits documenting the detectives taking cash from bar and nightclub owners. Collectively, the police detectives, who had the authority to shut down establishments over a number of license violations, accepted bribes to overlook operating infractions or extorted money with the threat of shutting down a business.

McCormick was convicted of accepting nearly $900 in bribes, and for his role with other officers in accepting $15,000 to perform an off-the-clock security detail for one business establishment that was never actually performed. US District Judge A. David Mazzone sentenced McCormick to three years in prison.

McCormick was among the lucky 140 who received a pardon from Bill Clinton on January 20, 2001. Representing him in his clemency request was Boston attorney Thomas E. Dwyer Jr. In addition to his reputation of being a successful lawyer, Dwyer had close personal connections to the Clintons. He was a bona fide Friend of Bill.[32]

Thomas Dwyer was a prolific fundraiser for Bill Clinton as well as other Democrats and various Democrat organizations. Between 1993 and 1996, Dwyer personally contributed more than $12,000 to just the Democratic National Committee. In January 1995, he was among a handful of prominent fundraisers who was invited to meet privately with Clinton in the White House Map Room.[33] That same year, Clinton appointed Dwyer to cochair the New England Lawyers for the Clinton-Gore '96 campaign committee. In December 1995, Dwyer joined Clinton for Christmas dinner.

Dwyer hosted a $2,000 a ticket Boston fundraiser for Hillary in December 1999 when she first ran for the Senate that raised $450,000.[34] Between 1997 and 2000, Dwyer personally contributed more than $30,000 to Democratic candidates and organizations. On his office desk sat a picture of he and Clinton, likely taken at some fundraising event.[35]

Dwyer also had indirect ties to the Clinton fundraising saga during Bill's tenure as Arkansas governor. Dwyer represented financial adviser Mark Ferber after he was indicted in a massive corruption scandal related to bond underwriting in Massachusetts. Ferber also became embroiled in the scandal-plagued Arkansas Development Finance Administration (ADFA).

Created when Clinton was the Arkansas governor, the ADFA was referred to as Clinton's "personal piggy bank." The ADFA doled out millions of dollars in bonds to businesses owned or operated by Clinton cronies, including family members of Hillary Clinton's Rose Law Firm partners. Ferber was questioned by authorities regarding suspect bond underwriting in Arkansas. In 1996, Ferber was indicted on seventy-nine counts of theft, fraud, and conspiracy in activities state authorities claimed cost taxpayers of Massachusetts $11 million.[36]

CHAPTER 4

Drug Dealers

"It's no secret that the ethical stoplights in the Clinton White House often worked erratically. On his final day in office they appear to have failed completely."[1]

BILL CLINTON ONCE freely admitted, "[W]hen I was in England I experimented with marijuana a time or two, and I didn't like it. I didn't inhale." Few people took Clinton at his word. Most believe he was insulating himself from being caught for lying about never having smoked—and inhaled—marijuana. Instead, he cleverly couched his words and offered a nuanced denial of ever having used marijuana aside from "a time or two" and he "didn't inhale."

Yet, one thing is certain. When William Jefferson Clinton was inaugurated in January 1993 as the forty-second president, the casual drug use culture arrived with attitude at 1600 Pennsylvania Avenue NW.

One of Clinton's first acts as president was to slash the size of the Office of National Drug Control Policy (the "Drug Czar") by 84 percent from a staff of 146 to a mere 24.[2] Enforcement of drug laws was de-emphasized. Casual drug use was considered as normal as drinking alcohol. The makeup of the White House staff epitomized the Clinton attitude of leniency toward drug abuse. For example,

Clinton White House spokesman Michael D. McCurry admitted that he had been an occasional drug user throughout his twenties.

Rumors were rampant about Clinton's own drug use even when he was the governor of Arkansas. Clinton's half-brother, Roger, was frank about Bill's cocaine use in a comment that was captured on audiotape by a police detective when Roger was negotiating a cocaine deal. He said, "I've got to get some for my brother, he's got a nose like a Hoover vacuum cleaner."[3]

Roger had been using hard drugs for years. He brazenly threw coke parties in the governor's mansion.[4] He was eventually caught, arrested, tried, and convicted in federal court for cocaine distribution and he spent time in prison.

There were other drug users and dealers in the Clinton clan and in the circle of close friends. Hillary's brother Tony was an admitted marijuana user.[5] Some of Bill's closest pals and political supporters were deeply involved in the drug trade. The most infamous was Danny Lasater.

Danny R. Lasater

It was Little Rock businessman Dan Lasater to whom Bill turned when he lost his first reelection bid as governor in 1980. Lasater had a reputation for throwing out-of-control drug parties that included plying high school girls with cocaine in return for sexual favors. Lasater developed a sexual relationship with a sixteen-year-old virgin after giving her cocaine and making it available for her to use as many as five dozen times.[6] By his own admission, Lasater gave cocaine to others on more than 180 occasions.[7]

The Clintons developed very close ties to Lasater, using his private jet to fly to various events. Hillary once used the jet to fly celebrities to a charity fundraiser she was hosting.[8] In return, Clinton sent millions of dollars in Arkansas state business to Lasater despite Lasater not having any experience in certain government contracts and services. In one example, in 1985, Clinton personally lobbied for the state to award more than $30 million in state bonds sales to Lasater to overhaul the state police communications system even though Lasater had no expertise in that line of work.[9] Lasater's former business partner, George E. Locke Jr., told the FBI that because "[Lasater] backed the right individual in Governor Clinton, Lasater & Co. received the contract."[10]

Lasater was eventually caught and tried in federal court for cocaine distribution. Roger Clinton was the star witness who provided key evidence against him. Lasater was convicted and in December 1986 he was sentenced to two and one-half years in federal prison. He only spent six months in prison, four months in a halfway house, and two months in house arrest. Fortunately for Lasater, Clinton was still the Arkansas governor and in November 1990, Clinton took care of Lasater by giving him a state pardon. Although Clinton's pardon did not wipe away the federal conviction, it did restore state rights to Lasater and arguably, the state pardon could allow Lasater to continue competing for Arkansas state contracts.

While in prison, Lasater turned over the reins of his operations to his trusted employee, Patsy Thomasson. He gave her power of attorney to run his business and personal affairs. In 1984, Lasater and Thomasson flew in Lasater's private jet to the Central American country of Belize, which happens to be a major transshipment point for cocaine and is a destination for money laundering. The pair claimed they were considering buying a Belize cattle farm.[11] Apparently, the couple were unaware there were countless cattle ranches in nearby Texas and Oklahoma.

White House Drug Policy

Thomasson followed the Clintons to Washington, DC, where she was appointed the director of the White House Office of Administration. Once in Washington, Thomasson became one of Hillary's "most trusted White House loyalists."[12] One of her major responsibilities was to manage the White House drug testing program. How appropriate.

White House staff members are required to undergo a rigorous FBI background check. Lower-level employees have their backgrounds investigated for the preceding fifteen years. Senior staff have their entire adult lives investigated. Part of the investigation includes a review of prior drug use. The Secret Service vets the completed investigation before permanent White House passes are granted and security clearances are given.

An FBI agent conducting White House background interviews in the 1990s reported casual drug use among Clinton staffers continued long after their college years. He observed, "[T]he Clinton staffers, older or younger, made no apology for their illegal drug use, which was more extensive, and included many 'heavy' drugs like cocaine, crack, LSD, and methamphetamine. Many were actually 'in your face' about it, using the FBI interview to try to debate me on the merits of making drugs legal."[13]

Associate White House Counsel William Kennedy III, a long-time Hillary Clinton confidante and Rose Law Firm partner, was stunned to learn that frequent and recent drug use were considered disqualifying factors for approving White House access. Kennedy told FBI Special Agent Gary Aldrich that he would not deny White House access or a security clearance to a staffer based on recent drug use.[14] Kennedy then issued a memo dated June 10, 1993, stating that drug abuse was a disability and current drug users could claim a right to work in the White House.[15]

Secret Service agents appearing before a House of Representatives panel in July 1996 testified that dozens of Clinton White House employees had engaged in recent hard narcotics drug use including using cocaine, crack cocaine, and hallucinogenic drugs—drug use that disqualified personnel from obtaining White House positions in prior presidential administrations was deemed acceptable by the

Clinton Administration. In fact, the Secret Service was instructed to clear individuals even if they were currently engaging in illegal drug activity "if they promised to quit *after* they were caught."[16]

More than one hundred Clinton appointees were initially denied permanent White House passes for undisclosed reasons although drug abuse was likely in most cases. Eventually, twenty-one top Clinton aides failed drug screening tests, but they were permitted to continue working in the White House as long as they took scheduled, biannual drug tests.[17] Patsy Thomasson had supervisory authority over the drug screening tests.

Consider the attitude of one of Clinton's cabinet members. The controversial surgeon general nominee who underwent a hard-fought confirmation in the Democrat-controlled Senate in 1993 was Joycelyn Elders. Elders worked for Clinton when he was the Arkansas governor.

Elders was an advocate for legalizing recreational drug use.[18] Her son was a longtime cocaine addict who was convicted of being a drug dealer. Underscoring the cavalier and pervasive attitude of arrogance that was prevalent among the Clinton crowd, Elders's son was caught buying cocaine in an undercover sting operation during the very same time his mother was undergoing Senate confirmation.

Bill and Hillary's acceptance of casual drug use among White House employees was not surprising given their own past. The Clintons' soft on drug abuse attitude continued throughout their eight years in Washington, DC, except when Bill ran for reelection in 1996. At that time, he asked Congress for an increase in drug law enforcement funding.

On Clinton's last day as president, he granted executive clemency to 176 recipients. Of those, a stunning number of pardons and commutations were given to individuals convicted of major drug crimes. Fifty people out of 176, or nearly one in three, received executive clemency despite committing drug crimes—major drug crimes in 96 percent of the cases.

Other presidents have granted clemency to individuals who received relatively harsh sentences for possessing small amounts of drugs intended for personal use. Forgiving someone for smoking a little weed or dabbling in minute amounts of addictive drugs was the purview of prior presidents. Freeing major drug kingpins—several, at that—did not occur. However, Clinton was different. He doled out clemency to hardened drug dealers involved in importing and selling large amounts of drugs, or in laundering drug cartel money.

Cocaine

Clinton's last day pardon and commutation recipients who were convicted of the importation or distribution of cocaine include Nicholas M. Altiere, Chris H. Bagley, David R. Blampied, Gloria L. Camargo, Charles F. Campbell, Donna D. Chambers, Roger Clinton, Loretta D. Coffman, Derrick A. Curry, Velinda Desalus, Antoinette M. Frink (a car dealership owner who provided cars to a major cocaine trafficker), Kimberly D. Johnson, Hildebrando Lopez, Belinda L. Lumpkin, Charles W. Morgan III, Vernon R. Obermeier, Miguelina Ogalde, Hugh R. Padmore, Pedro M. Riveiro, Richard W. Riley Jr., Anna L. Ross, Gregory L. Sands, Marlena F. Stewart-Rollins, Carlos A. Vignali (he conspired to ship eight hundred pounds of cocaine from California to Minnesota), Kevin A. Williams, and Mitchell C. Wood.

Marijuana

Those who were convicted of dealing marijuana were Scott L. Bane, David R. Chandler (he was also convicted of capital murder for arranging the slaying of a police informer), Donald R. Clark (he ran a $30 million drug ring), Rickey L. Cunningham, Marcos A. Fernandez, Robert I. Hamner, Jay H. Harmon, Jodie E. Israel, Michael J. Rogers, and Bettye J. Rutherford.

Heroin

Other recipients of Clinton clemency largesse included those who pushed heroin or traded in LSD, PCP, or methamphetamines. They included Lau C. Chin, Loretta S. Fish, Gerard A. Greenfield, Debi Rae Huckleberry, Billy T. Langston Jr., Kellie A. Mann, and Cory H. Stringfellow.

CLINTON CONTRADICTING CLINTON POLICY

Perhaps what is even more egregious than Clinton's lax view toward pardoning major drug dealers, traffickers, and money launderers was that granting them clemency ran counter to policies he claimed he favored just five years earlier.

A January 26, 1996, memo to the Justice Department from then White House Counsel Jack Quinn outlined additional restrictions Clinton had placed on favorable clemency consideration. Adoption of these restrictions made it *more difficult* for an applicant to get a pardon or commutation from Clinton than from previous presidents. The memo stated there were "certain categories of crimes which are so serious that the President *will not consider* granting a pardon for them under almost any circumstances [emphasis added]." Among the included crimes was "large scale drug trafficking" and "offenses involving central involvement in political corruption."[19]

It should not be overlooked that Clinton issued his memo in 1996. This followed the disastrous 1994 mid-term elections when Democrats lost control of both the House and Senate for the first time in forty years and Clinton was facing a potentially troublesome reelection bid. These political considerations may have had something to do with his "get tough on paper" attitude toward drug trafficking. Clinton conveniently ignored his tighter restrictions when he was issuing pardons and commutations willy-nilly in January 2001.

Cali Cartel Money Launderers

When the federal agents finally finished their two days of work in late November 1994, they had arrested a Cali cartel drug money laundering ring of nineteen people. Among those in the ring were partners in a Manhattan law firm, a pair of rabbis, a police officer, a firefighter, a diplomat, a bank manager, a stockbroker, husband and wife Swiss bankers, and a beer distributor. "Money became the narcotic. Even people in respectable professions yielded and succumbed to temptation," observed Special Agent William A. Gavin of the FBI's New York City office.[20]

The ring was one of the largest money laundering operations ever busted in New York.[21] It was the second largest money laundering operation ever prosecuted in Switzerland. The operation involved drug profits from the US, Canada, Puerto Rico and Europe.[22] As much as $100 million was laundered by the group from the time it began operation in October 1993 to when it was raided thirteen months later. In the ten months it was under surveillance, federal agents directly observed $15 million being laundered. During the surveillance, federal authorities seized $5 million from various couriers.

Robert Hirsch and Harvey Weinig, partners in the Manhattan law firm Hirsch-Weinig, and beer distributor Robert Spence, a former firefighter, were the ringleaders. The three ran the operation that involved cities as far away as Houston, Los Angeles, Miami, San Juan, and Zurich. Hirsch and Weinig used their firm's resources to direct the entire operation, including managing banking operations and money shipments.

Hirsch or Weinig would receive a phone call from Juan Guillermo Ocampo, a Cali representative in Germany, telling the lawyers that money was ready for pickup.[23] The amount would be in the tens to hundreds of thousands of dollars. The lawyers would contact Spence, who would send a courier. The main couriers were two Hasidic rabbis, Alexander Schwartz and Menashe Leifer, and Chaim Herman, a Spence acquaintance.

The couriers would fetch the money and bring it back to New York. Occasionally, it would be another regular courier such as Bronx police officer Michael Kalanz. One time, Kalanz stashed $1 million in his precinct locker for a brief period of time. On some occasions, the money would be stored in Weinig's apartment before being deposited in a bank account. Presumably, Weinig's wife, who was also an attorney and a law school professor, was not aware of the hundreds of thousands of dollars in cash her husband often kept in the apartment.

Others who served as couriers were Charles Bruno, a Queens firefighter; hospital administrator Gary Salerno; Donald Hayden, a Santa Monica, California stockbroker; and Latchezar Christov, a Bulgarian diplomat living in Los Angeles. Hayden and Christov would ship the money cross-country to New York using a package courier service. FBI agents who searched Salerno's home found a "hit man's kit" consisting of several weapons—including a garrote—ammunition, three pairs of handcuffs, and a law enforcement badge.

The courier, after making cash pickups in locations closer to New York, would lug the money in suitcases, duffel bags, or boxes, and would deposit the cash in a bank account managed by Spence. The bank account was opened by Hirsch and Weinig under the name of Transglobal Import Export Trading, Co., Inc. Patricia Dilluvio was the bank manager and an accomplice of the group who ensured the deposits occurred without difficulty. The money was then wire transferred to bankers Rachel and Leon Weinmann in Zurich, Switzerland. With the laundering operation completed, the Weinmanns would transfer the funds to banks in the US, Caribbean, or in Central America, where the Cali cartel would have access to it.

Hirsch, Weinig, and Spence collected a fee of 7 percent of the money they laundered. The couriers were paid between $1,000 and $6,000 per run. Federal investigators believe the ring transferred as much as $100 million during the time it was in operation. The Weinmanns told investigators the operation laundered at least $72 million.

During the surveillance, federal authorities learned the Cali cartel was furious over cash the money laundering ringleaders had stolen from them. Hirsch, Weinig, and Spence conspired to skim $2.5 million from the cartel by crafting an elaborate plan to fool the Colombians. The crooked lawyers drew up a fake indictment and seizure documents, claiming Spence and had been arrested, and the cash seized by federal agents. The Colombians did not fall for the story. They intended to get their money back from the three New Yorkers. They would use violence, if necessary.

Law enforcement authorities conducting surveillance of Weinig intercepted a telephone call in which Weinig explained to Hirsch his motive for taking the money from the cartel. Weinig said, "We're dealing with people who are total assholes, who are out of control, who are scumbag, lying cheats. And I am gonna be in this for the long haul? Fuck 'em! Fuck 'em! I'm taking a million dollars let's, let's see you get it from me."

The illegal activities did not end there. Spence and Weinig engaged in another criminal enterprise in November 1994. Spence had a shady business deal with a man named James Clooney that turned out badly. Spence claimed he lost nearly a quarter of a million dollars and he wanted to recover it from Clooney so, he kidnapped the man and demanded a ransom to make up for the money he lost. Weinig aided Spence in the ransom aspect of the kidnapping by ordering a pair of his law firm associates to draft legal papers transferring some of the kidnapping victim's assets to Spence that Clooney eventually signed.

It was not long after the conspirators were arrested and charged that nearly all of them offered to cooperate with federal authorities. Hirsch and Spence agreed to work with officials, but Weinig was steadfast in his refusal to cooperate. He was adamant in his alibi that he thought he was engaged in the sale of "gray market goods." He also refused to acknowledge the kidnapping of Clooney as a criminal act, instead referring to it in his clemency petition as an incident in which "a client of mine had detained an individual."

However, the voluminous transcripts compiled from hundreds of intercepted telephone calls provided ample evidence that Weinig knowingly engaged in laundering drug trade proceeds. Seventeen of the nineteen people in the ring pleaded guilty, but not Weinig. He waited until the eve of his trial before he admitted his guilt and requested to negotiate a deal, but by then Weinig's fate had been all but determined. Hirsch, Spence, and the Weinmanns provided authorities with ample evidence to gain a conviction of Weinig on most, if not all the thirty-eight counts he faced related to money laundering, and a separate count related to the kidnapping of Clooney.

One September 21, 1995, Weinig pleaded guilty to two counts related to his money laundering activities and he faced as much as twenty years in prison. On March 22, 1996, US District Court Judge Kevin T. Duffy sentenced Weinig to eleven years and three months in prison for his role in the drug money operation and kidnapping. Weinig was lucky. Another conspirator received an even longer sentence of twelve years and seven months.

Weinig's wife, Alice Morey, who was also an attorney, and a professor at the City University of New York Law School, hired a criminal defense attorney with close ties to the Clintons to lobby for her husband's release. Reid Weingarten had represented other infamous Clinton figures involved in various scandals or criminal activities including Ron Brown, Alphonso "Mike" Espy, Pauline Kanchanalak, and Yah Lin "Charlie" Trie. Kanchanalak and Trie were involved in the 1996 fundraising scandal when hundreds of thousands of dollars in illegal contributions were funneled into the Clinton-Gore reelection campaign. Weingarten also represented International Brotherhood of Teamsters President Ron Carey over the 1996 scandal when the union gave illegal contributions to Clinton's reelection committee in exchange for donations to Carey's union reelection fund.

Weingarten met with several Clinton insiders, including White House Counsels Bruce Lindsey and Beth Nolan and Clinton Chief of

Staff John Podesta, regarding Weinig's pardon request. Underscoring the reality that it was political ties that led to Weinig's clemency was Weingarten's admission to congressional investigators that he "never, ever, ever got into the facts of the case."[24]

Weingarten downplayed the seriousness of the kidnapping charge by claiming the victim was "fed steaks and whores." At best, Weingarten's claim was a gross mischaracterization of what really transpired. In fact, it was the abductors who patronized prostitutes while they were holding the victim hostage.

A written statement from Weinig supporting his clemency request was filled with misstatements and half-truths. The statement claimed Weinig played only a "minor role" in the money laundering scheme when, in fact, he was a ringleader. The petition included the assertion that Weinig thought he was engaged in legitimate business transactions. Such a claim defies belief since the entire operation dealt in tens of millions of dollars in cash with no receipts exchanged and it occurred without legal documents of any kind. As an attorney for two decades, Weinig would have known such transactions involved serious illegal activity of some kind.

Further, the petition requested a commutation to time served, claiming Weinig's eleven-year sentence was "unconscionably disproportionate" and that Weinig "has made and will make a positive contribution to society." The fact of the matter is Weinig received a sentence commensurate with the sentencing guidelines of 108–135 months, which was approximately half of the maximum of the 240 months he could have faced. Moreover, unlike nearly every other defendant in the case, Weinig refused to cooperate with prosecutors for nearly a year and only offered to do so on the eve of his trial. In addition, not a shred of evidence was offered to support unsubstantiated claims that Weinig had made a "positive contribution" to society. Weinig mistakenly believed offering free legal advice to his close friends qualified as a "contribution to society."

Deputy White House Chief of Staff Harold Ickes was one of the most partisan political operatives in the Clinton administration. Ickes was always looking for a political payoff in return for every presidential action. It just so happened that his children and Weinig's children attended the same school. Morey used that tie to ask Ickes to lobby for her husband's relief. Ickes obliged. No doubt Ickes realized currying favor and influence with wealthy and connected New Yorkers was good business for Hillary as she was running for a US Senate seat, representing a state in which she had never lived.

Weinig's wife went one better than simply hiring Clinton associate Weingarten and asking Clinton confidante Ickes to lobby on behalf of her husband. Morey's cousin was David Dreyer, a longtime senior Clinton White House official. Dreyer had served as White House deputy communications director and as senior adviser to US Treasury Secretary Robert E. Rubin. Dreyer took advantage of his close ties and White House access to ask Podesta to press Clinton for Weinig's release. Weingarten claimed Dreyer may have requested Clinton commute Weinig's sentence on as many as twenty occasions.

The entire criminal justice establishment viewed the Weinig clemency request as totally undeserving. Mary Jo White, who was appointed the US attorney for the southern district of New York by Clinton, had jurisdiction in the case. White was adamantly opposed to any clemency for Weinig. The pardon attorney, Roger Adams, opposed commutation for Weinig. The judge who sentenced Weinig noted that the 135-month sentence was appropriate and within federal guidelines. Deputy Attorney General Eric Holder recommended against commuting Weinig's sentence. Only Clinton's own White House Counsels (Beth Nolan, Bruce Lindsey, and Meredith Cabe) recommended a change to the sentence and they argued that it be commuted to 108 months, a reduction of twenty-seven months.

Nonetheless, presidential action on January 20, 2001, made Weinig a free man. Bill Clinton, acting contrary to the recommendations of the authorities involved in the case and contrary to his own Justice Department, commuted Weinig's sentence to just five years and nine months. Clinton lopped sixty-six months off Weinig's prison term, allowing him to leave prison after serving just barely more than half of his sentence for his key role in laundering as much as $100 million in drug money. Clearly, the lobbying by Podesta, Ickes, and Dreyer had achieved the results Weinig wanted: he was sprung from prison.

The international backlash was harsh and entirely predictable. Clinton's generous clemency for Weinig sparked outrage in Colombia. Colombian officials and citizens accused the US of hypocrisy and of practicing a double standard. Alfonso Valdivieso, Colombia's ambassador to the United Nations, was the country's top prosecutor of drug crimes during the 1990s. Valdivieso labeled Clinton's clemency action as "sordid." He further remarked, "For Colombia, this situation is quite disappointing and delivers the wrong message."[25]

Gustavo de Greiff was Valdivieso's predecessor as prosecutor general. He called Clinton's pardon of Weinig "monstrous."[26] He added, "What President Clinton has done, they criticized us for. And we offered sentence reductions to those who had not been captured yet, while the United States offers this to people who have already been caught."[27]

Former Foreign Minister Rodrigo Pardo complained, "This gives us the notion that the anti-drug fight is asymmetrical. The United States demands more from Colombia than it is disposed to do itself."[28]

Former Colombian president Ernesto Samper condemned the clemency. Samper observed, "What would have happened if, with just a few days left in my presidency, I had set free several drug traffickers arrested in Bogota, and if those same people were found to be helping people in my government?"[29] Samper clearly recognized the Clinton politics that were at play in freeing a major drug money launderer who had connections to the White House. Samper called Clinton's clemency of Weinig "repugnant."[30]

Similarly, Colombia's former National Police chief Rosso Serrano remarked, "They [drug traffickers] must be laughing at us. It's a terrible precedent for those of us who have openly fought this scourge [of drug trafficking]."[31] Serrano also said, "[Clinton] sent the wrong message to the anti-drug struggle, because it negates the suffering of all the families of those who died to fight [drug] trafficking."[32] Serrano was speaking from firsthand experience. It was the constant emotional pain from having attended the funerals of so many of his police officers killed in the war on drugs that led to Serrano's retirement in 2000.[33]

James T. Maness

When James T. "Tim" Maness was arrested in 1985 for selling prescription pills to a pair of undercover officers, they were surprised at the sheer quantity of pills he was peddling. He had so many Valium tablets that the police weighed them rather than counted them. Maness was attempting to sell twelve pounds of illegal Valium pills that had a value of about $200,000 in 1985 dollars.[34]

Maness' arrest in Memphis, Tennessee landed him in that city's US District Court where he was convicted of conspiring to distribute Valium. Surprisingly, he was let off with a sentence of only three years of probation, 120 days in a halfway program, and 150 hours of community service.[35] Maness actually lived in Arkansas, where other local drug dealers of the day, including Roger Clinton and Dan Lasater, had a political benefactor in Bill Clinton, who, as Arkansas governor and president, generously gave away state and federal pardons.

Maness received an unconditional presidential pardon from Clinton even though he did not submit a clemency petition to the Justice Department. If he had, and it were properly vetted, then investigators would have known that law enforcement authorities believed Maness continued in the drug trade after his arrest. Maness refused when offered a reduced sentence in return for cooperating with the police. "He wouldn't say a word. The only reason a drug dealer doesn't talk is because he wants to stay in business," said arresting officer Rick Jewel.[36] DOJ officials would have also learned that at the same time Maness was being considered for a pardon, he was embroiled in another legal controversy.

In 2001, Maness was a broker for NBC Capital Markets Group of Memphis, Tennessee and both Maness and NBC had been sued by New Mexico's Sandoval County government over investments for the county that resulted in steep losses.[37] The county's lawsuit alleged Maness and the brokerage house engaged in a scheme to defraud the county.[38] Despite his legal difficulties, and lingering suspicions over his possible continued involvement with illegal drugs, Maness had his criminal record wiped clean by Bill Clinton.[39]

The Cabinet Secretary's Son

Shortly after he was elected president in November 1992, Bill Clinton appointed Richard W. Riley Sr. to oversee political appointments to his new administration. Only days later, Riley's son, Richard W. Riley Jr., was indicted in a Greenville, South Carolina courtroom as part of a nineteen-person cocaine and marijuana distribution ring.

The elder Riley was confirmed as Clinton's first secretary of education in January 1993 and served in the capacity for all eight years Clinton was in office. It was not until later in 1993 that the younger Riley had his day in court. He was convicted of conspiring to distribute cocaine and marijuana and sentenced to house arrest. He was pardoned in January 2001 by Clinton without ever submitting a pardon petition to DOJ. In 2007, his father endorsed Hillary Rodham Clinton for president and served as her campaign cochair.

Cory H. Stringfellow

"For most of the perpetrators, the denial of any opportunity for parole from their lengthy sentences is simply cruel and a waste of taxpayer money," wrote Cory H. Stringfellow in a letter to the editor published in the November 2, 2002, edition of the *Deseret News*. The public should be "ashamed," he wrote, "that they continue to let such an important humanitarian issue go uncorrected." Stringfellow was arguing against mandatory minimum sentences and in favor of generous parole for drug convicts.

Stringfellow knew a little something about mandatory minimums and early release from prison. He also knew a little something about drug dealing. Stringfellow, a high school dropout, was not a minor player in the drug trade. He sold 5,100 hits of LSD to a customer who, in turn, sold some to an undercover police officer.[40] Stringfellow was arrested in October 1992 for dealing LSD. He reached a plea agreement with prosecutors to serve seven years in prison for conspiracy to possess and distribute LSD. On the morning of his September 1993 sentencing, Stringfellow had second thoughts, and he fled the country rather than serve time in prison for his crimes.

Stringfellow was captured in the United Kingdom in March 1995, one and one-half years after he became a fugitive, and was extradited to the states. Expecting to receive the same eighty-four-month sentence he agreed to nearly two years earlier, Stringfellow was shocked to have been sentenced for the drug dealing and the aggravating circumstances of fleeing the country.

In 1995, Stringfellow was convicted and sentenced to sixteen years in prison on the drug charges and a charge related to fleeing the country. His parents, Burton and Carol Stringfellow, began lobbying for their son's release, arguing that the sentence was excessive. After a lobbying visit, Burton Stringfellow, a University of Utah professor, remarked, "We believe in punishment, but we do not believe that punishment needs to be destructive of the human spirit."[41]

The parents got Ross C. "Rocky" Anderson, the Salt Lake City mayor, to take up the cause. A soft-on-crime Democrat, Anderson went to Clinton with a request Clinton pardon Stringfellow. Anderson first spoke with Mickey Ibarra, the director of Intergovernmental Affairs for the Clinton administration, and White House Counsel Beth Nolan. In December 2000, Anderson met with Clinton and personally pressed his case for the release of Stringfellow.

Stringfellow did not fit the profile of a repentant criminal looking for official forgiveness. While in prison, he wrote he had "never been a 'druggie'" and that he "merely used LSD and other psychedelics as part of my own spiritual quest." In addition, Stringfellow never accepted responsibility for his crimes. He claimed, "I committed a crime, but I am not a criminal." He promised that after his eventual release from prison he would work to free "all of the many thousands of victims of the drug war's injustices."

Rather than demonstrate contrition, Stringfellow claimed his release from prison was "vindication." Stringfellow never claimed he was unfairly convicted. In fact, he admitted to dealing in LSD. He simply believed that he should not have received anything more than a nominal sentence for his crime.

President William Jefferson Clinton commuted the drug dealing sentence of Cory H. Stringfellow to time served of about seventy months. A former fugitive from justice, Stringfellow left prison a free man after serving less than six years of his sixteen-year sentence. Federal prosecutors who had responsibility for the case were shocked Stringfellow was released. Justice Department procedures were never followed, and prosecutors and the courts were never notified that clemency was being considered for Stringfellow. "He flouted the courts," said Assistant US Attorney Gregory C. Diamond. "He should have been given more [prison] time."[42]

Ignatios Vamvouklis

Restaurant owner Ignatios Vamvouklis was one of fifteen people caught in a drug sweep in New Hampshire's seacoast area in 1990. The ring was involved in the distribution of as much as one hundred pounds of high-grade Colombian cocaine with accomplices allegedly using machine guns to collect drug payments. The ringleader received a thirty-year sentence and another accomplice was sentenced to twelve years. In contrast, Vamvouklis received an extremely light sentence that included no prison time.

Vamvouklis was convicted in 1991 of a misdemeanor charge of cocaine possession. He was fined and underwent drug rehabilitation. That aside, the circumstances surrounding his arrest suggest he got off with very little punishment considering the gravity of his crime. Even still, he got a January 2001 pardon from Clinton.

The Little People

Only two of the fifty people that Clinton pardoned or whose sentences he commuted in January 2001 for drug offenses were those who possessed relatively small amounts of drugs. They were the very people for whom other presidents would bestow executive clemency. One was Delores C. Burleson, who was convicted in 1978 for possession of marijuana.

The other one who was a relatively minor drug offender compared with the others Clinton pardoned was Velinda Desalus, who was arrested when she unknowingly went along with a friend on two cocaine deals with undercover narcotics officers. Desalus, the mother of two children, sat in the car during the second drug deal. A first-time offender, Desalus had served eight years of her mandatory ten-year prison term when Clinton commuted her sentence. Still, she did not get a complete break from her crime as Clinton had given to nearly all the hardened drug dealers he had pardoned. Desalus had to undergo mandatory drug testing during her supervised release.

CHAPTER 5

Arkansans and Whitewater Associates

"Whatever the merits of the individual pardons, the surreptitious haste was typical of the Clinton White House at its worst— sloppy, self-indulgent and with a whiff of corruption."[1]

WHEN BILL CLINTON finished his second term as president, he left more than fifteen hundred clemency petitioners in the lurch. He did not bother acting upon their pardon and commutation requests. However, Clinton did manage to cherry pick through 7,489 filings that were sent to him for action to ensure nearly two dozen petitioners from Arkansas—including some of his Whitewater associates—had their petitions granted on his last day in the White House.

The absurdity of the high percentage of clemency recipients who were from Arkansas cannot be overstated. According to the 2000 census, 0.94 of every one hundred Americans was from Arkansas, yet more than fourteen of every one hundred pardons and commutations Clinton gave on both December 22, 2000, and January 21, 2001, were from Arkansas.[2]

ARKANSANS

Tansukhial "Tom" Bhakta was a tax cheat who received a pardon from Clinton in 2001. He distinguished himself as a successful commercial real estate developer in Arkansas who left nothing to chance. Getting a pardon was no exception. Bhakta needed to seal the deal to ensure he got the pardon he wanted in spite of not filing a clemency request with the Justice Department. Ultimately, he got his pardon with relative ease.

Underscoring how little the Justice Department knew of Bhakta when Clinton gave him a pardon was the fact that his name was misspelled on his clemency award certificate. DOJ officials knew nothing about the offense he committed, the sentence he received, or even what state he lived in, let alone what his home address was. All of this information was absent from the clemency warrant save the simple sentence that Bhakta was granted a "full and unconditional pardon after completion of sentence."

Little about who received Clinton pardons was either coincidental or happenstance. Bhakta's pardon was no different. Bhakta's business partner in his real estate development business was lawyer Kenneth Mourton. One client Mourton represented was commodities broker Robert L. Bone.

In late 1978, Bone invested $1,000 in cattle futures for Hillary Clinton, whose husband was the Arkansas attorney general at the time and the front-runner for the 1980 governor's race, which Clinton won. That $1,000 investment was a phenomenal success as it mushroomed into a $100,000 profit in a matter of only months. Hillary referred to her amazing windfall as having "been fortunate."[3]

Hillary Clinton received highly unusual and preferential treatment of her trading account in violation of Chicago Mercantile Exchange rigid policies. She did not make the required $12,000 advance cash payment in accordance with the Exchange's rules governing margin call investments.[4] She closed her commodities account only six months after she opened it, but not before she was a recipient of a 10,000 percent profit.

Bone was a controversial figure in the commodities trading industry. He was disciplined on multiple occasions by the Chicago Mercantile Exchange and the Commodity Futures Trading Commission for various infractions and irregularities. After Clinton closed her account, Bone was fined $100,000 and suspended from trading for three years regarding his practice of improperly allocating winning trades to certain favored customers.[5] The vagueness of the bookkeeping records associated with Hillary Clinton did not allow investigators to determine if the $100,000 she received was really Hillary's or if it was misallocated by Bone from the account of another, unsuspecting client.

In late 2007, Mourton contributed the maximum primary election amount of $2,300 to Hillary's 2008 presidential campaign.

In October 2000, Bhakta, his wife, and their three children, twenty-one- and twenty-year-old daughters and a seventeen-year-old son, gave $5,000 in campaign contributions to Hillary Rodham Clinton's senatorial campaign. The family members were not election campaign contributors prior to the submission of Bhakta's clemency request, nor were they regular political donors following his pardon request, although the son gave a modest $250 campaign contribution in 2004 to a House candidate. Obviously, Bhakta remembered to be grateful for his Clinton pardon. He gave $1,000 to Hillary's presidential campaign in 2007.

The ties among Hillary, Robert Bone, Kenneth Mourton, and Tom Bhakta make it abundantly clear that being a "friend of a friend" was a surefire ticket to receiving a Clinton pardon. Contributing money to Hillary's political campaign was simply icing on the cake.

E. Harley Cox

When First South Federal Savings Bank failed in December 1986, it was the costliest savings and loan collapse in US history.[6] The failure cost the Federal Savings and Loan Insurance Corporation $1.68 billion.[7]

First South was guilty of "stunningly sloppy business practices, reckless real estate speculation and massive insider loans, many of them illegal."[8] First South had loaned hundreds of millions of dollars to stockholders and company insiders. Bad loans were hidden from the board of directors and federal regulators. All in all, First South epitomized the excesses of S&L debacle of the 1980s. At the center of the First South scandal was E. Harley Cox Jr.

Cox was a former president of the Arkansas Bar Association. He was a partner with the prestigious Pine Bluff law firm Ramsey, Cox, Lile, Bridgeforth, Gilbert, Harrelson & Starling. Cox served on the University of Arkansas Board of Trustees. He was also the legal counsel for First South, the S&L's primary attorney, and a member of its board of directors.

Cox was also involved in an elaborate daisy chain plan in which nonperforming First South loans were sold by the S&L to a succession of companies and were eventually "parked" in shell companies owned by Cox. Cox used new First South loans to finance his purchases of the failed loans. Initially, this allowed nonperforming loans to disappear from the First South books in an effort to mislead regulators and shareholders regarding the fiscal health of the S&L.

After a time, Cox sold the failed loans back to First South, reaping a profit in the process. According to federal officials, Cox made at least $681,000 from the sham transactions.[9] During this time period, Cox received $25 million in improper loans from the thrift beginning in 1983. By the time First South failed, Cox and his shell companies held more than $67 million in outstanding loans.[10] This amount exceeded the $46.3 million limit federal regulations placed on thrifts lending to a single borrower.[11]

The fallout from Cox's activities was widespread. In August 1989, Cox's law firm paid a $12 million settlement to the federal government for the roles of Cox and the law firm in the S&L's collapse. The firm's liability insurance carrier placed new restrictions on the firm following the legal settlement. This led to Cox resigning from the firm.

In February 1991, Cox was charged with fifteen counts related to the First South collapse. The prosecution presented overwhelming evidence of Cox's guilt during the April 1991 trial. Former bank executives who were accomplices in the affair testified against Cox. On May 3, 1991, the jury delivered guilty verdicts on all fifteen counts against Cox after deliberating a mere two hours. Cox faced up to five-year prison sentences and $250,000 in fines for each of the fifteen counts.

Assistant US Attorney Doug Chavis observed that Cox was "the only person who profited" from First South and as "a lawyer... [he] had an ethical obligation" to refrain from engaging in illegal activities.[12] In August 1991, US District Judge H. Franklin Waters sentenced Cox to just four years in prison and levied a fine of only $75,000. Cox was not even ordered to make restitution for the First South losses or the profits he made from the scam.

Ernest Harley Cox Jr. was no stranger to Bill Clinton. Cox was involved in suspect transactions involving the Arkansas Development Finance Authority (ADFA) when Clinton was the Arkansas governor. The ADFA had been called Clinton's "political piggy bank" because of the sheer number of low-interest bonds that went to Clinton insiders and cronies.

For example, a 1985 $2.75 million bond went to a company headed by Seth Ward, who was Webster Hubbell's father-in-law. Hubbell was a partner of Hillary Clinton at the Rose Law Firm. Another $1.77 million bond issue in 1985 went to the father of William Kennedy III, another Hillary law partner. A total of $11 million in bond issues went to Century Tube Corporations, a firm with political ties to Bill Clinton. Cox was the attorney who represented the firm in the deal.

The close business and political ties involving both Bill and Hillary Clinton and Harley Cox apparently did not pose an ethical dilemma for the forty-second president. Bill Clinton pardoned Ernest Harley Cox Jr., on January 20, 2001.

Robert Clinton Fain and James Lowell Manning

Robert Clinton Fain and James Lowell Manning were convicted on August 13, 1982, of aiding and assisting in the preparation of a false corporate income tax return. The pair filed a fraudulent income tax return for their restaurant business, International Ventures, Inc.[13] Fain was sentenced to six months in prison and Manning was given fifteen months. Both men were fined $5,000 each.

Fain's motivation for getting a pardon was he wanted to tell his family he was forgiven for his crimes. Manning claimed he wanted to get a hunting license. They began considering clemency petitions in late 2000. In spite of late submissions, they used a close Clinton associate to get them head-of-the-line privileges for consideration. They were advised on how to go about obtaining their pardons by Clinton confidante and friend, Harry Thomason. It was Thomason, a Hollywood TV producer, who produced the campaign film *A Man from Hope* that featured Clinton at the 1992 convention. Thomason referred the men to Harold Ickes who, in turn, told them to contact William Cunningham.

William Cunningham III, was a law partner in the New York firm of Meyer, Suozzi, English & Klein and a close friend of Harold Ickes, a longtime Clinton "dirty trickster"[14] and Hillary insider. Cunningham was also the treasurer for Hillary's Senate campaign committees, "Hillary Rodham Clinton for US Senate" and "Friends of Hillary." Cunningham completed clemency applications for Fain and Manning and then completely bypassed that pesky Justice Department process that would have engaged in bothersome activities such as vetting the applications for truthfulness and to determine if the applicants were not facing other legal difficulties.

Cunningham gave the pardon applications to Janice Enright, the business partner of Ickes who then filed the applications directly with the White House a mere four business days before Clinton was to leave office.[15] For his efforts, Cunningham was paid $4,062.50.

According to Ickes, he, too, had copies of the pardon applications that were delivered to the White House.[16]

Only Hillary Rodham Clinton could say with a straight face that Cunningham's clients did not receive preferential treatment despite the fact that fifteen hundred applications—some filed months and even years earlier—*were never acted upon*. Perhaps more absurd was the claim that Thomason, Ickes, and Cunningham had not communicated with either of Bill or Hillary Clinton regarding the pardon applications.

If none of the three spoke with the Clintons, as Cunningham claimed,[17] then what would have motivated two men in Arkansas to hire an expensive, high-powered, politically connected attorney from a fifty-five-lawyer firm in New York City? In fact, why would they have gone out of their way to hire an attorney who had absolutely no experience in preparing clemency petitions? Cunningham had never prepared a pardon request prior to being hired by Fain and Manning.[18] Certainly, there was no shortage of attorneys in Arkansas who could have completed the pardon applications for the two felons. Not surprisingly, it was later learned that Thomason had, in fact, spoken with Bill Clinton about Fain and Manning as he asked Clinton to "give it a fair hearing."[19]

Whatever hearing Clinton gave the applications was enough. He pardoned both men.

Lloyd George

Lloyd R. George was first elected to the Arkansas House of Representatives in 1962 and held his seat all but six years over the next thirty-four years. The longtime Democrat lawmaker resigned from the House of Representatives in September 1997 following his guilty plea in a mail fraud case. The case was over a fraud perpetuated by George, his close friend Arvie "Art" Lockhart, the director of the Department of Corrections, and Doug Vess, who was a John Deere tractor dealer. Governor Bill Clinton appointed Lockhart to the post of assistant director of the Department of Corrections in 1979. Lock-hart was elevated to the position of director two years later.

The fraud took place when George and Vess sold ten-year-old farm equipment to the Arkansas Corrections Department in 1991 at inflated prices. Lockhart facilitated the purchase in violation of state purchasing regulations. As a member of the Arkansas legislature, George had a requirement to report any goods valued $1,000 or more that he sold to any government agency. He did not.

George purchased the irrigation equipment in 1981 for $19,280. Ten years later, George and Vess conspired with Lockhart to sell the ten-year-old, used irrigation system to the Department of Corrections for $24,800. An Arkansas State Police investigator who investigated the transaction called the irrigation system "outdated and over-priced."[20] In addition, the irrigation system was for use with row crops and was completely unsuitable for the Department of Corrections' (DOC's) cattle pastures.

George purchased new farm tractors from Vess for $24,800. The two men then worked out an arrangement with Lockhart in which the DOC specified an irrigation system to purchase. George provided DOC procurement officials with the specifications for his used irrigation system. These became the bid specifications for the irrigation system the DOC was willing to buy even though George's row crops irrigation system was completely useless to the prison system.

The DOC received two bids. One was from Vess for $24,800 and the other from another company for an irrigation system at half the price. Lockhart directed DOC procurement officials to execute the purchase with Vess for $24,800, the exact amount owed to Vess by George. When the purchase was executed, George got his new tractors, Vess had his money, and the prison system had a worthless, second-hand irrigation system.

A federal grand jury indicted George, Lockhart, and Vess on April 11, 1996, on four counts of mail fraud since documents dealing with the fraudulent sale were sent through the US Postal Service. Much of the original investigative work that led to the indictments came from the independent counsel investigating the White-water scandal.

Other irregularities were uncovered during the independent counsel's investigation of officials tied to the Arkansas prison system. There were indications of misuse of a $13.9 million tax-exempt bond issue from the scandal-plagued Arkansas Development Finance Authority in the late 1980s to fund the building of a new prison. The Office of the Independent Counsel believed there may have been the diversion of state funds to various Arkansas politicians including Bill Clinton. However, not enough evidence was found to bring criminal indictments against the involved parties.

Shortly before the trial began, Lockhart and Vess struck plea deals with the federal prosecutor and agreed to testify against George. On September 2, 1997, only one day before his trial was to commence, Lloyd George changed his mind and struck a plea deal with prosecutors. George admitted his role in defrauding the state in return for prosecutors dropping three of the four counts against him.

When asked why by US District Judge James M. Moody, George replied that he knew a guilty plea would prevent him from holding public office. Hours after he left the courthouse, George was adamant that he would not resign his seat and intended on staying in the Arkansas legislature. "Why not?" he asked.[21] Succumbing to intense public pressure, George resigned his House seat two days later.

Judge Moody sentenced George on December 17, 1997, to two years of probation, including nine months of home detention, and fined him $25,000 for defrauding the state of Arkansas. Three years later, Bill Clinton pardoned Lloyd George even though five years had not elapsed since the completion of his sentence.

David Herdlinger

People driving on the streets of Springdale, Arkansas were not safer when David S. Herdlinger was the city attorney. That is because he allowed drunk drivers to remain on the road by dropping charges against them or by doctoring court documents to give the impression charges were dismissed.

Herdlinger contacted people who were to appear before the Springdale Municipal Court on charges of driving while intoxicated. He offered to reduce or dismiss the charges in return for cash payments. Authorities estimate he made about $10,000 from the scam between 1983 and 1985.

Unfortunately for Herdlinger, he used the US Postal Service in the bribery scam to collect payments and to return impounded drivers' licenses. He was charged under federal antiracketeering laws. His arrest resulted in an August 1986 guilty plea, the surrendering of his law license, and resignation from office. On October 17, 1986, US District Court Judge Morris S. Arnold sentenced Herdlinger to three years in prison and fined him $50.

Herdlinger was the Washington County chairman of Arkansas Governor Bill Clinton's 1986 reelection campaign when he was caught. No doubt Clinton remembered this fact when he pardoned Herdlinger in January 2001.

Charles Morgan

Charles Wilfred "Chuck" Morgan III, fit the image of the stereotypical trust fund baby. His grandfather was John Cooper, a multimillionaire real estate developer. His stepfather was another multimillionaire; George Billingsley imported products from third world Asian countries for Walmart, stores. Billingsley was also a major Democrat political donor, having given $42,200 to Democrats during the 1990s.[22]

Chuck Morgan was surrounded by money. Perhaps coming from a family that was flush with cash and not having established a stable career is why he slipped into a bout of alcoholism and was ultimately convicted in 1984 for dealing cocaine. He spent three years in prison for his drug dealing.[23] At twenty-seven years of age, Morgan was a spoiled rich kid with a criminal conviction.

By the time he reached his thirties, Morgan embarked on a career as a realtor, but the real estate business was never a good fit for him. In early 1994, he launched a new business in a relatively new industry: factoring. Chuck Morgan launched Morgan Financial Group, which traded in accounts receivable for mid-sized companies. Morgan was in the business of loaning money to cash-strapped companies by using their accounts receivable as collateral. After the accounts receivable were paid off, Morgan Financial would take a percentage of the payment. The practice has been called a "high-end pawn shop."[24]

Within three years of its launch, Morgan Financial was embroiled in various legal difficulties. In early 1996, it filed for involuntary bankruptcy to be entered against a client. The following year, Morgan Financial was defending itself against a lawsuit lodged against the factoring company.[25] In a matter of months, Morgan was involved in lawsuits and countersuits and the FBI had opened an investigation. The *Arkansas Business* described Morgan Financial as "lawsuit-plagued."[26]

The company, clients, several employees, and Chuck Morgan were swept up in various allegations of fraud. Compounding the difficulties facing Chuck Morgan and his company were claims that Morgan Financial was in violation of the state's usury laws by charging exorbitant interest rates. In some cases, Morgan Financial was alleged to have charged 38 percent interest on an annualized basis.

The legal entanglements proved to be too much. Morgan Financial Group went out of business. Morgan Financial's legal counsel for much of the company's operations was Hillary's former Rose Law Firm partner, William Kennedy III.

Kennedy had his own sketchy background. He was a veteran of shady and questionable activities. Kennedy conspired with Hillary Clinton, Vincent W. Foster Jr. and Webster Hubbell to oust from the Rose Law Firm C. Joseph Giroir Jr., the longtime managing partner who grew the practice from seventeen lawyers to more than fifty in the late 1970s to mid-1980s.[27]

Giroir was the firm's rainmaker, having landed all of the big accounts including Stephens, Inc., Tyson Foods, Walmart, and Worthen Bank.[28] That aside, Clinton, Foster, Hubbell, and Kennedy led a political assault on Giroir that finally caused him to leave the firm, taking several attorneys and major clients with him.[29] The trio of Clinton, Foster, and Hubbell seized control of the firm and installed Kennedy as the chief operating officer. With Giroir gone, they rewrote the firm's compensation rules, giving themselves a larger share of the profits by moving away from production-based criteria.[30]

In 1993, Kennedy followed his law partner, Hillary, to Washington, DC, where he was placed in the White House Counsel Office. Kennedy was embroiled in many of the early Clinton scandals, including Filegate and Travelgate.

Hillary's hand-picked White House security team had squirreled away several hundred FBI files on prominent Republicans shortly after Bill was inaugurated in a case of dirty politics that became known as Filegate. According to Leslie Gail Kennedy, Bill Kennedy's wife, he "brought FBI files from his White House office to their home in Alexandria [and]…[made] entries from the files into a database he maintained on his lap top computer."[31]

Kennedy was also knee-deep in the firing and subsequent cover-up of seven career White House Travel Office employees on trumped-up charges of illegal activities. Kennedy alleged a crime where one did not exist. The firings were part of an elaborate plan to install Catherine Cornelius, Clinton's cousin, in charge of the Travel Office and then direct airline charter business to a company partly owned by Harry Thomason. Thomason was the Hollywood executive who was in the circle of Clinton insiders.

Steering company business in the direction of cronies and relatives was a long-established practice of the Clintons during their Arkansas days. Attempting to turn the White House Travel Office responsibilities of booking travel arrangements for White House staff and accompanying press personnel into a profit-making venture for Clinton cronies became an instant scandal known as Travelgate.

Screw-ups in the two significant political scandals of Filegate and Travelgate made Kennedy a major embarrassment and a liability to the Clintons. His close ties to Hillary were to be severed if the Clintons had any chance of getting through their second full year in the White House.

By mid-1994, Kennedy was gone. In addition to his deep involvement in the Filegate and Travelgate scandals was the revelation that he failed to properly pay his federal income taxes in 1991 and 1992. Nor did he pay the appropriate employment taxes for a nanny he hired, despite the fact that nanny-hiring scandals embroiled two nominees early in the Clinton administration. To top things off, Kennedy's wife, Leslie, had had enough of their marriage and filed for divorce.[32]

After returning to the Rose Law Firm, Kennedy was again in charge. He was the firm's managing partner and he represented Morgan Financial. Kennedy's counsel did not keep Morgan Financial out of hot water. According to several Morgan Financial employees, Kennedy had a "hunch" that Morgan Financial's interest rates were "legally questionable."[33] Nonetheless, the controversial interest rates remained in place.

It was William Kennedy III, who requested Clinton pardon Charles Wilfred Morgan III. Clinton complied.

Jimmie Wilson

Jimmie Lee Wilson of Helena, Arkansas was a trial attorney and president of the Phillips County, Arkansas chapter of the National Association for the Advancement of Colored People. When decrying what he referred to as a lack of black representation on state boards and commissions, Wilson claimed that black nominees were held to a higher standard. He said, "When whites are appointed, they're just a run-of-the-mill redneck."[34]

Wilson also operated a farm. In 1981 and 1982, Wilson received various loans from the US Farmers Home Administration (FmHA) after he put up his farm crops as collateral. He later sold rice, soybean, and wheat crops that he had mortgaged to FmHA, and he pocketed the proceeds. Wilson attempted to evade detection by having payments for his crops made to his farm manager and his fifteen-year-old son. Wilson also used loans, which he received for farm operations, to instead buy himself a new Mercedes-Benz and to cover losses in his law practice.[35] In all, he defrauded the federal government of more than $775,000.[36]

Wilson was caught and charged in 1984 with conspiracy to defraud FmHA. He pleaded innocent and in early 1985, only days before his federal criminal trial was to begin, he filed a lawsuit against FmHA claiming he was targeted for a probe because he was black, and that he was targeted because of his involvement in a civil rights case.[37]

In March 1985, after a week-long trial, Assistant US Attorney Sandra Cherry was successful in her prosecution as a federal jury convicted Wilson of forty-one counts of defrauding the FmHA by his conversion of mortgage property to his own use.[38] Wilson was sentenced to thirty months in federal prison the following month.

Days later, US District Judge G. Thomas Eisele ruled the Federal Land Bank of St. Louis could foreclose on Wilson's farm for his 1979 default on a loan. Shortly thereafter, Wilson filed for Chapter 11 bankruptcy reorganization in order to stave off creditors. He listed more than $1.1 million in debts.

Wilson appealed his case to the Eighth Circuit Court of Appeals, arguing that some potential jurors in his criminal trial were kept off the jury due to race. Wilson was convicted by a mixed-race jury. Nonetheless, in April 1987, the appeals court ordered the trial judge to review the jury selection process.

Federal prosecutor Sandra Cherry and Assistant US Attorney Fletcher Jackson told Judge Eisele they used a peremptory challenge against one black potential juror because of reports that Wilson had friends who were going to tamper with the jury by approaching specific jurors. Eisele ruled the prosecutors acted properly. In a narrowly divided six-to-five September 1989 opinion, the Eighth Circuit disagreed and ordered the district court to retry the case.[39]

Wilson's legal difficulties did not dissuade him from running for state representative in 1990. He and his primary opponent disagreed on a proposal to convert the local community college into four-year institution. Wilson argued that with an 83 percent black enrollment and a faculty that was 16 percent black, converting Phillips County Community College to a four-year college would "just increase the plantation system."[40]

In August 1990, on the day he was to be retried, Wilson struck a plea deal with prosecutors in order to settle the nearly decade-long case. Wilson pleaded guilty to five counts of converting mortgaged crops and loan proceeds for his personal use.

Wilson's criminal convictions did not prevent him from being elected to the state legislature the following November in his court-ordered majority minority (64 percent black) district. Wilson was elected with a plurality of about 45 percent of the vote. He was opposed by a black Republican and a black independent.

In December 1990, US District Judge Stephen Reasoner sentenced Wilson to four and a half months in federal prison. Wilson was to report to prison in February 1991, which posed one of many problems because the legislature was to convene in January.

The Arkansas House of Representatives had the authority to refuse to seat Wilson and there was widespread public outcry against Wilson serving in the legislature. The state constitution disqualified anyone who was "convicted of embezzlement of public monies, bribery, forgery or other infamous crimes." Legislators decided the clause did not apply to Wilson and voted overwhelmingly eighty-eight-to-nine to seat all House members.

Jimmie Lee Wilson admitted he was surprised to have been pardoned by Bill Clinton since he had submitted his clemency petition shortly after Clinton entered the White House nearly eight years earlier.[41] Clinton did not see fit to grant Wilson's pardon request until he needed to pad his clemency list in January 2001.

Mitchell C. Wood

Mitchell Couey Wood traveled with the same drug crowd as Roger Clinton. It was likely the evidence that resulted in Wood's arrest and eventual conviction for cocaine distribution came from Roger Clinton.

Clinton was convicted and sent to prison in January 1985 for cocaine distribution and conspiracy to distribute cocaine. Federal prosecutors agreed to drop further criminal charges against Clinton in exchange for his cooperation against other conspirators. That day came in October 1986, when a drug ring of ten people was arrested. Roger Clinton was named as an unindicted coconspirator in the cocaine distribution ring.

Major participants in the cocaine distribution ring were longtime supporters of Bill and Hillary Clinton. These included Danny R. Lasater, who had been a financial supporter of the Clintons for years. Lasater was infamous throughout the 1980s for the massive drug parties he threw that included plying high school girls with cocaine in exchange for sexual favors. Lasater was a cocaine supplier for Roger Clinton and in return, Bill's half-brother was the errand boy and driver for Lasater.

Others indicted in the drug ring included George E. "Butch" Locke Jr. and David Collins. Those two men were partners with Lasater in the investment banking firm of Lasater, Locke and Collins. All three pleaded guilty to various charges of conspiracy to possess and distribute cocaine. To say they were surprised to have been prosecuted for recreational drug use and casual distribution to friends was an understatement. Collins complained, "Prosecution for recreational use and distribution of cocaine in a social setting was almost unheard of two years ago."[42]

George Locke would later team up with Roger Clinton and a third friend, Dickey Morton, to form a company called C. L. M., LLC. C. L. M. marketed to a number of potential customers several services, but it was most notorious for hustling pardons in 2000 to potential clients without actually delivering on their promises.[43] The trio made hundreds of thousands of dollars off gullible, pardon-seeking victims.

Mitchell Couey Wood pleaded guilty to a single count of conspiracy to distribute cocaine. He admitted in court that he was a cocaine user and he shared it with others, but denied he sold the drug. Wood was sentenced to four months in prison.

During Bill Clinton's first term as governor, from 1979 to 1980, Wood worked for the Arkansas Industrial Development Commission (AIDC). It was at the AIDC where Wood worked alongside James B. McDougal. A few years later McDougal would become Bill and Hillary Clinton's partner in the failed Whitewater Development Corporation.

Mitchell Couey Wood was pardoned by Bill Clinton even though he did not bother submitting a clemency petition to the Justice Department.

Whitewater

James B. McDougal was an old-time wheeler and dealer. He had been involved in Democratic party politics since at least 1960. He was fairly well connected to the Arkansas Democrat political machine, having entered into business arrangements with various politicians including the notorious segregationist Senator J. William Fulbright.

McDougal met Bill Clinton in 1968, when Clinton interned in Fulbright's office and volunteered for the Senator's reelection campaign. McDougal managed the Senator's Little Rock office. McDougal and Clinton became reacquainted after Bill returned to

Arkansas after college to pursue his political career. Jim McDougal became quite close to Bill Clinton and Hillary Rodham, attending their wedding in October 1975.

McDougal, his wife, Susan, and Bill and Hillary Clinton were equal partners in a land deal that became the Whitewater Development Corporation. Whitewater, as it had come to be known, was a scandal of epic proportions that led to numerous criminal convictions of fourteen prominent and some not so prominent people. The one common thread for the fourteen convicts was they were all friends, business partners or associates of Bill and Hillary Clinton. *Time* magazine referred to Whitewater as a "thorny bramble of failed land deals and shady bank loans."[44]

The people convicted of crimes related to Whitewater or stemming from discoveries of criminal activity as a result of the independent counsel investigation into Whitewater underscored the climate of bribery, graft, and corruption that was prevalent in the Clintons' circle of friends and acquaintances. Those convicted included Neal T. Ainley, Eugene Fitzhugh, David L. Hale, John Haley, Webster Hubbell, Larry E. Kuca, William J. Marks Sr., Charles Matthews, James B. McDougal, Susan H. McDougal, Robert W. Palmer, Stephen A. Smith, Jim Guy Tucker, and Christopher V. Wade.

Some swept up in the Whitewater scandal escaped conviction. Herbert Branscum Jr. and Robert M. Hill were a pair of bank officers accused of fraudulent banking activities. Their case ended in a mistrial in August 1996 when jurors deadlocked on several counts. Suzanna W. Hubbell, Charles C. Owen, and Michael C. Schaufele were indicted in April 1998 on mail fraud, tax evasion, and related charges regarding the criminal activities of Webster Hubbell, a close friend and law partner of Hillary Clinton. The independent counsel dropped the charges against them in June 1999.

The plan for Whitewater Development Corporation was the Clintons and McDougals had purchased 230-acres of land along the White River near the Ozark Mountains and subdivided it into forty-two individual lots. The lots were to be sold as inexpensive vacation and retirement homes for "snowbirds" from the north. Neither the Clintons nor the McDougals contributed any equity to the deal. The entire financing of the nearly $203,000 purchase price of the property was borrowed.

Rather than achieving the financial success the Clintons and McDougals had anticipated, Whitewater Development Corporation became a bust. By 1986, it lost nearly $194,000 and in spite of being fifty-fifty partners with the Clintons, the McDougals shouldered nearly the entire loss by putting up $158,000 to the Clintons' $36,000.

The $61,000 discrepancy between what the Clintons paid and what they *should have* paid as equal partners should have been reported by the Clintons as a loan, gift, or income from the McDougals. It would have become a debt for the Clintons if it was a loan or they would have incurred a tax liability if it was either a gift or income. The Clintons did not report the $61,000 in their income tax filings, nor did they ever repay the McDougals. The Clintons had cheated either the IRS or the McDougals.

Part and parcel of the Whitewater scandal was the involvement of the Madison Guaranty Savings and Loan Association that was owned by the McDougals. Hillary Clinton represented Madison Guaranty in legal matters, a fact she attempted to cover up during Bill's 1992 presidential run and after the Clintons were in the White House. Rose Law Firm legal papers related to Hillary Clinton's legal work on behalf of Madison Guaranty and Castle Grande (another land development scheme) were destroyed in 1988 as part of a "housekeeping effort," according to Hillary Clinton.[45] After the destruction of the legal papers, the Rose Law Firm billing records were the only documents known to remain in existence that shed any light on Hillary's deep involvement with Madison Guaranty and Castle Grande.

The original billing records at Rose Law Firm were destroyed on the orders of Hillary as Bill prepared for his candidacy for the White House. The absurdity of a law firm intentionally destroying its own legal papers and billing records cannot be overstated unless this was accomplished in an attempt to cover up wrongdoing. The only known remaining copies of the law firm's Madison Guaranty billing records belonged to Hillary. Her copies disappeared during the 1992 campaign and remained missing for more than four years in spite of three separate subpoenas to produce the billing records.

Underscoring that the Clintons knew there was something seriously wrong with Whitewater was their blatant omission of any mention of Whitewater in mandatory financial disclosures the Clintons had to submit when Bill announced his candidacy for the presidency. Hillary had final approval over completion of the financial disclosure forms. When news broke that the Clintons were 50 percent partners in a major land development deal that was not properly disclosed, they claimed their failure to disclose it was an error.

One troubling aspect of the Clintons' involvement in Whitewater was the improper income tax deductions they took for their Whitewater investment in 1984 and 1985. The questionable deductions plagued Vince Foster in preparing the Clintons' 1992 income tax return. Although Foster was officially deputy White House counsel, he acted in a capacity befitting a personal attorney for the Clintons. Facts and figures did not match the Clintons' claims and suspicions that Whitewater was simply a vehicle to illegally funnel money to the Clintons, and Bill's political campaigns appeared well placed.

The growing scandal surrounding the Clintons and their involvement in Whitewater is believed to have been a contributing factor, if not the major factor, behind Vince Foster's suicide. Foster was found dead in Fort Marcy Park in northern Virginia in July 1993 with a gunshot wound to the head.

The McDougals purchased Madison Guaranty Savings and Loan Association in 1982. In April 1985, McDougal held a political fundraiser for Clinton's reelection campaign in the offices of Madison

Guaranty. The event raised $35,000 with one-third of the proceeds coming in the form of cashier's checks from Madison Guaranty, suggesting Clinton may have been the recipient of illegal campaign contributions.

Madison Guaranty quickly became the McDougals' personal piggy bank. In 1985, Jim McDougal launched a residential property development project near Little Rock known as Castle Grande. McDougal's partner in Castle Grande was Seth Ward, the father-in-law of Webster Hubbell, Hillary's partner at the Rose Law Firm.

The purchase price of the one-thousand-acre property was $1.75 million. McDougal did not have the money and he only could borrow a maximum of $600,000 from Madison. So, he conspired through a series of transfers and shady business arrangements to procure the remaining $1.15 million in funding from Madison.

The fraud was discovered in 1986, and by 1989, the Castle Grande venture had completely failed, costing taxpayers about $4 million.[46] Castle Grande did not collapse alone; Madison Guaranty failed in its wake. The S&L's collapse cost the US taxpayers $73 million.[47]

One of the many convictions that occurred as a result of the independent counsel investigation into Whitewater was that of Webster L. Hubbell. He was serving as Clinton's associate attorney general when it was discovered he defrauded Rose Law Firm clients of nearly $500,000 by billing them for work not performed. Additionally, he did not report all of his income to the Internal Revenue Service.

Hubbell pleaded guilty to mail fraud and tax evasion and was sentenced in June 1985 to twenty-one months in prison. Immediately thereafter, Clinton cronies lined up $700,000 in "consulting" work for the disgraced lawyer. It appeared to objective observers that hush money had been arranged to keep Hubbell from talking to investigators about what he knew about Whitewater.

Contrary to their claims, the Clintons were not cleared of any wrongdoing regarding their Whitewater involvement. Instead, the independent counsel's final report indicated that available evidence was "insufficient to prove to a jury beyond a reasonable doubt" that the Clintons had engaged in illegal activities.

For example, Bill Clinton testified under oath that he "never borrowed any money from Madison Guaranty," "never caused anybody to borrow any money for (his) benefit," and "never had any personal loan with Madison Guaranty at any time." However, a Madison Guaranty loan check found in the trunk of a car following a July 1997 tornado indicated otherwise. The check was made payable to "Bill Clinton" in the amount of $27,600 and was dated November 15, 1982.[48]

A second check found among banking microfilm copies in the amount of $5,081.82, drawn on the account of James B. McDougal Trustee and dated August 1, 1983, was made payable to Madison Guaranty. The second check was signed by Susan McDougal and the memo line read "Payoff Clinton."[49]

The amount of the second check was the exact amount of the remaining principal and interest that would have been due on August 1 on a loan amount of $27,600 from the previous November 15.[50]

This evidence did not lend itself "to prove to a jury beyond a reasonable doubt" that Clinton lied under oath because although both checks had been deposited and processed, neither check had an endorsement signature from Clinton and the identity of the fingerprints on the first check was inconclusive.[51] Luckily for Bill Clinton, he dodged a bullet.

On May 28, 1996, James B. McDougal was convicted of eighteen felonies related to Madison and Whitewater. His wife, Susan H. McDougal, was convicted on four felony counts. Clinton's lieutenant governor, Jim Guy Tucker, who became governor when Clinton was elected president, was convicted of conspiracy and mail fraud regarding failed real estate development schemes. Susan McDougal faced a maximum of seventeen years in prison and a $1 million fine.

The three were defendants in a three-month-long case in a Little Rock federal courthouse. The prosecution brought in a seemingly endless stream of more than thirty witnesses and presented over six hundred exhibits. In contrast, the defense had only Jim McDougal and Bill Clinton (who testified via videotape) testify in their behalf. The defense strategy of using Clinton's star power in his home turf of Arkansas to sway the jury did not work.

Susan McDougal was sentenced to two years in prison plus three years' probation for her role in obtaining millions of dollars in illegal loans. Among these was a $300,000 loan she received from David Hale for her small advertising company. A former municipal judge, Hale operated a business backed by the Small Business Administration. He testified at the trial of Tucker and the McDougals that Bill Clinton had pressured him to loan the money to Susan McDougal. Clinton denied he pressured Hale, but the money was, in fact, loaned to McDougal. Instead of going to her advertising company, some of the money was placed in Whitewater business accounts, a development that benefited Bill and Hillary Clinton.

Amazingly, Susan McDougal claimed she had no knowledge of the $300,000 loan although there was indisputable evidence that she received it and spent much of the money. During a follow-on grand jury empaneled to further investigate the Whitewater deals, Susan McDougal refused to answer any questions. US District Judge Susan Webber Wright cited McDougal for civil contempt of court and sent her to jail. McDougal served the maximum of eighteen months of incarceration from September 9, 1996, until March 6, 1998.

McDougal immediately began serving her two-year criminal sentence on March 7, 1998, but she was released only four months later in July 1998. US District Judge George Howard Jr. ordered her released early from prison because her back had been bothering her. Susan McDougal was pardoned by Bill Clinton in January 2001. McDougal intentionally skipped submitting a clemency request through the Justice Department and instead went straight to Clinton.[52] Clinton did not need to pardon James McDougal. He passed away in March 1998.

Robert W. Palmer

Robert William Palmer was a Little Rock appraiser who found plenty of work conducting property appraisals for Madison Guaranty starting in 1984. The legal difficulties with Palmer stemmed from the fact that he grossly inflated property appraisals.[53] This particular skill of Palmer came in handy when Jim McDougal arranged for a fraudulent $825,000 loan to a Whitewater accomplice to purchase three parcels of land from David Hale. Palmer overvalued the land in order to justify the loan amount. Hale made almost $500,000 from the sale. Palmer was involved in other appraisals that inflated the value of properties in order to obtain fraudulent loans.

Palmer testified during his March 1996 trial that he was told that guidance to inflate property appraisal values came from "all the way to the top." When he asked if that meant McDougal, he gave the answer "higher," implying that it was Governor Clinton who wanted Palmer to fudge the facts. That Clinton was behind the request to deliver the bogus appraisals was a reasonable conclusion for Palmer to reach because he knew that McDougal was close to Clinton and had actively campaigned and fundraised for Clinton.[54]

Palmer pleaded guilty on December 5, 1994, to one felony count of conspiracy for filing false real estate appraisals for Madison Guaranty Savings and Loan. He was sentenced to one year of home detention, three years of probation, and he was fined $5,000. In spite of not reaching the Justice Department minimum of five years since the completion of his sentence, Palmer was pardoned by Bill Clinton.

Stephen A. Smith

Stephen A. Smith was an Arkansas state senator prior to becoming the chief of staff to first-term Attorney General William J. Clinton in 1976–78. Smith followed Clinton to the state house when Clinton was elected governor in 1978. Smith served as the governor's executive assistant from 1979 to 1980 when Clinton was defeated for reelection. Smith was also a business partner with Jim Guy Tucker and James McDougal in the ownership of the Bank of Kingston, which preceded the McDougals' purchase of Madison Guaranty.[55]

Smith was one of a long trail of Clinton friends, politicians and business partners who defrauded the Small Business Administration on loans received from David Hales' Capital Management Services. Hale used his SBA-backed small business investment company to lend money to borrowers for a variety of inappropriate uses.

Smith misused a $65,000 loan he borrowed for the purposes of operating his consulting business. Instead, Smith used the money to settle a business debt incurred in a real estate deal he entered with Tucker and the McDougals.

Smith pleaded guilty on June 8, 1995, after he was caught during the independent counsel investigation. He agreed to a plea deal that resulted in lesser charges in return for his cooperation in the case against Jim Guy Tucker and the McDougals. US Magistrate John Forster sentenced Smith to perform one hundred hours of community service at his place of employment, the University of Arkansas.

President William J. Clinton gave Stephen A. Smith a pardon on January 20, 2001.

Christopher V. Wade

Christopher V. Wade was owner of Ozark Realty Company, and he was the real estate broker for McDougal. Wade was also a major shareholder and director of Citizens Bank and Trust that lent money to the McDougals and Clintons for the purchase of property that became known as the Whitewater Development Corporation. Of note, the president of Citizens Bank also happened to have been an officer with the development company that sold the Whitewater property to the McDougals and the Clintons. How convenient.

In 1978, Wade partnered with the McDougals and Clintons to sell the Whitewater property that had been subdivided into forty-two lots. Throughout their business relationship, Wade, the McDougals, and the Clintons were involved in a series of confusing property swaps, land purchases, loans, and loans paying off prior loans. For example, a Whitewater Development Corporation loan taken out in the name of James McDougal was paid off by a loan in the name of Bill Clinton. Clinton's loan was paid off by loan made to Wade. The Wade loan was paid off by a Whitewater Development Corporation check that was drawn on insufficient funds, but was covered by a loan from Flowerwood Farms, Inc., that was owned by McDougal.

Wade and his wife filed for Chapter 11 personal bankruptcy reorganization in November 1989. While the bankruptcy was pending, Wade purchased Whitewater lot #7 using John H. and Marilyn B. Lauramoore to conduct the "straw" purchase. In June 1991, Wade again turned to the Lauramoores to make a "straw" loan on his behalf. Wade was going to use the loan proceeds to build a home on lot #7. Wade and the Lauramoores conducted a second straw loan in September 1991.

The straw purchase of lot #7 was not the Lauramoores first business transaction involving Whitewater. In 1988, the Lauramoores bought a different Whitewater lot from Hillary Rodham Clinton for a mere $100 "and other good and valuable considerations."[56]

In March 1995, Wade pleaded guilty to a single felony count of bankruptcy fraud and one felony count of false application and certification to a financial institution. In December 1995, US District Court Judge Susan Webber Wright sentenced Wade to fifteen months in prison, three years of probation, and levied a fine of $3,000.

As with Clinton's other Whitewater associates, Christopher V. Wade had his criminal record wiped clean as Clinton gave him an unconditional pardon in January 2001. As with so many others, Wade did not meet the minimum criteria for consideration of clemency.

Chapter 6

Christmas Clemencies

"Mr. Clinton granted pardons or commutations without proper consultation with federal prosecutors, often to reward friends or political allies or gain future political advantage."[1]

ON DECEMBER 22, 2000, only three days before Christmas, Bill Clinton issued fifty-nine pardons and three commutations. Although the holiday season is a logical time to grant clemency requests, it also fits neatly into the longtime Clinton practice of taking highly unpopular or controversial action only hours before a long holiday weekend was to begin. December 22nd fell on a Friday and the family travel plans and vacations that coincided with Christmas (which fell on the following Monday, a federal holiday) meant that Clinton's clemencies would receive very little attention. There is little doubt this was intentional.

Clinton issued a total of sixty-two pardons and commutations that day. Seventeen of those, or more than one in four, went to drug felons convicted of importing, dealing or conspiring to distribute drugs including cocaine (eight clemency recipients), marijuana (six recipients), anabolic steroids (one), methamphetamines (one) and prescription drugs (one). Drug dealers who received pardons were Harlan R. Billings, William R. Carpenter, Philip V. DiGirolamo,

105

Peter W. Dionis, Peter B. Gimbel, Daniel W. Keys, Larry R. Killough, Pierluigi Mancini, Edward F. McKenna III, Andrew K. Mearns III, Philip J. Morin, Anthony A. Schmidt, Stephanie M. Vetter, Thomas A. Warren, and Charles Z. Yonce Jr., Dorothy M. Gaines and Kemba N. Smith had their prison sentences commuted for their convictions for conspiracy to distribute cocaine. John R. Raup was the only recipient convicted of simple marijuana possession.

Eight of the Christmas 2000 clemency recipients were from Arkansas. Several more had close political ties to Bill and Hillary Clinton or were "friends of friends." Other clemency recipients were political allies and campaign donors.

DANIEL D. ROSTENKOWSKI

Bill Clinton's Christmas pardons were generously lavished on several of his political cronies. None of the political cronies were bigger than Congressman Dan Rostenkowski.

Daniel D. Rostenkowski was the stereotypical Chicago politician. Figuratively and literally, he was the offspring of a Chicago ward boss. He not only was part of Mayor Richard Daley's notorious Cook County Democrat political machine, but he also came from a political family. His father was a ward boss, one of the many political power brokers who controlled nearly all aspects of daily life in Chicago.

Rostenkowski himself was a ward boss as he served as Chicago's 32nd ward Democrat committeeman for several years even while he was a sitting member of Congress. His career in Congress lasted for thirty-six years. Twenty-two years after he first entered Congress, Rostenkowski became chairman of the powerful House Ways and Means Committee, the committee that creates US tax policy. Rostenkowski served as the committee chairman from 1981 to 1994.

In a testament to his political prowess, Rostenkowski is credited with enacting legislation in 1972 that required Medicare to assume the costs of kidney disease treatment for all patients including all those under Medicare's minimum treatment age of sixty-five years. According to reports, Rostenkowski pushed for enactment of the legislation that would require Medicare to pick up the tab for those under sixty-five because he had a young relative suffering from kidney disease.

Rostenkowski's political career began to unravel in 1993, when he was implicated in the infamous House Post Office scandal. In April 1991, US Capitol Police began investigating reports of embezzlement by a House Post Office employee. Post Office employees reported the disappearance of a fellow worker and thousands of dollars. During the investigation, it became apparent that the scandal was deeper and more widespread than just a single staff employee. This development led House Speaker Thomas Foley (Democrat, Washington) to order the Capitol Police investigation closed.

The US Postal Service picked up the investigation where the Capitol Police left off. A completed investigation report was given to Foley in 1992. Foley refused to publicly disclose the findings until a public outcry forced him when word finally leaked out there was widespread corruption involving several congressional employees and elected officials.

The scandal over the cover-up perpetrated by House Democratic leaders pressured Foley to reluctantly forward the matter to the Committee on House Administration to conduct its own investigation. Committee members and staffers conducted inquiries and interviewed personnel implicated in the Post Office scandal. The Democrat-dominated committee whitewashed the entire affair and issued a statement stating the matter was closed and no further investigation was warranted.

The matter did not end there. Outgoing US Attorney Jay Stephens, who was appointed by President George H. W. Bush, had launched his own investigation. In July 1993, House Postmaster Robert V. Rota pleaded guilty to one count of conspiracy and two counts of embezzlement. Rota accused Rostenkowski and Representatives Austin Murphy (Democrat, Pennsylvania) and Joseph Kolter (Democrat, Pennsylvania) of cashing in official postage stamps and office expense vouchers for money they kept for themselves.

The Stephens investigation of Rota was nearly derailed when US Attorney General Janet Reno demanded the resignation of all ninety-three US Attorneys in March 1993. It was thought Stephens' prosecution of Rostenkowski was one investigation the Reno firings was meant to shut down.[2]

After a year of foot-dragging by House leaders, the public outcry over the House Post Office scandal and the Democratic leadership's cover-up reached fever pitch. A resolution to publicly release the entire investigation was introduced by US Representative Robert H. Michel (Republican, Illinois). Eric H. Holder Jr., who was the new Clinton appointee to the position of US attorney for the District of Columbia, had virulently opposed the public release of the Committee on House Administration investigation into the scandal. Public opinion forced Holder to drop his resistance to the disclosure of the investigation's results. On July 10, 1994, the resolution passed 399-2.

(Four years later, in 1997, Clinton appointed Holder to the post of deputy attorney general, the second most senior position in the Justice Department. Holder became embroiled in the notorious Marc Rich pardon when he urged former Clinton colleague and Rich's attorney, Jack Quinn, to bypass the Justice Department in seeking a pardon for Rich.)

As a result of the Rota allegations, an investigation was launched regarding the conduct and financial affairs of Dan Rostenkowski. That investigation uncovered Rostenkowski's misuse of federal funds for his own financial gain and that of his friends. He accomplished this by keeping payroll money set aside to pay phantom employees, using official funds to buy gifts, leasing vehicles for his personal use, and cashing in official postage and office expense vouchers. His actions resulted in a theft from the US government of about $700,000. Prosecutors referred nearly twenty felony counts against Rostenkowski.

Demonstrating that gall knows no bounds, one of Rostenkowski's defense attorneys, Howard Pearl, argued that Rostenkowski's false statement charges should have been dismissed. Pearl claimed the pertinent law prohibiting false statements during the course of an inquiry applied only to executive branch officials and not to members of Congress.[3]

In May 1994, Rostenkowski faced seventeen felony counts dealing with his widespread corruption, although four counts were dismissed by US District Judge Norma Holloway Johnson as the trial date neared. Facing the prospect of serving a considerable amount of time in prison Rostenkowski instead pleaded guilty on April 10, 1996, to two charges of mail fraud in return for the dismissal of the remaining eleven charges. The two charges he pleaded guilty to were related to Rostenkowski giving gifts to political supporters that were purchased with taxpayer funds and for the fraud of having phantom employees on his payroll. He was convicted and sentenced to seventeen months in prison and fined $100,000.

Moments after he was sentenced, Rostenkowski was unrepentant. He delivered a stinging public statement accusing prosecutors of "unprecedented" misconduct. He denied he stole public money, misappropriated funds, or obstructed the investigation. Perhaps he felt comfortable making those claims since those very charges were dismissed as part of his plea agreement. Rostenkowski also denied committing the two crimes for which he had pleaded guilty only minutes earlier.[4]

Daniel D. Rostenkowski was released from prison after serving fifteen months. Not surprisingly, Bill Clinton gave Rostenkowski a pardon on December 22, 2000. The pardon was more than old-fashioned cronyism at work. The pardon was Clinton payback to a close political ally. Rostenkowski was widely considered to have been something of a mentor to Clinton during his freshman year in the White House. Rostenkowski was also credited with helping ensure the passage of Clinton's massive tax hike bill in the Democratically controlled House in early 1993. The controversial tax bill passed with a slim six vote margin, largely due to the efforts of Rostenkowski.[5]

PHILIP GRANDMAISON

Nashua, New Hampshire Alderman Philip J. Grandmaison was a staunch Bill Clinton supporter in the mid-1980s when Clinton was testing the political waters for a possible presidential run. Grandmaison organized a luncheon featuring Clinton in April 1987 that had several influential New Hampshire elected officials in attendance. Establishing close ties with the Democratic political machine in the state holding the first-in-the-nation primary was extremely valuable to Clinton if he were to launch a presidential bid. Grandmaison had effusive praise for Clinton following the luncheon.[6]

Grandmaison was disappointed Clinton did not run in 1988, but he was behind the Arkansas governor when Clinton did run four years later. Grandmaison served as a Clinton delegate to the 1992 Democratic National Convention. His brother, J. Joseph Grandmaison, was another invaluable Clinton supporter and donor. Joseph Grandmaison served as Chairman of the New Hampshire Democratic Party and was the 1990 Democratic nominee for governor. He was rewarded for his unwavering support of Clinton. Joseph Grandmaison was an eight-year Clinton appointee as director of the US Trade and Development Agency from 1993 to 2001. Such longtime, dedicated Grandmaison family support of Clinton paid off for Philip in December 2000.

Grandmaison was not a stranger to charges of conflicts of interest. Concerns arose in 1989 over Grandmaison's ties to a waste services company and an apparent conflict involving his alderman responsibilities of awarding contracts to such companies. Grandmaison was employed by ASG Disposal Services, Inc., a company owned by his cousin, Ansel Grandmaison. A second company owned by Ansel had contracts performing waste disposal services for Nashua.[7] Because of Philip Grandmaison's aldermanic duties, his employment by his cousin and his cousin's contracts with the city, the city attorney gave an opinion to city officials that "an appearance of impropriety may exist."[8]

In an interesting twist, Ansel Grandmaison was elected to the board of the Department of Public Works in 1990 and served in that position for seven years before losing reelection. In 1999, his trash disposal company was sued by the city of Nashua over $50,000 in unpaid bills.[9]

Philip Grandmaison had risen to the position of president of the Nashua board of alderman when he was charged in 1993 in a corruption scandal. Two years earlier, the board of aldermen awarded a $6.5 million renovation project to Eckman Construction Company. Grandmaison happened to have been the marketing director for Eckman Construction when the contract was awarded. Nashua Aldermen Steve Kuchinski and Thomas Magee admitted to having accepted cash and other valuables from Grandmaison in return for their support of the Eckman contract bid.[10]

Grandmaison was convicted and sentenced on February 8, 1995, for mail fraud. US District Judge Steven McAuliffe sentenced him to eighteen months in prison. Grandmaison appealed his case and the US Court of Appeals for the First Circuit overturned the eighteen-month sentence. An appeals court ruling allowed the district court judge to ignore mandatory sentencing guidelines and to resentence Grandmaison to a shorter term in prison. Grandmaison eventually spent nine months in prison.[11] Bill Clinton pardoned him in December 2000.

Currying the favor and support of powerful movers and shakers in the New Hampshire Democratic Party cannot be overemphasized. The Granite State holds the first-in-the nation presidential primary and is often the springboard toward a party's presidential nomination.

MARTIN J. HUGHES

Martin J. Hughes was an old-style labor boss. He was the president of the Cleveland American Federation of Labor and Congress of Industrial Organizations (AFL-CIO) Labor Council, an organization of 125,000 members. He was also the District 4 (Midwest region) vice president of the Communication Workers of America. Hughes's two union leadership positions gave him considerable clout with countless Democratic politicians, particularly in his home state of Ohio. He was a member of the Ohio state Democratic Executive Committee.[12] The influence and power of Martin Hughes extended well beyond the Ohio border. Hughes was on a first-name basis with John Kennedy, Lyndon Johnson, and Hubert Humphrey. He was a frequent White House guest of Jimmy Carter.[13]

In July 1987, Hughes was convicted of committing four felonies and ten misdemeanors regarding the improper reporting of CWA political contributions. Twenty-three other counts were dismissed during the month-long trial.

Hughes gave $300,000 in CWA political contributions to various Democratic candidates and covered up the political donations by accounting for the disbursements in more than five hundred wage and expense vouchers claiming they were legitimate union expenses. Hughes prepared vouchers to make it appear each of the candidates had performed some unspecified work for the union. Hughes' attempted subterfuge did not stand up to scrutiny. Several of the Democratic candidates told law enforcement officials they did not perform any work for the CWA.

Hughes' sole defense during his trial was that the phony campaign contribution bookkeeping practices were routinely performed by the union. Hughes claimed the CWA had been accounting for its political contributions in this manner for forty-seven years.[14] Hughes was sentenced in 1987 to two years of probation, fined $10,000, and was banned from seeking union office until the year 2004.

Hughes went back to work for the Cleveland office of the AFL-CIO Federation of Labor committee in the capacity of making political endorsement recommendations to the group. Hughes' work with the AFL-CIO did not violate his court-ordered ban from holding a union office because technically the AFL-CIO was not a union, but instead was an association of labor unions.[15]

Bill Clinton gave Hughes a pardon on December 22, 2000. However, the drama involving Hughes did not end there. Ten months after he was pardoned, Hughes was sued by Union Eye Care Center, Inc. of Cleveland.

In October 2001, Hughes was sued along with the United Telephone Credit Union, Inc. Hughes had been employed as the president of Union Eye Care before he was abruptly terminated in May 2001. He was simultaneously the manager and treasurer of the credit union. According to Union Eye Care, the credit union had improperly used Eye Care funds to pay about $400,000 in expenses and benefits incurred by credit union officers and directors. The credit union reimbursed Union Eye Care approximately $36,000 but still owed a balance of about $363,000 that it would not pay.

A little more than three months later, and thirteen months after he was pardoned, Hughes was at the center of yet another dispute. Hughes was specifically named by three women who filed complaints with the Ohio Civil Rights Commission on February 5, 2002.

According to Deborah Ann Fannin, Gay Griffith, and Cheryl Ortoski, employees of United Telephone Credit Union, Hughes had been sexually harassing them.

According to the women, Hughes would ask if he could accompany them to the bathroom, he threatened to spank one of them, and he suggested he might visit Planned Parenthood to discuss the sexual history of one of the three. One of the women alleged Hughes advised her that in the event she was to be raped, she would "need to lay there and enjoy it."[16]

The Ohio Civil Rights Commission presented Hughes with the allegations and gave him until November 15, 2002, to offer a response. The process was known as conciliation and it was intended to resolve disputes in informal channels. Hughes never replied to the Commission, forcing the government body to refer the matter to the Ohio attorney general.[17] Shortly thereafter, Hughes relocated the six-thousand-member credit union's headquarters over a mid-December 2002 weekend without disclosing to the three women the new location. State regulators ordered Hughes to return the credit union headquarters to its original location.

The various allegations involving Hughes led a state examiner to inspect the operations of United Telephone Credit Union commencing in early July 2002. Three months later, the state examiner issued a preliminary report that the credit union demonstrated "a considerable lack of oversight over management and its operation of the credit union, which has resulted in unsafe and unsound practices."

Among the operating discrepancies, the state examiner found that Hughes had deposited about two-thirds of the credit union funds (about $5.5 million) in a bank owned by his wife's family. Hughes used credit union funds to pay his personal expenses, including restaurant charges, beauty salon expenses, legal bills, and grocery store trips. The eighty-one-year-old had an employment agreement with the credit union that ran until he was ninety-three years old. The agreement included paying his wife a death benefit in excess of $400,000 upon his death. Hughes also gave preferential loan treatment to at least one local elected official.[18]

State regulators gave Hughes a second chance to remain in charge of the credit union. He was required to sign a "supervisory agreement" in which he promised to make several changes to improve credit union operations to include eliminating suspect operations and money mismanagement. But the second chance did not last long. Changes in operating procedures that state officials had ordered the bank to undertake the previous year were never put into practice.

In February 2003, state officials removed Hughes and the credit union directors (his wife, Natalie, a cousin, two neighbors, and a fifth individual) over the discovery of further mismanagement issues. A state examiner learned that in November 2001, United Telephone Credit Union sold 1,742 shares of the credit union's holding of Fahey Banking, Co. stock to his wife, Natalie Hughes, at only one dollar per share for a total sale price of $1,742. The actual value of the stock when it was sold was $2.2 million. Additionally, Hughes refused to turn over a credit union checkbook he had been using to pay personal expenses.

After the removal of Hughes and the board of directors, state officials installed a conservator to manage the credit union until state officials would be comfortable the financial institution was on solid financial footing.[19]

Martin J. Hughes died on March 8, 2006, at the St. John West Shore Hospital in Cleveland at the age of eighty-five. According to a *Plain Dealer* obituary, he "was not repentant" regarding his criminal convictions.[20]

RICK HENDRICK

One of the most popular spectator sports in America is the National Association for Stock Car Auto Racing or NASCAR. Started in 1948, NASCAR had become the second most widely viewed sporting event on television about the time Clinton was leaving the presidency. Many NASCAR drivers have become as well known as athletes in longer established professional sports.

One of the most successful NASCAR ownership groups is Charlotte, North Carolina-based Hendrick Motorsports, headed by Joseph Riddick "Rick" Hendrick III. Rick Hendrick had experience in all aspects of the sport. In addition to his being a team owner, he had worked as a crew chief and occasionally served as a driver. He had co-owned a team with actor Paul Newman. Some of the drivers who worked for Hendrick Motorsports included Ken Schrader, Ricky Rudd, Terry Labonte, and Jeff Gordon. Hendrick had the pleasure of watching some of his cars enter victory lane after winning prestigious races. He owned cars that won two Winston Cup championships.

Hendrick was also successful outside of the racetrack. He was a cofounder of the National Basketball Association's Charlotte Hornets franchise in 1987 with its first season beginning in the fall of 1988. He served on the board of directors of NationsBank Corporation, one of the country's largest banks. By the mid-1990s, Hendrick owned more than five dozen auto dealerships across the country; the dealerships generated nearly $2 billion in revenue.[21] He was the single largest owner of Honda and Saturn dealerships. And, according to Justice Department officials, Rick Hendrick was also a criminal.

In March 1994, Justice Department officials arrested fifteen current and former automobile executives who were part of a widespread bribery and influence peddling scandal. At the heart of the scandal was the awarding of new car dealerships and the allotment of automobile inventories.

During the 1980s, an import regime existed that limited the number of Japanese automobiles that could be shipped into the US. One of the hottest selling brands was Honda. Due to low supply and high demand, cars could be sold from dealers' lots at premiums that were thousands of dollars over the manufacturer's suggested retail price.

Auto dealers who could get a new Honda franchise or would receive as many cars as they could sell were virtually ensured of becoming financially successful. This set of circumstances led to US Honda officials collecting upwards of $15 million in bribes in order to select new franchisees and allot car deliveries.[22] According to federal authorities, Rick Hendrick was one of the dealers who paid bribes or offered gifts and gratuities to influence American Honda officials. Between 1978 and 1992, Hendrick acquired twenty-eight

Honda and Acura dealerships.[23] Acura is the luxury automobile line owned by Honda.

In return for a new dealership in California, Henderson lent one Honda executive more than $250,000 to help finance a new home purchase. Some Honda executives' family members were on the Henderson payroll or simply received cash payments in order to provide Hendrick with a higher allotment of new car deliveries. In a completely bizarre case of brand disloyalty, a very senior US Honda executive drove a brand new BMW owned by Hendrick that he just so happened to have stored at the Honda executive's home. As many as seventeen Honda dealerships owned, in part or in whole, by Hendrick were implicated in the scandal.[24]

By early February 1995, twenty people including sixteen current and former Honda executives pleaded guilty to charges resulting from the scandal investigation. Two more executives were convicted in criminal trials in April 1995.

One prominent Honda executive, Stanley Cardiges, gave evidence resulting in the indictment of Hendrick on December 4, 1996. Cardiges told investigators that Hendrick helped him finance the purchase of two homes and would periodically send him overnight delivery packages stuffed with as much as $20,000 in cash at a time. Hendrick was indicted on thirteen charges of money laundering, one count of mail fraud, and one count of conspiracy. His brother, John, who also worked in his auto business was indicted on single count of conspiracy.

If convicted, Hendrick faced maximum sentences of ten to twenty years in prison and fines between $250,000 and $500,000 for each count of money laundering and five years and $250,000 fines for the conspiracy and mail fraud charges. Compounding matters was the fact that Hendrick faced at least sixty civil lawsuits filed by various automobile dealers.[25]

Hendrick's initial defense was that he loaned money or gave cash and gifts to Honda executives as a friendly gesture and not to gain influence. In some cases, he claimed he paid money to Honda executives who he alleged were extorting him. However, the evidence and testimony against Hendrick was overwhelming and he changed his claim of innocence to a plea of guilty in relatively short order. In December 1997, Rick Hendrick pleaded guilty to mail fraud and was sentenced to one year of home detention, three years of probation, and was fined $250,000.

On December 22, 2000, Hendrick received a full and unconditional pardon from Bill Clinton. Hendrick had filed his clemency request the previous September. His lawyer was John Arrowood, who was a campaign coordinator for Clinton's 1992 presidential race and had been a regular donor to Democrat candidates and organizations, at least since 1990. Hendrick gave $10,000 to the Democratic Senatorial Campaign Committee in 1996. According to Federal Election Commission records, Arrowood also gave more than $6,500 to Hillary's political campaigns after Hendrick received his pardon.

One of the most influential people who lobbied Clinton for a pardon for Hendrick was Bank of America chairman and CEO Hugh L. McColl Jr. of the Bank of America, one of the largest banks in the US, which merged with NationsBank in 1998. McColl was previously the top executive at NationsBank and he assumed the same position at Bank of America after the merger. Hendrick was a former member of the board of directors at NationsBank when McColl was in charge.

While McColl's letter to Clinton may have helped Hendrick gain a pardon, it was more likely an announcement McColl made two weeks earlier that did the trick. In remarks he gave on December 7, 2000, McColl announced that Bank of America was giving $500,000 to the William J. Clinton Presidential Library.[26] The bank's $500,000 contribution was significant since the William J. Clinton Presidential Foundation had raised only a paltry $3.1 million the year before toward the library's $200 million fundraising goal.[27]

RALPH E. MECZYK

Operation Greylord was a joint federal investigation that was conducted in the 1980s by the Federal Bureau of Investigation and the Internal Revenue Service Criminal Investigation Division into corruption in the judicial system of Cook County, Illinois. Nearly one hundred judges, prosecutors, defense attorneys, court personnel, and police officers were indicted as a result of the investigation. More than eighty were convicted. One of those convicted was trial attorney Ralph E. Meczyk. Although Meczyk was not convicted in the bribery dragnet, he was one of more than one dozen who were caught cheating on their taxes.

Meczyk and his law partner did not report substantial income during the tax years of 1980 and 1981. They were charged in March 1987 and pleaded guilty the following July to filing a false partnership income tax return and false individual returns. Meczyk attempted to excuse his criminal actions by offering, "We had an incredibly horrible bookkeeping system."[28] US District Judge Marvin Aspen sentenced both men to thirty days of work release in federal prison, four years of probation, fined each $500, and ordered them to each perform five hundred hours of community service. Remarkably, Meczyk was able to continue practicing law.

When Meczyk returned to his legal profession, he went back to doing what he did best. He represented some of the most notorious defendants of some of Illinois' most sensational crimes. Among these was Roy Caballes, whose traffic stop conviction was appealed all the way to the US Supreme Court, where he lost. Caballes believed the K-9 in the police squad car that alerted police to the 282 pounds of marijuana Caballes had in the trunk of his car represented an illegal search. In a 2005 decision, the Supreme Court justices ruled otherwise.

Perhaps Meczyk's most infamous defendant was David Dowaliby who was convicted of murdering his seven-year-old stepdaughter in 1990. The child's birth mother was acquitted of the charges. Dowaliby later had his sentence overturned by the state appeals court.

In 1993, Meczyk defended mob family soldier James "Big Jimmy" Coniglio. And he lost the case.

Other infamous defendants on Ralph Meczyk's client list included Bryant Capiz who was charged in 1998 with breaking laws protecting certain endangered wildlife. Capiz attempted to smuggle more than two dozen rare tarantulas through Chicago's O'Hare Airport.

Meczyk withdrew from a 1999 case in which his client, Chicago police officer Joseph Miedzianowski, was accused of aiding a major organized cocaine operation. Prosecutors wanted to call Meczyk as a witness for the prosecution.

Beniss Mooshol ran into a small problem when he embezzled four million dollars from his employer, claimed authorities. Nineteen-year-old Jada Saenz drugged girls as young as twelve years old so that he could videotape himself having sex with them. Mooshol and Saenz relied on Ralph Meczyk to represent them in 2000 and 1994, respectively.

Meczyk was identified by name in a March 2002 *Chicago Tribune* article titled "Inept Lawyers Still on List for Capital Cases; Reforms Fail to Weed out Problems." The main complaint of the *Tribune* article was that lawyers with criminal and disciplinary records were still permitted to defend critical life-and-death capital punishment cases.[29]

Meczyk client Mohammad Azam Hussain was arrested in 2004 for immigration violations when he lied about his ties to a terrorist group. Meczyk also represented his own law partner, Lawrence Hyman, in 2006 over allegations of complicity stemming from Hyman's days as an assistant state attorney, when a suspect was savagely beaten.[30]

In 2006, Meczyk criticized what he saw was a trend by authorities in pursuing criminal charges against political figures. He remarked, "Prosecutors have taken what were traditionally political acts and made them criminal. Every day, garden-variety acts—political patronage and helping your friends and supporters—are now crimes."[31] Illinois must have been so fortunate to have someone of the caliber of Ralph E. Meczyk working in the criminal justice system.

Meczyk lost another case in 2007 involving defendant Anthony "Twan" Doyle, a retired Chicago cop who worked for organized crime. Nor did Meczyk's client Jeremy Dozier fare any better in the courtroom. The Illinois State Trooper was convicted in 2006 of forcing drivers during traffic stops to strip and urinate in public for his entertainment in exchange for not receiving a traffic ticket.

Meczyk received his pardon from Clinton in December 2000. Perhaps Clinton saw fit to pardon Meczyk as a payback to the tax-cheating lawyer who contributed money to Bill Clinton's Whitewater legal defense in 1995.[32]

ARCHIBALD R. SCHAFFER

Archibald R. Schaffer III, was an early and one of the most vociferous critics of the independent counsel investigation of Alphonso "Mike" Espy. In retrospect, Schaffer opposed the investigation for good reason. He was one of the crooks the independent counsel caught as a result of the investigation. Schaffer was a senior vice president with Arkansas-based Tyson Foods when he was caught up in the bribery and illegal gratuities scandal involving Espy.

Mike Espy served as Bill Clinton's secretary of agriculture from 1993 to 1994. He stepped down shortly after a corruption investigation began. Immediately after he assumed the duties as Agriculture Secretary, Espy became embroiled in an influence peddling and bribery scandal.

Although Espy was not convicted of soliciting and accepting illegal gifts and gratuities, the various lobbyists and corporate executives who provided the largesse were not so lucky. A dozen entities and individuals pleaded guilty or were convicted in federal trials. (See Chapter 3.) Nearly all of them were pardoned by Clinton in January 2001. Archie Schaffer received his clemency gift a month earlier, on December 22, 2000.

Schaffer was convicted on June 26, 1998, of one count of violating the *Meat Inspection Act of 1907*. The act prohibited the agriculture secretary from receiving anything of value from any "[a] ny person, firm, or corporation, or any agent or employee of any person, firm, or corporation" he regulated, such as Tyson Foods.

Schaffer was charged with violating the 1907 Act because he gave Espy $2,556 worth of air transportation so that Espy and his girlfriend, Patricia Dempsey, could attend a May 1993 birthday party in Arkansas for a pair of girlfriends of Tyson executives.[33] Schaffer headed government relations for Tyson. In other words, Schaffer was Tyson's head lobbyist whose job was to influence government officials.

This was how Bill Clinton attempted to explain away the pardon of Schaffer in his autobiography, *My Life*. Clinton wrote, "[Schaffer] was facing a mandatory jail sentence for violating an *old law* Schaffer *knew nothing about*, because he had made travel arrangements, as instructed, so that Espy could come to a *Tyson retreat* [emphasis added]."[34]

The "old law" was the basis on how the Department of Agriculture regulated the entire meat packing industry. The 1907 act was a direct result of the public outcry that erupted regarding Upton Sinclair's *The Jungle,* the 1905 book that presented a most vivid and disturbing portrait of the meat packing industry at the time. Every executive in the entire industry—especially at Tyson, the nation's largest poultry producer—knew about the Meat Inspection Act. In addition, as the senior vice president in charge of lobbying, Schaffer, more than any other single person at Tyson, undoubtedly knew that giving thousands of dollars in free plane tickets to a government official—and the Agriculture Secretary, at that—was illegal.

Lastly, the "Tyson retreat" was no business event. It was a wild and raucous party thrown for the girlfriends of a couple of Tyson executives. It was completely shameful for Clinton to attempt to portray the event as anything other than what it was: a party for executives and their girlfriends. Mike Espy and his girlfriend, Patricia Dempsey, were invited attendees.

Schaffer had twice appealed his 1998 conviction and was awaiting a rehearing of his case in late 2000, when Clinton issued him a pardon. One individual who heavily lobbied Clinton in favor of clemency for Schaffer was Dale Bumpers, a patriarch of Arkansas politics. Bumpers was a former Arkansas governor (1971–1975) and a US Senator (1975–1999) and was highly regarded among Arkansas' Democratic elite. In the US Senate, Bumpers succeeded J. William Fulbright, for whom Bill Clinton worked as a college intern and campaign volunteer. Bumpers also happened to be the uncle of Archibald R. Schaffer III.

Larry R. Killough

Dr. Larry R. Killough of Searcy, Arkansas was indicted in October 1984 on thirteen counts of illegally distributing prescription drugs and another two counts of bribery. Killough was accused of writing illegal prescriptions. Killough wrote several prescriptions to Thomas H. Williams in just over a month's time for 330 tablets of the opioids Demerol and Dilaudid and the stimulant Preludin, which was ten times more tablets than a patient should consume during that time period.

Doctors like Killough became known as "pill mills" because they would write prescriptions for unnecessarily large amounts of controlled narcotics. These doctors were part of the cause of the opioid epidemic that was taking tens of thousands of lives each year only three decades later.

It was also alleged Killough attempted to bribe Williams, who was the star witness against him, on at least two occasions.

In his May 1985 trial, federal prosecutors introduced as evidence a hidden camera videotape that captured Killough in a

1984 motel room negotiating with undercover state police officer, Chris Anderson. Killough was trading prescriptions for the opioid Dilaudid to Anderson in exchange for what Killough thought were stolen diamonds.[35]

Killough's meeting with Anderson was set up after Williams was arrested on unrelated drug charges and he told law enforcement authorities that Killough had been writing illegal prescriptions. Williams reported to the police that Killough had been selling illegal prescriptions to him since 1978.

Williams inexplicably confessed to Killough in September 1984 that the police were investigating Killough. That led to Killough giving $5,000 to Williams to leave the country to avoid cooperating in the investigation. Killough later paid Williams an additional $2,000 to not cooperate in the investigation. Williams never left the country.

During the trial, prosecutors dropped five of the thirteen illegal distribution counts and the two bribery charges against Killough. On May 14, 1985, a federal jury convicted Killough of the remaining eight counts of illegally distributing prescription medication. US District Judge G. Thomas Eisele sentenced Killough on June 18, 1985, to twenty months in prison and fined him $40,000. Killough argued before his sentencing, "Incarceration would waste my skills." Eisele replied, "A prison sentence is absolutely required in this case."[36]

Killough voluntarily surrendered his medical license to the state medical board on July 1, 1985, prior to entering prison in an attempt to dissuade the board from suspending or revoking it. Nevertheless, the state board voted to suspend Killough's license and offered that he could reapply for a license once he was out of prison.

The board reinstated Killough's license in April 1986 once he was released from the Texarkana Federal Correction Institute, but while he was still in federal custody. He had three months in a halfway house to complete his sentence. US Attorney George W. Proctor was appalled the board reinstated Killough's license calling the action "an insensitivity to the drug epidemic in Arkansas."[37]

After Killough was released from prison, the Drug Enforcement Agency revoked Killough's DEA permit to write prescriptions for controlled narcotics. Killough initially appealed that decision but then dropped his appeal in November 1987.

Less than three years later, Killough was back in a federal courtroom again facing multiple counts of writing illegal prescriptions. Killough was caught writing prescriptions using the DEA permit belonging to another doctor.

Killough's defense in his August 1990 trial was that DEA attorney Stephen Stone at the agency's Washington, DC headquarters had given him verbal permission over the telephone to write prescriptions on another doctor's permit. Killough claimed Stone also gave him written permission in a letter, but that he had lost the correspondence. In his court testimony, Stone denied he ever gave such permission. Killough's son, Larry Jr., who was an attorney, claimed Stone also told him on the phone that his father could write prescriptions on another doctor's DEA permit. On August 16, 1990, a federal jury acquitted Killough of all twelve charges.

A decade later, Bill Clinton gave Killough a full and unconditional Christmas season pardon. However, controversy surrounding Killough and illegal prescription drugs did not end with his pardon. In a sad but ironic turn of events, Killough's grandson died from an overdose of prescription medication. Seventeen-year-old James Webb Killough, the son of Larry Killough Jr., died on May 12, 2006, from an overdose of methadone in an apartment parking lot. The source of the prescription narcotic was never publicly disclosed. Larry Jr. knew of his son's drug experimentation and said he thought he was properly dealing with the problem.[38]

TOMMY BROOKS

Much of the public believes there exist politicians who brazenly sell access and influence. Mississippi Senate President Pro Tempore

Tommy Brooks was one who actually did. Brooks had served for three decades in the Mississippi legislature when he was arrested in February 1985 for attempting to extort $50,000 in exchange for passing proposed legislation.

At issue was a bill that would have allowed residents in Jackson and Tunica counties to vote on legalizing horse racing. The horse racing bill sailed through the Mississippi House, failed to pass in the Senate, but remained active on the political docket under a procedure known as reconsideration. After initially accepting $16,000 to get the measure passed the first time the bill appeared for a Senate vote, Brooks passed word through an intermediary to the Mississippi Horse Racing Association President Jim Newman that it would take $50,000 to revive the bill on reconsideration and ensure its passage. Newman contacted the FBI and offered to cooperate with the federal agency.

The man in the middle between Brooks and Newman was Robert Q. Houston. Houston had conspired with Brooks to extort money from the racing association. According to a secret audio recording of their meeting, Brooks told Newman to work with Houston and "do whatever Mr. Houston said" if the association wanted the horse racing bill passed.[39] After his arrest, Houston agreed to work with the FBI and he later agreed to testify against Brooks.

There was evidence that Brooks was working hard to get the horse racing bill passed. During the trial in late May 1985, Mississippi Senator David Smith testified Brooks told him he would be a fool if he turned down money to vote in favor of the proposed legislation.[40]

After Brooks upped the ante to $50,000 in order to get the bill passed, Houston conveyed to Brooks a response from the association that the horse racing group could only raise $15,000 on such short notice. Unbeknownst to Brooks, the FBI had already arrested Houston and he was cooperating in the investigation. Houston was videotaped passing to Brooks a brown bag consisting of 150 one-hundred-dollar bills that was supplied by federal law enforcement officials.[41]

Brooks was convicted in June 1985, and in August, he was sentenced to nine years in prison for extortion. Houston received one year of probation and was fined $10,000 for his role in the extortion. Robert Q. Houston was pardoned by Bill Clinton in December 2000.

JERE W. JOHNSON

It was the nation's largest corruption case involving public officials when it was investigated in the 1980s. There were 162 current or former commissioners in sixty-one of Oklahoma's seventy-seven counties who were convicted after a four-year investigation. Another sixty-two suppliers and salesmen were convicted alongside them. One of the government officials convicted was Garfield County Commissioner Jere Wayne Johnson. In 1982, he was sentenced to three years of probation and was fined $2,000 for accepting kickbacks between 1976 and 1981.[42]

The details of the kickback scheme were identical in nearly every case. It was a routine practice for salesmen, who were selling products and services to the county governments, to pay the county commissioner 10 percent of the value of the contract amount right off the top. If the contracted product or service the salesman was providing to the county was in excess of the county's needs, then the commissioners and the salesmen split the contract sales proceeds fifty-fifty. Prosecutors noted that officials in one county had purchased enough lumber "to rebuild every bridge in the county four times." In fact, no such lumber existed. The sales existed only on paper.[43]

The extent of the unneeded additional purchases was so large that counties experienced major spending reductions after the corruption was discovered. For example, highway construction costs fell by as much as 40 percent following the successful prosecutions.[44] Johnson received his pardon from President Bill Clinton in December 2000, two years after he requested one.[45]

PADDING THE PARDON LIST

One trend of the clemencies given out during the waning weeks of the Clinton presidency was some went to recipients that previously had their pardon and commutation requests denied. Other recipients were petitioners whose requests Clinton ignored for several years or throughout his entire presidency. Bill Clinton then resurrected clemency petitions he previously turned down or those he ignored in order to hand out pardons. Clinton did this when he needed a few "normal" petitions to pad his clemency lists to obscure the reality there were so many atrocious pardons.

There is little doubt Clinton was padding his clemency lists in an effort to detract attention from undeserving clemency recipients. Several of the Christmas clemency recipients were surprised to learn Clinton was interested in giving them pardons years after he turned down or completely ignored their original requests. The lucky pardon recipients included William Carpenter, Peter Dionis, James Rogers, Dent Snider Jr., and Charles Yonce.

William Robert Carpenter of Michigan's Upper Peninsula pleaded guilty in 1988 to possession of marijuana with intent to distribute. He did not attempt to deny his guilt. Carpenter believed he should suffer the consequences for his crime. He was sentenced to one year of probation in 1991.

Carpenter filed a pardon request when Bill Clinton assumed the presidency that Clinton denied in 1994. Carpenter thought that was the end of it and his opportunity to get a presidential pardon was forever lost. So, it was understandable that Carpenter was shocked when he was approached by Clinton officials in late 2000 who wanted to know if he still wanted a pardon. Of course, he replied. Carpenter was among the December 2000 batch of pardon recipients.

Similarly, Peter Dionis was convicted in 1975 for drug trafficking. Dionis was caught smuggling hashish into the US from Morocco. The drug was hidden in the false bottom of a suitcase.

After serving an eighteen-month federal prison sentence, Dionis returned to Ft. Lauderdale and lived a law-abiding existence for the next two decades. Then he applied for a pardon right after Bill Clinton assumed the presidency. Clinton denied his clemency petition. Dionis also thought that was the end of his chances. Yet, Dionis, as with William Carpenter, received a telephone call out of the blue. The call came *nearly eight years* after he submitted his pardon application. A Justice Department official asked him if he still wanted to get a pardon. Dionis received a Christmas pardon from Bill Clinton only days later.

Operation Fast Hit was an eighteen-month-long undercover operation run out of the FBI Field Office in Columbia, South Carolina office. The plan was to uncover corrupt state and local officials.[46] Operation Fast Hit began in early 1980 and ran through mid-1981. One of those officials arrested was James W. Rogers Jr., the Berkeley County Sheriff. Rogers had received $4,000 in bribes in 1981 from the operator of an illegal gambling operation in exchange for protection from law enforcement authorities.[47]

Rogers reached a plea agreement and pleaded guilty to conspiracy to commit racketeering in return for the prosecutor dropping all other charges. In January 1982, Rogers was sentenced to fifteen years in prison. He spent two years in prison and began rebuilding his life after his release. More than a decade passed. Then Rogers submitted a clemency petition request shortly after Clinton was reelected to his second term. After a few years passed, Rogers forgot about the pardon request until he received a telephone call from a Justice Department official notifying him that his years-old request had been approved.[48]

Dent E. Snider Jr., had the bad luck of arranging a cocaine sale to someone who was part of an undercover operation in 1973. Snider was living in Hawaii at that time, but he moved to Colorado before he was apprehended. He was arrested seven years later in Denver. Snider worked out an agreement with prosecutors and escaped an almost certain prison term by pleading guilty to a lesser charge of using a telephone to arrange a drug sale. He was sentenced to four years of probation.[49]

Snider sent a clemency application to the Justice Department right after Bill Clinton was sworn in as president. Snider's case was tailor-made for a pardon. He was among the very few that Clinton pardoned that fit profile of someone actually deserving of a second chance. He had kicked his drug habit, become sober, and begun working as a social worker. He counseled drug addicts in Santa Cruz, California. For six years, Snider's pardon application sat dormant until he finally received word in 1999. His pardon request was denied. "It was devastating," said Snider.[50] He was deeply disappointed to have not had the opportunity to wipe away the last vestige of his youthful misbehavior.

Then Clinton needed to pad his pardon list in order to obscure countless undeserving Christmas clemencies. Snider received a telephone call on December 23, 2000, he described as "out of the blue."[51] A Justice Department official told Snider that his name was on a pardon list that was released the day before.

Charles Z. Yonce Jr. headed off to federal prison on April 27, 1988, to serve a six-month sentence. He was convicted of conspiracy to possess cocaine with intent to distribute, and of aiding and abetting a conspiracy. He also faced five years of probation. He was released from prison in August 1988.

Hoping to capitalize on the generosity of President George H. W. Bush, Yonce sent a clemency application to the Justice Department in early 1993 just days before Bush left the White House. Bush never acted upon Yonce's request. Neither did Bill Clinton. For *nearly eight full years*, Yonce's application languished in Clinton's

Justice Department.[52] Then it was revived when Clinton needed to pad his December 2000 clemency list. Yonce got a pardon.

Padding his clemency list was a practice Clinton continued the following month when he handed out pardons and commutations in the dead of night during his last hours in office. Clinton pardoned Willie Pruitt on January 20, 2001, for his 1954 Air Force court-martial for being absent without leave. Pruitt had died the year before.[53]

Former Arizona Governor John Fife Symington III was in the midst of a felony fraud investigation when Clinton told Symington's attorney during a chance December 2000 meeting that Clinton would "entertain a petition for a pardon."[54] Symington did not seek a pardon, but eager to pad his list, Clinton was still anxious to give him one on his last day as president. And he did.

CHAPTER 7

Hugh Rodham, the Drug Kingpin, and the Huckster

"Hugh says this is very important to him and the First Lady as well as others."[1]

CARLOS A. VIGNALI

The first raid was carried out on November 9, 1993. It was the culmination of several months of undercover police work and investigation. Several suspects were arrested. Subsequent arrests were made over the ensuing months. When it was over, thirty-one people were arrested. A massive drug ring that conspired to ship eight hundred pounds of powder cocaine from Los Angeles to Minneapolis to process into crack cocaine had been broken. It was the largest drug investigation in the history of Minnesota.

The evidence was overwhelming. The government had conducted court-approved wiretaps of numerous residential and cellular telephones. One of the conspirators reached a plea deal with the prosecution and agreed to tell the prosecution all he knew. Twenty-seven of the thirty-one who were arrested pleaded guilty to a variety of drug-related charges. Carlos A. Vignali and three others opted to go to trial.

After a six-week trial, the jury found Vignali guilty on three counts. He was found guilty of conspiring to manufacture, possess, and distribute cocaine; of aiding and abetting the use of a facility in interstate commerce with the intent to distribute cocaine; and of aiding and abetting the use of communication facilities for the commission of felonies. Vignali was sentenced to fourteen years and seven months in federal prison. In comparison, Todd Hopson, a low-level dealer in the Vignali drug ring, received a twenty-three-year prison sentence.[2]

Carlos Vignali had his prison sentence commuted to time served on Clinton's last day in office. Hopson, who remained incarcerated while Vignali walked free, observed, "I didn't have anybody walk my application up to the White House and put it in front of the president. I didn't have those connections."[3] Vignali had the most powerful connection to arrange his release: Hillary Rodham Clinton.

White House officials who later argued that Vignali's sentence was unduly harsh and was deserving of clemency were unperturbed that lower-level participants in the drug ring still languished in prison. Several were serving sentences longer than the mere five years Vignali eventually served.

Four major issues set Vignali apart from the other thirty conspirators in this case. First, he was a kingpin of the drug ring. Most of the other participants were small-time drug hustlers. Second, Vignali was Hispanic, whereas most of the others were black. Vignali's father was Argentine and his mother was Puerto Rican. This fact came into play during his trial. The third issue was that Hillary Clinton's brother, Hugh Rodham, was paid more than $200,000 to arrange for a favorable executive clemency decision from his brother-in-law. Fourth, Vignali had his sentence dramatically shortened by President William J. Clinton while the others had to serve out their sentences.

Hugh Rodham, described by *Time* as the "sartorially impaired sometime golfing partner of [Bill Clinton],"[4] played the key role in effecting the commutation of Vignali. If not for Hugh Rodham, Carlos Vignali would have likely served out his prison sentence.

Contributing to Vignali's clemency was his father, Horacio Vignali, a rich Los Angeles entrepreneur who gave more than $160,000 to influential California politicians, nearly all of whom were Democrats, and many of whom lobbied Clinton asking for clemency for Carlos Vignali. Horacio Vignali, who gave only a modest amount of campaign contributions before his son was arrested, began writing checks for tens of thousands of dollars at a time after the younger Vignali was arrested. Recipients of his largesse included California Governor Gray Davis, to whom he directly contributed $49,400.[5] Vignali raised an additional $75,000 for Davis from other donors just months before Clinton commuted his son's sentence.[6] Vignali also gave $10,000 to the Democratic National Committee.

There was nothing about Carlos Vignali that justified the commutation he received from Clinton. He was not a small-time drug peddler nor an occasional recreational user who faced a disproportionately long prison sentence from the possession of a very small amount of narcotics. Vignali was a drug kingpin directing a conspiracy to ship to Minneapolis nearly half a ton of cocaine that was destined to become crack cocaine. Vignali, known as "C-Low," was allegedly the West Coast supplier of cocaine to Minneapolis drug dealers. Prosecutors tied Vignali to more than fifteen pounds of crack cocaine that he said he personally converted from powder.[7]

"He was not a minor player; he was not a street level dealer. This guy was a major source in keeping a drug organization here [in Minneapolis] being fed with dope from California," according to US Attorney Todd Jones.[8] It was Jones' office that prosecuted Vignali.

Moreover, Clinton could not argue that Vignali received an unfair sentence due to sentencing disparities between powder and crack cocaine trafficking without exposing himself as a hypocrite. Clinton supported tougher sentences for crack traffickers. He opposed the Federal Sentencing Commission in 1995 when it proposed equalizing the sentences between powder and crack cocaine.[9] Moreover, US sentencing guidelines called for a minimum sentence of at least five years for trafficking in five hundred grams, a little more than one pound, of powder cocaine. Vignali had conspired to traffic in more than seven hundred times the amount of powder cocaine that would fetch a minimum of five years in prison.

Vignali would have never received a favorable clemency decision from the president if Clinton had adhered to his own policy. A January 26, 1996, memo to the Justice Department from then White House Counsel Jack Quinn outlined additional restrictions Clinton had placed on favorable clemency consideration. Adoption of these restrictions would have made it *more difficult* for an applicant to get a pardon or commutation from Clinton than from previous presidents. The memo stated there were "certain categories of crimes which are so serious that the President *will not consider* granting a pardon for them under almost any circumstances [emphasis added]." Among the included crimes was "large scale drug trafficking" and "offenses involving central involvement in political corruption."[10]

Andrew Dunne was one of the assistant US attorneys who prosecuted Vignali. Dunne was staunchly opposed to clemency for Vignali and wrote a very strong letter to the White House stating that fact. Dunne reported that Vignali did not meet the bare minimum for consideration of executive clemency because he had never acknowledged responsibility, nor had he shown any remorse for his crime. In the same January 1996 memo, Quinn underscored Clinton's position that "acceptance of responsibility, remorse and atonement"[11] by the perpetrator for a crime was critical toward any favorable consideration of clemency petition.

US District Judge David Doty, the judge who tried Vignali, also opposed clemency. Doty was not a "hanging judge" who believed in lengthy prison sentences. In fact, Doty was a longtime critic of mandatory sentences. He gave Vignali a sentence that fell in the middle of the sentencing guidelines of thirteen to sixteen years. "I hit him the middle…I didn't max him out," said Doty. "Carlos deserved what he got."[12]

This reality underscored the absurdity of Clinton's claim that Vignali was unfairly victimized by mandatory minimum sentences. Vignali was given an appropriate sentence that fit the crime by a judge who was an outspoken critic of mandatory minimums. Doty, like US Attorney Dunne, pointed out that Vignali was not repentant for his crimes.

Vignali's trial defense was absurd. First, he played his own version of the race card and then he concocted a preposterous defense of vague accusations that was sketchy on the details and was devoid of facts.

Danny Davis, the attorney for Vignali, told the jury in his opening statement that "this conspiracy, the evidence will show, really comes down to a black drug dealing network…. My client is not [black]."[13] Vignali's defense was that he, a Hispanic, could not possibly be complicit in selling illegal narcotics to black men and women.

Second, Vignali claimed that recorded conversations discussing his drug transactions were misinterpreted. He claimed that discussions regarding drug money were really about $20,000 he alleged he lent to a friend to buy Christmas presents and to invest in a business deal with some professional basketball players. When asked how he had $20,000 in cash to lend with only a reported annual income of less than $14,000 a year while working at his father's auto body shop, Vignali claimed it was his life's savings he kept stashed in his bedroom closet.[14] It proved difficult for Vignali to convince a jury that he lent money to a man he claimed he hardly knew more than two thousand miles away for an investment that was short of details.

Vignali was untruthful when he claimed that he eked out a meager salary working in his father's auto body shop. Federal authorities reported he could lose as much as $200,000 on a gambling trip to Las Vegas without batting an eye.[15]

Every single defendant in the Vignali drug ring, including Vignali, had either pled guilty or was convicted with the exception of one relatively minor player. In spite of the mountains of evidence, the prosecution witnesses, and the recorded conversations, Vignali did not accept his conviction and immediately appealed the jury's finding hoping for a different outcome. He lost before the US Circuit Court of Appeals for the Eighth Circuit. The appellate court ruled unanimously against Vignali and upheld the district court's finding.

After the failed appeals court ruling, Horacio Vignali began lining up a letter writing campaign for his son. The elder Vignali pulled strings and urged well-connected political friends, particularly those with whom he showered with political contributions, to urge White House officials to review his son's conviction.

The first letter to the White House in 1996 came from former California Assembly speaker Antonio Villaraigosa, who would later be elected mayor of Los Angeles. Fabrications and falsehoods in Villaraigosa's letter would be repeated again and again in other letters, and later, and in documents supporting Vignali's executive clemency application. Villaraigosa falsely claimed, "Mr. Vignali has no prior criminal record." In fact, Carlos Vignali had an extensive criminal record with multiple arrests and convictions.

When first questioned about his support of the drug kingpin, Villaraigosa falsely stated that he wrote only the appeals court, asking the judge to review the matter. When it was later learned that Villaraigosa actually wrote the White House and not an appeals court judge, Villaraigosa then claimed he had simply confused the details of his own involvement.[16]

It was not until after there was a public uproar over the Vignali commutation that Villaraigosa expressed regret over writing his letter. He admitted that he had not spoken to the prosecutors in the matter and did not have the facts of what had actually transpired in the drug case. Villaraigosa claimed the nearly $3,000 Horacio Vignali had given to his political campaigns had no bearing on his support for a commutation for Carlos Vignali.[17]

Los Angeles County Sheriff Lee Baca lobbied the White House on behalf of Vignali. Baca wrote at least two letters and spoke with the White House counsel's office in favor of clemency.[18] Coincidentally, Horacio Vignali held several fundraisers for Baca, including a 1999 fundraiser at Vignali's downtown auto body shop.[19] Horacio Vignali contributed $11,000 to Baca's political campaigns.[20] In addition, Vignali gave $1,000 in cash to Baca as a wedding gift when Baca married his second wife in 1999.[21]

Many of the letter writers expressed regret that they sent letters on behalf of Vignali's clemency appeal, but only after the public became aware of the extent of Vignali's prior criminal record, the cushy ties his father had with several public officials, and the amount of political fundraising dollars that changed hands.

Roman Catholic Cardinal Roger Mahony publicly apologized for writing his letter of support, acknowledging that he knew neither of the Vignalis. "I broke my decades-long practice of never sending a letter on behalf of any person whom I do not know personally," said Mahony in a prepared statement.[22] Mahony said he wrote the letter after lobbying by Villaraigosa, Baca, and US Representative Xavier Becerra.[23]

Congressman Becerra was prolific in not only writing to Clinton, but also in calling White House and Justice Department officials on multiple occasions. He "peppered the White House with calls."[24] Becerra even phoned the White House during the evening of January 19, the eve of Clinton's departure from office. In that telephone call, Becerra pressed White House officials for the status of Vignali's clemency request.

Becerra defended his actions as the sort of service he would provide to any constituent.[25] He later conceded that the Vignalis were not even constituents of his. That aside, Becerra disputed that

Horacio Vignali's $15,000 in campaign contributions to Becerra and his political committees[26] and Vignali family contributions totaling $3,500 to Becerra's Los Angeles mayoral campaign[27] had any influence on why he had taken such active interest in Vignali.[28]

Becerra stated another reason why he became involved in the Vignali case was to combat racism because "justice is not yet blind to color in America."[29] That was a remarkable statement coming from the Hispanic Becerra, who was a sitting member of Congress and who, at the time, was a leading candidate to be elected mayor of the second most populated city in America. Moreover, the federal prosecutor's office in Minnesota that prosecuted Vignali was led by Todd Jones, a black man who was appointed as US attorney by Clinton. Clearly, race had not been a hardship as Becerra had suggested.

Becerra, who worked feverishly to help free a convicted drug kingpin, was elected the California attorney general, the state's top crime fighter, in 2016.

In a very highly unusual move, Alejandro N. Mayorkas, the US attorney for the central district of California, called the White House counsel urging Clinton to commute the sentence of Vignali. As a rule, US attorneys do not intervene in cases outside their district. Because Vignali was prosecuted in Minnesota, his case was under the jurisdiction of US Attorney Todd Jones. Commenting on Mayorkas's actions, Margaret Love, the Clinton administration's pardon attorney until 1997 stated, "The US Attorney in Los Angeles should have had no role. It's peculiar for him to become involved at all. What business is it of his?"[30]

Jones reported that Mayorkas telephoned him at least two times in early 1999 and suggested to Jones that the Minnesota prosecutor may have made a mistake in prosecuting Carlos Vignali. According to Jones, Mayorkas was involved in the younger Vignali's clemency efforts at the request of the elder Vignali.[31] Mayorkas later expressed regret for his actions and he admitted that he "should not have made that call to the White House."[32]

Appearing on the February 18, 2001, edition of NBC's *Meet the Press*, Clinton's former chief of staff, John Podesta, claimed it was the involvement of US Attorney Mayorkas in advocating on behalf of Vignali that was crucial to the commutation decision. Podesta failed to mention that Todd Jones, the US attorney whose office had jurisdiction in the Vignali matter and had prosecuted the case, vigorously opposed clemency.

Mayorkas's persistence in pursuing freedom for Carlos Vignali led to suspicions of heretofore unknown ties between Mayorkas, appointed as US attorney in 1998 by Clinton, and the elder Vignali. In his two and a half years as US Attorney, Mayorkas had eschewed pursuing narcotics and organized crime in favor of "hate" and environmental crimes.[33]

Mayorkas's actions also led to the resignation of one of his superstar deputies. Assistant US Attorney Duncan DeVille resigned from his job noting that Mayorkas's actions in support of a major drug supplier hampered DeVille's ability to effectively fight the narcotics trade. In a terse resignation letter DeVille wrote, "I frequently place in danger both my life and, more importantly the lives of law enforcement agents, in the pursuit of drug dealers. Accordingly, I cannot support your recent actions in assisting in the pardon [of Carlos Vignali]."[34]

Because of the Vignali clemency, DeVille had been labeled a hypocrite. He was in Armenia and Russia working with the respective governments on ties to ethnic organized crime in southern California when the Vignali clemency became public. DeVille's main point to Armenian and Russian law enforcement authorities was their responsibility to enforce the rule of law. Then news broke that DeVille's immediate boss was assisting, rather than prosecuting, an organized crime figure in the US. "When this broke, the Clinton pardons, they threw it in my face, saying, you're a hypocrite," said DeVille. "Look, your government does the same thing. And I think the worst station in life may be that of a hypocrite."[35]

Villaraigosa's successor as California Assembly speaker, Robert Hertzberg, also wrote a letter to Clinton, urging he commute the sentence of Carlos Vignali. Hertzberg, who received $4,000 in campaign contributions from Vignali wrote Clinton that "neither guns, drugs or drug money was found in Mr. Vignali's possession"[36] and "It is time to return Carlos Vignali to his family."[37]

Others who wrote to Clinton included California Senator Richard Polanco, who was a candidate for the Los Angeles City Council at the time, Los Angeles City Councilmen Richard Alatorre and Mike Hernandez, and Los Angeles County Supervisor Gloria Molina. Polanco received more than $20,000 in campaign contributions from Vignali and Alatorre received $1,500.[38] Molina said she succumbed to "a constant barrage of requests" and "begging" from Horacio Vignali before finally agreeing to write a letter.[39]

Polanco, who was the Democrat floor leader in the California Senate, had been running a race for a seat on the Los Angeles City Council. He abruptly ended his candidacy and dropped out of the race the day the story broke of his involvement in the Vignali clemency.[40]

The falsehoods did not end with the letters from family-connected politicians. Congressman Dan Burton (Republican, Indiana), whose committee investigated the commutation of Vignali's federal sentence observed that Vignali "lied in his pardon [clemency] application."[41] The application listed only two of the four times he had been arrested and it failed to note his admission to law enforcement authorities that he had been a member of the violent West Covina gang.[42]

After the failed appeals court effort, the elder Vignali requested Danny Davis, his son's attorney during the criminal trial, to prepare an executive clemency petition. Davis turned down the request telling the father that his son's chances of getting a favorable clemency decision were "like a snowball in Hades." Apparently, during Bill Clinton's last day as president, Hades had a snowstorm. Clinton commuted the sentence of Vignali even though officials from Clinton's own Justice Department strongly recommended disapproval of the clemency petition.[43]

After Vignali walked from the Federal Correctional Institute in Safford, Arizona a free man, Margaret Love reacted with the comment, "It's not plausible; it makes no sense at all."[44] Love was the US pardon attorney for much of Clinton's administration.

In the days following the release of Carlos Vignali from prison, his father denied he had asked any politicians to write letters pressing Clinton for clemency for the younger Vignali.[45] The elder Vignali claimed he had no knowledge of who had written to the White House on behalf of his son's clemency request. Vignali answered, "Nope," when asked if Hugh Rodham had any involvement in his son's release.[46] Horacio Vignali's denials, it turned out, were not true.

The elder Vignali also falsely stated he did not know of Rodham's involvement in managing the petition,[47] even though Vignali paid $204,280 Rodham to lobby Bill Clinton to rule favorably on the clemency request.[48]

After it became public that Hugh Rodham was paid more than $434,000 to influence his brother-in-law for the commutation for Vignali and a pardon for A. Glenn Braswell (to be addressed in a later section), Bill and Hillary both addressed the matter. The Clintons did not deny they were aware of Rodham's involvement.

On February 22, 2001, Bill Clinton said, "Yesterday I became aware of press inquiries that Hugh Rodham received a contingency fee in connection with a pardon application for Glenn Braswell and a fee for the work on Carlos Vignali's commutation application. Neither Hillary nor I had any knowledge of such payments. We are deeply disturbed by these reports and have insisted that Hugh return any monies received."[49]

A confidential source who was a longtime Clinton adviser reported that Clinton did know of Rodham's role in the clemency petitions but that "he did not know that Hugh [Rodham] would be compensated."[50]

The same day, Hillary stated, "I was very disturbed to learn that my brother, Hugh Rodham, received fees in connection with two clemency applications."[51] She further remarked, "I don't have any memory at all of talking to my brother about this."[52]

In typical Clinton fashion, Bill and Hillary's comments were carefully crafted to address very specific knowledge and narrow topics. Bill Clinton did not deny knowing that Rodham had been paid. Instead, he denied knowing the specifics of how Rodham's fees were structured. In addition, he expressed disappointment for "these reports" from the media. Clinton was not disappointed in Rodham. He was disappointed in the media reports. An incurious national press corps did not press Clinton on the matter.

Hillary did not deny knowing that Rodham was lobbying for clemency for Vignali and Braswell. Instead, she claimed that she did not speak directly with her brother about these two specific applications.[53] She didn't have "any memory" of speaking with him about it.

This claim is remarkable in and of itself. Hugh had been spending a considerable amount of time living at the White House in the waning months of Clinton's presidency. In fact, Hugh had nearly as much stuff to be moved from the White House in January 2001 as did Chelsea Clinton, the first daughter.[54] Rodham was offered nearly a half a million dollars—50 percent in contingency fees to be paid only if he were successful—in securing favorable clemency decisions by his brother-in-law. It defies credulity to believe that Hugh Rodham did not discuss Vignali and Braswell with Bill and Hillary Clinton.

As a matter of fact, Hugh joined Bill Clinton and half-brother Roger Clinton for regular get-togethers including threesome golf outings in the waning months of the Clinton presidency. As one Clinton staffer observed, Hugh had "the kind of access we couldn't do a thing about."[55] There is little doubt Rodham pressed Clinton for clemency for his clients, especially Braswell. Rodham would not have earned Braswell's $200,000 "success fee" unless he was successful.

Fortuitously, direct communication between the Clintons and Hugh Rodham was not necessary. Rodham had been working with Bruce Lindsey, the Deputy White House Counsel, a decades-long confidant of Bill and Hillary, and the Clinton administration official managing the pardon process, especially those clemency applicants who escaped Department of Justice scrutiny. Rodham had only to make his desires known to Lindsey, the Clintons' longtime fixer,[56] who would have likely informed the president and the first lady to allow them to assert plausible deniability.

Yet in a maneuver typical of the Clinton administration, Lindsey claimed he could not recall if he had spoken with Clinton about Rodham's involvement.[57] A spokesman for the former president stated Clinton "[didn't] recall ever discussing Mr. Rodham's views on the Vignali pardon application."[58] It was telling that neither Clinton nor Lindsey offered an unqualified denial. Instead, they both "could not recall" discussing a clemency application that reached the White House just days before a commutation was issued.

Unfortunately for Lindsey, Rodham did remember speaking to him about the Vignali clemency request. In fact, Rodham admitted he spoke with Lindsey on at least three occasions regarding Vignali.[59] It defies logic that Lindsey claims he could not recall discussing with Clinton the involvement of the president's very own brother-in-law in a controversial clemency request.

Unless there is a deathbed confession, it is likely the public will never know what was said between Rodham and the Clintons regarding the Vignali and Braswell clemencies. Rodham had free reign to come and go as he pleased at the White House personal quarters. Rodham spent considerable time with Clinton in the waning weeks of his presidency including at the White House and at Camp David, Maryland.[60]

After it became public that Rodham had profited handsomely from his family ties in lobbying Clinton to issue the Vignali commutation and the Braswell pardon, both Bill and Hillary made a big show of insisting Rodham return the payments. Rodham claimed he would do so, and the press immediately gave him credit for refunding the money he had taken. It was later learned that he returned only $300,000 of the money and instead kept $134,000 with a promise through his attorney that the balance would be returned at some later date.[61] There is no evidence the remaining balance was ever returned.

According to *Time*, Rodham may have been liable for civil charges if he had not properly registered as a lobbyist. As *Time* reported, Rodham should have registered as a lobbyist because he met at least two of the criteria requiring mandatory registration as delineated under the Lobbying Disclosure Act of 1995. Satisfying any single criterion triggered mandatory registration.

The criteria requiring registration are an individual who (1) spends at least 20 percent of their time for a particular client on lobbying activities; (2) has multiple contacts with legislative staff, members of Congress, or high-level executive branch officials; and (3) works for a client paying more than $5,000 over six months for that service. Rodham met the last two criteria.[62] He likely satisfied the first criterion, as well. Aside from his pardon lobbying activities, Hugh Rodham spent the rest of his time loafing about the White House.

The elder Vignali had not been without controversy. Not only was his son Carlos a high school dropout and drug trafficker, but two of his other three children were drug addicts.[63] Local and federal drug enforcement officials had long believed Horacio Vignali had been deeply involved in the illegal drug trade.

There was other legal controversy surrounding Vignali. Less than two years before Carlos had his sentence commuted, two of his father's automobile repair businesses were sued by the California and Farmers Insurance Exchange allegedly for padding insurance repair bills and putting in claims for phantom work. Vignali settled with the insurers. Terms of the settlement were confidential.[64]

Officials from federal and state law enforcement agencies had long suspected the elder Vignali of extensive involvement in smuggling and selling illegal narcotics since at least the mid-1970s. Moreover, this very information was available to both the White House and Justice Department yet, Clinton gave a commutation to Carlos Vignali in spite of it.[65]

According to the Drug Enforcement Agency, Horacio Vignali smuggled heroin into the US where it was hidden in the drive shafts of automobiles he transported from Mexico. The Bureau of Alcohol, Tobacco and Firearms reported he had tried to sell a machine gun to ATF agents and bragged about how he smuggled heroin into the U.S.[66]

The Federal Bureau of Investigation, the criminal investigation division of the Internal Revenue Service, and the California Bureau of Narcotic Enforcement had information tying Horacio Vignali to illegal drug activity.[67]

Federal prosecutors in Minneapolis were convinced Horacio Vignali was the drug supplier to his son. Carlos Vignali turned down prosecutors' offer for a reduced sentence in return for information on his drug supplier. According to Todd Jones, the US attorney for Minneapolis, "He did not want to snitch on his dad." Todd added, "He was willing to go to prison for [his dad], for a long time."[68]

Law enforcement authorities also believe that Horacio Vignali was part of a much-larger drug ring operated by George Torres. Vignali and Torres had been longtime business partners and had numerous business deals between the two of them.

Bill Clinton was practicing the old adage "ask me no questions and I will tell you no lies." By studiously avoiding the rigorous Justice Department scrutiny that clemency applicants are supposed to undergo, Clinton got the very answer he wanted: Carlos Vignali was the victim of an overly aggressive criminal justice system and harsh sentencing guidelines. Clinton didn't want to know that federal, state, and local law enforcement suspected the Vignalis of longtime drug dealing activity. By circumventing rigorous scrutiny of the Vignalis, Clinton apparently felt justified setting Vignali free.

At least six federal, state, and local law enforcement agencies detailed ties between Torres and illegal narcotics activity.[69] According to the DEA, Torres had been involved in drug trafficking since at least the 1980s and by the 1990s was smuggling hundreds of kilograms of cocaine into Los Angeles from Mexico.[70] Torres, authorities alleged, was distributing as much as one hundred kilos each month.[71]

Torres operated Numero Uno, a chain of local supermarkets located in Mexican neighborhoods in southern California. Authorities believed he smuggled cocaine in tractor-trailers making deliveries from Mexico with the illicit drugs hidden among grocery products. Further, authorities alleged Torres used the supermarkets to launder the money from drug sales.[72] Torres had a lot of baggage. He had twice been convicted of illegal gun charges. And he was a named suspect in two murders.

Numerous police informants had implicated both Horacio Vignali and George Torres in major drug trafficking, although authorities had been unable to build a strong case against either man by the time Clinton freed Carlos Vignali. That changed after young Vignali was set free.

The media attention focused on the Vignali commutation and the spotlight focused on alleged illegal narcotics activity by Vignali and Torres inspired thirteen federal, state, and local law enforcement authorities to take a closer look at the facts. That closer look was revealing.

According to informants, George Torres engaged in theft, bribery, extortion, racketeering, and even murder. There were claims against Torres of intimidation, beatings, illegal alien smuggling, and the use of drug dealers to carry out violent crimes including murder.

The investigation was very thorough. When completed, it resulted in a fifty-nine-count federal indictment in June 2007 listing offenses against Torres including murder, solicitation of murder, bribery of a public official, illegal alien smuggling, and tax evasion.

The indictment detailed an allegation that Torres arranged for a drug dealer named Ignacio Meza to perform a hit against the Primera Flats street gang that Torres believed was responsible for a Numero Uno employee's murder in 1993. Meza was wanted in Alabama in connection with cocaine trafficking in that state.[73]

The indictment also laid out the chain of events when Torres allegedly ordered Meza to kill a member of the so-called Mexican mafia that was reportedly trying to shake down one of Torres' stores.

Further, the indictment noted that Torres was alleged to have arranged with yet another drug dealer to kill Meza when Torres suspected Meza of having stolen money from him. Meza disappeared shortly thereafter, and he is presumed by law enforcement to have been killed on Torres' orders.

It was shocking that the Clinton White House did not take into consideration any information from the Drug Enforcement Agency regarding the largest narcotics case ever prosecuted in the state of Minnesota when Clinton decided to set Carlos Vignali free.

HUGH RODHAM

Hugh Rodham lived a spectacularly unremarkable existence as an assistant public defender in Miami. His lackadaisical life contrasted sharply with his sister, who was driven to achieve her lofty goals. Yet Hugh was very close to his sister and brother-in-law. In fact, Hugh and brother, Tony, joined Bill and Hillary on their honeymoon to Mexico.

Hugh's stumbling through life changed when his brother-in-law was elected president and his sister invited Hugh and younger brother Tony along for the ride to partake in the White House gravy train. The brothers' chutzpah knew no bounds. Hugh and Tony Rodham solicited corporate sponsorship of private parties they planned to hold immediately following Bill Clinton's 1993 inauguration.[74] They held a party at the Renaissance Mayflower Hotel, but came up short in paying for it, causing the Democratic National Committee to cover the expenses.[75]

Hugh Rodham attempted to duplicate Hillary's political success. He ran as the Democrat nominee to the US Senate against Republican Connie Mack in the 1994 election and lost by a landslide. Even the *New York Times*, which was reliably sympathetic to the Clintons, described Rodham's candidacy as a "quixotic bid" which he ran "in sweetly hapless fashion."[76] He was so inept that his campaign manager, Michael Copperthite, admitted "Hugh'd sleep until noon, one o'clock" instead of being out campaigning.[77]

Rodham was later criticized by consumer activist Ralph Nader for his engaging in personal lobbying of Bill and Hillary when the White House was formulating a plan on tobacco lawsuits in which Rodham would personally profit. Rodham had signed on to one group of lawyers in a class action lawsuit and stood to make a windfall profit of millions of dollars, but that group's settlement deal fell apart during congressional deliberations on a national settlement plan.

The most powerful quality Hugh Rodham had going for him was access. Longtime friend Clayton Kaiser observed, "He can go to the President and get serious attention paid."[78] That one-of-a-kind access paid handsomely for Rodham. In fact, it paid more than $430,000 when he parlayed his immediate access to Bill and Hillary into presidential clemency for Carlos Vignali and Glenn Braswell.

GLENN BRASWELL

When Almon Glenn Braswell Sr., received his presidential pardon from Bill Clinton, he was already knee-deep in another federal criminal investigation. The US attorney for Los Angeles had been investigating Braswell for a year and a half over allegations of money laundering and tax evasion.[79] This was the first time in history that a president handed out a pardon to a convicted felon who was under active investigation for committing additional felonies.

The allegations of further crimes committed by Braswell were not unfounded. In fact, the evidence against him was overwhelming. Two years after Clinton gave him a pardon, Braswell was indicted and arrested in January 2003. He admitted to the charges and pleaded guilty. Fortunately for Braswell, Clinton's pardon of his earlier crimes wiped his record clean, establishing him as a first-time offender and allowing him to escape punishment that was more fitting for a twice-convicted felon.

Braswell received the Clinton pardon for 1983 convictions for perjury and mail fraud regarding claims he made regarding a hair baldness potion he was peddling through the US Postal Service. Braswell had falsified photographs misrepresenting the success of his claimed baldness cure.[80] Braswell's assertion that he was falsely convicted in 1983 had little standing as his conviction was appealed all the way through the legal system where the US Supreme Court declined to hear the case. Braswell served only seven months of his three-year federal prison sentence.

Braswell had been dogged by controversy for three decades. The US Postal Service filed 139 complaints against him.[81] The US Food and Drug Administration had placed a ban on the importation into the US of his products. Dr. Stephen Barrett, who heads Quackwatch, a nonprofit organization affiliated with the Consumer Federation of America at that time and whose mission is to "combat health-related frauds, myths, fads, fallacies, and misconduct," had been closely following Braswell's snake oil salesman escapades and was scruti-nizing the activities of Braswell's company, Gero Vita International. Barrett reported, "I have file on this guy that is 14 inches thick."[82]

The trade group the National Council for Reliable Health Infor-mation called Gero Vita's marketing brochures "quackish" and referred to the company's "blatant, exaggerated claims" to "prevent or treat disease." The National Council Against Health Fraud called him a "health huckster" and claimed Braswell was "perhaps the biggest direct marketer of bogus health products."[83] Under a 1983 court-filed consent judgment with the Federal Trade Commission, Braswell was permanently barred from making any restorative claims regarding his baldness products.[84]

Even the mildest of skeptics would have steered clear of Braswell's products because of the outlandish claims. Gero Vita products included "10 different 'sexual enhancers,' and 'mind extenders' for 'accelerated thinking' using herbs allegedly 'dating to the days of the Chinese Imperial Court.'"[85]

In spite of a trail of criminal and regulatory violations, Braswell was extremely successful from peddling his products. According to critics, he was a huckster of the highest order who preyed on the elderly, selling them bogus products, and relieving them of their retirement nest eggs.

Braswell had civil as well as criminal difficulties. He was sued by sports celebrities NASCAR driver Richard Petty; Hall of Fame baseball player Stan Musial; and NFL great Len Dawson. The sports figures alleged Braswell wrongfully used their photographs in advertising a prostate remedy.[86] In a civil trial that took place only four months before Clinton rewarded him with a pardon, Braswell invoked his Fifth Amendment right against self-incrimination 196 times.

Braswell was also viewed as a troublemaker and nuisance in his own hometown. He hired a Florida law firm and lobbyist to win approval from Miami-Dade County officials to chop down 428 trees inside a mangrove cluster. He claimed the trees blocked the view of Biscayne Bay from the back porch of his home in a seven-acre compound in the exclusive Coconut Grove section of Miami.

He went through a messy and very public divorce in 1999. Braswell and his estranged wife, Renee Covington, fought over the custody of their infant son and money. At one point during their prolonged divorce proceedings, Covington slugged Braswell's female dinner companion.

As was the case in dozens of other Clinton clemency actions, Braswell's pardon application bypassed the Justice Department's normal review process and did not adhere to the DOJ's clemency application guidelines. Nor did his application undergo rigorous scrutiny by the Federal Bureau of Investigation.[87] Had Braswell undergone even the most basic procedures for review "Then the FBI would [have] cut off the background investigation and end[ed] it,"[88] claimed John Stanish, the pardon attorney under former president Jimmy Carter.

Eight months after he was pardoned, Braswell appeared before the Senate Special Committee on Aging chaired by John Breaux (Democrat, Louisiana) on a hearing regarding whether Braswell's company was one of the "bad apples in the supplement industry." In his opening statement at the September 10, 2001, hearing, Breaux stated that the congressional role was "help protect American citizens, particularly our elderly, who are preyed upon by modern-day snake-oil salesmen."[89]

Breaux referred to the *Journal of Longevity*, a marketing brochure disguised as a medical journal, and produced by Braswell's company, as "an elaborate, misleading advertising tool." Breaux said some of the journal's articles "simply prey on the fears of the elderly."

Braswell refused to answer any questions during the hearing, and he invoked his Fifth Amendment right against self-incrimination. Michael O'Neill, the former chief financial officer of Braswell's G.B. Data Systems, another company involved in the sale of fake remedies, had previously testified that Braswell's products were "laden with lies and deception."[90] O'Neill testified he was fired after only six months of working for Braswell when he pressured Braswell to cease deceptive advertising.

O'Neill testified that he had grown disillusioned with trying to expose Braswell's practices after he was fired by Braswell until he learned that Clinton had pardoned the supplement magnate. O'Neill became outraged that Clinton had given official forgiveness to Braswell, whose companies continued to make more $200 million profit each year on its sales of miracle products. O'Neill told the Senate panel that in addition to selling questionably effective products, Braswell utilized a Canadian return address that had no employees in order to create an obstacle that would prevent upset customers from contacting company officials who were actually located in Marina del Rey, California.[91]

It turned out Braswell used a Mail Boxes Etc. mailbox address that gave the appearance his company owned a brick-and-mortar operation in Canada. In fact, it was simply a mail drop that allowed him to obfuscate the company's real location from irate customers.

Nearly two years to the day after he was pardoned by Clinton, Braswell was arrested by Special Agents of the Internal Revenue Service on charges that he evaded paying more than $13 million in federal taxes. Braswell was arrested at his Florida home on January 13, 2003. He was named in a thirteen-count grand jury indictment alleging he avoided paying more than $9 million in personal income taxes and $4.4 million in corporate taxes.

According to federal investigators, Braswell's company evaded paying taxes by inflating its deductible expenses and in funneling millions of dollars to offshore accounts that Braswell controlled.

The scam, as described in the federal indictment, was accomplished by moving money from Braswell's two US companies, G.B. Data Systems and Gero Vita International, to a sham company based in Bermuda under the pretext the companies were paying legitimate business expenses. Phony invoices were sent from Deleon Global Trading in Bermuda to the two American firms, purporting to show that Deleon sold products to G.B. Data Systems and Gero Vita International. These false expenses reduced the tax liability of the companies in which Braswell was the sole shareholder. Then, Braswell used Deleon as his personal piggy bank, dispensing money to himself whenever he wanted without claiming it as income.

In May 2003, just months after his indictment and arrest, the Federal Trade Commission filed a nine-count complaint against Braswell and his companies alleging they engaged in a "deceptive practice" and in "making of false advertisements" in promoting the sale of various miracle cures and products including dietary supplements that purported to treat or cure respiratory disease, diabetes, Alzheimer's disease, obesity, and erectile dysfunction.[92]

The FTC complaint sought a ban against Braswell participating in future business dealings related to the advertising or sale of dietary supplements and other health-related products. FTC spokesman Howard Beales accused Braswell's organization of having "built their businesses on false and outrageous claims."[93]

Braswell agreed to pay a million-dollar fine and turned over assets totaling $3.5 million to settle the charges brought by the FTC. He was also banned from ever participating in the direct response marketing of food items, supplements, and other unapproved drugs.

Gaining the Hugh Rodham-engineered pardon from Bill Clinton was more valuable to Braswell than just simply satisfying his ego or restoring his right to vote. Wiping away prior convictions benefited him in future convictions when courts take into account prior illegal activity in determining the severity of a sentence. Officially, Braswell had a clean record and would be treated as first-time offender.

That Clinton pardon came in handy because Braswell pleaded guilty to tax evasion. Braswell admitted to a scheme to overstate the business expenses of one of his companies. He agreed in court that the total of his underpayment together with penalties and interest amounted to more than ten million dollars. Braswell had been so wildly successful in profiting from peddling miracle cure products that he agreed to pay the Internal Revenue Service the entire amount due of $10,455,367 within three weeks. According to federal authorities, Braswell had been "squirreling away" large amounts of money in foreign accounts in the eventuality that he would flee the country to avoid arrest. He deposited $52 million in an account in Liechtenstein.[94]

As part of Braswell's plea agreement, he was sentenced to only eighteen months in prison for what was in reality a second conviction for committing various federal crimes. The Clinton pardon undoubtedly spared Braswell a longer prison sentence. US District Judge Margaret Morrow, who sentenced him, stated that Braswell could have been sent to prison for at least thirty-three and up to forty-one months.[95]

Hugh Rodham did not prepare Braswell's pardon application. Another Florida lawyer, Kendall Coffey, had prepared the application. Coffey was appointed by Clinton in the early 1990s to serve as the US attorney in south Florida, but he was forced to step down in 1996 when he bit a stripper at a Miami nude bar. Coffey represented Vice President Albert Gore Jr. in late 2000, when the Democrat presidential candidate lost the Florida election and recount.[96]

Rodham's task, for which he was paid nearly one-quarter of a million dollars, was to prod his brother-in-law into issuing the pardon. On this task, Rodham was successful. According to a published report, Coffey did not complete Braswell's pardon application until January 17, just three days before Clinton left office.[97] The speed with which the application worked its way through the White House underscored the reality that Clinton knew full well that his wife's brother was fully involved in the Braswell pardon application.

According to a Justice Department official, Braswell's pardon application was so sketchy on the details that it did not even include a current address for the former felon. The Justice Department had to use other means to track down Braswell in order to mail him a copy of his actual pardon announcement.[98]

One of the many unconscionable aspects of the Braswell pardon was how the Clintons allowed Al Gore to take the fall for pushing it forward. When news broke that the mail order swindler, who was already under federal investigation for further crimes, received an undeserved pardon, the question arose as to how it came about.

The Clintons were well aware that Hugh Rodham was behind Braswell's pardon, yet they and their former staff remained silent when suspicions fell on the ties between Coffey and Gore. "[Braswell] has no apparent ties to the former president or to the Democratic Party. The only known connection seems to be that his attorney, Kendall Coffey, represented Vice President Gore in the Florida recount," said correspondent Jackie Judd on ABC's February 6, 2001, episode of *World News Tonight*. It would be more than two weeks later before the public learned of Rodham's deep involvement and Bill and Hillary were forced to respond.

Hugh Rodham was paid more than $434,000 to arrange for the commutation for Carlos Vignali and the pardon for Glenn Braswell. Even at the exorbitant rate of $600 per hour, Rodham would have had to have worked continuously and exclusively on these two applications for more than eighteen forty-hour weeks in order to earn his fee.

Sadly, "Bill and Hillary created a climate in which Mr. Rodham felt free to peddle his influence for pay."[99] Yet there was a more troubling issue. Vignali and Braswell were able to buy clemency from Bill Clinton. That it was a Rodham and not a Clinton that profited was immaterial. As one Durham, NC *Herald-Sun* editorial writer observed, "Chicanery is a genetic strain in the enormous extended family called Friends of Bill."[100]

All did not end well for Braswell. The multimillionaire peddler of miracle cures, dietary supplements, and life-extending tonics died at the age of sixty-three. He was found dead in his Miami Beach condo on October 28, 2006, by some of his employees. His brother, Joel, announced that Braswell would be cryogenically frozen so that he could one day return to life.[101]

CHAPTER 8

Tony Rodham's Circus Act

"From wacky business schemes to ill-fated Senate runs, the Brothers Rodham—as they were known among White House staffers—engaged in one embarrassing shenanigan after another, often brazenly cashing in on their connections to the Clintons. As one former White House official recalled in 2001, 'You never wanted to hear their names come up in any context other than playing golf.'"[1]

THE HAZELNUT SCHEME

Located along the southern reaches of the Caucasus Mountains, the country of Georgia became independent when the Soviet Union dissolved in 1991. Eduard Shevardnadze, an ethnic Georgian long familiar to the public as the Soviet Foreign Minister under USSR leader Mikhail Gorbachev, became the second Georgian president in 1995. He was elected in a landslide victory.

Under Shevardnadze, Georgia quickly became oriented toward the West. Georgian leaders in the capital of Tblisi expressed an interest in joining the European Union and NATO. The country began receiving generous foreign aid from the West. Importantly for the US, Georgia was viewed as an important counterbalance to Russian influence in the Transcaucasus region, and the southern republic became closely allied with the United States.

Yet independence for Georgia came with a cost. The nation was beset with several problems, including rampant corruption and a fractious political relationship between the capital of Tblisi and three separate ethnic regions in the country. One of the three separatist areas was Ajara, an autonomous region located in southwestern Georgia along the Black Sea and populated predominantly by Muslims. Ajara encompasses about 1,200 square miles and has a population of about one-half million.

Ajara was led by Aslan Abashidze, who was the main political opponent to Shevardnadze. Abashidze's politics were not the only thing that worried US officials. He was also a local strongman suspected of embezzlement and murder, a regional leader in organized crime, and he was suspected of close ties to Grigori Loutchansky, a Russian mobster.[2] Loutchansky was long suspected by US authorities of drug trafficking and of smuggling nuclear materials.[3] Loutchansky was also known for his role in the questionable and highly suspect sell-off of Russian commodities in the early days after the fall of the Soviet Union.[4]

Loutchansky even had an American connection, of sorts. He had close ties to the billionaire fugitive, Marc Rich,[5] who fled the US ahead of a fifty-one-count federal indictment for tax evasion and other crimes, including trading with the enemy when he was secretly negotiating deals with Iran while Muslim revolutionaries held fifty-two Americans hostage.

Abashidze reached an accommodation with Shevardnadze, who turned a blind eye toward the mobster's criminal activities as long as Abashidze maintained peaceful relations between Ajara and the national government in Tblisi.

The de facto truce did not hold. Abashidze had posed a continuing problem for Shevardnadze, proving to be the Georgian president's biggest challenge to power, testing Shevardnadze's control of the country and allowing corruption to flourish in the western regions of the country.

Abashidze would later flee to Russia to seek refuge after being ousted from office. He was convicted in absentia in an Ajarian court in 2007 for embezzling nearly $60 million from the provincial government. He also faced murder charges for allegedly killing his deputy in 1991.

It was against this political backdrop that Hillary's brothers, Hugh and Tony Rodham, traveled to Ajara in August 1999 to negotiate a trade deal with Abashidze.[6] A major agricultural crop and export of the region is hazelnuts. Hugh and Tony were officials with Argo Holdings International, a firm that was to invest as much as $118 million in producing and exporting hazelnuts from western Georgia to world markets.

Shevardnadze put on a brave face in public and welcomed the business investment when the presidential brothers-in-law arrived in the country. Privately, Shevardnadze was seething. Urgent missives were sent between officials in Tblisi and Washington, DC regarding the Rodhams' visit.[7] An editorial in the *Washington Post* called the brothers' visit "the Clinton administration's confused response to corruption and political disarray in the former Soviet Union."[8]

The meeting between Abashidze and the Rodhams was viewed as politically damaging to US ally Shevardnadze. The Georgian President's suspicions were confirmed when Abashidze issued a statement following the visit by the Rodhams of "the possibility of political support rendered to him by US President Bill Clinton."[9] Abashidze also claimed his role in the hazelnut deal would land his venture "an office near the White House."[10]

Immediately following the trip, Tony Rodham willingly stood in as the godfather in the baptism of Abashidze's grandson, which made Rodham a close relative in accordance with Georgian custom. Rodham became an active participant in Abashidze's challenge to Shevardnadze's hold on power.

This was an affront and a deeply disturbing political challenge to Shevardnadze, whom the US viewed as an important, strategic ally in the region. The Rodhams visit led to a hastily arranged visit to Georgia by the First Lady to conduct diplomatic damage control. According to a Georgian news agency, Hillary Rodham Clinton was making the trip in response to her brothers having "met with the Ajarian leader, Aslan Abashidze."[11]

In a stroke of pure irony, the National Democratic Institute had recognized Hillary Clinton and Eduard Shevardnadze in late September 1999 as the corecipients of an award recognizing their democratization efforts.[12] Shevardnadze was installing democratic reforms in Georgia at the same time Hillary's brothers became the de facto symbols of Clinton administration ties to Shevardnadze's biggest political threat to democratic stability.

The close ties between Abashidze and Loutchansky, one a suspected mobster and the other a well-known mobster, should have been embarrassing for the Rodhams. Yet, it apparently was not, because brother-in-law Bill Clinton had already set the bar extremely low when it came to socializing with Russian mobsters. Clinton met with the Russian organized crime leader at one of his 1993 political fundraisers where Loutchansky was an attendee and was photographed with Clinton at his side.[13] Loutchansky was unable to attend a subsequent $25,000 a plate[14] Clinton fundraiser in 1995 when the State Department refused to issue Loutchansky a visa over concerns of his role in Russian organized crime.[15]

Loutchansky's attendance at the 1993 fundraiser wasn't Clinton's last brush with Russian organized crime. In 1997, Tony Rodham arranged a meeting between National Security Adviser Samuel R. "Sandy" Berger and Moscow Mayor Yuri Luzhkov to pump up US support for launching a debit card company in Moscow. The debit card company was the project of Rodham client, Gene Prescott.

Berger willingly accommodated the younger Rodham's request to entertain the meeting when Rodham pitched a business plan on behalf of a client. Tony Rodham also arranged for brother-in-law Bill to sit in on the meeting in spite of the fact that Luzhkov was suspected of mob ties[16] and may have played a role in the unsolved murder of an American businessman with whom Luzhkov had a quarrel.[17] The White House scheduled the meeting to take place on a Saturday, hoping the press would not find out.[18] Rodham even received information from the National Security Council's Russia Desk to assist him in the business venture.[19]

Another shady character involved in the hazelnut export plan was the Rodhams' Georgian partner, Vasili Patarkalishvili. Early in the 1990s, Patarkalishvili launched Liberty Bank to operate in both the US and Georgia. The plan was to use Liberty as an offshore bank for Georgians to conceal their money from Georgian government tax collectors. However, US regulators shut down the bank after it was learned Liberty was not registered to conduct banking in the US.

Hillary, despite knowing of her brothers' trip to Georgia beforehand, expressed no concern over the planned visit.[20] The third partner in the fledgling venture was Stephen Graham, who worked for Hillary for several years as an advance man. Hillary offered the preposterous claim she was ignorant of the details of the trip by her brothers and her own employee to one of the more politically sensitive far reaches of the world, even though the Ajarian public knew in advance that the brothers were going to meet with Abashidze.[21]

Hillary's denials aside, the White House acknowledged that it urged the trio to first stop off in the Georgian capital of Tblisi instead of flying direct to Ajara, as was their original plan.[22] This underscored that the Clinton White House knew a lot more about the visit, including the identities of Georgians with whom the Rodham brothers were going to meet, than Hillary would admit.

As Keelin McDonell of *The New Republic* accurately observed, "[T]he most curious aspect of the Brothers Rodham is not their penchant for bad behavior but Hillary's track record of turning a blind eye to it."[23]

However, when news accounts emerged in the US press the following month, National Security Adviser Berger, with the approval of Hillary, reportedly urged the brothers to drop their hazelnut scheme.[24] The Rodham brothers claimed in mid-September 1999 they had withdrawn from the hazelnut venture, although Ajarian officials confided this was not the case and the Rodhams were moving ahead with their imported nut operation.[25]

Three months later in December, after the initial furor had died down, the Rodham brothers were back in Ajara, traipsing through Aslan Abashidze's political base of Batumi in an effort to revive their project. A Clinton administration official later admitted that Tony Rodham was moving ahead with the hazelnut venture.[26] When asked if he was going to cancel the business deal in accordance with the request from Berger, Tony Rodham responded "Why should I? I'm a private businessman."[27] After being confronted with the fact that the Rodham brothers were still attempting to strike up a business deal with the primary domestic threat to Georgian leader Eduard Shevardnadze, Hillary Clinton commented, "They're my brothers, I'm not their keeper."[28]

Then in mid-January 2001, Tony Rodham hosted a dinner for Abashidze at the Monocle Restaurant on Capitol Hill. Later, Abashidze was escorted by Rodham to Andrews Air Force Base, where Abashidze was a guest of the Clintons at their farewell tribute immediately following the inauguration of President George W. Bush.[29]

EDGAR AND VONNA JO GREGORY

The hazelnut scheme was one of the projects Tony presented to Edgar and Vonna Jo Gregory as an investment opportunity. A year before he traveled to Georgia, Tony signed a contract with the Gregorys' circus company, United Shows of America, Inc. and several related businesses to serve as their "independent consultant."

According to the Gregorys, Tony Rodham would bring investment opportunities to the company. Aside from the hazelnut scheme, in which Rodham would financially benefit, and an overseas telecommunications proposal, Rodham did not bring any other opportunities to their attention.

Perhaps not coincidentally, the Gregorys negotiated the "independent consultant" contract with Rodham at the same time they decided to pursue presidential pardons. Edgar and Vonna Jo Gregory were convicted over their role in draining the savings from the First Bank of Macon County and the Wilcox County Bank, a role in which they had controlling interests in order to fund risky loans for their personal benefit.

The Gregorys were eventually convicted of a variety of banking charges including conspiring to misapply bank funds, the misapplication of bank funds, and wire fraud. Edgar received a two-year federal sentence and Vonna Jo was given three years' probation. An appeals court upheld part of the verdict and overturned another part on procedural grounds. Rather than return to court, the Gregorys instead admitted guilt and agreed to a plea deal netting Edgar five years of probation and Vonna Jo, three.

Independent consultant Tony Rodham was unsuccessful in securing a business investment from Edgar and Vonna Jo Gregory. His only success involving the circus owners was in hustling presidential pardons for the pair in March 2000.

The Gregorys were not strangers to the Clinton clan. They were financial backers of Bill when he first ran for president in 1992. They donated hundreds of thousands of dollars to the political campaigns of Bill and Hillary Clinton and to various Democrat political parties during the eight years Bill was in Washington, DC. In the two years leading up to their pardons, the Gregorys, their children, and their company and key employees contributed nearly $300,000 to political campaigns, with nearly all of it going to Democratic causes.

Those campaign fundraising checks were not the only checks the Gregorys wrote. From the time he signed on as an independent consultant, Tony Rodham received nearly a quarter of a million dollars in "consulting fees." When pressed by congressional investigators after the pardon scandal broke, the Gregorys were unable to produce a single document that supported any work Rodham produced on their behalf except the solicitation for them to invest in his hazelnut scheme and the telecommunications venture, and the good fortune of staging a pair of modest circus events at the White House in 1998 and 2000. This was hardly the sort of business activity that was worthy of the $244,769, including a $25,000 signing bonus the Gregorys paid to Rodham. Additionally, the Gregorys provided Rodham with health care benefits and use of a 1995 Chevrolet Suburban.

The most important task Rodham arranged for the Gregorys was executive clemency, although the Gregorys and Rodham claimed the payments, benefits, and vehicle use had nothing to do with the Clinton pardons. Their protests aside, Edgar Gregory admitted that his money gave him access. "I do believe that that does make a difference,"[30] he said.

Edgar and Vonna Jo Gregory were keen to get pardons because their criminal history was damaging their ability to compete for government-sponsored fairs and circuses. Often, the bid process to stage state, local, and county fairs included a provision that barred operators who had a criminal record. The Gregorys were convicted felons. They wanted to wipe their records clean so they could compete for circus, fair, and carnival contracts.

In 1998, the Gregorys were informed that their criminal records posed an obstacle to winning the contract in future years to manage the Florida State Fair, one of their largest revenue generators. This revelation was immediately followed by the "independent consultant" contract they negotiated with Rodham in June 1998.

The Gregorys began the executive clemency application process and submitted their pardon application through proper channels to the Justice Department with a copy sent directly to President Clinton in November 1998. The Justice Department maintained periodic contact with Gregorys, directly and through their attorneys at the law firm of Greenberg Traurig, frequently asking for amplifying information in support of the pardon application.

By late 1999, approximately one year and a half after they submitted their pardon applications, the Gregorys became impatient with waiting. So, they approached Tony Rodham, gave him a copy of the clemency petition, and pressed him to get deeply involved in their pardon request. "I did ask him after we weren't on that Christmas pardon list of '99 if he could help us, and I don't see anything wrong with that,"[31] explained Edgar Gregory.

After the 2001 pardon scandal broke, the Gregorys attempted to convince a skeptical public that Rodham played no role in their March 2000 pardons. However, Rodham contradicted them when he conceded on CNN's *Larry King Live* in March 2001 that he asked Bill Clinton to pardon Edgar and Vonna Jo Gregory. "Yeah, I talked to my brother-in-law. I told him that Ed Gregory is a good guy, he is a guy that, you know, this was hurting his business. He needs it, his business, to support his family, and he is the kind of person that the pardon system was designed for."[32]

Rodham also admitted that he informed his sister ahead of time that he was seeking a pardon for the Gregorys. When asked if Hillary Clinton knew of Rodham's lobbying for a pardon on behalf of the Gregorys he told King, "Yes—she—I talked to her about it."[33]

Tony Rodham not only lived in the shadow of his highly driven sister, but he epitomized those baby boomers that stumbled through life without ever achieving a stable career or home life. A college dropout and sometimes marijuana user,[34] Rodham drifted from job to job, seemingly incapable of maintaining meaningful employment. He failed at his attempt at a "power marriage" to the daughter of California Senator Barbara Boxer.

In 2002, his estranged wife accused him of being a deadbeat dad for not meeting timely child support obligations, alleging that he fell behind in payments by as much as six months.[35] By the end of 2007, Rodham owed his ex-wife $75,000 in child support payments and another $55,000 in alimony. In spite of legal rulings against him, Rodham had not paid up.[36]

During the latter half of the Clinton White House stay, Tony Rodham began yet another career as he anointed himself an "independent consultant." He announced in a televised interview that his job was "just bring different peoples together. I help them negotiate deals. I solve problems for people."[37]

Rodham began hustling for business clients eager to cash in on his White House ties. In fact, he found being the brother of Hillary Rodham Clinton to be his most valuable asset. It opened doors for him and provided him the potential to make money from a variety of wacky ventures. Yet he apparently was unable to bring any scheme or business venture to fruition except for those related to his kinship with Bill and Hillary Clinton.

Tony Rodham benefited from his family relationships as doors were opened to him as Hillary's brother. He would often plow ahead in his pursuit of money even when conventional wisdom indicated he was making grievous mistakes.

In 1997, he contemplated arranging a meeting between Paraguay President Juan Carlos Wasmosy and Bill Clinton in return for a six-figure payment, and eventually claimed he pursued the meeting without receiving any payment.[38] He pursued investment opportunities in Cambodia only days before the contested 1998 national elections where he palled around with Prime Minister Hun Sen, who was criticized by the US for human rights abuses.[39] Yet it was Hillary's longtime advance man Steve Graham who felt compelled to defend Tony's Cambodia visit, calling it "just a trade possibility."[40] Hillary said nothing about Tony's Cambodia trip.

Rodham also visited other far-flung countries such as the United Arab Emirates and Taiwan where, it was speculated, he was fishing for campaign contributions for his sister's Senatorial campaign.[41] His biggest payoff appears to have been when he received $351,769 in salary and personal loans from the Gregorys in their successful bid for pardons.

The Gregorys knew exactly what they were getting when they hired Tony Rodham. It was access. "You've got a man that is the brother-in-law of the president of the United States," said Edgar Gregory as he gave the reason why he hired Tony Rodham. He added, "He's the brother of the First Lady of the United States and certain people are going to know his name."[42] Certainly, everyone on the White House staff and the Justice Department knew exactly who Tony Rodham was.

As far as the Gregory pardons were concerned, no one aside from Tony Rodham was in favor them. They failed to meet objective Justice Department guidelines of accepting responsibility for their crimes.[43] Jeff Sessions, who was the US attorney whose office prosecuted the Gregorys for bank fraud in 1982, was appalled they had received pardons.[44] He was never even consulted, as required by Justice Department guidelines.[45] Ginny S. Granade, who was the assistant US attorney that tried the case commented, "They drained the banks that they were majority shareholders in and just ran them into the ground for this interconnecting web of companies they owned. They ran those banks with an iron fist."[46]

The trial judge was opposed to clemency[47] as was the Justice Department.[48] Even Bill Clinton's own White House counsel was not in favor of pardons for the Gregorys. Everyone was against Clinton granting executive clemency for the Gregorys, yet Hillary's brother wanted the pardons and Bill granted them.

The Gregorys' pardons are clear examples of a quid pro quo. The Gregorys were longtime, generous campaign contributors to the Clintons and other Democratic candidates and causes, and it was no secret Hillary had designs on running for president one day. The Clintons could not continue to benefit from the Gregorys' largesse unless the Gregorys' businesses continued to be extremely profitable.

The growing trend by state, county, and local governments to place restrictions on awarding contracts to business owners with criminal convictions had stymied the Gregorys' business opportunities. The Gregorys told Tony they needed to have pardons no later than February 2000 if they were to continue to operate the Florida State Fair. The March 2000 presidential pardons wiped the slate clean and gave them the opportunity to continue bidding for the Florida State Fair contract.

Every entity involved in the Gregorys' pardon process from the prosecuting attorney to Clinton's own Justice Department opposed granting them pardons. Yet Clinton acquiesced to Tony Rodham, who was handsomely paid to ensure presidential pardons were given to Edgar and Vonna Jo Gregory. In the process, the Clintons could continue feeding from the Gregorys' campaign contribution gravy train just as Hillary began her own career in elective politics. Edgar and Vonna Jo Gregory had already contributed more than $15,000 to Hillary's Senate campaign before everything began to unravel for them after the scandal over their pardons erupted.

A year and a half after the Clintons left office was when the Gregorys truly hit bottom. News of the pardons led to several creditors reassessing their business relationships with the Gregorys and their companies. Dateline NBC reported that in the 1990s games in the Gregorys' United Shows of America were rigged against the public and there were concerns the Gregorys had made false representations in order to gain investors in various projects.

Many creditors began calling due loans and by August 2002, Edgar Gregory and several of his businesses entered bankruptcy protection.[49] One creditor accused Edgar Gregory of making false representations about business opportunities in which the creditor invested $2.9 million.[50] The Gregorys' bankruptcy case listed more than two hundred creditors.

Edgar Gregory's death from natural causes in April 2004 may have ended his fallout from the pardon fiasco, but it only continued trouble for Tony Rodham.

Michael Collins was designated the US trustee overseeing the bankruptcy of United Shows of America. Among the United Shows papers were documents showing that the Gregorys had loaned at least $107,000 to Tony Rodham, right after they were given the pardons. Collins learned that Rodham had yet to pay back any of the loans. Collins demanded Rodham repay the original loan amount plus $46,034 in interest for a total debt of $153,034.

By now, Rodham's version of events had changed significantly. No longer was the money given to him after the Gregorys received their pardons considered a loan, he claimed. Rodham made this assertion despite the fact the word "loan" was written on the memo line of all sixteen Bank of Nashville checks that were made out to Anthony D. Rodham.[51] Instead, Rodham argued, it was payment for unspecified "consulting services."

Neither the Gregorys, United Shows of America, nor Tony Rodham offered any documentation that supported Rodham's contention that he performed any services after the pardons were received that justified the payments from the Gregorys. Moreover, Rodham could have easily ended disagreement over the nature of the payments if he had simply provided copies of his income tax records documenting he had claimed the $107,000 as income. That he did not proffer his tax records supported Collins' assertion the money was a loan.

There was another insidious issue possibly at play. There was no documentation that Rodham had made any repayments toward satisfying his debt or that the Gregorys and United Shows had pursued Rodham's repayment of the loans. This strongly suggests there was never any expectation by either party that Rodham would repay any of the "loans." In other words, Rodham and the Gregorys may have conspired to allow Rodham to keep the money without having to report it to the Internal Revenue Service and to avoid paying taxes on it as income by claiming it was a "loan." A loan they never expected he would repay.

In March 2006, Collins won a judgment against Rodham for the money owed. Bankruptcy Judge Marian F. Harrison signed the judgment in favor of Collins as the Chapter 11 Trustee for the total amount of $153,034. Rodham appealed the case and it dragged into the following year. In his own court filings, Rodham claimed the $107,000 was for unspecified work he performed for the Gregorys. He further claimed the Gregorys owed him $130,000 beyond the $244,000 he had already been paid for consulting work he performed. Rodham further charged that the Gregory estate owed him additional money although he could not document any consulting work performed.

Tony Rodham was able to finally close the sordid "pay for no work" chapter of his life when he reached a settlement regarding the money that he owed the Gregorys' estate in September 2007, just before the case was to go to trial. Details of Rodham's repayment were kept confidential as part of the settlement agreement.

CHAPTER 9

Roger Clinton and the Heroin Trafficker

"To dismiss Roger Clinton's activities as merely the comical bumbling of Bill Clinton's less-gifted half-brother, however, runs the risk of seriously undermining public confidence in the integrity of the government."[1]

ON FEBRUARY 17, 2001, less than one month after being pardoned by his brother, Roger Cassidy Clinton Jr. was arrested in Hermosa Beach, California for creating a disturbance outside a beachside bar and for suspicion of driving while intoxicated. The arresting officer observed Clinton driving erratically. Clinton smelled of alcohol and he failed a balance and coordination test and breathalyzer test.[2] He measured just over the 0.08 blood alcohol content threshold to be considered driving while intoxicated.[3]

Before he went to trial, Roger Clinton told CNN's Larry King that he was set up because he was Bill Clinton's brother. "They're not out to help me," he argued. "If they were wanting to help me, they'd have called me a cab that night. It just stinks."[4]

In August 2001, he pleaded guilty to a lesser charge, was fined $1,350, and was placed on probation for two years. Clinton was not in the courtroom when the sentence was handed down as he was already enrolled in a four-week program at the Cottonwood de Tucson rehabilitation facility in Arizona for treatment of cocaine addiction.[5]

In the classic film *The Godfather*, Virgil "The Turk" Sollozzo asks Don Vito Corleone to join him in selling heroin. Corleone turns him down, saying, "Drugs is a dirty business." Corleone does not believe he should involve the Corleone crime family in the drug trade because it is bad for the neighborhoods. Don Corleone's oldest son, Sonny, disagrees and shows keen interest in joining the drug trade.

Sometimes life does imitate art. Don Carlo Gambino ran the Gambino crime family, one of the original "Five Families" that operated out of New York and whose organized crime syndicate was present through much of the US. At one point, he was the undisputed "boss of bosses." Carlo Gambino was vehemently opposed to becoming involved in the drug trade. However, a relative of his, Rosario Gambino, did not have the same reservations about selling illegal narcotics.

ROSARIO GAMBINO

Rosario Gambino and brothers, Giuseppe and Giovanni, were known as the "Cherry Hill Gambinos." Born in Palermo, Sicily, they emigrated to the US in the 1960s. In Italy, they were "made men," members of the Sicilian mafia. In the US, they engaged in major heroin trafficking and ran most of their operations from the Cherry Hill, New Jersey area. Law enforcement authorities believe Rosario Gambino was the Italian mob's key figure behind the Italy-to-US heroin trade.

Rosario had frequent brushes with the law. In March 1980, he and five others were charged with conspiring to smuggle into the US aboard an Alitalia jetliner from Milan, Italy forty kilos of heroin.[6]

The drugs had a wholesale value of $10 million and a street value of tens of millions of dollars more. Gambino was indicted in both the US and Italy for the drug conspiracy. His first trial in the US resulted in a hung jury, and he was acquitted in his second trial. However, he was convicted in absentia (but represented by legal counsel) by an Italian tribunal and sentenced to twenty years in prison. The US and Italy had an extradition treaty in place, but US officials believed extraditing to him to Italy, after having been acquitted in the US, constituted double jeopardy.

Gambino was also implicated in providing safe refuge to Michele Sidona, the reputed treasurer and money launderer for the Sicilian mafia.[7] In 1979, Sidona was indicted in the US and Italy for bank fraud in excess of $400 million related to the collapse of New York's Franklin National Bank, but he failed to make his September 1979 trial date after a staged kidnapping. In reality, he was hiding out in a safe house belonging to the Cherry Hill Gambinos.[8]

By late 1983, a pair of FBI agents working undercover had infiltrated the Cherry Hill Gambino drug ring as a couple of drug buyers looking to establish ties to a reliable source of heroin. The two agents started off by making purchases of modest amounts of heroin, indicating they were trying to find a supplier that could deliver large quantities for their growing heroin trade in California.

The Gambino heroin ring was known as the "pizza connection" because pizza restaurants were used as heroin distribution points. In each purchase by the undercover agents, Rosario Gambino was consulted by his crew, and his permission was received before a deal was completed.

In March 1984, after the completion of a six-month investigation, federal agents arrested nine members of the Cherry Hill Gambinos. Among those arrested was Rosario Gambino.

On December 7, 1984, Rosario Gambino was sentenced to forty-five years in federal prison for heroin trafficking after his conviction on six different counts two months earlier. His accomplices and relatives Erasmo Gambino, Antonio Gambino, and Anthony Spatola received sentences ranging from thirty to thirty-four years. Gambino lost appeals of his sentence at both the US Court of Appeals for the Third Circuit in 1988 and the US Supreme Court the following year.

Rosario's brothers, Giovanni and Giuseppe, were indicted in 1990 for their roles in the drug ring. According to US and Italian authorities, the pair were involved in the shipment of more than one-half ton of heroin into the US from Italy from late 1978 to mid-1979.[9]

In 2000, sixteen years after Rosario Gambino's conviction, President Bill Clinton's half-brother was lobbying the forty-second president to pardon the heroin trafficker. However, Roger Clinton's relationship with the Gambino crime family began years earlier.

Roger began lobbying for the release of Rosario Gambino from federal prison in early 1996. Clinton claimed he became involved after having been persuaded by Rosario's son, Tommaso Gambino, whom Roger considered a close friend. Tommaso operated a pay telephone installation business, placing pay phones in public establishments. His partner in the venture was Dominick "Donnie Shacks" Montemarano, a mobster convicted in 1987 for racketeering, bribery, and extortion.[10] Tommaso provided Roger with dozens of documents, which Clinton read to familiarize himself with the case.

Clinton first contacted Commissioner Carol P. Getty of the Kansas City, Missouri regional office of the US Parole Commission in January 1996 to get Gambino released early from prison at an impending parole hearing. The Kansas City regional office had previously recommended against an early release of Gambino. Clinton told Getty that he supported early release for Gambino, and he informed her he would visit her later in the month. Then Clinton completely unsettled Getty by telling her he was aware that the Kansas City regional office was scheduled to be shut down and that her job as a commissioner might be in jeopardy.

Disturbed by Clinton's telephone call, Getty contacted fellow commissioner Michael J. Gaines in the agency's Maryland headquarters and relayed her concerns over the impropriety of the president's brother directly contacting the Parole Commission regarding a pending hearing.

Gaines addressed the substance of Getty's concerns in a memorandum that he sent to Sharon Gervasoni, the Parole Commission's designated agency ethics officer. Gaines wrote, "I do not know Roger Clinton, and I have not spoken to him about this matter[.]"[11]

Gaines followed up Getty's telephone call to him with a call of his own to the White House Counsel's office. Gaines told Trey Schroeder in the White House Counsel's office he thought it was necessary the White House Counsel knew of the contact of the Parole Commission by Roger Clinton. Schroeder abruptly ended the conversation with Gaines with "Okay, thanks."

The following day, on January 17, 1996, Roger Clinton contacted Sam Robertson of the Kansas City parole office. Robertson was the hearing examiner assigned to the Gambino case. Clinton informed Robertson that he was no longer planning on visiting the Kansas City office and would instead take up his concerns directly with the US Parole Commission headquarters in Maryland.

Clinton called the office of Commissioner Gaines on January 30. Unable to speak directly with Gaines, Clinton left a message with Gaines' assistant asking the commissioner to return his call. The message read "Roger Clinton, very important...ASAP, re: brother recommended meeting."

Gaines, who was from Arkansas, knew the contact by Clinton was highly inappropriate so he had Parole Commission General Counsel Michael Stover return Clinton's telephone call. Stover asked Gervasoni to participate in the return call. Stover intended to inform Clinton that his efforts to communicate with agency officials regarding a pending case were improper. Stover's notes from the telephone call with Clinton were stunning.

"Roger Clinton…began the conversation by informing me that his brother '…is completely aware of my involvement,'" Stover documented. "Roger Clinton stated that his brother had recommended to him that he not meet with the Commissioner Getty (as Roger Clinton had originally sought to do) because Commissioner Getty's Kansas City Regional Office was about to be closed. Roger Clinton informed me that his brother suggested that he contact Commissioner Gaines instead."[12]

Stover informed Clinton that his contact with the commission was inappropriate, the Privacy Act barred the agency from discussing Gambino's case with Clinton, and that all communications on a matter between the commission and legally designated representatives must take place within a regularly scheduled hearing. Clinton reacted poorly, according to Stover's notes from the call. Stover noted:

> "Roger Clinton evinced his strong disappointment upon learning that he could not meet with Commissioner Gaines about this case.... I informed him that such a meeting would not have been appropriate. Roger Clinton then asked me how it could be that the President would be misinformed as to the law, and [Clinton] emphasized that the President had suggested that he should meet with Commissioner Gaines, '...a friend of ours from Arkansas.' Roger Clinton professed his bewilderment as to how the President would not be knowledgeable as to the law with respect to the propriety of this suggested meeting. He stated that he would have to inform his brother that his brother had been wrong.... During this colloquy, however, Roger Clinton's voice rose, and betrayed the fact that he was upset with what I was saying."[13]

In a memorandum for the record, Stover wrote, "[Sharon Gervasoni] and I are disturbed at the tactic employed by Roger Clinton of repeatedly invoking his brother as having (allegedly) recommended that he meet with Commissioner Gaines on the basis of that Commissioner being '…a friend of ours from Arkansas.' The US Parole

Commission must not permit itself to be subjected to improper attempts to exercise political influence over its procedures."[14]

There is no record of Clinton attempting to contact the Parole Commission again for nearly two years. Then something curious happened. Previously, the parole commissioners constituted the only politically appointed positions at the commission. In late 1997, Marie Ragghianti became the first person to have ever become a political appointee to a nonpolitical position when Bill Clinton appointed her to be the agency's chief of staff. This unprecedented political appointment occurred after Roger's failed entreaties to the Parole Commission.

By then, Gaines, who was originally from Arkansas, had been elevated to Commission chairman. It was after the hiring of Ragghianti and the appointment of Gaines to the chairmanship that Roger Clinton again called Gaines. Still avoiding Clinton, Gaines asked Ragghianti to take care of him.

Rather than put him off as others at the commission had done before her, Ragghianti instead called Clinton and agreed to meet with him on December 23, 1997, to discuss the Gambino case. She even gave Clinton her home telephone number, which Clinton used on at least four separate occasions to call Ragghianti.

The agency's director of case operations, Tom Kowalski, joined Ragghianti for her scheduled meeting with Clinton. Afterward, Ragghianti and Kowalski separately prepared memos detailing the meeting with Roger Clinton. Kowalski documented that Clinton pressed his case that Gambino "[was] not an organized crime boss," Parole Commission General Counsel Michael Stover was "discriminatory" toward Gambino, and that the "Commission [was] being too harsh with [Gambino]."

In a later interview with congressional investigators, Kowalski corroborated what Stover had previously experienced. Kowalski reported that Clinton was pushy and insistent the Parole Commission adopt his point of view. Kowalski noted that Clinton continually "mentioned his brother" and Clinton emphasized he was supporting

Gambino "with his brother's knowledge." Kowalski added that Clinton "threw it in your face that he was staying at the White House." In other words, Roger Clinton was attempting to cower the commission officials by underscoring that the President was supportive of his efforts to secure an early release for Rosario Gambino.

Kowalski later recalled that during the meeting with Clinton, "I thought to myself, 'Lord, Lord, Oh Lord, why would the President want to get involved in the case of this guy?'"

A reading of Ragghianti's memo left one wondering if she and Kowalski had attended the same meeting. Ragghianti wrote:

"Mr. Clinton was articulate. His questions and comments were thoughtful and appropriate, which is to say that he in no way came across as wishing to capitalize on his name. Instead, he apologized for taking our time. He appeared to be a genuinely caring person, not only for the 3 individuals he was seeking advice for, but in general."[15]

Clinton was not only pressing for parole for Gambino, but he also requested furlough be granted for a felon named John Ballis and he asked for a pardon for another felon whose name Ragghianti had forgotten. (Roger Clinton would later include Ballis' name among at least five other names of people he wanted his brother to pardon.)

Following that initial meeting, Clinton began regular communications with both Ragghianti and Kowalski regarding the Gambino case. Clinton sent an ominous sounding handwritten letter to Kowalski dated February 13, 1998. He warned Kowalski, "We need someone to 'step up to the plate' on this one…. This man deserves to be released to return to his family after 14 years. He did the crime and he has done his time. We all deserve a second chance! I am living proof of that. Please help us achieve what is right!" Included in the letter were several handwritten pages of notes containing "points of emphasis" Roger Clinton wanted the Parole Commission to take under consideration at a February 18 parole hearing for Gambino.

Clinton met with Ragghianti and Kowalski a second time in the spring of 1998. The substance of that meeting was similar to the first meeting of December 1997.

Between May 1998 and July 1998, Clinton averaged nearly one call a week to Ragghianti and Kowalski, having made eleven telephone calls during that time. Ragghianti and Kowalski met with Clinton a third time in July 1998. That meeting went much like the previous two, with Clinton pressing the case for Gambino's early release from prison.

In spite of the inappropriate nature of the contacts, Ragghianti did not inform the agency's general counsel of her ongoing meetings and phone calls with Roger Clinton. As the agency's chief of staff, Ragghianti should have steered herself clear of Clinton since the Parole Commission was ruling on the Gambino's parole requests.

In yet another phone call to Kowalski, Clinton renewed his request to meet with Chairman Gaines despite having been told on several previous occasions that it was inappropriate for him to meet with any of the commissioners. In response to the most recent efforts by Roger Clinton, Stover drafted a letter that Ragghianti reviewed and heavily edited before sending it to Clinton. The letter was addressed to Clinton, care of a commercial mailbox address in Los Angeles that actually belonged to Tommaso Gambino.

In September 1998, FBI agents were conducting a routine review of Gambino's criminal and prison record at the Parole Commission and found notes relating to Clinton's various attempts to contact several Commission employees. Concerned over the impropriety of such contacts, the FBI opened an investigation. After she was informed of the FBI's interest in Clinton, Ragghianti wrote a memorandum for the file in which she justified her overfriendly communications and meetings with Clinton, and she excoriated the commission's general counsel Michael Stover. Ragghianti wrote "Mr. Stover had, in the past, been gratuitously rude to Mr. Clinton." When questioned later by congressional investigators regarding that statement, Ragghianti could not provide a single example to back up her claim that Stover had been "gratuitously rude" toward Clinton.

In early November 1998, Hearing Examiner Sam Robertson recommended a possible reduction in the time Gambino was to serve in prison. Learning of this, Clinton became overjoyed, not understanding that this was merely Robertson's recommendation and that a final decision would be made by all the Commissioners. Nonetheless, Clinton sent a thank you letter to the Commission dated November 17, 1998, erroneously noting that Gambino would be released on January 15, 1999. Clinton's letter stated, "I have marked that date on my calendar as a day of celebration."

It was not until January 1999 that the Parole Commission ruled against Robertson's recommendation and voted to set March 2007 as Gambino's parole date. Chairman Gaines recused himself from participating in that decision due to the extensive attempts by Roger Clinton to contact him. (Gambino was eventually released from prison on September 14, 2006.)[16]

Back in November 1998, Clinton did not know or apparently even understand that the Commission would turn down Robertson's recommendation the following January. In November, Clinton was convinced Gambino was going to be freed early from prison.

Curiously, something else occurred in November. Roger Clinton started depositing into his bank account unendorsed money orders in various large amounts. Unendorsed means the purchaser of the money orders did not enter his name nor add his signature to the money orders. Such identifying information would have allowed the purchaser to file a claim if the money orders were lost or stolen. Perhaps more noteworthy, not endorsing the money orders made it nearly impossible to ascertain who sent them and for what reason they were sent.

In November and December 1998, Clinton deposited seven money orders totaling $164,000. Months later, Clinton would again begin depositing money orders in various amounts. By late 2000, Clinton deposited into his bank account twenty-seven unendorsed money orders totaling $335,000. Roger Clinton later refused to tell congressional investigators the source and the reason for the mysterious payments.

In January 1999, while FBI Special Agent Jackie Dalrymple was working at the Parole Commission, Roger Clinton left voice mail messages for both Ragghianti and Kowalski regarding the Gambino case. Dalrymple was alerted, listened to the messages, and later recorded them as part of the bureau's ongoing investigation into Roger Clinton's activities. Dalrymple then proposed Kowalski agree to meet with Clinton and introduce him to another Commission staff member who could possibly help Clinton with the Gambino case. The newly introduced commission staffer would, in fact, be an undercover FBI agent who would determine if Clinton was illegally attempting to influence the Commission regarding the Gambino case.

Ragghianti completely rejected the proposal and insisted the Parole Commission would not assist the FBI in the matter. According to commission notes of a discussion that took place regarding the FBI request, Ragghianti questioned the legality of the FBI recording any comments by Clinton and likened the FBI effort to the "Linda Tripp debacle." Tripp was the woman who recorded the comments by Monica Lewinsky, the White House intern who carried on a sexual relationship with President Bill Clinton.

In September 1999, a year after opening an investigation into his improper contacts with the Parole Commission, a pair of FBI agents approached Roger Clinton at his home. They interviewed him regarding his relationship with Tommaso Gambino and his efforts to influence the Parole Commissioners. According to the agents' notes from that interview, "Clinton stated he did not tell his brother, the President of the United States, specifically what he was working on. He believes, however, that the President knew he had some business with the US Parole Commission, but did not know specifically what he was working on. He did not tell his brother that he was working on the Rosario Gambino case. He did not seek advise [sic] or referrals from the President in his efforts to contact the Parole Commission on behalf of Rosario Gambino."[17]

At least three different Parole Commission officials, Stover, Gervasoni and Kowalski, in separate accounts claim that Roger Clinton stated unequivocally that the president was aware of his lobbying efforts at the Commission. According to all three accounts, Roger Clinton also claimed that he was making contact at the Commission based on the President's recommendation. In addition, Clinton left a telephone message for a fourth Commission official, Commissioner Gaines, that stated his "brother recommended meeting."

It is entirely possible that Roger Clinton did not tell the president what he was up to and it was possible he did not receive any advice from Bill Clinton. In which case, Roger Clinton lied to the various Commission officials.

However, Clinton also told the two FBI agents "he did not represent to anyone on the Parole Commission that his brother was aware of his efforts to assist the Gambino family or that the President was supporting his effort to assist in getting Rosario Gambino released from prison."[18] In fact, Clinton represented to nearly everyone he spoke with at the Parole Commission that his brother "is completely aware of my involvement." Clinton also "emphasized that the President had suggested that he should meet with Commissioner Gaines." Roger Clinton's statements to the FBI were bald-faced lies. Lying to federal agents in the course of an investigation is a federal offense.

During his FBI interview, Roger Clinton mentioned that Tommaso Gambino had offered to loan him money for down payment on a home he was in the process of buying. That very same day Clinton deposited a check, dated September 29, 1999, from Anna Gambino, the daughter of Rosario Gambino, in the amount of $50,000. A month later, Clinton purchased a home in Torrance, California for $570,000 with a down payment of $114,000. Yet the money Clinton used to finance the down payment did not come from

Gambino, but instead was apparently from a loan he received from another acquaintance.

Gerard Guez, the CEO of the Tarrant Apparel Group, wired $100,000 to Clinton just four days before Clinton withdrew from his bank account the funds necessary to make his down payment. Clinton repaid the $100,000 to Guez with separate $50,000 checks drawn on his personal checking account, one dated December 17, 1999, and the second dated January 6, 2000. There is no record of Clinton ever repaying the $50,000 from the Gambinos, which he claimed was a loan. This also raises the question if Clinton ever reported the $50,000 as income.

A few weeks before the FBI interview, Roger Clinton was playing golf with three other men he met at the Rancho Park golf course in Los Angeles. During the round, a man drove up in a golf cart and handed to Clinton a box containing a brand new gold Rolex watch. After the man drove off, Clinton explained to his golfing partners that the man was Tommaso Gambino, and that he was helping Gambino's father. Unbeknownst to Clinton, two of the other three golfers were US Air Force officers who found the entire episode troublesome. Accordingly, they informed the FBI of what they observed.[19]

When the FBI agents asked Clinton about the Rolex, he denied the incident ever took place. Then he changed his story, claiming Gambino only showed him a watch that he was wearing on his wrist. Clinton changed his story a second time and claimed he did have a watch which he bought from Hollywood celebrity George Hamilton.[20] Then he changed his story a third time and admitted he received a watch from Gambino, but that he did not know where the watch was and that he thought he might have returned it because it was a "fake."[21]

When the Gambino payment of $50,000 became public after Bill Clinton left office, Roger Clinton's attorney refused to answer questions regarding the purpose of the payment. "'Tommy Gambino is a friend of Roger Clinton's and has been for many years,' [Clinton attorney Bart H.] Williams told the [*Newark Star-Ledger*]. 'I'm not going to comment on what the payment is for or about. I am going to say it was not related to Roger Clinton's assisting Tommy Gambino's father in his parole efforts or any other effort.'"[22]

In discussing Clinton's efforts to help free Rosario Gambino, a person close to Tommaso Gambino told the *New York Times* that Clinton led the Gambino family to believe that Rosario would be pardoned. "Whatever he [Roger Clinton] said to him [Tommaso Gambino] made Tommy Gambino think it was a lock."[23] However, the pardon never came through.

ROGER PEDDLING PARDONS

Roger Clinton did not stop with attempting to free Rosario Gambino from prison early. According to a spokesman for Bill Clinton, Roger submitted to his brother a list comprising fewer than ten names of individuals Roger wanted his brother to pardon.[24] "I put the names on it. I put down their relationship to me. And I said they had all gone through the Justice Department and they were deserving," Clinton told the *Los Angeles Times*. He added, "I put [the list] into a stack of papers on a table in the White House where he would see it."[25]

Clinton claimed his list "consisted of only my best friends I've known for 20 years or more."[26] One name on the list was George E. "Butch" Locke Jr., a former Arkansas state senator who served in federal prison alongside Roger Clinton for their roles in a cocaine distribution ring. The other names on the list were J. T. Lundy, Blume Loe, John Ballis, Steve Griggs, and Mark St. Pé.[27]

In November 1999, Lundy asked for Roger Clinton's aid in getting a pardon in return for stock in a Venezuelan coal business. Lundy offered to transfer the stock to Dan Lasater, a close friend of Bill and Roger Clinton, who was convicted on the strength of testimony from Roger for involvement in a 1980s cocaine distribution conspiracy. Such a transfer would have allowed the stock to be liquidated and the cash proceeds passed to Roger without him having to declare it as income. On November 30, 1999, Roger Clinton deposited in his bank account exactly $100,000 in money orders purchased overseas, with some of the money orders having been obtained in Venezuela.[28]

Blume Loe's wife claimed surprise that Roger Clinton would seek a pardon on her husband's behalf since they had met him twenty years earlier in college and she said they did not consider him a close friend.[29] The reality was that Loe traveled in the same circles as Bill and Roger Clinton throughout the 1980s. Lundy, Loe, and the Clintons were very close friends and business associates of Lasater, a longtime political supporter and fundraiser for Bill Clinton's political campaigns. Lasater was infamous for his lavish cocaine parties in which he traded cocaine to high school girls in return for sexual favors.[30] He would eventually be convicted and sentenced to federal prison for cocaine distribution. Fortunately for Lasater, then governor Bill Clinton gave him a state pardon for an earlier state of Arkansas conviction in order to restore his state rights.

Jon Ballis pleaded guilty to paying $371,000 in kickbacks to a savings and loan president in return for nearly $7 million in loans. Ballis was the man for whom Roger Clinton unsuccessfully sought a furlough from the US Parole Commission a few years earlier. Like the others, Ballis had close ties to Lasater. Ballis' wife was a Lasater employee.

According to his lawyer, Steve Griggs, whose name was also on Roger's list, barely knew Clinton, however, the Griggs family paid Clinton to arrange a pardon for him. Just after New Year's Day 2001, the Griggs family sent an overnight letter to Roger Clinton in care of the White House. Bill Clinton noticed the envelope before his brother received it because he marked on the outside of the envelope "Meredith, looks like a case for commutation pls check out—BC," which he then passed on to Meredith Cabe, a White House lawyer who was working on pardon requests.[31]

The lawyer for Mark St. Pé also sent a letter to Roger Clinton in care of the White House shortly after New Year's Day 2001 requesting Roger lobby the President to pardon St. Pé. The lawyer stated that neither he nor St. Pé knew Roger Clinton, but that he communicated with the president's half-brother as he explored all avenues for clemency. It defies logic that Roger Clinton would campaign for a pardon on behalf of a man he never met—only days before his brother left office—without having received any compensation.

According to multiple sources, Roger Clinton approached several convicted felons and offered to secure pardons in exchange for cash payments. Eugene O'Daniel, a Little Rock, Arkansas lawyer, notified the Justice Department in early 2001 that Roger Clinton approached his client, Phillip David Young, and asked for $15,000 in return for a pardon. Young turned down Clinton.[32] The Justice Department did not take any action against Roger Clinton despite being forewarned before Bill Clinton left office.

Longtime friends of the Clintons, Dickey Morton and George Locke operated a company called C.L.M., LLC. The company derived its name from the initials of the last names of the firm's three partners, Roger Clinton, Locke, and Morton. C.L.M. marketed to potential customers several services, including pardons.[33]

Roger Clinton knew Locke from the 1980s, when the two were in the same cocaine distribution ring. Clinton was an unindicted coconspirator when the ring was arrested in October 1986. Additional charges against Roger Clinton (beyond those he faced in 1985) were dropped in return for his testimony that resulted in the arrest of Locke and nine others.

GARLAND LINCECUM

A Texas businessman reported he met with Clinton, Locke, and Morton to discuss a pair of business deals. Richard Cayce claimed he first had to pay $35,000 in cash to the trio before they would discuss efforts to obtain diplomatic passports Cayce wanted to use in an overseas business venture and efforts to secure a pardon for Garland Lincecum, an acquaintance of Cayce's who had been convicted, but not yet sentenced to federal prison. Cayce was told the total price to get a pardon for Lincecum was $300,000.

In August 1998, Morton sent a facsimile to Cayce outlining what steps he had to take in order to get an audience with Roger Clinton. The fax instructed Cayce to make first class airline reservations for Roger Clinton and his wife to fly from Los Angeles to Dallas. Cayce was instructed to bring "1/3 of cookies ($) that we discussed or 33,000 cookies ($) will be delivered by your representative or you, cookies need to be ready to eat." In other words, Cayce was to make a one-third down payment toward a total payment of $100,000 in order to initiate business dealings with Clinton, Locke and Morton.

Cayce brought $35,000 in cash to the early August meeting that he handed over to Clinton in an airport hotel room. The attorney for Locke and Morton later told congressional investigators they split up the money with Clinton taking $18,000 as his share. Clinton later claimed the $35,000 was not related to selling pardons, but instead was reimbursement for his time and business advice.[34] Only in the world of the Clintons was it quite natural to pay for time and business advice with a wad of cash in an airport hotel room. Banking records show that only days later, Cayce made a wire transfer of an additional $70,000 (for a total of $105,000) to the bank account of C.L.M., LLC.

By November 1998, Garland Lincecum had been sentenced to seven years in prison for fraud, but he had not been ordered to report to prison. He was desperate to get a pardon before his April 1999 report date. He asked relatives to cash in retirement and savings accounts in order to pay Clinton, Locke, and Morton $200,000, in addition to the $105,000 Cayce had already paid them, to secure a pardon for him.

According to Lincecum, Morton and Locke met with him in the atrium of a Dallas airport hotel and finalized the offer to get the pardon in return for the total payment of $305,000. Clinton stood on a nearby balcony looking down on Lincecum while the meeting took place. In a follow-up telephone call, Clinton told Lincecum, "We're working to solve your problem…I can get anything from my brother." Lincecum was told his name would be among a list of six names that Roger Clinton was going to have pardoned before Bill Clinton left office.[35] Lincecum never received the pardon.

When interviewed on CNN's *Larry King Live* in June 2001, Roger Clinton gave a cleverly couched response to Lincecum's allegations. "No, sir, I'm not saying he's lying. I'm not saying he's lying. I said there was no—let me clarify: there was no money exchanged with me. And I never heard one word about a pardon."[36] Technically, Clinton may have been telling the truth. Lincecum did not personally give the money to Clinton, but rather, one check was mailed to C.L.M. and a second check was hand-delivered to Clinton's business partner Dickey Morton through Lincecum's brother, Guy. Standing on a balcony overlooking the atrium meeting, Clinton would have likely been out of earshot.

Banking records confirm that two checks for $100,000 each were made out to C.L.M., LLC. According to a bank notation on one check, it was drafted on behalf of Alberta Lincecum, Garland's eighty-two-year-old mother. The other check was drawn on behalf of Guy Lincecum's retirement account at the Edward Jones investment firm. Alberta wiped out her life savings while Guy liquidated his retirement account. Both checks were deposited at First National Bank of Crossett in Arkansas in the account belonging to C.L.M., LLC. Neither Clinton, Locke, nor Morton ever adequately explained what services they performed that warranted a total payment of $305,000 from Garland Lincecum and Richard Cayce other than to claim the money was for some unspecified "public appearances" by Roger Clinton.

Clinton fronted some of the meetings on behalf of C.L.M., yet he later claimed he had no involvement in C.L.M., he had not heard of the company, and that if Locke and Morton used his name, they did so without his permission. There is no record Clinton ever took action against Morton and Locke for improperly using his name, as he alleged. More significantly, C.L.M. bank records disclose that Clinton received three checks (two dated December 10, 1998, for $10,000 and $5,500 and a third check dated January 7, 1999, in the amount of $10,000) totaling $25,500 from C.L.M. even though he claimed he had never heard of the company.[37]

Roger Clinton became so aggressive in his influence peddling that he even reached out to Rita Lavelle, who had been an Environmental Protection Agency official during the Reagan administration. Lavelle was convicted of perjury in the 1980s. A third party approached Lavelle, allegedly on behalf of Clinton, and offered to arrange a pardon for her in return for a $30,000 payment. Lavelle turned him down, although she did submit a pardon request. On the last night Bill Clinton was in office, Roger contacted Lavelle and asked, "Do you have $100,000 to get this through?" She again turned him down. Lavelle did not receive a pardon.[38]

CHAPTER 10

The Puerto Rican Terrorists

"They seem to want to kill people." [1]

—*Police official surveying the carnage from the Fraunces Tavern bombing*

The FALN

Wednesday, December 11, 1974, was Angel Poggi's first day as a New York City police officer. It ended tragically.

A telephone call was made to the New York City police department that day claiming a dead body was found at an abandoned tenement building at 336 East 110th Street in East Harlem. Poggi responded to the call to investigate the reported dead body.[2] When Poggi opened the outside door to the building, a booby-trapped device detonated.[3] It cost Patrolman Poggi an eye. Responsibility for the blast was claimed by Fuerzas Armadas de Liberación Nacional (Armed Forces of National Liberation), also known by the initials FALN.[4]

The blast that permanently disabled Poggi was one of approximately 130 bombing events attributed to or conducted in the name of the FALN and its sister organization, Los Macheteros, between 1974 and 1983.[5] FALN activities resulted in dozens of actual bombings, numerous attempted bombings, several bomb threats, dozens of incendiary attacks, resulting in eight deaths, more than one hundred injuries, and over $48 million in property damage.[6]

It was only two months prior to Poggi's disfiguring bomb blast that the FALN publicly announced its existence. It did so in an October 26, 1974, English language communiqué taking credit for a series of bombings that day and earlier in the year resulting in more than one million dollars of damage. The communiqué stated:

> *"Today, commando units of the FALN attacked mayor [sic] Yanki [sic] corporations in New York City...These actions, along with the bombing of major department stores, for three consecutive days in late spring, and the dynamite blasts at Newark Police Headquarters and City Hall, demonstrate what we have said since 1969: that the Puerto Rican people organizing and arming in order to form a Peoples [sic] Revolutionary Army which will rid Puerto Rico of yanki [sic] colonialism [sic]. We have opened two fronts, one in Puerto Rico and the other in the United States, both nourished by the Puerto Rican people and allies within Northamerica [sic]."*

The FALN claimed it was fighting for Puerto Rican independence, however, the organization demanded much more than the independence of the Caribbean island from the United States. The FALN also demanded the immediate and unconditional release of five violent and dangerous felons the group referred to as "political prisoners."

The "political prisoners" the FALN wanted freed were Puerto Rican nationalists Oscar Collazo, Andres Figueroa Cordero, Lolita Lebrón, Rafael Cancel Miranda, and Irving Flores Rodríquez who were serving time in US prisons. Three of them were serving sentences of at least seventy years each, one a sentence of fifty-six years, and one was serving a life sentence.

Collazo was one of two Puerto Rican nationalists who attempted to assassinate President Harry S. Truman in the early afternoon of November 1, 1950. The other would-be assassin was Griselio Torresola. The pair traveled to Washington, DC, from the Bronx on October 31. Because of ongoing renovations to the White House, Truman and his family were living in the Blair House, just across the street from the White House near Lafayette Park.

Collazo and Torresola attempted to shoot their way into Blair House in order to kill Truman who was inside at the time taking a nap. The pair traded gunfire with White House policemen and Secret Service agents in front of the home. The gunmen managed to shoot three White House policemen, Donald Birdzell, Leslie Coffelt, and Joseph Downs. Coffelt died that day from his wounds while Birdzell and Downs survived. One of the federal agents managed to shoot and kill Torresola; Collazo was seriously wounded just as he made his way to the front steps of Blair House.

Collazo was captured, charged, tried, convicted, and sentenced to death. A compassionate Truman commuted his sentence to life imprisonment.

On March 1, 1954, Andres Figueroa Cordero, Lolita Lebrón, Rafael Cancel Miranda, and Irving Flores Rodríquez unfurled a Puerto Rican flag from the visitors' gallery on the House side of the US Capitol, Lebrón yelled "Puerto Rico is not free," and then the four sprayed the House chamber with gunfire in the direction of 243 Representatives who were debating legislation at the time. The four fired dozens of bullets, striking five Congressmen. Wounded were Alvin M. Bentley (Republican, Michigan), Clifford Davis (Democrat, Tennessee), George Fallon (Democrat, Maryland), Ben F. Jensen (Republican—Iowa) and Kenneth A. Roberts (Democrat, Alabama).

Congressman James Van Zandt (Republican, Pennsylvania), a Navy veteran of World Wars I and II, ran from the House floor to the gallery where he managed to wrestle to the ground two of the gunmen. A tourist in the gallery disarmed a third gunmen. Cordero, Lebrón, and Miranda were immediately arrested. The fourth terrorist, Rodríquez, was arrested at a bus station in Washington, DC.

Four of the Congressmen suffered serious injuries; however, Bentley was critically wounded and was fighting for his life. It took several hours of emergency surgery to save him.

After being tried and convicted, the four Puerto Rican gunmen were each sentenced to death. President Dwight D. Eisenhower later commuted their sentences, with three of them each facing at least seventy years in prison. Lebrón had her sentence reduced to fifty-six years in prison.

In September 1979, President Jimmy Carter commuted the sentences of Collazo, Lebrón, Miranda, and Rodríquez to time served and they were immediately released from prison. Carter released Cordero two years earlier, as Cordero was dying from cancer. The terrorists granted clemency by Carter eventually went back to Puerto Rico, where Collazo died in 1994.

The four released by Carter did not show any remorse for their actions. They appeared at a New York City rally the day after their release and vowed to continue a campaign of violence against the US, if necessary, in order to achieve independence.[7] The freed terrorists then traveled to Havana, Cuba, where they were received as the personal guests of Fidel Castro.

Twenty-five years after her release, Lebrón still demonstrated not an ounce of remorse. She announced, "I am proud of what I did" and she considered the US "the most terrorist country in the world!"[8]

The FALN had a sister organization wreaking terror in Puerto Rico. Los Macheteros ("the machete wielders") was cofounded by Juan Enrique Segarra-Palmer, a Harvard University-educated son of well-to-do parents, and Filiberto Inocencio Ojeda-Ríos, a suspected agent of Cuban intelligence.

Los Macheteros was a violent paramilitary group that espoused the same claim of FALN that they were fighting for Puerto Rican independence. Yet, independence was a position favored by only a very small minority of the island's citizens. Less than 3 percent voted for nationalist candidates beginning in the 1932 elections and voters consistently cast about 3 percent of their votes for independence candidates or for the independence of Puerto Rico in referendums throughout the 20th century.

Ninety-seven percent of the Puerto Rican voters desired either statehood or the continuation of commonwealth status affiliated with America.[9] Even US Representative Herman Badillo from the Bronx, a leader among New York's Puerto Rican community, was not sympathetic to the FALN during their 1970s bombing campaign. He urged the Puerto Rican community to instead cooperate with the authorities in order to stop the FALN.[10]

Fervent in their demand of independence for Puerto Rico and the unconditional release of the five Puerto Rican felons, the FALN embarked on a bombing campaign that was indiscriminate toward who was targeted. Government officials, police officers, corporate employees, office workers, restaurant patrons, and passersby were all affected. The FALN averaged nearly one bomb each month during its decade-long campaign of terror. The bombing campaign became so prolific and sustained that mid-1977 became known as the "summer of violence" in New York City.[11]

A little more than a month after rookie Patrolman Poggi was severely wounded, the most devastating and deadly FALN bombing occurred at a national historic landmark.

Built in 1719, the Fraunces Tavern is the oldest surviving building in Manhattan. It is listed on the National Register of Historic Places. Entrepreneur Stephen Fraunces purchased the three-story brick mansion at 54 Pearl Street in 1762 to use as an inn. The Fraunces Tavern quickly developed a reputation as a popular tavern and meeting place. It became a landmark of note because of its rich history.

The New York state Chamber of Commerce was founded in the tavern in 1768. The Sons of Liberty, the group of advocates who exhorted their fellow countrymen to support the colonies' fight for independence, gathered there. After a meeting in 1774, the Sons of Liberty raided an English trading ship at the East India pier and threw its shipment of tea into the harbor.

George Washington became a frequent guest and close friend of proprietor Stephen Fraunces. Washington delivered his farewell to the Continental Army at the Fraunces in 1783, just days after the last British troops left US soil, and before Washington traveled to the Continental Congress in Annapolis, Maryland to resign his commission. When New York City was the nation's capital from 1785–1790, Fraunces Tavern served as headquarters for the Departments of State, Treasury, and War.

On January 24, 1975, the historic Fraunces Tavern was the location where Frank Connor, Charlie Murray, and William Newhall of Morgan Guaranty Bank were entertaining three clients. Connor had a busy schedule planned for the entire day. That evening, he and his wife were planning to celebrate the ninth and eleventh birthdays of their sons, Tom and Joe. Frank Connor never made it home for the party.

A bomb ripped through the ground floor of the Fraunces Tavern, killing thirty-three-year-old Connor and two of the clients, James Gezork, aged thirty-two, and twenty-eight-year-old Alejandro "Alex" Berger. The blast wounded more than sixty other restaurant patrons, employees, and passersby and it created more than $300,000 in property damage.[12] Most of the damage occurred in the tavern's ground floor and in the second floor Anglers Club dining room.

The FALN claimed responsibility in a communiqué claiming that attack was against "reactionary corporate executives inside [the restaurant]."[13] The FALN further explained, "The targets of our attack were bankers, stockbrokers, and important corporate executives of monopolies and multi-national corporations. These are not friends of the working people. But the enemies of humanity everywhere."[14]

Also killed in the Fraunces blast was sixty-six-year-old Harold Sherburne, an investment banker and partner of the New York firm Bacon, Whipple and Company, who was dining in the Anglers Club. One of the four patrons killed in the explosion was completely decapitated.[15]

The FALN struck again in New York on April 2, 1975, with four near simultaneous bombs exploding against banks and insurance companies. The bombs detonated at the New York Life Insurance building, the Metropolitan Life Insurance building, Bankers Trust Company building, and at a restaurant adjacent to American Bank and Trust Company of New York City. The FALN bombing campaign was well underway and law enforcement authorities knew very little about the FALN other than officials suspected there were very few members in the group. At the time, authorities believed the FALN only numbered about ten.[16]

It was the beginning of summer in June 1975 when the FALN conducted its first bomb attack in Chicago. After New York City, Chicago had one of the largest Puerto Rican populations in the mainland United States. The United American Bank and the First National Bank buildings located in the downtown Loop area were rocked by powerful bomb blasts.[17, 18]

The FALN then embarked on an effort to apparently show how sophisticated the group had become. On October 27, 1975, bombs went off against nine targets including the US Mission to the United Nations, and National Westminster, First National City, First National, and Chase Manhattan banks in New York City; Continental National Bank, IBM Plaza, the Sears Tower and the Standard Oil building in Chicago; and the Department of State and the Bureau of Indian Affairs offices in Washington, DC.[19, 20]

In the middle of 1976, the FALN added incendiary devices to its arsenal of weapons. The FALN set off incendiary devices in ten

New York City department stores, including branches of Macy's, Gimbels, Lord & Taylor, Altman's, Korvettes, and Ohrbachs the day the Democratic National Convention convened.[21, 22] The incendiary devices set numerous fires that caused considerable damage.

The FALN suffered its first major setback when one of the group's bomb-making factories was discovered by law enforcement authorities in Chicago on November 3, 1976. A drug addict broke into the apartment serving as the bomb-making factory, stole dynamite, and attempted to sell it to an undercover police officer.[23]

When the police raided the apartment, it was unoccupied, but the discovery led to the identification to several key FALN members. Ida Luz Rodríguez, Oscar Lopez-Rivera, and husband and wife Carlos Alberto Torres and Marie Haydee Torres were identified as FALN soldiers. Additionally, it was learned that Luis Rosado-Ayala, Adolfo Matos, William Gillermo Morales, and Dylcia Pagan were FALN members deeply involved in the New York City bombing campaign.

However, the Chicago bomb-making factory discovery did not slow down the FALN. Its members simply abandoned their public lives, went underground, and continued their attacks. Three months later, on February 18, 1977, a pair of bombs went off in the Merchandise Mart and the US Gypsum Building in downtown Chicago.[24] The Merchandise Mart suffered $1,335,000 in damage.[25]

By late summer, the FALN set off another bomb in New York that would take innocent life. On August 3, 1977, the late morning was interrupted when an explosion occurred at the Mobil Oil Company office. Charles Steinberg, a cofounder of Viva Temporary Services, an employment agency in the building, was killed. Nine others were wounded.[26] A second blast detonated in the Transportation building near city hall.[27] Bomb threats by the FALN also caused the evacuation of as many as one hundred thousand office workers from various city skyscrapers.

A bomb planted at the American Metal Climax building in New York's Rockefeller Center was discovered and successfully disarmed on August 8. Laboratory analysis revealed that dynamite in the bomb was from the same batch of dynamite that was recovered from the Chicago apartment rented by Carlos Alberto Torres.[28, 29]

The following spring, the FALN again demonstrated its ability to carry out coordinated attacks. On the morning of May 22, 1978, three incendiary devices detonated and started fires at LaGuardia and John F. Kennedy airports in New York City and at New Jersey's Newark International Airport.[30] About the same time, a bomb went off near the Constitution Avenue entrance of the US Department of Justice headquarters building in Washington, DC. A bomb threat was also called in claiming an explosive device would go off at the Hilton Hotel near Chicago's O'Hare International Airport, although no device was ever found.[31]

Then the FALN suffered its second major setback on July 12, 1978. A pipe bomb being assembled by an FALN member exploded in a New York City bomb-making factory. William Gillermo Morales was the bomb maker, and the explosion severely wounded him by blowing off much of both his hands. He was found alive among the ruins. Morales' injuries were so severe that after he was arrested, he had the remaining portions of his hands amputated.

The authorities also found several bombs with affixed timers in the apartment, suggesting Morales and the FALN was only hours away from launching another bombing wave. The police confiscated sixty-six sticks of dynamite; over 350 pounds of incendiary chemicals and explosive powder; blasting caps; four weapons, including a sawed-off shotgun; one thousand rounds of ammunition; and bomb-making components.[32] According to the police, it was the "biggest haul of explosives ever recovered in New York City." About the time of the bomb factory explosion, a pair of bombs detonated in Macy's and Korvettes department stores elsewhere in New York City.[33,34]

The New York bomb-making factory was in an apartment rented to a couple believed to have been Carlos Alberto Torres and his wife, Marie Haydee Beltran Torres. Marie Torres was already wanted in connection with the August 1977 Mobil Oil Company blast that killed Charles Steinberg. Her fingerprints were found at the bomb site.

William Morales went to trial in early 1979 and was convicted in late February of unlawful possession of pipe bombs and a sawed-off shotgun. In April, he was given the maximum sentence of ten years in prison on the federal charges. At his sentencing, Morales was unrepentant. He told US District Court Judge Eugene Nickerson, "Judge, if I survive this sentence and get out, I will do it again. But I'll do it by writing books and pamphlets. I urge my followers to have courage and continue the fight."[35]

Days after his federal sentence was handed down, Morales was sentenced in New York state court on the explosives charges. He was again found guilty and this time he received a much longer sentence. Morales faced twenty-nine to eighty-nine years in state prison. However, a month later, Morales was free.

After his sentencing in state court, authorities had taken Morales to New York's Bellevue Hospital prison ward to be fitted with prosthetic hands. He was left unsupervised in his hospital room and on May 21, the day after his arrival, he was gone. The window screen had been cut and a pair of wire-cutting shears was left behind. It was believed Morales climbed out the third story window and slid forty feet to the ground using a makeshift rope.[36]

Neither of the bombing discoveries seriously slowed down the FALN or the sister group, Los Macheteros. In fact, the two groups became more brazen in their operations. On August 24, 1978, Los Macheteros members killed San Juan Police Officer Julio Rodriguez Rivera while attempting to steal his police car.

The next fourteen months were the quietest period in the terror campaign of the FALN and Los Macheteros. Then the quiet solitude was shattered when the FALN launched another coordinated attack in Chicago, New York, and Puerto Rico.

On October 18, 1979, bombings occurred simultaneously in Chicago at the Cook County building housing county and city government offices and in a building at Great Lakes Naval Training Facility north of Chicago. A third bomb was detected and disarmed at building housing a Republican party committee and a presidential campaign office for Massachusetts Senator Edward M. Kennedy.

That same day, four bombs exploded at the US Customs building, a US Coast Guard radio tower, a Reserve Officers' beach club, and at a monument in Puerto Rico. A fifth bomb was discovered before it detonated.[37] At the same time, four fake bombs were found in the Democratic and Republican party offices in downtown Manhattan.[38]

The following month a bomb was discovered and disarmed at the International Tractor building in Puerto Rico. Then, in late November, bombings occurred at two military recruiting offices and at a National Guard armory in Chicago.[39]

December 3, 1979, was another very deadly day in the campaign of terror. Los Macheteros gunmen launched another brazen attack, this time against a US Navy bus outside a Navy communications facility in Toa Baja, Puerto Rico. The gunmen killed two sailors, twenty-nine-year-old John R. Ball and Emil L. White, aged twenty, and wounded ten others, including five women.[40]

The aggression against innocent bystanders continued a month later. As many as nine armed FALN members forced entry into the National Guard Armory in Oak Creek, Wisconsin on January 14, 1980. They held a National Guardsman and a janitor hostage to gain access to the weapons vaults. Home to two National Guard battalions, the Oak Creek Armory vaults were a repository for various weapons including heavy machine guns and bazookas. The FALN intruders fled after they were unsuccessful in gaining access to the locked vaults.

In mid-March 1980, the FALN stormed the Chicago campaign offices of President Jimmy Carter and Vice President Walter Mondale. Seven campaign workers were bound and gagged. At the same time, ten workers at the George H. W. Bush presidential campaign offices in Manhattan were also tied up and gagged after a FALN takeover. FALN members spray painted slogans on the walls and ransacked the offices of both presidential candidates.

The activities of the FALN began to unravel on April 4, 1980, in Evanston, Illinois when eleven members, six men and five women, were captured shortly before they were about to rob an armored truck. The FALN members arrested were Carlos Alberto Torres, Maria Haydee Beltran Torres, Elizam Escobar, Ricardo Jimenez, Adolfo Matos, Alfredo "Freddie" Mendez, Dylcia Pagan (the wife of William Gillermo Morales), sisters Ida Luz Rodríguez and Alicia Rodríguez, Luis Rosa, and Carmen Valentín.

The FALN members had been under surveillance after neighbors notified the police of suspicious activity near a parked van that turned out to have been stolen. Neighbors watched as two people dressed in jogging suits made multiple trips to the van. After the police arrested the suspicious pair, they found the other nine FALN members inside the van. All of the suspects were armed. They had ten shotguns and pistols in their possession.

The arrest of the FALN terrorists led the police to safe houses in Milwaukee and Jersey City. Authorities found postal worker uniforms and FALN correspondence in the Milwaukee safe house. In Jersey City, authorities recovered details of Madison Square Garden leading to speculation the FALN was planning to attack the Democratic Presidential nominating convention that was going to be staged at the Garden during the summer.

The FALN members' radical beliefs were on full display after their apprehension. At their first court appearance just days after being arrested, the eleven FALN members shouted at Circuit Court Judge William Kelly that they did not recognize the court. They demanded they be treated as prisoners of war. Judge Kelly thought otherwise.

Maria Torres was separated from the others and was moved from Chicago to New York to be tried for her role in the Mobil Oil building bombing. Torres carried out the attack by hiding the bomb in a coat rack while visiting Charles Steinberg's employment office and pretending to be a job applicant. Torres was convicted of the bombing and was given a life sentence. Declaring herself to be a prisoner of war, Torres refused to attend her own trial, and she instead sat in a courthouse holding cell.

Alicia Rodríguez and Luis Rosa had their own separate trial, as well. The pair had robbed an Evanston, Illinois car rental agency. They were convicted in Illinois state court on August 4, 1980, and sentenced to thirty-year prison terms for armed robbery and conspiracy.

In their state trial, Carlos Torres, Elizam Escobar, Ricardo Jimenez, Adolfo Matos, Alfredo Mendez, Dylcia Pagan, Ida Rodríguez, and Carmen Valentín were found guilty of possessing a sawed-off shotgun and conspiracy to commit armed robbery. Illinois Circuit Court Judge Francis Mahon sentenced each of them to a total of eight years in state prison.

Ten of the eleven FALN members arrested in Evanston were also indicted on thirteen counts by a federal grand jury on December 10, 1980, for their roles in twenty-nine bombings in the Chicago area. Also indicted with the ten was fugitive FALN member Oscar Lopez-Rivera. An unindicted coconspirator was Maria Torres, who was not tried because she had already been given a life sentence for the Mobil Oil office bombing in New York City.

The ten FALN members went on trial and were convicted in federal court in early February 1981. They were sentenced later that month to prison terms ranging from fifty-five to ninety years. Their convictions included charges of armed robbery, weapons violations, interstate transportation of stolen vehicles and seditious conspiracy. The seditious conspiracy charges stemmed from their conspiring to bomb twenty-nine buildings during the 1970s.

The convicted terrorists showed no remorse. "You are lucky that we cannot take you right now. Our people will continue to use righteous violence. Revolutionary justice can be fierce, mark my words," Carmen Valentín shouted at US District Court Judge Thomas R. McMillen during her sentencing.[41]

The arrests put the FALN out of business, however, sister group Los Macheteros still posed a serious threat. In fact, Los Macheteros was responsible for the most spectacular terrorist attack in terms of the highest dollar amount loss. This was due to bombing damage at Puerto Rico's Muñiz Air National Guard base on January 12, 1981. Bombs were set off causing more than $45 million in damage to ten A-7 Corsair jet aircraft and to an F-107 Starfighter that was on static display. In all, eleven aircraft were badly damaged or destroyed. [42,43] Los Macheteros, led by Juan Enrique Segarra-Palmer and Filiberto Inocencio Ojeda-Ríos, was responsible for the attack.[44]

Another Los Macheteros attack that had wide-ranging repercussions occurred three months later when the organization bombed a main power plant outside San Juan, Puerto Rico, plunging most of the Caribbean island into darkness. Nearly all of the island's 3.3 million citizens were left without electricity for about twelve hours through the night of April 11 and morning of April 12.

The island-wide blackout led to looting. This forced Governor Carlos Romero Barcelo to declare an island state of emergency and he activated a call-up plan for off-duty police officers and firemen. He also placed the National Guard on alert.

The power plant was bombed after Los Macheteros members kidnapped the plant's chief of operations, Manuel Vasquez Santiago. He was bound in chains and had his head and eyebrows shaved off. A star, the FALN logo, was painted on his forehead before he was driven to a remote field and released, otherwise unharmed.

The next violent attack to occur in the mainland US was when four bombs exploded in New York on the night of February 28, 1982 on Wall Street. Rocked by blasts were the Merrill Lynch stock brokerage, the headquarters of Chase Manhattan bank, the New York Stock Exchange, and the American Stock Exchange.[45] No one was injured because the explosions occurred prior to midnight on a Sunday. A communiqué was left behind claiming the FALN perpetrated the attacks.

The final hurrah attributed to the FALN occurred on New Year's Eve, December 31, 1982 in New York. A wave of bombings took place during an evening when the city's streets were crowded with hundreds of thousands of revelers.

The first explosion occurred at 9:27 PM at the 26 Federal Plaza, the location of a Federal Courthouse, the FBI, and other federal agencies. Fortunately, no one was injured.

Hearing of the explosion, Police Officer Rocco Pascarella, who was on duty at One Police Plaza near City Hall, began to scour the building area. He approached a suspicious package, which detonated as he neared. He lost his leg below the knee when that bomb went off at 9:55 PM. Pascarella was also blinded and became deaf in one ear. He was hospitalized for two months, underwent six surgeries, and received more than forty stitches to his face and ear.

Minutes later, a third bomb exploded outside the US District Courthouse at Cadman Plaza in Brooklyn. No one was injured in that blast.

A pair of bombs were discovered near the Manhattan office of the US Attorney for the Southern District of New York and the Federal courthouse St. Andrew's Plaza. Police officials were concerned with disarming the bombs because the area was packed with throngs of New Year's Eve celebrants.

Detectives Salvatore Pastorella and Anthony Senft of the New York City bomb squad were examining one of the bombs when it went off. Pastorella lost all the fingers of his right hand and suffered serious injuries to his eyes, leaving him blind. He would eventually need thirteen major operations to reconstruct his face. Senft was only slightly luckier. He sustained major eye and facial injuries that left him blind in one eye and missing most of his left ear. Other bomb squad members safely deactivated the fifth and last bomb.

Subsequent information and analysis indicated that the last two major bombings on Wall Street in February and on New Year's Eve that were attributed to the FALN were instead carried out by terrorist group the May 19th Communist Organization in the FALN's name.

After May 19th member Sylvia Baraldini was arrested for her role in the 1981 Brinks armored car robbery, authorities found in her apartment a carbon copy of the FALN communiqué claiming credit for the February 28 blasts. That communiqué expressed solidarity with the Brinks robbery gunmen and accomplices.[46] Forensic analysis determined that the New Year's Eve bombs were built using explosive material from dynamite stolen by May 19th Communist Organization members.[47]

THE WELLS FARGO ROBBERY

It was 9:30 PM on Monday, September 12, 1983, when the armored truck backed into the Wells Fargo loading dock. Moments later, Victor Manuel Gerena placed a revolver to the head of security manager James McKeon and threatened to blow his head off unless McKeon and Timothy Gerard obeyed him. Gerard was the driver of the truck and Gerena was the security guard who rode with him.

The pair had just completed a day of cash pickups that began in Springfield, Massachusetts and ended in the Wells Fargo garage in West Hartford, Connecticut. Gerena bound and gagged McKeon and Gerard and then injected them both with a solution that Gerena claimed would make them drowsy.

Over the next ninety minutes, Gerena made several trips from the Wells Fargo vault to his car and loaded it with $7,017,151 in various denominations.[48] That amount became the second largest cash robbery in US history. The haul weighed about nine hundred pounds. Gerena then drove off. The twenty-five-year-old Gerena eventually fled to Cuba.

It was not until nearly two years later in August 1985 that a federal grand jury handed down indictments in the case. A grand jury in Hartford, Connecticut indicted seventeen people, fourteen of whom were already in federal custody, on conspiracy charges stemming from the robbery. Sixteen of those indicted were members of the Los Macheteros. Among those in custody were Filiberto Inocencio Ojeda-Ríos and Juan Enrique Segarra-Palmer, whom federal authorities identified as the mastermind behind the heist.

Ojeda-Ríos already had a criminal record. He had been arrested in 1970 for planting bombs in the hotel district of San Juan. He fled while on bail and had been a fugitive ever since. He was also a suspect in the bombing of Fraunces Tavern in 1975.[49]

An informant identified Segarra-Palmer as the planner behind the December 3, 1979, machine gun attack against a Navy bus outside a Navy communications facility in Toa Baja, Puerto Rico in which two sailors were killed and ten others were wounded.[50] According to the FBI, Segarra-Palmer was also tied to the attack at the Muñiz Air National Guard in Puerto Rico that resulted in $45 million in damage to eleven aircraft.[51]

Segarra-Palmer, Ojeda-Ríos, and Gerena were identified as the three responsible for planning and carrying out the robbery. After the robbery, Segarra-Palmer moved the money to Massachusetts and stored it in the bedroom of a woman with whom he has having an affair. He later drove Gerena and the cash to Mexico in a motor home.[52] The other fourteen under indictment were identified as accessories to the robbery after the fact.

Segarra-Palmer and Ojeda-Ríos were the founders and key members of the group Los Macheteros. It was a violent organization closely aligned with the FALN. Their plan was to use the stolen money to finance Los Macheteros terror attacks against government facilities and corporate entities in Puerto Rico.

The big break in the investigation occurred as a result of more than 2,300 telephone calls made during 1985 that the FBI monitored under a court-approved wiretap. All of the calls were made to the home of Anne Gassin, the only indicted coconspirator who was not a member of the Los Macheteros.

Gassin had an intimate relationship with the married Segarra-Palmer and she was helping the group launder the stolen money. Authorities dropped robbery charges against her when she agreed to cooperate with the prosecution.

Juan Enrique Segarra-Palmer, his wife, Luz Berrios Berrios, Antonio Camacho-Negron, Robert J. Maldonado Rivera, Carlos M. Ayes Suarez, Norman Ramirez-Talavera, and Paul S. Weinberg were the first seven defendants to go to trial. The rest were to go to trial later as the prosecution and defense attorneys battled over the admissibility of the taped conversations.

When his trial began, Segarra-Palmer announced he would not take the stand in his own defense. He said, "I don't recognize the legitimacy of the court or the whole proceeding."[53] However, his wife, Luz Berrios Berrios, and attorney Paul S. Weinberg struck deals with prosecutors the day jury selection began. Berrios admitted her role in the conspiracy. "I didn't do anything physical. I only helped out and I knew the details [regarding] transporting the money and what was to be done with it," she said.[54]

Weinberg pled guilty to aiding in the transportation of stolen money and was sentenced to one year in prison and fined $1,000. Weinberg was a friend of Segarra-Palmer and loaned several vehicles to him knowing they were used to move the stolen Wells Fargo money. Berrios received a five-year sentence for her role in the robbery.

In opening arguments, Segarra-Palmer's attorney admitted his client had advance knowledge of the Wells Fargo robbery, received the stolen money and distributed some of it to Los Macheteros. However, the lawyer argued, Segarra-Palmer should be acquitted because he did not carry out the robbery himself.

Two witnesses for the prosecution and his own words were damaging to Segarra-Palmer's defense. Gassin testified that the money was first moved to Massachusetts where it was kept under her bed for a period of time. It was later split up and moved to Mexico, Puerto Rico, and Cuba.

Kenneth Cox, a convicted felon and longtime friend of Segarra-Palmer, testified he accompanied Segarra-Palmer to Hartford, Connecticut a month before the robbery in order to plan the heist. According to Cox's testimony, Segarra-Palmer bragged that he would pull off "one of the biggest robberies" in US history.[55]

Further implicating Segarra were his own words. The FBI taped a conversation between Segarra-Palmer and Ojeda-Ríos after the robbery in which the two debated if they should send the fiancée of Victor Gerena, the Wells Fargo gunman, to live with him in Cuba.[56]

The prosecution prevailed in the trial. Segarra-Palmer, Camacho-Negron, Maldonado Rivera, and Ramirez-Talavera were found guilty on nearly all counts. As he left the courtroom, Segarra-Palmer plunged his clenched fist skyward and yelled in Spanish "Long live free Puerto Rico!" Moments after he was acquitted, Ayes Suarez vowed, "We will continue to do whatever is necessary to free our country."[57]

Segarra-Palmer showed no remorse for his actions at his sentencing when he told the court his "conscience is clear." He then shouted, "Puerto Rico Libre!" after he was sentenced to sixty-five years in prison and fined $500,000. Camacho-Negron was given a 15-year sentence and Maldonado Rivera and Ramirez-Talavera were each sentenced to five years in prison. In spite of their passion for their cause, very few Puerto Ricans supported the goal of Los Macheteros. Only 3 percent of Puerto Ricans voted for independence in a referendum that was conducted a few months earlier.

THE CLEMENCY

The mid-1999 commutation of the sentences of the Puerto Rican terrorists was a total surprise. Bill Clinton had received 3,448 clemency petitions requesting commutations since taking office until August 1999. He only approved three commutations.[58] Clinton denied 99.9 percent of the commutation requests until the day he decided to award clemency to the sixteen FALN and Los Macheteros terrorists. Perhaps even more amazing was that Clinton offered commutations to the sixteen, even though not a single one of those convicted terrorists petitioned for his or her own release.

An organization calling itself Ofensiva '92 first submitted a clemency request for the terrorists to Clinton shortly after he took office.[59] During those six years, Clinton never saw fit to grant clemency. That all changed when it was clear his wife Hillary would become a candidate for the US Senate for the state of New York. Puerto Rican voters represented a sizable voting bloc in New York. Mayor Rudolph Guiliani, who would be the GOP candidate for Senator (although he later withdrew from the race when he was diagnosed with prostate cancer), was very popular in the Puerto Rican community. Guiliani captured 43 percent of the Puerto Rican vote in his last mayoral election in 1997.

On August 11, 1999, Clinton shocked the entire law enforcement community, the hundreds of victims of Puerto Rican terrorism, and the public by offering executive clemency to the Puerto Rican terrorists. Clinton offered clemency in spite of the fact that his own Justice Department recommended *against* clemency two and one-half years earlier on December 16, 1996. Clinton did not see fit to grant the clemency request until after it became clear the release of the Puerto Rican terrorists had value to the political campaigns of Hillary and Vice President Al Gore, who was running to succeed Clinton as president.

In return, Clinton asked the clemency recipients to renounce violence. He even gave them an entire month to mull over his offer. Their acceptance, it turned out, was easier said than done.

A small group of activists supporting clemency for the terrorists, led by Bronx Congressman Jose Serrano, were livid Clinton had placed *any* conditions on the clemency. "I am shocked by the conditions he [Clinton] set on their release," exclaimed Serrano.

Lolita Lebrón, the terrorist and would-be congressional assassin released from prison by Jimmy Carter in 1979, announced "The [conditions] are onerous, an insult to the dignity of a people that has an inalienable right to fight for its liberation."[60]

As far as law enforcement authorities knew at that time, an agreement by the terrorists to renounce violence would have amounted to little more than a Trojan horse. The US Bureau of Prisons had secretly and legally taped conversations among the terrorists. The group vowed to continue using violence once they were released.[61] Remarkably, the White House claimed it did not know of the existence of the tapes while simultaneously claiming it conducted an exhaustive four-year review of the clemency request.

Perhaps even more stunning was that Clinton offered clemency to a group of bombers a mere four years after the 1995 bombing of Oklahoma City's Alfred P. Murrah Federal Building, and while convicted bomber Timothy McVeigh awaited his execution on death row.

The reason for Clinton's generous offer of clemency was explained by Clinton's longtime political adviser, Dick Morris. According to Morris, "The key difference between New York politics and those of any other state in America is its balkanization into a dozen or more ethnic voting blocs."[62] Morris noted that Puerto Ricans and Hasidic Jews had broken with automatically supporting Democratic politicians and had increasingly turned toward Republicans. Morris observed "these groups are key targets for anyone seeking political office. Every politician caters to them, as one might expect, with patronage, promises, and platitudes. But only Hillary and Bill gave them pardons."[63]

The immense political value of the clemency offer in boosting Hillary's Senate candidacy in the Puerto Rican community was apparent to the Clinton administration. In an interoffice memorandum, White House staffer Mayra Martinez-Fernandez wrote, "most Puerto Ricans agree that their sentences should be commuted."[64] She continued, "The release of these Puerto Rican men and women… will have a positive impact among strategic Puerto Rican communities to the US [read, voters]."[65]

Notes from a White House meeting on the topic of potentially releasing the FALN terrorists underscored the political considerations at work. According to the notes, the White House staff recognized the FALN release was a "high priority for the P[uerto] R[ican] communities in the U.S."[66]

In 1998, speculation mounted that former New Jersey senator Bill Bradley would challenge Gore for the 2000 Democratic nomination for the presidency. Bradley established a presidential exploratory committee that year. In July, Gore met with the Hispanic Caucus of the House of Representatives in a likely effort to shore up support among that constituency. One of the major talking points drafted by White House staff for Gore's use was a discussion of the status of the FALN terrorists.[67]

The Clinton administration refused to publicly release any of the clemency recommendations made by the law enforcement community. This was because the Justice Department, the Federal Bureau of Prisons, US prosecutors, the FBI, and state and local police officers were universal in opposing Clinton's clemency offer.

Guiliani came out forcefully against the clemency pointing out the terrorists were tied to the Fraunces Tavern bombing that killed four. Yet, Hillary Clinton waited nearly a month after her husband's clemency offer before she made her first statement on the affair. This delay gave Hillary Clinton ample time to measure the widespread public disapproval of the clemency offer. A month after Clinton's clemency offer, Hillary claimed she had "no involvement in or prior knowledge of the decision."[68] Hillary's assertion was a complete lie. Two days before her husband offered the clemency, Hillary was personally presented with material in support of the clemency by New York City Councilman Jose Rivera. The packet of material included a letter from Rivera asking Hillary to "speak to the president and ask him to consider granting executive clemency."[69]

On September 8, 1999, US Representative Vito Fosella (Republican, New York) introduced House Concurrent Resolution 180 titled "Expressing the Sense of Congress That the President Should Not Have Granted Clemency to Terrorists." Forty-three members of the House cosponsored the resolution. The resolution had bipartisan support. It received an overwhelming 311 votes when it went to a vote on the House floor although forty-one members voted against the measure and another seventy-two voted "present" rather than take a position in favor or against the bill.[70] The 113 members who voted "present" or "nay" were all Democrats with the exception of the Socialist Bernie Sanders of Vermont.

There was a similar resolution in the Senate introduced by Senator Trent Lott (Republican, Mississippi). Senate Joint Resolution 33 resolved "That making concessions to terrorists is deplorable and that President Clinton should not have granted clemency to the FALN terrorists." The resolution passed overwhelmingly by a ninety-five-to-two vote. The two Senators who voted against the resolution were Daniel Akaka (Democrat, Hawaii) and Paul Wellstone (Democrat, Minnesota).

The absurdity of Clinton's claim that the released terrorists were not involved in violence cannot be overstated. Gilbert G. Gallegos, National President of the Grand Fraternal Order of Police accurately observed that the murderous gangster Al Capone was never imprisoned for any violent crimes. Capone was convicted of tax evasion.[71] Yet, every single American knew just how violent Capone was and the number of people who died because of his actions.

Not surprisingly, once the FALN terrorists were in custody, the major FALN bombing campaign came to an abrupt end. A few minor bombings occurred that were initially attributed to the FALN, but ties were never proved. Two larger bombing waves in 1982 were the work of the May 19th Communist Organization, whose members tried to attribute them to the FALN. Law enforcement discoveries and forensics made it clear that May 19th was responsible for the blasts.

The hypocrisy of Clinton's generous clemency offer to the Puerto Rican terrorists who blew up buildings, set fires, and conducted shootings killing eight and wounding nearly one hundred was underscored about a year earlier when he forcefully denounced similar terrorism.

"I have said many times that terrorism is one of the greatest dangers we face in this new global era," said Clinton in televised remarks when he announced air strikes launched against a pharmaceutical factory in The Sudan and a vacant training camp in Afghanistan. "We saw its [terrorism's] twisted mentality at work last week in the embassy bombings in Nairobi and Dar es Salaam, which took the lives of innocent Americans and Africans and injured thousands more," he continued."[72] Clinton falsely claimed that the region's largest medicine factory was manufacturing chemical weapons for Al-Qaeda. The strikes were ordered the same day Monica Lewinsky testified before a federal grand jury regarding her sexual relationship with Clinton.

Twelve of the terrorists accepted Clinton's clemency offer and signed statements agreeing to refrain from engaging in violence after their release. Not one of the convicted felons ever apologized for their actions or expressed any remorse for those killed, maimed or injured, nor did they apologize to anyone who lost loved ones.

Even before the ink on their commutations was dry, the group refused to accept any responsibility for their crimes. Speaking on their behalf, their attorney Jan Susler said, "They are no criminals.

They are political people."[73] The about-to-be freed Puerto Rican terrorists delivered a big "Screw you" to the American public.

Eleven of those granted clemency were to be immediately released. Juan Enrique Segarra-Palmer, the cofounder of Los Macheteros, the Wells Fargo robbery mastermind, the man who engineered the machine gun attack that killed two US Navy sailors, and the leader responsible for $45 million in damage to several military aircraft, had only served ten years of his fifty-five-year sentence. Clinton reduced Segarra-Palmer's sentence to fifteen years, allowing him to go free in only five years' time.

The eleven who were granted clemency and were immediately released were Edwin Cortes, Elizam Escobar, Ricardo Jimenez, Adolfo Matos, Dylcia Pagan, Alicia Rodríguez, Ida Luz Rodríguez, Luis Rosa, Alberto Rodríguez, Alejandrina Torres and Carmen Valentín.

After he was released from the federal penitentiary in Lewisburg, Pennsylvania, Cortes announced that the terrorists were not "criminals," but instead "were patriots."[74]

Roberto Maldonado Rivera and Norman Ramirez-Talavera also accepted the clemency offer. They had been released from prison years earlier and Clinton's clemency offer allowed them to walk away from paying the fines they received in their federal sentencing. Maldonado was fined $100,000 and Ramirez-Talavera $50,000.

Two of the terrorists, Oscar Lopez-Rivera and Antonio Camacho-Negron, refused to renounce terrorism and forfeited their opportunity for executive clemency—under *this* President Clinton.

Margaret C. Love, the pardon attorney in the Justice Department from 1990 to 1997, disapproved of Clinton's politicization of the commutation and pardon process. She said, "Now clemency has been taken hostage in the war on crime."[75]

LIST OF SELECTED TERRORIST ACTS BY FALN AND LOS MACHETEROS

August 31, 1974—bomb goes off in Damrosch Park, New York.[76]

September 28, 1974—bombs go off at Newark, New Jersey police headquarters and city hall.[77]

October 26, 1974—five bombings against Marine Midland Bank, office building housing Exxon and Chemical Bank, Banco de Ponce at Rockefeller Plaza, Lever Brothers House, and Union Carbide offices.[78]

December 11, 1974—police officer loses eye in East Harlem tenement blast.

December 31, 1974—Puerto Rico's Government Electrical Agency transformer is destroyed by bomb;[79] two branches of the Chase Manhattan Bank are bombed; two additional bombs are found unexploded.[80]

January 24, 1975—lunchtime blast at Fraunces Tavern, Manhattan's oldest building, killed four and wounded sixty.[81]

April 2, 1975—four separate bombings damage New York Life Insurance building, Metropolitan Life Insurance building, Bankers Trust Company building and a restaurant adjacent to American Bank and Trust Company of New York City.[82]

June 14, 1975—first bombings in Chicago, Illinois; United American Bank and First National Bank buildings rocked by blasts.[83,84]

June 15, 1975—bomb discovered at Federal building in Chicago before it detonates.[85]

October 27, 1975—bombs went off against nine targets including US Mission to the UN, National Westminster, First National City, First National, and Chase Manhattan banks in New York City; Continental National Bank, IBM Plaza, Sears Tower and Standard Oil building in Chicago; and the Department of State and Bureau of Indian Affairs offices in Washington, DC.[86, 87]

November 9, 1975—bombing of First National City Bank in New York City.[88]

December 29, 1975—bombing of LaGuardia Airport.[89]

June 7, 1976—bombing of John Hancock building, Bank Leumi Le Israel, and First National City Bank Plaza and police building in Chicago.[90]

June 19, 1976—bombing of Marshall Fields Department Store in Chicago.[91]

June 21, 1976—bombing of Marshall Fields Department Store in Chicago.[92]

June 25, 1976—four bombs explode at Pan Am Building, South Bronx police station, Chase Manhattan Bank, and Citibank in New York.[93]

July 12, 1976—Incendiary devices explode in ten New York City department stores including branches of Macy's, Gimbels, Lord & Taylor, Altman's, Korvettes, and Ohrbachs the day the Democrat National Convention convened.[94,95]

September 10, 1976—bombing of Holiday Inn in Chicago.[96]

September 19, 1976—bombing of Marshall Fields Department Store in Chicago.[97]

September 21, 1976—bomb explodes at New York Hilton Hotel.[98]

February 18, 1977—two bomb blasts rock the Merchandise Mart and US Gypsum Building in downtown Chicago.[99]

February 18, 1977—bombs detonate outside the Gulf & Western and Chrysler buildings, injuring two passersby.[100]

March 20, 1977—bombs explode outside New York City headquarters of FBI and the currency printing plant of the American Bank Note company.[101]

April 9, 1977—eight incendiary devices started small fires in Macy's, Gimbels and Bloomingdales department stores in Manhattan.[102]

June 4, 1977—bomb explodes outside Mayor's Office in Cook County Building in Chicago.[103]

August 3, 1977—midday bombing against Mobil Oil Company officer killed one and wounded nine;[104] a second blast detonated near a Defense Department office in the Transportation building near City Hall.[105, 106]

August 4, 1977—New York Commodity Exchange is bombed.[107]

August 8, 1977—bomb is disarmed at the American Metal Climax building in New York's Rockefeller Center; the dynamite matches that found in an FALN apartment in Chicago.[108,109]

October 7, 1977—statue commemorating US landing in Puerto Rico is bombed.[110]

October 11, 1977—pipe bomb explodes outside the main branch of the New York Public Library; a dynamite bomb is discovered and defused outside General Motors building in Manhattan.[111] Bombs explode at Gimbels and Macy's department stores.[112]

October 12, 1977—bomb detonates under a New York City police car.[113]

October 15, 1977—Three children notify authorities after discovering a timer-detonated bomb before it exploded at National Guard Armory in Chicago.[114]

November 15, 1977—attempted bombing of Iran Air office in New York.[115]

January 12, 1978—an incendiary device explodes in Macy's department store in New York.[116]

January 31, 1978—two pipe bombs explode under a police cruiser and by the Consolidated Edison Company headquarters in New York City.[117]

February 8, 1978—attempted bombing of New York City power transmitter.[118]

February 16, 1978—attempted bombing of Manufacturer's Bank in New York.[119]

March 12, 1978—four are arrested for carrying a 36-calibre pistol into a Bronx courtroom during an arraignment for a colleague.[120]

March 24, 1978—a series of explosions occur through a 26-block of the South Bronx sewer system.[121]

May 22, 1978—three incendiary devices detonate and start fires at LaGuardia, John F. Kennedy, and Newark International Airports;[122] Chicago's O'Hare International; a bomb goes off at US Department of Justice headquarters in Washington, DC.[123]

June 24, 1978—bombs go off in the J.C. Penney, Marshall Fields and Sears department stores in Schaumburg, Illinois.[124]

July 12, 1978—explosion in New York City FALN bomb factory severely wounded FALN bomb maker.

July 12, 1978—bombs detonate in New York Macy's and Korvettes department stores.[125]

August 24, 1978—Los Macheteros killed a San Juan, Puerto Rico police officer during a car theft.[126]

August 29, 1978—bomb goes off in Macy's Department Store in New York.[127]

October 18, 1979—a pair of bombings occur simultaneously in Chicago at the Cook County building housing government offices and in a building at Great Lakes Naval Training Facility north of Chicago; and three explosive devices detonate causing damage at federal offices and facilities in Puerto Rico.[128] Four fake bombs are found in the Democrat and Republican party offices in downtown Manhattan.[129]

November 24, 1979—bombings take place at two military recruiting offices and at a National Guard armory in Chicago.[130]

December 3, 1979—Los Macheteros gunmen attack a Navy bus and kill two sailors while wounding ten others outside a Navy communications facility in Toa Baja, Puerto Rico.[131]

January 12, 1980—as many as nine armed FALN members stormed the National Guard Armory in Oak Creek, Wisconsin, overpowering one National Guardsman and a janitor in an unsuccessful effort to get access to automatic weapons.[132]

March 12, 1980—Los Macheteros gunmen attempt to kill three faculty from the ROTC unit at the University of Puerto Rico.[133]

March 15, 1980—FALN gunmen storm presidential campaign offices of Jimmy Carter in Chicago and George H. W. Bush in New York; several Carter campaign employees are bound and threatened prior to the offices being ransacked.[134] A list of convention delegates is stolen and threatening letters are sent to them.[135]

April 11, 1980—San Juan, Puerto Rico power plant is bombed causing a blackout of most of the Caribbean Island.[136]

June 3, 1980—bomb goes off in museum of Statue of Liberty.[137]

November 3, 1980—FALN protestors seize Carter-Mondale campaign office in Los Angeles and storm Reagan-Bush offices in San Francisco.[138]

December 21, 1980—two pipe bombs explode in lockers at New York's Penn Station during Christmas holiday travel rush.[139]

January 12, 1981—$45 million in damage to 10 A-7 Corsair jet aircraft and an F-107 Starfighter static display at Puerto Rico's Muñiz Air National Guard base.[140,141]

February 28, 1982—coordinated bomb attacks against the New York Stock Exchange, the American Stock Exchange, Chase Manhattan Bank, and the Merrill Lynch and Company headquarters.[142]

September 20, 1982—bomb explodes at Bankers Trust building in New York City.

December 31, 1982—bombings of a police headquarters, two Federal office buildings, and a Federal courthouse seriously injure three police officers.[143]

CHAPTER 11

The New Square Swindlers

"Every politician caters to them, as one might expect, with patronage, promises, and platitudes. But only Hillary and Bill gave them pardons." [1]

THE ELECTION OF SENATOR HILLARY RODHAM CLINTON

Hillary Rodham Clinton held a private meeting with Grand Rabbi David Twersky in his home in the New Square community of New York's Rockland County on August 8, 2000. New Square is a Hasidic Jewish village located about thirty miles north of New York City. Clinton had her work cut out for her as she campaigned for the US Senate. It was expected that New Square residents, like every other Hasidic community, would overwhelmingly vote for the Republican nominee to the US Senate.

Clinton was deeply unpopular with New York's Orthodox and Hasidic Jewish communities. This was due to her stand on several key issues, including her support for abortion on demand, her opposition to school vouchers, her antagonistic stand toward Israel and

Israel's security, and her call for Palestinian statehood. During a 1998 satellite address to a Middle East audience Clinton said, "I think that it will be in the long-term interest of the Middle East for Palestine to be a state."[2]

Hillary had more recently embraced groups fighting Israel. The American Muslim Alliance, a group sympathetic to militants using armed force against Israel, held a $50,000 fundraiser for her in Boston in June 2000.[3]

Hillary invited Muslims opposed to Israel's existence to several White House receptions. One such guest, Abdurahman Alamoudi the founder of the American Muslim Council (not to be confused with the American Muslim Alliance), stated, "We are the ones who went to the White House and defended what is called Hamas."[4] Hamas was the main culprit behind suicide bombings in Israel.

Alamoudi criticized Al Qaeda's execution of the 1998 car bomb attack on the US Embassy in Kenya that killed 213 because "many African Muslims have died and not a single American died."[5] He publicly supported Hizballah and 1993 World Trade Center bombing mastermind Sheikh Omar Abdul Rahman. He referred to Hamas as a "freedom-fighting organization" just days after it took responsibility for a deadly 1997 suicide bombing in Jerusalem.[6] Even with that history of support for terrorism against the US, Alamoudi was a frequent visitor to the Clinton White House.[7]

From 1997 through 2000, Alamoudi worked as a US State Department goodwill ambassador under Secretary of State Madeline Albright. When not traveling to the Middle East representing America, he was in the US leading anti-Israel rallies across from the White House.[8]

Hillary Clinton's political organization attempted to cover up Alamoudi's May 2000 $1,000 contribution to her Senatorial campaign by listing his employer as the "American Museum Council" rather than the American Muslim Council on official Federal Election Commission documents.[9] Alamoudi would be arrested in 2003[10] and later sentenced to twenty-three years in prison on terrorism-related charges, including plotting to assassinate Crown Prince Abdullah of Saudi Arabia.[11]

It was not until four months after the Boston fundraiser that Clinton announced she would return the money to the American Muslim Alliance, and then only after a public outcry had erupted. "All $50,000, every penny of it, is going back," Clinton said.[12] She claimed she had no idea the Muslim group was behind the fundraiser. Unfortunately for Hillary, a photograph of the event surfaced in which she held a plaque given to her by the group that was inscribed with the American Muslim Association name[13] in large type.[14] According to financial disclosure records filed with the Federal Election Commission, Clinton returned just over $33,000 of the $50,000 she received from the AMA fundraiser.[15]

Hillary's embrace of radical Muslims wasn't her only problem. She was something of an anti-Semite herself. Hillary had a long history of using derogatory terms regarding Jews.[16] She once referred to a former campaign worker as "a f**king Jew bastard."[17] Yet, it was Clinton's kiss and hug of Suha Arafat, the wife of Palestinian Authority President Yasser Arafat, at a November 1999 joint appearance with Arafat in the Palestinian town of Ramallah that had most recently enraged Orthodox and Hasidic Jews.

Clinton kissed Yasser Arafat's wife moments after Suha Arafat had accused Israel of poisoning 80 percent of Palestinian water and of releasing toxic gas on Palestinian women and children. Arafat said, "Our [Palestinian] people have been submitted to the daily and intensive use of poisonous gas by the Israeli forces, which has led to an increase in cancer cases among women and children."[18] This was Hillary Rodham Clinton's political baggage.

Neither Clinton nor Twersky ever divulged all of what was said during their private meeting on that August 2000 day. Clinton denies they talked about Twersky's most pressing issue, his request for executive clemency for four New Square members who were imprisoned after they had swindled US taxpayers out of more than

$44 million. However, a confidential source said that trading executive clemency for votes was the focus of the meeting.[19]

Clinton's Republican opponent, US Representative Rick Lazio, was wildly popular among Orthodox and Hasidic Jews. He was a member of the House Republican Israel Caucus and was a staunch supporter of Israel. He was applauded for voting in favor of generous foreign aid to Israel each year. He supported school choice and he was opposed to abortion, particularly late-term partial birth abortion, which Hillary favored.

On Election Day, *every single* Hasidic Jewish community in New York voted overwhelmingly for Lazio except for one.[20] New Square village voted for Hillary fourteen hundred to twelve.[21]

Immediately after the August Clinton-Twersky meeting, New Square leaders began campaigning for Clinton. They even drove cars with loudspeakers outside the community blaring endorsements of Clinton.

The month after Clinton was elected as the next US Senator from New York, Twersky made his first visit to the White House for a private meeting with President Bill Clinton and Senator-elect Hillary Rodham Clinton. According to New Square officials, Twersky requested executive clemency for the New Square con men and asked Clinton to ensure the safe return of fugitive Chaim Berger who sought refuge in Israel. Hillary claimed she sat silently and took no position on the clemency request even though it came from a powerful constituent who delivered to her 99.15 percent of the vote from his village! Such a statement is perhaps the most incredulous comment to have ever been uttered by Hillary Clinton.

New Square is a Skverer Hasidic community located in the town of Ramapo in Rockland County. It was settled in 1954 when several Skverer families in Brooklyn relocated to a dairy farm where they wanted to shut out the "evils of American society."[22] The community was incorporated as New Square village in 1961, becoming New York state's first community to be governed by a specific religious group.

The Skverer Hasidic sect of Judaism began in the eighteenth century in what is now present-day Ukraine. Hasidism originated when some Jews believed that most expressions of Jewish life had become too intellectual. Hasidism emphasizes the heart, joy, and spirituality of Judaism. Skverer Hasidism stresses religious as opposed to academic study of the Torah, prayer, and abstention from excessive earthly pleasures in order to achieve purity of heart and mind.

In 2000, New Square was led by Grand Rabbi David Twersky, who was also the international spiritual leader of one of two offshoots of Skverer Hasidism. Twersky inherited this powerful leadership position from his father. New Square village is a closed community that is served by a single synagogue. No house of worship representing any other religion, nor any other sect of Judaism exists. Similarly, no other schools exist in the village except for New Square's Jewish school system operating under the banner of Yeshiva Avir Yaakov.

Yiddish is the primary language spoken throughout the community. The approximately six thousand New Square residents are subject to a beth din, a rabbinical court in which three rabbis serve as judges. New Square has elected officials, including a mayor and trustees, but the positions are largely ceremonial and carry very little power aside from managing village administration and finances. All candidates for elected office are selected by the Grand Rabbi and they run unopposed. The real power rests in the hands of the religious hierarchy. As Grand Rabbi, Twersky was the law of the land.

New Square was relatively anonymous for most of the first forty years of its existence. The revelation that prominent village leaders, including New Square cofounder Chaim Berger, had bilked taxpayers out of more than $44 million of federal and state tax dollars in an elaborate swindle put New Square firmly in the public eye. Clinton's commutation of the prison sentences of the fraud's ringleaders ensured the public spotlight remained on the community.

New Square later garnered worldwide ridicule in 2003 when a fishmonger claimed to have heard a twenty-pound carp shout out apocalyptic warnings to him in Hebrew. Zalmen Rosen claimed the carp began yelling at him that the end is near, and that Rosen should pray and study the Torah.[23]

According to the sixty-four-count federal indictment, the swindle involved seven major players and included many coconspirators from the village. Six New Square men, Nathan Adler, Chaim Berger, his son Benjamin Berger, Jacob Elbaum, Avrum David Friesel, Kalmen Stern, and David Goldstein of Brooklyn (and formerly of New Square) hatched an elaborate plan in which they fraudulently obtained tens of millions of dollars from various federal and state aid programs. These were the Pell Grant program, Small Business Administration loans for minority-owned businesses, funds from the federal government's Housing and Urban Development Section 8 housing subsidy program, grants from the New York state Tuition Assistance Program, and the old-age benefit program of the Social Security Administration. In addition, the conspirators defrauded the Internal Revenue Service by concealing their income.

PELL GRANTS

Created in 1972 by Senator Claiborne Pell (Democrat, Rhode Island), the Federal Pell Grant Program was originally known as the Basic Educational Opportunity Grant program. The goal of the program is to provide need-based grants to low-income undergraduate students and, in some cases, to select graduate students. The intention is to promote access to post-secondary education. Over the course of a decade, the New Square con men fraudulently obtained grants on behalf of students who were not low income, did not meet enrollment status requirements, did not attend a school or were enrolled in multiple schools.

The conspirators collected $11.6 million from fraudulently obtained Pell Grants by using the nearby Rockland County Community College. Chaim Berger established a mentor-based Judaic independent studies program ostensibly to be operated in New Square and loosely associated with Rockland College enabling the fraud to be carried out. According to the scheme, mentors would guide students through independent studies to include periodic examinations. The independent studies program did not require the students to attend any formal classes. Successful completion of the independent studies program would allow students to receive Rockland College course credit. To make the fraud complete, most of the mentors were New Square residents who were in on the scam.

The fraud committed at the nonexistent Toldos Yakov Yosef seminary in Brooklyn was nearly identical. The conspirators created the fake seminary with each of them playing various roles. Chaim Berger served as president and chairman of the board. David Goldstein pretended to be the dean. Avrum Friesel, the son of New Square Mayor Mattus Friesel, claimed to be the financial aid officer. Kalmen Stern played the role of registrar when accreditors inspected the school.[24] Nathan Adler, Benjamin Berger, and Jacob Elbaum pretended to be members of the seminary's administration, faculty or staff.[25]

Berger, Stern and Goldstein created fake resumes, phony minutes of board meetings, and bogus student progress reports in order to fraudulently qualify for the federal grant money. An accomplice in the case testified for the prosecution. Alan Berkowitz testified in court that Toldos Yakov Yosef had no program, no classes, or no academic grading. He testified he assisted the conspirators in creating the necessary fake documents to make the school look legitimate.

Berkowitz testified that his efforts helped the seminary gain accreditation from the Accrediting Council for Continuing Education and Training (ACCET).[26] The ACCET accreditation gave the school the legitimacy needed to participate in the Pell Grant and New York State Tuition Aid Program.

As with the Rockland College scam, Toldos Yakov Yosef offered a mentor-based independent studies program leading to either a six-year rabbinical certificate or a five-year Judaic studies certificate.

The "independent studies" aspect of the program gave the conspirators the excuse they needed to explain why the seminary did not have any classrooms.

Thousands of Jewish students from New Square and Brooklyn were enrolled in the nonexistent seminary. Nearly every single student was awarded a Pell Grant although the students never actually received the grant money. The conspirators kept it. From 1987 to 1992, the fictitious Toldos Yakov Yosef received more than $10.3 million in Pell Grant funds on behalf of its phantom students.

Once the school programs were established, the conspirators created a steady enrollment of "students." This was achieved in numerous ways. Students attending the Yeshiva of New Square high school, who were ineligible due to their high school student status, allowed their names to be used. Hundreds of New Square residents lent their names for the scam while other New Square residents were paid to fake student status.[27]

In some instances, the conspirators used biographical information purchased from brokers who specialized in selling fake identities. Additionally, Russian immigrants who did not speak English had their names and biographical information used without their knowledge. New Square residents who moved out of the country also had their identities used. In all, thousands of fake students were enrolled in both schools. More than three thousand mostly New Square residents enrolled in just Rockland County Community College alone.

Pell Grant applications were submitted on behalf of the "students" attending Rockland County Community College and Toldos Yakov Yosef seminary by two organizations controlled by officials of New Square community. The Yeshiva of New Square Higher Learning and the Student Placement Center were organizations that completed and then submitted applications for student financial aid. Chaim Berger was the president of the Yeshiva of New Square Higher Learning, and he assisted in the establishment of the Student Placement Center.

Once the grant applications were approved, the Department of Education wired the grant money to each of the schools to be applied to the students' accounts. Money sent to Rockland College was passed on to the New Square personnel, who allegedly were paying the mentors and were administering the Judaic studies program. The money was never applied to any student's account because no student was actually attending either school. The conspirators pocketed the money or directed it elsewhere. Coconspirator Avrum Friesel received Pell Grants in his own name over the course of a decade.

The Rockland College fraud was first uncovered during a 1992 state audit of the college. This eventually led to the US Attorney's investigation of the entire New Square fraud ring.

According to officials with US Department of Education, which administers the Pell Grant program, the New Square swindle was "one of the largest cases of fraud in the history the program."[28]

Rockland College and Toldos Yakov Yosef seminary may not have been the first academic grant frauds perpetrated by this group. Federal investigators believed the New Square swindlers may have pulled a similar con in the 1980s with the Derach Ayson Seminary.

SMALL BUSINESS ADMINISTRATION INVESTMENTS

The fraud against the Small Business Administration was accomplished through the establishment of the Square Deal Venture Capital Corporation (SDVCC). The SDVCC was launched as a small business investment company, licensed by the SBA, to make equity investments and long-term loans to qualifying small, minority-owned businesses. The SBA funded and guaranteed the loans so the SDVCC was actually "investing" the taxpayers' money.

Federal regulations prohibit small business investment companies, such as the SDVCC, from making investments in a company in which any official or a relative of an official of the small business investment company has a direct or indirect relationship. The SDVCC, with Chaim Berger as one of its directors, made investments in a variety of companies and businesses in which the New Square conspirators had direct ties.

Berger also fraudulently applied for SBA loans listing Yeshiva of New Square as the recipient. As a not-for-profit organization, the yeshiva was ineligible to receive funds from this federal subsidy program, which is intended to help entrepreneurs launch for-profit businesses.

HUD Section 8 Housing Subsidies

The conspirators defrauded the Department of Housing and Urban Development by applying for and receiving Section 8 housing subsidies intended to benefit low-income tenants. The conspirators accomplished this in two ways. They applied for rent subsidies for themselves by falsely reporting their real income and portraying themselves as living below the poverty level.

Friesel, Stern, Elbaum, and Benjamin Berger received rental subsidies from the Section 8 housing program. The subsidies were distributed by the New Square Public Housing Authority, in which, coincidentally, Chaim Berger was an official and he had access to its bank accounts.

The conspirators also received rental subsidies as the owners of "rental" property. They executed contracts with the New Square Public Housing Authority to provide low-income housing. They covered up their actual ownership of the properties by using front companies and fake owners. HUD money was then transferred to the front companies and fake owners on behalf of the tenants. In some cases, the "low-income tenants" who occupied the rental property were actually family members of the conspirators. In one case, one of the con men applied for government subsidies for himself as both a tenant and as a landlord.[29]

The Section 8 money was deposited in bank accounts the conspirators opened in the names of the phony owners. The conspirators then withdrew money from these bank accounts or wrote checks on the accounts in order to pay their personal expenses.

SOCIAL SECURITY ADMINISTRATION

The conspirators defrauded the Social Security Administration by applying for benefits on behalf of ineligible recipients. They used the names of the phony owners that were used to hide their ownership of properties that received Section 8 rental subsidies. The conspirators created fake documents including income tax returns, W-2 forms and employment histories in order to create an employment record of the phony owners and to qualify them for Social Security benefits. Money from the Social Security Administration would be deposited in the bank accounts previously opened by the conspirators in the names of the phony owners. Of course, this gave the conspirators immediate access to the Social Security funds.

INTERNAL REVENUE SERVICE

The conspirators' complex fraud also included their filing of dozens of fake and forged Internal Revenue Service documents. The conspirators cheated the IRS by not reporting the actual income they received from their various illicit deals.

THE CONSPIRATORS

Chaim Berger cofounded New Square village and he served on its board of trustees. He cofounded and served on the board of directors of the New Square Local Development Corporation, which was under contract to administer development programs for New Square village, using federal loans and grants. Berger served on the board of the Yeshiva of New Square and was president of the Gruss Girls Seminary. He served as president of the Yeshiva of New Square Higher Learning, an entity that managed Pell Grant and Tuition

Assistance Program monies on behalf of "student" applicants for post-secondary school education. He was president and chairman of the board of the Toldos Yakov Yosef seminary.

Berger was a director the Square Deal Venture Capital Corporation, a private company licensed by the Small Business Administration to administer SBA-guaranteed loans to minority-owned businesses operating in New Square. He was also a member of the New Square Public Housing Authority. Berger had signature authority for numerous bank accounts associated with nearly every one of those entities and organizations. Berger had access to most federal grant and loan monies that flowed into New Square. Berger's son, Benjamin, was principal of the Yeshiva of New Square elementary school.

In addition to his being the mayor's son, Avrum Friesel was also the New Square Village Clerk.[30] Friesel administered several of the New Square education programs and he signed documents as an administrator of the Derach Ayson Seminary, where an earlier fraud likely occurred.

Kalmen Stern and Jacob Elbaum worked for Chaim Berger at New Square Higher Learning. Elbaum was also a director of the New Square Local Development Corporation.

Berger was the mastermind behind the swindle. The other six were major coconspirators, but the seven were not able to pull off such a big fraud without help. There were scores of accomplices. There were countless unindicted coconspirators. Thousands of New Square residents posed as fake students and phony low-income tenants in a scheme that resulted in more than $44 million in fraudulently obtained grants, loans and aid funded by US taxpayers. More than three thousand "students" were involved in just the Rockland County Community College scam alone from 1982 until 1993.[31] A sizable number of the New Square community apparently was in on the con. The widespread involvement of community members in the New Square swindle gave life to the title of Hillary Rodham Clinton's book *It Takes a Village*.

Assistant US Attorney Joanna C. Hendon would later tell a jury these men were "looting [government programs] through a web of deceit so clever and so sophisticated that for many, many years, nobody figured out what was really going on."[32]

NEW SQUARE VILLAGE

Commenting on the claims that Grand Rabbi Twersky was ignorant of the swindle, another Hasidic rabbi, who wished to remain anonymous, said, "Everything that happens in that community happens with the rebbe's [Twersky's] guidance."[33]

New Square village spared no expense in coming to the aid of the indicted. It put together a high-priced legal defense team for the con men that the Jewish daily newspaper *Forward* described as "rival[ing] the defense of O.J. Simpson."[34] The village also engaged the services of public relations hired gun Howard Rubenstein in order to spruce up the community's public image.

Other Jewish leaders were critical of the bad publicity caused by New Square's activities. Referring to New Square village, Rabbi Avrohom Pam of Yeshiva Torah V'daath and Rabbi Yaakov Perlow, both of Agudath Israel of America, said, "Orthodox individuals and institutions have been tarred with the brush of illegal activity."[35] They called for a return of "honesty and integrity" to Orthodox Judaism.

William Helmreich is a sociologist at the City University of New York. An expert on Orthodoxy and the yeshiva world, he is also an Orthodox Jew. Helmreich observed that a deeply pious community such as New Square could rationalize a fraud of epic proportions if it were to further the Skverer community's goal of studying the Torah. In other words, for some Hasidics, the end justifies the means when the end goal is furthering their religious studies. Helmreich observed that communal lying and stealing "can become justifiable - because they have decided that if it raises money so they can study Torah, then it's OK to try and get as much as they can."[36]

Commenting in a different but similar matter of the devoutly religious breaking the law, Orthodox rabbi Irving Greenberg said, "In the Orthodox community there is too much closing ranks and a 'no one rock the boat' mentality." Greenberg, president of the Jewish Institute for Learning and Leadership, observed, "There is authoritarian leadership, and dissent is not tolerated. Criticism is seen as disloyalty."[37]

In addition, abuse of tuition aid programs by yeshivas was not an unusual phenomenon. According to a Government Accounting Office report, New York City yeshiva operators were adept at abusing the Pell Grant program.[38] In 1993, the GAO investigated twenty-three New York City area yeshivas and found every one of them had used false documentation to support ineligible Pell Grant applications. This included the use of "ghost" students, ineligible high school students, biographical information belonging to individuals without their knowledge, and misrepresentation of academic eligibility criteria.

New Square had long been a fortunate recipient of government largesse in the form of rent subsidies. The *New York Daily News* reported that New Square received $4.1 million in Section 8 housing subsidies in 2001. An average monthly subsidy of $785 went to 435 of the community's 550 households. According *Daily News* analysis, the average subsidy was more than the average monthly rent suggesting "taxpayers may be covering the full rent for nearly every village resident."[39]

During three years of a grand jury probe, New Square leaders refused to cooperate with authorities. Administrators of the Yeshiva of New Square, one recipient of the illegal loans and grants, defied subpoenas and refused to turn over financial records to federal authorities. Investigators wanted to examine the yeshiva's records because many schools and congregations that were associated with the Yeshiva of New Square school system had been implicated in the swindle. These included the Congregation B'nai Yacov Bardichov,

Congregation Chasdei David, Congregation Chasdei Yoinah, Gruss Girls School, Kolel Avrechim of New Square, Mosdos Square and Toldos Yakov Yosef.

Yeshiva of New Square accrued $3.2 million in federal contempt of court fines levied by US District Court Judge Leonard B. Sand over the course of one year by refusing to comply with subpoenas.[40] In December 1995, Judge Sand appointed New York attorney Melvin Stein as a federal receiver. Stein seized yeshiva property to serve as collateral to force the seminary to pay its fines. Stein appointed Rabbi Eliyahu Safran, an Orthodox Jew, to administer the business operations of the Yeshiva during the receivership.

During a visit to the school, Safran was confronted by several yeshiva rabbis, and they pressured him to turn over the remaining funds in the school's bank account. He complied.[41]

Once the bank account was empty, New Square authorities abruptly shut down Yeshiva of New Square, Inc. in January 1996 and reopened the school system under a new name, Yeshiva Avir Yaakov, with a different set of school directors. Rather than pursue the organizational sleight of hand, the federal government instead reached an arrangement with New Square leaders. The village paid less than one million dollars toward its $3.2 million fine and the federal receiver returned the seized collateral. Authorities left the new school alone.

During the same timeframe, federal investigators were threatened whenever they visited the community and a pair of Internal Revenue Service agents made a frantic call for police assistance after they were threatened by residents.[42] When FBI agents attempted to deliver subpoenas, a truck with a mounted loudspeaker trailed them, urging residents not to open their doors.[43] At the behest of New Square leaders, rabbis in Israel issued edicts ordering the residents of New Square to refuse to cooperate with investigators. This action allowed New Square officials to avoid federal obstruction of justice charges.

New Square community leaders were critical of US authorities after the six men were indicted on May 28, 1997. Leaders attempted to play the religious victim card in a released statement claiming that indictments were delivered "in a manner remindful of the Holocaust that many in this community endured decades ago."[44] That reference was to Chaim Berger, a Hungarian immigrant and Holocaust survivor and a mastermind behind the swindle. "[Prosecutors] have imposed a reign of terror on this entire community," claimed New Square spokesman Rabbi Mayer Schiller.[45]

Community leaders claimed the federal government had a "vendetta" against New Square without elaborating on their allegation other than to say it was because they were Hasidic Jews.[46] This was a totally absurd claim considering their indictments occurred in the most heavily Jewish city in the world.

THE CONVICTIONS

Benjamin Berger, Elbaum, Goldstein, and Stern appeared in court on June 5, 1997, in order to enter pleas in their cases. Chaim Berger, Friesel, and Adler went on the run. Accompanied by his wife, Berger fled to Israel, which offered him safe refuge. It was generally believed that both Friesel and Adler also sought refuge in Israel. Friesel left behind a wife and seventeen children.

After a nearly three-month trial that began in late 1998, Benjamin Berger, Jacob Elbaum, David Goldstein, and Kalmen Stern were convicted on January 25, 1999, on twenty-one counts including conspiracy, embezzlement, and wire and mail fraud. US District Court Judge Barbara Jones described the swindle as "sophisticated, long term and brazen in its execution."

In October 1999, Kalmen Stern, a leading figure in the swindle, was sentenced to seventy-eight months in prison; David Goldstein of Brooklyn received seventy months; Jacob Elbaum was given fifty-seven months; and Benjamin Berger received a sentence of thirty months. All four received considerably less than the maximum sentence allowed and collectively, they received sentences that fell short of the sentencing guidelines of five to twenty years.

The four were also ordered to pay the government 10 percent of their monthly salaries after their release from prison toward repaying the millions of dollars they stole. Stern owed the government $11.2 million, Elbaum, $11.1 million; Goldstein, $10.1 million; and Berger, $523,000.[47] In 2000, their convictions and sentences were upheld by the US Court of Appeals for the Second Circuit prompting New Square officials to seek executive clemency through Hillary Clinton in return for votes for her Senate candidacy.

THE FUGITIVE MASTERMIND

New Square founder Chaim Berger was a jeweler who emigrated to the US from Hungary, where he had escaped the Holocaust. He had settled in the Williamsburg area of Brooklyn and practiced Skverer Hasidism. At the time, the Skverer Grand Rabbi was Jacob Joseph Twersky, whose son David would later assume his spiritual leadership position.

Grand Rabbi Jacob Twersky inspired Berger and a handful of others to move from Brooklyn and start a closed Jewish community that could separate them from the evils of American society. In 1957, Berger cofounded New Square. The village incorporated in 1961, becoming the first Jewish incorporated community in America.

Berger became a powerful elder in New Square. He served as a village trustee and he served on the community's public housing board of directors. He would later become the chairman of the board of the phony Toldos Yakov Yosef seminary in Brooklyn.

Berger sought refuge in Israel after he fled when the indictments were handed down in 1997. The US sought his extradition, but Israel granted Berger citizenship, making him immune to extradition. Responding to US requests, Berger was placed into custody by Israeli authorities in February 1999 pending the outcome of US insistence he be extradited. He was released from custody the following month after New Square officials raised money to post a $3.5 million bail.

Then in April 1999, Israel enacted a new law that allowed Israeli citizens to be extradited for crimes committed in other countries. Before Berger could be extradited to the United States, however, the Israeli Parliament considered legislation that would exempt fugitives aged seventy and older from being extradited. Berger was seventy-four years old at the time. The legislation, written specifically to protect Berger, became known in Israel as the "Berger Bill."

The bill was passed in committee but failed to win passage in the full Knesset. Critics cried hypocrisy and warned that a similar law on the books in other countries would prevent the extradition of Nazi war criminals.[48]

Berger's efforts to fight extradition to the US were far from over. He appealed to the Israeli Supreme Court, arguing that as an Israel citizen he should be permitted to serve his sentence in Israel rather than in the US. At the same time, New Square spokesman Rabbi Mayer Schiller went on the offensive and accused the US of perpetuating "human suffering" by pursuing "a 75-year-old Holocaust survivor."[49] Schiller neglected to mention that Berger was the mastermind behind a more than $44 million swindle of US taxpayer money.

Berger lost his Israeli Supreme Court appeal in August 2001 by a narrow four-to-three ruling and he was ordered sent to the US for trial.[50] He was finally extradited to the US in November 2001.

The evidence against Chaim Berger was overwhelming. In January 2002, he admitted in a US courtroom in Manhattan that over several years, he and his accomplices repeatedly defrauded federal and state grant, loan, and aid programs for tens of millions of dollars for their personal gain, for the financial benefit of relatives, and to benefit specific entities in the New Square community. He also admitted to concealing his income from the Internal Revenue Service.

Berger pleaded guilty to conspiracy and mail fraud charges and was sentenced in May 2002 to six years in prison and was ordered to pay 10 percent of his earnings after his release from prison[51] toward $11.65 million in restitution for stealing more than $44 million in federal aid money.[52] During his sentencing, US District Court Judge Barbara Jones noted that Berger "was responsible in this case for a meticulously planned, complex and massive fraud on the government over 15 years."[53]

During sentencing, Judge Jones responded to Berger's call for leniency offering the justification that he did not spend the money on a lavish lifestyle. Jones replied, "The notion that Chaim Berger did not benefit himself or his family is also not true. There is no possible justification for...[the decision] to defraud the United States so he could spend millions of dollars his way, achieve his goals and his chosen lifestyle."[54]

Suffering from cancer, Berger was sent to the Federal Medical Center prison in Butner, NC to serve out his sentence in the prison hospital. Chaim Berger died in March 2004 before he repaid any of the stolen money.

THE COMMUTATIONS

US Attorney for the Southern District of New York Mary Jo White was notified by the White House only days before Bill Clinton was going to commute the sentences of Benjamin Berger, Jacob Elbaum, David Goldstein, and Kalmen Stern. White was given just one day to submit an input. Not surprisingly, she recommended against Clinton granting them clemency. It was the Manhattan US attorney's office that had been involved in the case since it was first investigated right up until the four convicts' failed appeals court bid of the previous year.

Neither US District Court Judge Barbara Jones nor were any prison officials asked for their recommendations in the clemency request, in accordance with US Department of Justice guidelines. Bill Clinton did not consider any victim impact statements. Ultimately, the victims of the swindle were the US taxpayer and the thousands of eligible students who did not receive Pell Grants and other educational aid, the small businesses that went without low-interest loans, and low-income families who did not receive rent subsidies because the money instead ended up the pockets of the New Square con men and their accomplices and associates.

Other victims of the swindle included the Department of Education, Department of Housing and Urban Development, the Social Security Administration, the Internal Revenue Service, and the Small Business Administration. It was their grant, loan, and aid money that was obtained by fraudulent means.

One can only imagine how unsuccessful the executive clemency request would have been had New Square residents followed the pattern of every other Orthodox and Hasidic community in New York and instead voted for Rick Lazio.

CHAPTER 12

The Billionaire Fugitive

"Some of the former aides who are loyal to the former president said they are upset with the former first lady, believing the decision to accept such a large number of lavish gifts— apparently to help furnish two new homes—bore Hillary Clinton's imprint, as did some of the pardons that went to politically well-connected New Yorkers." [1]

FOR NEARLY FIFTY years, Marc Rich traded with dictatorships, rogue nations, and terrorist states. Rich and his business enterprises struck up financial deals with Fidel Castro when a US embargo was in effect;[2] with Ayatollah Ruhollah Khomeini while fifty-two Americans were being held hostage;[3] with Colonel Muammar Qadhafi when Libya was a state sponsor of terrorism, including the bombing of Pan Am flight 103 that killed 189 Americans and eighty-one others;[4] with the hermit kingdom of North Korea;[5] and with Iraq's Saddam Hussein when United Nations sanctions were in place.[6]

Rich became a trading partner of South Africa during the apartheid era;[7] of Angola when under the rule of Cuban-advised dictators;[8] of Romania when Nicolae Ceausescu was plundering the country;[9] of Serbia when its leaders were practicing genocide against Bosnian men, women and children;[10] and of the Russian mafia.[11] Rich sold grain to the Soviet Union in violation of an American embargo.[12] Some of Rich's associates have been implicated in scandals in Venezuela and Nigeria.[13] It appears Rich would not pass up a single deal, no matter how reprehensible the trading partner, if it meant he could profit from it.

In addition, Rich was reportedly involved with the corrupt Bank of Credit and Commerce International (BCCI). Federal regulators and government investigators found that BCCI was involved in money laundering, bribery and terrorism. BCCI was formed "to commit fraud on a massive scale"[14] and its activities included the financing of sales in "nuclear weapons, gun running, [and] narcotics dealing."[15] When the fraud was uncovered, BCCI became the biggest banking scandal of all time.

Rich was also tied to the Russian Grigori Loutchansky, whom US authorities had been watching due to his ties to Russian organized crime.[16] Loutchansky "[had] been accused of drug trafficking and smuggling nuclear materials."[17] Loutchansky was known for his role in the questionable and highly suspect sell-off of Russian commodities in the early days after the fall of the Soviet Union.[18] According to the CIA, Loutchansky was suspected of plotting to launder $10 billion through the Bank of New York.[19] Rich was also implicated.[20]

Incidentally, Loutchansky was also a Clinton acquaintance, having attended a political fundraiser for the president in 1993. He missed out in attending a $25,000 dinner in honor of Clinton in 1995 when the State Department refused to issue him a visa due to his ties to organized crime.[21]

In addition to dealing with dictators, thugs, and criminals, Rich was known to engage in his own despicable practices. A standard business tactic for Rich was to bribe government officials and commodities executives with money,[22] drugs,[23] and prostitutes.[24] One of his former traders said, "[a senior Rich executive] once told me to take a lot of petty cash out to take some of our South American customers out for whores. It made me sick. I came back the following morning and told my boss that I would never do that again. I knew right there that my career was over at Marc Rich."[25] There was no low to which Marc Rich would not stoop in order to make money.

According to US Marshal Howard Safir, who attempted to serve an arrest warrant on Rich, "He sees himself as a citizen of the world, unencumbered by the laws of sovereign nations. His view is that everything and everyone can be bought and sold, and government is irrelevant."[26] Rich was just as successful in securing a pardon from Clinton as he had been in bribing third world government officials to complete illegal commodities trades. Clinton was as easily manipulated as a small nation despot when he rewarded Rich with an unconditional pardon.

Then there was the not-so-minor issue of Rich owing the city of New York and New York state $137 million in back taxes, penalties, and fees.[27] Rich left damage in his wake no matter where he traveled and what he did.

Five days after Clinton pardoned Rich, he was at it again. Marc Rich + Co. Investment A.G. was buying oil from worldwide pariah Saddam Hussein as part of the corrupt Oil-for-Food program.[28] Marc Rich + Co. directed its French bank to not disclose the company's identity to US authorities.[29] According to the Independent Inquiry Committee into the United Nations Oil-for-Food Programme (the "Volcker Commission"), Marc Rich + Co. paid nearly one million dollars to Saddam in illegal surcharges.[30]

Congressional investigators learned that "Saddam paid $25,000 rewards to the families of Palestinian suicide bombers…[from the] kickback money Saddam demanded from suppliers to his regime."[31] Saddam was generous when it came to his rewarding the relatives of those who killed Jews. According to Palestinian sources, Saddam paid in excess of $35 million to the families of suicide bombers.[32] Investigators into Saddam's activities believe that money from the kickbacks and surcharges that were routinely paid to Saddam as a precondition for executing oil deals with Iraq may have been funding the post-Iraq war insurgency.[33]

Marc Rich became one of the FBI's Top Ten Most Wanted international fugitives in 1983 when he and business partner Pincus Green fled the United States and sought refuge abroad. Rich and Green were facing a fifty-one-count federal indictment for tax evasion and other crimes, including trading with the enemy that could have led to a maximum sentence of 325 years in prison. The indictment resulted from an extensive two-year investigation into the operations of Rich, Green, and their companies by the US attorney for the southern district of New York. At the center of Rich's activities was an elaborate scheme by which his companies fraudulently sold oil that came under price controls. By implementing this scheme, Rich evaded paying at least $48 million in federal taxes, making him the biggest tax cheat in US history.

Rich participated in a scheme known as "daisy chaining," in which oil that came under the price controls that were in effect during the 1970s and early 1980s was fraudulently relabeled and resold, sometimes several times and on occasion between the same two parties, outside of the price controls mechanism reaping huge profits.[34] As many as four hundred million barrels of oil may have been sold under the "daisy chaining" scam between 1973 and 1981.[35] The illegal profits from the deals were deposited in offshore accounts "using sham invoices and Panamanian front companies"[36] in order to avoid paying taxes.[37]

Eventually, the US Justice Department became involved. The Department of Energy raised the alarm when it could not account for two hundred thousand barrels of price-controlled oil each day that had "vanished" somewhere between the wellhead and the refinery.[38] It was clear the price-controlled oil was being resold outside of the price control regime. In addition, someone was not paying the US government for the taxes on the illicit profits.

Morris "Sandy" Weinberg Jr., a US attorney, was assigned as the lead prosecutor in the Rich fraud case in mid-1981. Weinberg subpoenaed over four dozen witnesses and two hundred thousand pages of documents during the initial phase of his investigation.

Rich and Green were uncooperative. They had been immensely successful in bribing third world government officials in order to achieve their goals and their attitude toward Weinberg's investigation was no different. The pair thought they could negotiate, barter, or buy their way out of any serious legal difficulties.[39]

During the first year and a half of the investigation, Rich hired a battery of high-priced lawyers to argue point after point, thus delaying Weinberg. Rich refused to comply with subpoenas to produce more than one million pages of documents and financial records. His lawyers argued that turning over company records during the course of the investigation amounted to industrial espionage. The US District Court judge overseeing the case ruled otherwise.

Rich lost an appeal to the Second Circuit Court of Appeals as it affirmed the district court judges' ruling. Rich appealed to the US Supreme Court, which refused to hear the case. The lower court ruling stood. Still, Rich refused to comply with the court order to turn over his documents so, the judge found his company in contempt of court and fined it $50,000 a day—a mere pittance compared with the amount of money Rich's company allegedly hid from the Internal Revenue Service. In fact, Rich's company paid approximately $21 million in contempt fines throughout the course of Weinberg's investigation rather than produce the subpoenaed documents. This underscores the sheer magnitude of Rich's illegal profits if he was willing to allow his company to spend $21 million to conceal his ill-gotten gains.

Rich's international headquarters of his American company was located in Switzerland. When his company was presented with the subpoenas for the critical documents, a Swiss prosecutor allegedly had the documents seized. The Swiss prosecutor claimed that Rich company papers stored in Zug, Switzerland, were protected under that country's trade secrets laws. It did not appear bothersome to Swiss officials that the prosecutor, Rudolf Moismann, who ordered the seizure of Rich's documents and who made the trade secrets claim was also on Rich's payroll. Moismann was a director of the Swiss-based company Marc Rich A.G.[40]

Rich was refusing to cooperate in the investigation; fortunately, prosecutors received a lucky break. Acting on a tip in August 1983, federal agents boarded a jetliner at John F. Kennedy International Airport and seized a Rich paralegal and two steamer trunks loaded with documents that had been subpoenaed by Weinberg, but instead were en route to Switzerland. Rich and Green had fled to Switzerland a few weeks earlier.[41] Rich's attorneys were offered the opportunity to refute the counts that were under consideration by the grand jury, but instead Rich and Green chose to flee the country.

The following month in September 1983, Weinberg released a fifty-one-count indictment against Marc Rich, Pincus Green, Clyde Meltzer (who managed the details of the oil fraud scheme), Marc Rich + Co., A.G., and Marc Rich + Co., International, Ltd. The charges included tax evasion, mail fraud, wire fraud, racketeering and conspiracy.[42] Unfortunately for prosecutors, Rich and Green were safely ensconced in their luxurious villas outside Zug, Switzerland where Mayor Othmar Kamer said that Rich was one of "six large tax contributors who influence our financial budget."[43] The Swiss were not about to honor a US extradition request. Similarly, Israel refused to extradite Rich, allowing him to freely travel to and from that country.[44]

According to the indictment, Rich had concealed $71 million in illegal profits. Weinberg later amended his indictment of Rich and his cronies by tacking on an additional fourteen counts. The new counts included charges of wire fraud and mail fraud as part of the defendants' efforts to defraud the IRS and Department of Energy. The new charges arose from investigations that continued after Rich and Green became fugitives from justice.

The charges against Rich and Green also included their trading with Iran when it was illegal to do so. Muslim radicals stormed the

US Embassy in Tehran in early November 1979 and captured sixty-three American diplomats and staff. Several hostages were released, but fifty-two Americans were held for more than fourteen months. Shortly after the hostage taking, President Jimmy Carter issued Executive Order #12205, which imposed a trade embargo against Iran, and Executive Order #12211 that prohibited the payment or transfer of funds to Iran. The Department of Treasury issued regulations governing the embargo.

The embargo did not stop Rich from seeking to profit from Iran's newfound pariah status. Marc Rich + Co., A.G. entered into a contract with the radicals that were in charge of the Iranian government to purchase crude and fuel oil from the National Iranian Oil Company. The first deal was the purchase and subsequent resale of more than $200 million of Iranian oil in spite of the embargo. Rich's company concealed the identity of the recipient of the oil payments from the US banks involved in the deal in order to keep the banks from reporting Rich's activities.

Rich's illegal deals with Iran provided much-needed cash during the early days of the Iranian revolution. Rich was a de facto financial backer of a country that was to become a major state sponsor of worldwide terrorism and one of the most destabilizing influences in the Middle East over the next three decades.

Sanctions busting was business as usual for Rich. In the 1980s, he was the middleman that provided hard currency to the Soviet Union by purchasing its oil and reselling it to South Africa when the apartheid nation was under international sanctions. He laundered the sales transactions through several companies based in locations such as Monaco, Liechtenstein and the Cayman Islands.[45]

Rich also negotiated a weapons deal with North Korea to purchase gyroscopes for resale to Iran to outfit their antiaircraft missile systems.[46]

The evidence against the defendants in Weinberg's indictment was overwhelming.

Because the case against them was so strong, the two corporate entities, Marc Rich + Co. A.G., and Marc Rich + Co. and International, Ltd, and fellow defendant Clyde Meltzer pleaded guilty to the charges in the indictment. In an October 1984 court proceeding, US attorney for the southern district of New York, Rudolph Guiliani, offered a settlement in the case. A.G. pleaded guilty to forty counts and International pleaded guilty to thirty-eight counts, and the two companies agreed to collectively pay $200 million in back taxes and penalties to the US government in order to settle the case.

During the court hearing, Peter Fleming, the attorney representing International, admitted Rich's company "generated millions of dollars of income from crude oil transactions which International should have disclosed but intentionally did not disclose to the Internal Revenue Service and the Department of Energy." Meltzer pleaded guilty to filing false invoices regarding oil sales, with approximately $50 million in illegal profits having been transferred to Marc Rich's offices in Switzerland.

Guiliani informed the judge that the $200 million settlement "constitute[d] the largest amount of money ever recovered by the United States in a criminal income tax evasion." While the criminal indictments against Meltzer and Rich's two companies had come to an end, the case continued against Rich and Green as the pair remained fugitives from justice.

On September 3, 1982, a year before he was indicted and in a possible effort to avoid extradition should the need have arisen, Rich secretly renounced his US citizenship. US officials later learned of the renunciation after Rich became a fugitive from justice. The US State Department refused to accept his renunciation. Yet, in an October 1992 letter to the US Consulate in Zurich, Switzerland, Rich pressed his claim that he was no longer under US law, writing, "I had expatriated myself and that I am not—nor do I have any wish to be—a US citizen."[47] Rich also gained Israeli citizenship in the 1990s.[48] Rich's accomplice, Green, similarly attempted to renounce his US citizenship when he became a naturalized citizen of Bolivia in May 1983 and he surrendered his US passport to Bolivian authorities.[49]

According to Rich, he did no wrong. He was indicted, he claimed, because "I was successful, [and] I was Jewish."[50] The absurdity of Rich's claim that he was persecuted because he was a Jew cannot be overstated. Rich was prosecuted by Morris Weinberg, also a Jew, who was working as a US attorney in the most heavily Jewish city in the world. There is probably no safer place in the world to be a Jew than in New York City. Rich was playing the anti-Semitism card in an effort to garner sympathy and support. His second wife, Gisela Rich, offered a different defense, claiming her husband was the victim of a media conspiracy.[51] Rich had carried on an affair with Gisela that contributed to the breakup of his first marriage.[52]

Rich launched a determined battle to get a full pardon during the waning days of the Clinton presidency. In July 1999, Rich retained the services of lawyers Jack Quinn and Kathleen Behan from the Manhattan law firm of Arnold & Porter at a minimum retainer in the amount of $55,000 per month "in connection with Mr. Rich's potential negotiations and/or communications with the Department of Justice."[53]

Quinn had previously served as White House counsel in the Clinton administration and his lobbying for Rich's pardon was in direct violation of Executive Order #12834 issued by Clinton on January 20, 1993. Executive Order #12834 prohibited senior White House employees from lobbying the White House for a period of five years after leaving the administration. Quinn had left Clinton's staff only three years earlier. Not surprisingly, Clinton rescinded his executive order only days before he left office.[54]

Emails, text messages, correspondence, contemporaneous, and extemporaneous note-taking, and sworn testimony of activities during the period of time Quinn lobbied Bill Clinton revealed a dramatic and egregious departure from the established pardon process. Neither Marc Rich nor Pincus Green met any of the pardon guidelines as set by the Department of Justice.[55] Nonetheless, Bill Clinton gave Rich and Green full and unconditional pardons on January 20, 2001.

First, a pardon connotes forgiveness for the commission of a federal crime. Yet both Rich and Green refused to admit any responsibility, but instead they "demonstrate[d] an utter lack of remorse and/or contrition"[56] for their crimes. Second, a five-year waiting period must have elapsed following the completion of a sentence before the petitioner becomes eligible for a pardon. As fugitives from justice, Rich and Green never served a single day of punishment for their crimes.

During the same time Rich was seeking a pardon, the US pardon attorney informed the attorney for petitioner Fernando Fuentes Coba that Coba was not eligible for a pardon because he was a fugitive from justice. Pardon Attorney Roger C. Adams wrote, "Because Mr. Coba has served none of his prison sentence, he fails to meet this most basic eligibility requirement for pardon consideration."[57] In his prepared February 2001 testimony before the US Senate Committee on the Judiciary, Adams emphasized this point. "A person who has not yet been convicted or has not fully served the sentence for the federal crime for which a pardon is sought is ineligible for pardon under the regulations that guide the Department of Justices' processing of pardon requests."[58]

Third, inputs are to be requested from the prosecuting attorney. In the Rich case, it would have been the US attorney for the southern district of New York who should have offered a recommendation in the Rich and Green pardon requests. Neither the incumbent prosecutor Mary Jo White nor Rudolph Guiliani, who originally prosecuted the case, were asked for inputs; moreover, Deputy US Attorney General Eric Holder failed to fulfill the most basic tenets of the Justice Department's pardon guidelines. Holder withheld from

US Attorney White information that pardons were being considered for Rich and Green.

Fourth, the sentencing judge should be asked for a recommendation. As was the case with the US attorney for the southern district of New York, US District Judges Leonard B. Sand and Shirley W. Kram, who presided over the case, were not notified that Clinton was considering giving executive clemency to Rich and Green.

The fifth guideline is to seek the input of the victim. In this case, it would have been the Internal Revenue Service as the federal agency that did not receive the proper tax payments. The IRS was never consulted.

According to protocol, pardon petitioners are to have demonstrated they have not broken the law since their crime[s] for which they are seeking a pardon. Also, they must prove they are of good character and are deserving of the official act of forgiveness. Rich was anything but a man of good character. After his 1983 indictment, he escalated his practice of "deal-making and sanctions-breaking"[59] with rogue nations and in "hiding profits in a thicket of offshore companies."[60]

Rich traded with Libya in violation of US law when sanctions were in place following the Pan Am airline bombing over Lockerbie, Scotland, in December 1988 that killed 189 Americans and eighty-one others.

According to an executive with the Egyptian company INCOME, "Marc Rich has been INCOME's 'agent' [oil trader] since 1990."[61] INCOME was conducting oil deals with Iraq even though trade sanctions had been in place against Iraq following that country's unprovoked invasion of Kuwait in 1990.

Illicit deals also occurred between Rich and other bad actor countries such as Iran, Serbia, Romania, Angola, and with Russian organized crime between the time Rich fled from justice and when Clinton gave him a pardon. Rich was also a major trading partner of the Soviet Union during the height of the Cold War. Rich had betrayed the country that "had sheltered him in 1942, as the child of a Belgian Jewish family that had fled Europe amid the Nazi onslaught."[62]

The pardon attorney, Roger Adams, who had the primary responsibility of vetting clemency requests first received notification that Clinton was considering pardons for Rich and Green just after midnight during the early morning hours of January 20, 2001, the day the pardons were issued. Adams' office was able to conduct only the most cursory investigation of Rich and Green, consisting of a simple internet search. A brief communication with the FBI revealed that Rich and Green were wanted fugitives for a variety of charges including arms trading, tax evasion, and mail and wire fraud.

Adams was not aware of the clemency petitions from Rich and Green because Holder, the number two official in the Department of Justice, had secretly urged Quinn to deal directly with Clinton and to cut the Justice Department's pardon attorney out the process.

After the midnight pardons were announced, a public outcry erupted. Critics assailed several of the last-minute pardons, noting that Rich and Green were wanted fugitives. New York City Mayor Rudolph Guiliani, who was the US attorney that pursued Rich and Green before they fled the country, was attending Bush's inauguration on January 20 when he received the news of the pardons. Certain what he was told was incorrect, Guiliani asked an aide to verify his information. When the aide confirmed that Clinton pardoned Rich, a stunned Guiliani said, "[I]mpossible, the president would never pardon a fugitive, especially Marc Rich."[63]

Two days after leaving office, Clinton defended his pardons of Rich and Green to reporters outside a Chappaqua, New York deli. Clinton said, "You're not saying people didn't commit the offense, you're saying they've paid—they've paid in full—and they've been out enough after their sentence to show they're good citizens."[64] Yet nothing could be further from the truth. Rich and Green had not faced their accusers, let alone paid for their crimes. Their conduct was disgraceful and atrocious; however, Clinton's pardoning of them was even worse.

After completing personal identifying information such as name, address, age, height, weight, and so forth, the first question on the Justice Department's pardon petition application is "Are you a United States citizen?" Clinton pardoned two men who renounced their US citizenship, and, in the case of Rich, he made it clear he "[did not] have any wish to be…a US citizen."[65]

Clinton had no problem pardoning the billionaire Rich, who was no longer a US citizen who was living abroad. In contrast, Clinton denied a pardon request to Michael Bransome. In 1969, when he was eighteen years old, Bransome vandalized a Silver Spring, Maryland draft board office. While on furlough, he fled the country and eventually settled in Sweden where he married, raised a family and became a doctor.[66]

In his 2000 pardon request to Clinton, Bransome wrote, "With your help, I can follow your entreaty to come home and offer my hands 'to help bind the wounds, to heal and to build.'…Please, Mr. President, please bring me home."[67] Clinton turned down Bransome's pardon request. A State Department spokesman stated that Bransome's pardon request was unacceptable because he was living out of the country. Yet Clinton pardoned the nonresident, *noncitizen billionaire* Marc Rich.

Clinton wrote in his autobiography *My Life* that he turned down one pardon applicant's request because he "had not been out of jail for the usual period [of time] before being considered for a pardon."[68] Yet Clinton pardoned Rich who not only "had not been out of jail for the usual period," but had *not* even served *any time*. Moreover, Rich refused to accept any responsibility for his crimes.

The evidence against Rich and Green was overwhelming. They should never have been pardoned. No doubt there are more, better-suited candidates worthy of a pardon besides a billionaire living a lavish lifestyle while on the lam in Switzerland.

One only has to follow the money to understand why Clinton pardoned Rich. Marc Rich's ex-wife Denise Rich made numerous personal pleas to Clinton to pardon her ex-husband.

Denise was more than just another socialite supporter of Bill and Hillary Clinton. She was a frequent guest at the White House,[69] having visited the White House on nineteen occasions, including sleepovers in the Lincoln Bedroom[70] and Clinton visited the attractive, multimillionaire divorcee in her Manhattan penthouse.[71] She was also a major fundraiser for the Clintons, including for Hillary's 2000 Senate race, the Clinton Library, Bill and Hillary's defense fund, and the Democratic Party. In addition, Denise Rich showered the Clintons with gifts as they were leaving the White House.

Denise Rich, who was responsible for $3 million in fundraising lunches and personal donations,[72] personally gave more than $1 million to Democratic causes[73] including $450,000 to the Clinton library,[74] $120,000 to Hillary Clinton's Senate campaign,[75] $40,000 to underwrite the entertainment at Hillary's October 2000 birthday bash,[76] $10,000 to the Clintons' legal defense fund,[77] and $7,375 in gifts to Hillary.[78]

In mid-1998, Rich held a hush-hush soft money fundraiser for the Democratic National Committee featuring Bill and Hillary Clinton as the special guests. The event was held in Rich's very exclusive Fifth Avenue penthouse apartment and the price of admission was $100,000 per couple. The event was limited to a mere one hundred attendees.[79]

In a December 6, 2000, letter drafted by Rich's attorneys,[80] Denise Rich pleaded for Clinton to pardon her ex-husband who she falsely claimed had been in "exile." Marc Rich had not been exiled (that is, banished) from the United States. Instead, he fled America to avoid standing trial. His ex-wife characterized his flight from justice in softer terms by writing, "he had no choice but remain out of the country." Rich claimed her former husband was incapable of ever having a fair trial in the US and that for that reason, he chose to not return.

Rich's legal team crafted yet another letter, purportedly written by Denise Rich from the heart, that she was to personally deliver to the president. She accomplished this at a White House holiday dinner party when she "buttonholed Mr. Clinton about the pardon at a White House party on Dec. 20 after wresting him away from Barbra Streisand."[81]

Those aware of Denise Rich's longtime bitter feelings toward her ex-husband after their nasty 1996 divorce may have been surprised by her sudden change of heart toward him when it came to her supporting the pardon request. The change of heart may have been driven by a pledge from Marc Rich and Pincus Green to contribute $1 million each year to her G&P Charitable Foundation for Cancer Research. Her ex-husband had not previously contributed to the foundation.[82] The G&P Charitable Foundation was in honor of her daughter Gabrielle, who died of leukemia, and Denise Rich was very serious about supporting it.[83]

Attorney Jack Quinn personally delivered Rich's pardon application to the White House in early December 2000. In an accompanying letter addressed to Clinton, Quinn claimed "that a grave injustice has been done that can only be rectified by you through an act of Executive Clemency." Quinn argued that a fair trial for Rich would be "highly unlikely" and that "a pardon in the interests of justice is a reasonable end to all of this."

In a subsequent letter to White House Counsel Bruce Lindsey, Quinn made the preposterous claim that Rich and Green were not fugitives. The pair simply "chose not to return to the US for a trial," wrote Quinn. However, Denise Rich undermined Quinn's assertion by what she told television interviewer Barbara Walters. Denise Rich reported that Marc Rich fled the country to avoid being prosecuted.

She claims he said to her, "I'm having tax problems with the government. And—and I think that we are going to have to leave."[84]

In a second letter to Clinton dated January 5, 2001, Quinn made the mutually exclusive argument that the case against Rich was shaky, yet a fair trial for him was "impossible." How can an attorney argue that criminal charges are "meritless," yet his client has no possible way of being exonerated? It makes no sense.

The fact of the matter was the charges did have merit. If Rich and Green believed they had acted within the law, as they asserted, then they would never have illegally relabeled oil shipments, sold and resold oil several times between the same two parties, created false documents, established Panamanian front companies, and maintained off-the-record bookkeeping practices. These are not the actions of traders who believe they are practicing the normal course of business affairs.

In yet another letter to Clinton dated January 18, Quinn made a new offer to Clinton. According to Quinn, Rich and Green would "willingly accept a disposition that would subject them to civil proceedings" and that "they seek relief from criminal sanctions only." In other words, Rich and Green were willing to accept civil punishment (i.e., fines) for committing criminal acts.

In a fourth letter sent the following day, Quinn offered to Clinton that Rich and Green "waive any and all defenses which could be raised to the lawful imposition of civil fines or penalties" and they would waive the "statute of limitations." The offer of accepting responsibility for civil violations, according to Weinberg, was "an empty promise, because there is no individual civil liability for what this indictment was about."[85] Weinberg noted that it was the corporations that assumed a civil liability for breaking the law because corporations cannot be sent to jail.

Rich and Green's final offer to Clinton was they were each willing to accept a conditional pardon. Despite that meaningless offer, Clinton gave them each "a full and unconditional pardon."

The behind the scenes negotiations revealed a well-connected attorney and former Clinton White House counsel, Jack Quinn, teaming up with major Democratic and Clinton fundraisers supporting a billionaire fugitive who knew how to get favors in the form of support for his clemency request. Keeping the pardon request secret from the US pardon attorney, the lead prosecutor, the judge and, most importantly, the public aided their efforts immensely.

In late December 2000, Robert Fink, an attorney assisting Rich in his pardon request, emailed Quinn, "I think we benefit from not having the existence of the petition known, and do not want to contact people...who would create press or other exposure."

On December 27, Avner Azulay, a senior employee and confidante of Rich, suggested Quinn, and other attorneys, line up New York Senator Charles Schumer to support the pardon request. Azulay emailed, "I have been advised that HRC [Hillary Rodham Clinton] shall feel more at ease if she is joined by her elder senator of NY who also represents the Jewish population." Rich's public relations specialist Gershon Kekst suggested they pursue Schumer through his top campaign contributors, possibly to include Bernard L. Schwartz. Schwartz was one of the single largest campaign contributors to the Democratic Party in the 1990s and he was CEO of the Loral Corporation, which was selling prohibited missile technology to China.

In a January 10, 2001 email, Azulay informed Quinn that Beth Dozoretz "got a call from potus...and that he wants to do it [give Rich the pardon]." POTUS is shorthand for "President of the United States." A three-time divorcee who married into wealth with her fourth husband,[86] Dozoretz was a former finance chair for the Democratic National Committee who raised millions of dollars for the Democrat Party. She was a very close friend of Hillary.[87] Dozoretz gave $7,000 in gifts to the Clintons during that two-month window between the November 2000 election when Hillary was elected to the Senate and the January 2001 Senate swearing-in, at which time

Hillary would be prohibited from accepting such gifts.[88] Dozoretz had pledged to raise at least $1 million for the Clinton Library.

Dozoretz's promise of $1 million and Denise Rich's contribution for $450,000 were especially critical since the William J. Clinton Presidential Foundation had raised a paltry $3.1 million in 1999 toward the library's $200 million fundraising goal.[89] It is an understatement to say that Dozoretz had considerable influence with Clinton.

The outcry over the Rich and Green pardons finally led Clinton to write an op-ed for the *New York Times* defending his action. Clinton gave a litany of reasons for executive clemency, all of which did not apply to Rich and Green. Clinton wrote "a pardon or commutation is warranted for several reasons: the desire to restore full citizenship rights, including voting, to people who have served their sentences and lived within the law; a belief that a sentence was excessive or unjust, personal circumstances that warrant compassion; or other unique circumstances."[90]

Rich and Green both attempted to renounce their citizenship, so restoring voting rights was an absurd reason. The pair never served a single day of a sentence and they continued to flout US and international law including internationally recognized sanctions and embargoes.

The prospect of a guilty verdict and resulting sentence would not have been unjust as the other defendants in the criminal case quickly pleaded guilty. The argument that no one had been prosecuted for the same crimes since the Rich and Green case was specious because, as noted by Weinberg, "Back in 1980, we didn't have a money laundering statute that would have covered these offenses. We do now."[91] Years later, Rich and Green would have been prosecuted under a completely different statute. The case in the 1980s was so solid that attorneys representing Rich's two companies pleaded guilty to a combined seventy-eight counts *and* they paid a $200 million settlement. These are hardly the actions of the wrongly accused.

Clinton later tried to make the case in his 2004 memoir *My Life* that Rich "had not owed any taxes"[92] because the government erred in computing the taxes. Clinton further claimed that the "Justice Department ordered US attorneys to stop doing it."[93] That is, that in the future no one should be prosecuted under the same statutes as Rich because the statutes did not really apply. If all of the foregoing was correct, then Rich could have simply returned to the US and cleared his name. He did not. That is because Clinton's 2004 claims, just like his 2001 claims, were all lies.

What about compassion? It would be difficult, even for Clinton, to argue with a straight face that Rich needed compassion. He was a billionaire living in a luxurious villa in Meggen, Switzerland, with a ski chalet in nearby St. Moritz and a lavish estate in Spain. He traveled around the world by private executive jet trailed by body-guards and stayed in five-star resorts. He had the financial resources many times over to fly his children and grandchildren to visit him, should he have chosen to do so. Yet, the self-indulgent Rich did not even bother to visit his daughter Gabrielle in 1996 when she was dying from leukemia, nor did he attend her funeral. The argument that being a fugitive prevented him from seeing his immediate family was a lie. He simply put legal difficulties (that were of his own doing) ahead of sharing final moments with his dying daughter.

In his op-ed, Clinton also misrepresented several facts surrounding his decision to pardon the pair. He noted that companies indicted alongside Rich and Green had their cases disposed of as a civil rather than a criminal matter. Technically, Clinton was correct. That is because companies cannot be sent to jail. They settle legal matters by paying fines. Clinton also claimed that Deputy Attorney General Eric Holder was "neutral, leaning for," yet, the fact that the US pardon attorney—the designated expert authority on granting clemency—was intentionally cut out of the loop by the backdoor scheming of Holder should have set off alarms for Clinton.[94] After all, Clinton was a lawyer although he was barred from practicing law after losing his law license on January 19, 2001, for committing perjury.

Clinton lied to the *New York Times* readers that "three distinguished Republican attorneys" were actively involved and had "reviewed and advocated" the pardon application. This was a classic Clintonian fabrication. Although the attorneys he listed, Leonard Garment, William Bradford Reynolds, and I. Lewis Libby, had represented Rich in various matters, they were not participants in the Quinn-led pardon request. Clinton recycled this lie and used it again in *My Life*, implying that Libby was involved in Rich's pardon efforts. As observed in *Yediot Achronot*, Israel's largest daily newspaper, "Clinton has never been known as one for whom truth lights the way."[95]

One of the most troublesome Clinton claims was his final reason for granting the pardon: "importantly, many present and former high-ranking Israeli officials of both major political parties and leaders of Jewish communities in America and Europe urged the pardon of Mr. Rich." That statement rankled much of the Jewish community in the US, even though it was true that numerous influential Jews advocated for Rich's pardon. Among them were Abraham Foxman, head of the Anti-Defamation League; Rabbi Irving "Yitz" Greenberg, chair of the US Holocaust Memorial Council; Marlene Post, the former international president of Hadassah; and Nobel laureate Elie Wiesel.[96] Yet others were appalled at the pardons and Clinton's shifting the blame to the Jewish community.

As Jonathan S. Tobin wrote for the *Jewish Exponent*, "Clinton seemed to be telling the world, 'Don't blame me: The Jews made me do it.'"[97] In an editorial for the *Daily News*, Zev Chafets made a similar claim, "at least one Bill Clinton operative has been calling journalists with a message: The ex-President didn't really want to pardon Marc Rich. The Israelis or the Mossad or the Jews made him do it."[98]

Placing Jews and Israel at the center of the pardon controversy was unnerving. It also led to serious backpedaling by several
of Rich's prominent Jewish advocates. Greenberg and Post later
claimed they had mistakenly used organizational stationery when
they sent letters of support. Coincidentally, Rich pledged $5 million
to Birthright Israel, an organization headed by Post, but Post denies
Rich's generous contribution had any bearing on her support for his
pardon request.[99] Foxman admitted he made a mistake after it came
to light the ADL received a $100,000 contribution from Rich imme-
diately after Foxman became involved in Rich's pardon efforts.[100]

Rabbi Eric Yoffie, leader of the Reform Movement's Union of
American Hebrew Congregations, wrote a scathing op-ed addressing
the pardons. "The moral stain of this sordid affair has begun to
engulf us," he lamented.[101] Yoffie argued that certain prominent
Jewish leaders had been "bought" with large contributions.

Not all letters of support for Rich's pardon request that were
sent to Clinton were legitimate. Michael Schneider of the American
Jewish Joint Distribution Committee was "very surprised" to learn
that a thank you note the organization sent to the Rich Foundation
in response to a generous donation was included in the petition as
support for the pardon request.[102] Jonathan Halevy of the Shaare
Zedek Medical Center in Jerusalem also reported to having been
misled when he was asked to write a letter honoring Rich. He had no
idea it was to be included in Rich's pardon petition.[103]

The American Jewish Congress turned down a Rich overture to
speak favorably in support of Rich's pardon request in return for a
sizable contribution to the organization.[104] According to one report-
er's inquiries, only one of six letter writers contacted who were
among the fifty-two letters attached to the petition request knew that
their letters were going to be used for that purpose.[105] Only twenty-one of the seventy-three letters sent to the president in support of
Rich's pardon request actually contained language stating as such.[106]

Clinton's showstopper defense was that Israeli Prime Minister Ehud Barak had pressured him for Rich's pardon. That assertion unraveled when congressional investigators made public the verbatim transcripts of the three telephone calls Clinton had with the Israeli prime minister in which Marc Rich's clemency petition was discussed. Barak's support of Rich could be described as cautious, at best. The official White House transcript of verbatim remarks between Clinton and Barak regarding Marc Rich follows.

December 11, 2000.

Barak: One last remark. There is an American Jewish businessman living in Switzerland and making a lot of philanthropic contributions to Israeli institutions and activities like education, and he is a man called Mark [sic] Rich. He violated certain rules of the game in the United States and is living abroad. I just wanted to let you know that here he is highly appreciated for his support of so many philanthropic institutions and funds, and that if I can, I would like to make my recommendation to <u>consider</u> *his case. [emphasis added]*

January 8, 2001.

Barak: Let me tell you last but not least two names I want to mention. [Redacted]. The second is Mark [sic], the Jewish American.

Clinton: I know quite a few things about that. I just got a long memo and am working on it. It's best that we not say much about that.

Barak: Okay. I understand. I'm not mentioning it in any place.

Clinton: I understand.

Barak: I believe it could be more important [gap] not just financially, but he helped Mossad on more than one case.

Clinton: It is a bizarre case, and I am working on it.

Barak: Okay. I really appreciate it.

January 19, 2001.

Clinton: [Redacted] I'm trying to do something on clemency for Rich, but it is very difficult.

Barak: Might it move forward?

Clinton: I'm working on that but I'm not sure. I'm glad you asked me about that. When I finish these calls, I will go back into the meeting on that but I'm glad you raised it. Here's the only problem with Rich; there's almost no precedent. He was overseas when he was indicted and never came home. The question is not whether he should get it or not but whether he should get it without coming back here. That's the dilemma I'm working through. I'm working on it.

Barak: Okay.

It should be worrisome to anyone if Clinton truly believed the mild position of Barak in those telephone calls could be characterized as *pressuring* Clinton.

There certainly was a foreign policy component to the status of Marc Rich, and it had nothing to do with Israel. During congressional hearings that took place after the pardons were issued, the Central Intelligence Agency provided the following declassified summary to House investigators:

"If President Clinton had checked with the CIA, he would have learned that Marc Rich had been the subject of inquiries by various foreign government liaison services and domestics government agencies regarding their ongoing investigations of criminal activity."

By intentionally keeping the Rich pardon request secret and by excluding government agencies and offices outside of the White House from having any knowledge of the clemency deliberations,

Clinton limited the amount of accurate—yet derogatory—information regarding Rich and his activities.

Clinton's pardon of Marc Rich may have been the payback for the valuable financial support he and Hillary received from Rich's ex-wife, Denise Rich and the much-needed financial support the Clintons would get from Beth Dozoretz in the future. Or perhaps the payback would be heading the Clintons' way after he issued the pardons.

Bill Clinton preoccupied himself with a stunning schedule of overseas speaking engagements and trips abroad.[107] In her Senate ethics disclosures, Hillary Clinton reported her husband made $43 million from the various fees and honoraria he collected between 2001 and 2005. The financial windfall likely exceeded their wildest expectations.

What may never be known is what financial remuneration, if any, Clinton received that his wife never reported. It would have been easy for a bank account to be established in Clinton's name in a country such as Switzerland that has the kind of banking secrecy laws that would allow him to collect the funds without the Internal Revenue Service or the American public ever knowing.

Regardless of who was paying back whom, the reality is that Marc Rich and his partner Pincus Green never deserved presidential pardons.

CHAPTER 13

The Black Liberation Army

"I never believed in my heart he [Clinton] would do this. After [the federal office building attack in] Oklahoma, how could you pardon anybody who was caught in this country with weapons of mass destruction?"
—Diane O'Grady, widow of Edward O'Grady Sr.[1]

MAY 23 WAS the perfect spring day. There was not a cloud in the sky. Twenty thousand guests sat in Navy-Marine Corps Memorial Stadium near the US Naval Academy campus in Annapolis, Maryland. They watched as 952 Midshipmen comprising the class of 1997 graduated and received their commissions as Navy ensigns or as second lieutenants in the Marine Corps.

The first choice of every service academy is to have the president as the commencement speaker as he is also the commander in chief. In 1997, President Bill Clinton would deliver remarks to graduating West Point cadets. Vice President Al Gore was the featured guest of the graduating Midshipmen.

After Gore spoke, the nearly one thousand graduates stood, raised their right hands, and simultaneously swore their oath of office.

Then six F/A-18 Hornets comprising the Blue Angels flight demonstration team flew directly overhead, leaving six perfectly aligned contrails of smoke to honor the just-commissioned officers.

One newly minted ensign soon to head off to basic flight training at Naval Air Station Pensacola, Florida was Edward O'Grady Jr. Among the guests who watched young O'Grady's graduation were his mother, Diane, and his two sisters, Patricia and Kimberly. His father, Edward Sr., was not there to witness the proud moment. That is because more than fifteen years earlier in the autumn of 1981, Police Sergeant Ed O'Grady lay in a pool of blood, mortally wounded. Lying nearby was his partner, Officer Waverly Brown, who was dead. Members of the extremist Black Liberation Army aided by an offshoot group of the notorious Weather Underground gunned down the two police officers in a street ambush.

Minutes earlier, the same group of radicals shot and killed armored car courier Peter Paige and wounded his partner, Joe Trombino. The two men were couriers with the Brinks Company. The gunmen and their accomplices made off with more than $1.5 million in a brazen daylight armed robbery. One of the key planners behind the October 1981 armored car heist was Susan L. Rosenberg.

Perhaps it was fitting that Clinton was not the commencement speaker to address young O'Grady and his Naval Academy classmates in May 1997. In January 2001, Clinton commuted the fifty-eight-year prison sentence of Rosenberg and set her free after she served less than sixteen years in prison. There is little doubt regarding Rosenberg's role in several violent acts. Seven years after Rosenberg received clemency from Clinton, O'Grady commented, "Some people are good, and some people are bad. It's that black and white."[2]

May 19th Communist Organization

The Weathermen was a radical group with communist sympathies that advocated the revolutionary overthrow of the US government and an end to capitalism. The Weathermen had its birth on college campuses where like-minded students and nonstudents engaged in campus protests, often demonstrating against what the group claimed were American imperialism and institutional racism. It is generally acknowledged the Weathermen organization was launched in June 1969 at the Students for a Democratic Society (SDS) national convention.[3] Many of the Weathermen's members came from the SDS. Its members pledged militant action and violence to bring about changes to society.

According to a Top Secret (and now declassified) report prepared by the Chicago Field Office of the Federal Bureau of Investigation, the Weathermen had "an unremitting commitment to armed struggle as the ultimate necessity to seize state power."[4]

The Weathermen idolized the worst examples of the world community: Angola, Libya, Cuba, and China, to name a few. Several Weathermen traveled to Cuba to meet with Cuban and North Vietnamese government officials. One Weathermen member, Linda Sue Evans, actually visited North Vietnam.

After her return from North Vietnam in August 1969, Evans spoke of her three-week trip and of being given the opportunity to hold an antiaircraft gun. In her remarks, she stated she wished an American aircraft had flown over at that moment she was holding the antiaircraft gun.[5] She claimed that Americans held as prisoners of war by the North Vietnamese were receiving humane treatment.[6]

Among the earliest known violent events linked to the Weathermen was a September 1968 arson attack against the Navy ROTC building at the University of Washington that destroyed much of the building.[7]

An October 1969 rally of several hundred in Chicago, promoted by the Weathermen and known as the "Days of Rage," became violent when attendees smashed storefront windows and damaged several cars. The instigators arrived prepared for violence by wearing motorcycle helmets, steel-toed boots for kicking, and carrying steel rebar for fighting.

The Weathermen were comfortable with violence. The Weathermen claimed credit for the bombing of police cars in Chicago and Berkeley, California in late 1969 and early 1970. The group is suspected of a bombing that killed a San Francisco police officer in early 1970, and of responsibility for a police precinct bombing in Detroit.

Other bombings in 1970 that were tied to the Weathermen were at the National Guard Association building in Washington, D.C.; New York City police headquarters; San Francisco's Presidio army base; the Marin, California courthouse; a Queens, New York traffic courthouse; and on the campus of Harvard University.

During the next few years, the Weathermen were complicit in several more bombings, including at the US Capitol, the Pentagon, the US State Department, Massachusetts Institute of Technology in Cambridge, Massachusetts, several federal and state government buildings, as well as private business offices. In all, the group was believed to have been responsible for at least forty bombings during the period of 1969 to 1975.[8] Many of its members advocated violence as the sole tactic to achieve the group's goals.

The Weathermen received unwanted scrutiny in March 1970 when a bomb-making factory located in a Greenwich Village townhouse next door to actor Dustin Hoffman blew up.[9] Three Weathermen died in the explosion. Two women escaped with minor injuries. One was wearing clothes left in tattered shreds and the other had her clothes completely blown off.[10] The group changed its name to the Weather Underground as its members went underground in an effort to avoid detection and capture.[11]

An offshoot of the Weather Underground was a group linked to acts of even more violence, including murder. The May 19th Communist Organization derived its name from the May 19th birthdays of Malcolm X and Ho Chi Minh. Most of the May 19th members were white women who were looking for revolutionary causes to support. They settled on two causes. One was the FALN, and the other was the violent Black Liberation Army. The May 19th members decided to ally their organization with the Black Liberation Army, forming a group that became known as the "Family."

BLACK LIBERATION ARMY

The Black Panther Party for Self-Defense formed in Oakland, California in 1966 following the death of Nation of Islam official Malcolm X. The Black Panthers espoused a militaristic doctrine of armed resistance against what its membership claimed was a racist and imperialistic American society.

The group, which later shortened its name to the Black Panther Party, adopted a Socialist doctrine. Cofounder Huey P. Newton declared, "The Black Panther Party is a Marxist-Leninist party."[12] Panther Minister of Information Eldridge Cleaver stated the mission of the BPP was "to fight a revolutionary struggle for the violent over-throw of the United States government and the total destruction of the racist, capitalist, imperialist, neo-colonialist power structure."[13]

The BPP was an especially violent organization responsible for the deaths of dozens of party members, police officers, and civilians. The Panthers reserved much of their venom for law enforcement offi-cers. A 1968 headline of the organ's newspaper *The Black Panther,* referring to the police, stated "Pigs Want War."[14]

The party began to disintegrate when several national Panther leaders faced criminal charges. Newton and fellow cofounder Bobby Seale were arrested and tried for separate murders. Cleaver fled the country, spent several months in Cuba, and eventually settled in Algeria. When the national Black Panther Party finally fell apart, several Panthers joined other groups and causes.

The Black Liberation Army formed from the members of the New York City chapter of the Black Panthers. Its membership was made up of almost all black men. As with the Weather Underground, the BLA preached an armed struggle that included any number of violent acts, including shootings and bombings, to achieve the group's goals. One of the goals was a separate black nation formed from the southern United States. A frequent target of the Black Liberation Army was police officers. The BLA took credit for the brutal slaying of a pair of police officers, one white and one black, on May 21, 1971, and of the murder of a second pair of black and white police officers on January 28, 1972.

THE FAMILY

The BLA's partnership with the May 19th Communist Organization was a combination not previously observed by law enforcement authorities: groups of predominately black men and white women engaged in indiscriminate violence against a perceived enemy they believed was a racist, white society. In this relationship, the BLA called all the shots and the May 19th group performed supporting roles. Many of the BLA members referred to the May 19th members as "crackers."

The Family perceived several institutions and organizations as obstacles to its goal of creating a separatist black nation made up from the southern states. The Family wanted to eliminate these obstacles, so it compiled a hit list of organizations and institutions it would target with violence. Among those on the list included the International Association of Police Chiefs, the FBI-New York City Police Department Joint Terrorist Task Force, and the United Jewish Appeal.[15]

In order to achieve its goal, the Family needed to raise money. Lots of it. The Family intended to raise the needed money through robbery. It also wanted to achieve the kind of notoriety of its predecessor groups, the Black Panthers and the Weather Underground.

One of the first activities of the Family was to garner publicity for the new and unknown group. The Family planned the prison escape of Assata Shakur, the only female member of the BLA. Like most BLA members, she preferred to use her "African" name,

Assata Shakur, instead of her "slave name" given at birth, which was JoAnne Byron. Shakur was suspected of involvement in BLA orchestrated cop killings in 1971 and 1972. She was sentenced to prison for the shooting death of New Jersey State Trooper Werner Foerster and the wounding of State Trooper James Harper on May 2, 1973.

The May 19th members became actively involved in the Family's criminal activities by supplying safe houses and acting as getaway drivers after armed robberies.[16]

THE BRINKS ROBBERY

On the afternoon of October 20, 1981, a Brinks armored car made its last stop of the day to pick up $839,000 at a branch of the Nanuet National Bank in a Rockland County shopping mall in Nyack, New York. That pickup and money from earlier pickups totaled $2.9 million. Circling the area was a red Chevy van loaded with several BLA members. They used their African names rather than their slave names. Kuwasi Balagoon (Donald Weems), Jamal Baltimore (Edward L. Joseph), Solomon Bouines (Samuel Brown), Chui Ferguson-El (Cecilio Ferguson), Mutulu Shakur (Jeral Williams) and Mtayari Sundiata (Samuel Lee Smith) were in the van.

Brinks guards Peter Paige and Joe Trombino exited the shopping mall with a handcart loaded with moneybags. Moments after the guards began loading the money into the armored truck, the red Chevy van pulled alongside. Gunmen leapt from the back and immediately began firing weapons. "'They didn't even ask them to hand over the money,' declared an incredulous witness. 'They just blasted away.'"[17] One BLA member had an M-16 automatic and another had a shotgun. Paige was immediately killed and Trombino was seriously wounded. The BLA members snatched $1.6 million, about half of the money in the back of the armored car, loaded it into the Chevy van, and sped off. The entire incident was over in a matter of moments.

Minutes later, the gunmen pulled alongside a U-Haul rental truck and a tan Honda Accord waiting in a remote parking lot. The gunmen with their weapons and the money climbed into the back of the U-Haul and the Honda, abandoning the Chevy van, which had been stolen. In the cab of the U-Haul was a white couple. David Gilbert was behind the wheel and Kathy Boudin was in the passenger seat. Boudin had been in hiding since the day she fled from the Greenwich Village townhouse that had blown up in 1970 from an accidental explosion during bomb-making. The U-Haul and Honda then sped off, but not before an eyewitness watched the suspicious events unfold and notified police.

A short while later, four Nyack police officers pulled over the first U-Haul truck they came across. Gilbert and Boudin stepped out of the truck and attempted to convince the officers they were innocent of any wrongdoing. The officers heard police radio transmissions that the gunmen were black males, so they let down their guard when speaking with the white couple driving the rental truck. Officer Brian Lennon climbed into his cruiser to return to its rack the shotgun he was carrying.

Then a half dozen black men burst from the back of the U-Haul, firing automatic weapons at the police officers. Officer Waverly "Chipper" Brown was shot by M-16 fire and fell to the ground. Another gunman shot Brown with a 9-millimeter pistol as he lay on the ground. Brown died within minutes. Firing back, Sergeant Edward O'Grady Sr. managed to strike the gunman who shot Officer Brown. Chui Ferguson-El, the man with the M-16, fired and struck O'Grady. The police sergeant would die a short while later in a hospital emergency room.

The gunman O'Grady had shot was unhurt because, it was later learned, he was wearing a bulletproof vest. That gunman climbed into a nearby white Oldsmobile sedan, which sped off. Detective

Artie Keenan was shot twice by BLA gunmen but survived. Officer Lennon was trapped in his police cruiser returning his shotgun to its rack when the gun battle erupted. He was still in the cruiser trying to get out when the gunmen rammed it with the U-Haul before driving away. In a matter of minutes, Brown was dead, O'Grady lay dying, and Keenan was seriously wounded.

Boudin, who acted as a decoy by riding in the cab of the U-Haul, fled on foot when the shooting started. An off-duty corrections officer witnessed the shooting and saw Boudin running away. Instinctively, he gave chase and captured Boudin.

Boudin's involvement with the Family was not entirely unexpected. She grew up among radical activists. Her father, Leonard Boudin, was the attorney who represented Dr. Benjamin Spock, the pediatrician-turned-activist, and Daniel Ellsberg of Pentagon papers notoriety. Boudin family friends included the radical lawyers Leonard Weinglass and William Kuntsler. Leonard Boudin had been in frequent contact with his fugitive daughter ever since the Greenwich Village townhouse explosion. Among the visitors she received in prison after her arrest were Spock and the hero of the liberal intelligentsia, Noam Chomsky.[18]

It was reported to the police that some of the gunmen from the U-Haul later piled into a white Oldsmobile sedan. The white sedan sped off with the tan Honda. Nyack Police Chief Alan Colsey, who was en route to the shooting scene, spotted the Honda closely followed by a white Oldsmobile and he gave pursuit. The Honda crashed during the chase. In the vehicle were David Gilbert, the U-Haul driver, Solomon Bouines, one of the black gunmen, and Judith Clark, who was behind the wheel. Gilbert and Clark were May 19th members. Colsey held the suspects at gunpoint until backup arrived.

The white Oldsmobile got away. In it was Mtayari Sundiata who shot Officer Waverly Brown with the 9-millimeter pistol as he lay dying on the ground. It was Sundiata who was shot during the gun battle by Sergeant O'Grady. The Oldsmobile getaway driver was Susan Rosenberg. It was Rosenberg who did the preliminary work and scouted the Brinks armored car pickup route before the robbery was attempted.[19]

After Gilbert, Bouines, and Clark were arrested, a police inspection of the tan Honda turned up a semiautomatic pistol and $800,000 from the armored car heist. The radicals were frantically trying to locate the pistol, which had fallen to the floor during the crash, when Colsey ordered them to place their hands in view. Forensic evidence linked Gilbert and Bouines to the gun battle that killed O'Grady and Brown.

Police traced the license plate of the white Oldsmobile that got away to an apartment belonging to Marilyn Jean Buck, a self-proclaimed revolutionary, Weather Underground fugitive, May 19th member, and prison escapee living under an assumed name. She was not at home when the police arrived at her address. Information the police found when they searched Buck's apartment led them to another apartment that served as a "safe house." Clothing and weapons from the Brinks robbery and the shoot-out were found in the safe house.

Two days later, police officers spotted a Chrysler LeBaron they believed had ties to the Buck apartment. In the Chrysler were Mtayari Sundiata and Sekou Odinga (Nathaniel Burns). When the police officers attempted to pull over the Chrysler, the car sped off, resulting in yet another police pursuit. As with the Honda, this pursuit also ended in a crash. Sundiata and Odinga fled on foot and began firing at the officers. Officers fired back and Sundiata was struck and killed. Odinga was captured alive. He was in possession of two 9-millimeter pistols. Sundiata was wearing a bulletproof vest that had previously been struck by a bullet found in Sundiata's pocket. Forensics determined the round came from O'Grady's handgun. Sundiata was the gunman O'Grady had shot two days earlier.

This was not the Family's first armored car robbery that ended tragically. Months earlier on June 2, 1981, the Family robbed a Brinks armored car in the Bronx. The Family stole $292,000 and shot and killed armored car guard fifty-nine-year-old William Moroney and seriously wounded J. M. "Michael" Schlacter.[20] Witnesses reported that three black gunmen leapt from a yellow station wagon and immediately began firing weapons in the direction of the guards. As was their modus operandi, the gunmen switched to another series of cars a short distance away. Rosenberg was one of the getaway drivers.[21] Brinks offered a $100,000 reward for information leading to the arrest of those responsible for the Bronx armored car heist.[22]

SUSAN L. ROSENBERG

Susan Lisa Rosenberg was subpoenaed by a grand jury when it was considering charges against several captured Family members in 1982, but before authorities knew the extent of her involvement in the Family's activities. She became a fugitive when she fled rather than appear before the grand jury.

Three years after the Brinks robbery, law enforcement benefited from a fortuitous event. Called to settle a dispute at a public storage facility, police officers captured fugitive Susan Rosenberg and Timothy Blunk on November 29, 1984. Blunk was the husband of Family member Sylvia Baraldini and he was a prime suspect in a supermarket robbery that occurred two months earlier.[23]

Rosenberg and Blunk were moving 780 pounds of weapons, ammunition, and explosives,[24] including fourteen rifles and pistols, an Uzi machine gun and a Browning semiautomatic pistol,[25] and 640 pounds of dynamite into a storage locker when the police arrived. The pair was using a trailer rented in New Haven, Connecticut to haul the weapons and ammunition. Two years later, authorities would find a large amount of dynamite in an abandoned rental unit in New Haven. The dynamite Rosenberg and Blunk were caught moving was part of a massive cache of explosives stolen in Austin, Texas in March 1980. The dynamite found in New Haven was likely from the same source.

In their investigation of Rosenberg, the police learned that Marilyn Jean Buck, one of her fellow Brinks robbery getaway drivers, frequently stayed in Rosenberg's New Haven apartment during the previous year.[26] Rosenberg was wanted in connection with her role in the Brinks holdup. Her fingerprints were found in one of the getaway cars, the white Oldsmobile.[27]

There was ample evidence of Rosenberg's involvement in the Nyack Brinks robbery. Testimony during a June 1983 trial of some of the Brinks robbery defendants implicated Rosenberg in the crime. One of her fellow accomplices turned state's evidence. Kamau Bayete operated an acupuncture clinic in Harlem that was used as a meeting place and a location to store weapons for use in various crimes. The clinic was also the central location from which Family members used to buy cocaine to support their heavy drug habits.[28]

Bayete testified that a seriously distraught Rosenberg arrived at the clinic during the evening of the Brinks shoot-out seeking assistance for some of those involved in the day's crime spree who were holed up in a safe house.[29] Rosenberg demanded Bayete provide medical attention to Buck, who had accidentally shot herself in the leg during the gun battle with the police officers when she tried to remove her semiautomatic pistol from inside her boot. Bayete was an acupuncturist with no real medical training, so he was only able to provide rudimentary first aid.

Rosenberg later brought Dr. Alan Berkman, an actual MD, to administer more substantial medical attention to Buck. Berkman was committed to the radical cause. He was an old hand when it came to administering medical aid to terrorists. He was the personal physician of Fuerzas Armadas de Liberación Nacional terrorist William Gillermo Morales, who was seriously injured when a pipe bomb he was assembling exploded in July 1978.[30]

Law enforcement officials were after Rosenberg for more than just her role in the Brinks heist. She and two other fugitives, Mutulu Shakur and Cheri Dalton, were included in a five-count indictment unsealed in September 1982 along with Chui Ferguson-El, Jamal Baltimore, and Sekou Odinga, who were in custody by then.

According to the government, the six were involved in at least four armed robberies, attempted murder, and conspiracy. They were suspected of being behind a Manhattan armored car heist on April 22, 1980; the attempted murder of a guard in an unsuccessful armored car robbery on March 23, 1981, in Danbury, Connecticut; the armored car robbery on June 2, 1981, in the Bronx; and the holdup of a Navy Federal Credit Union in Arlington, Virginia on November 23, 1981.[31]

The six radicals were also suspected of conspiring to murder two of their own. In March 1982, Rosenberg and the others thought gang members Solomon Bouines and Kuwaida (Yvonne Thomas), an on-again off-again girlfriend of Mtayari Sundiata, might have been susceptible to cooperating with the police.

Another despicable player in this was Susan Tipograph, a self-described "overweight, Jewish, lesbian, lefty lawyer" who said one "had to support armed struggle and the killing of cops as legitimate tactics in the liberation of Black people."[32] She had been Rosenberg's roommate at one time. Tipograph, a reputed May 19th member, was friends with many of the radicals including Rosenberg, Berkman, Clark, Gilbert and Evans, and she legally represented some of them in their various trials. There was the strange coincidence in which clients who were supposed to have been meeting with Tipograph kept disappearing only to become fugitives from justice.

Two decades later, Tipograph would represent another activist lawyer and fellow National Lawyers Guild member, Lynne Stewart. The National Lawyers Guild calls itself a "progressive" bar association. For many years since its 1937 founding, the NLG was a front for the Communist Party.

Stewart would be convicted in 2005 of providing aid to jailed 1993 World Trade Center bombing planner Sheikh Omar Abdel Rahman. Stewart was found guilty of passing messages from the "Blind Sheikh" to his followers as they were carrying out terrorist plots. Stewart defended Weather Underground members and Black Panthers alongside Tipograph in the 1980s.

Rosenberg and Tipograph had been arrested for assaulting a police officer at the 1979 trial of Fuerzas Armadas de Liberación Nacional bomb maker William Morales. The Puerto Rican terrorist Morales was captured when a pipe bomb he was assembling exploded on July 12, 1978, nearly blowing off both of his hands.

Morales was convicted of federal charges in early 1979 and he received a ten-year prison sentence. He was later convicted of state charges and was sentenced twenty-nine to eighty-nine years in state prison. Tipograph aided Morales in his May 1979 escape from Bellevue Hospital when he was being fitted for prosthetic hands. She smuggled in the wire cutters that were used to cut the screen covering his window in the hospital's prison ward, allowing him to slip away one night.[33]

Rosenberg would later be indicted along with Mutulu Shakur, Sekou Odinga, and Sylvia Baraldini for their participation in the November 2, 1979, prison break of cop-killer Assata Shakur, who was serving a life sentence at the time. Rosenberg was among the May 19th members who protested at Shakur's trial two years earlier.

According to authorities, two prison employees at the Clinton Correctional Institute in Clinton, New Jersey were kidnapped by the Family and then exchanged in return for the release of Assata Shakur. Rosenberg drove one of the getaway cars; Marilyn Jean Buck drove the other.[34] After her prison escape, Shakur hid out in Pittsburgh for several months before she made her way to Cuba, where she was given asylum.

During her December 12, 1984, arraignment on the explosives and weapons charges, Rosenberg told a judge she was innocent of any crimes. She thought of herself as a prisoner of war and not as a criminal. Rosenberg claimed she and her accomplices were "revolutionary guerillas and have been captured in the course of building a resistance to this government."[35] Nearly all associates of Rosenberg had been actively involved in a "resistance" to the government. Most of it was violent.

Rosenberg was found guilty at her trial and received a lengthy prison sentence for her crimes. At her May 20, 1985, sentencing, Rosenberg said, "We were busted because we vacillated on our politics." That statement was thought to have meant Rosenberg and Blunk could have easily escaped capture if they simply had killed Cherry Hill, New Jersey police officer Mark DeFrancisco, who had arrested them.[36] At the time of her arrest, Rosenberg told DeFrancisco it was his "lucky day" that she did not kill him.[37]

Citing Rosenberg's fifty-eight-year prison sentence on the explosives and weapons charges, US attorney for the southern district of New York Rudolph Guiliani dropped the charges against her for her participation in the Brinks robbery and murders. Guiliani reached the conclusion there was no need for the government to try Rosenberg for her role in the Brinks shoot-out as she was not likely to be released from prison until she was in her eighties.

Guiliani did not anticipate that after completing only about one-sixth of her fifty-eight-year sentence, Rosenberg began demanding to be released from prison, claiming she had a change of heart.[38] Her demand came only a few years after she was still professing herself to being "guilty of revolutionary and anti-imperialistic resistance."[39] Rosenberg's rapid conversion from years of crime and violence to a claimed status of law-abiding citizen may have occurred after her realization that a prison sentence of fifty-eight years would be a very, very long time.

When her parole request was denied, Rosenberg launched an executive clemency effort. No one thought she had a remote chance of being granted clemency—even from Bill Clinton. "This is a woman who has taken lives," said Diane O'Grady, the widow of Police Sergeant Ed O'Grady, who was killed during the Brinks holdup.[40]

Gregory Brown was seventeen years old when Rosenberg's fellow gang members gunned down his father, Waverly Brown. "That day has affected my life and my family forever," said Brown.[41]

Even New York Senator Charles Schumer weighed in, telling the Justice Department he was personally opposed to clemency for Rosenberg.[42]

John Castellucci covered the Brinks robbery for the *Rockland Journal-News* newspaper. According to Castellucci, Rosenberg was "one of the most fervent, almost rabid members of the group when it comes to the question of whether violence should be used in the furtherance of revolutionary goals."[43] To demonstrate her mettle, Rosenberg challenged a black Family member on whether she would have the courage to kill a police officer, implying that Rosenberg could and would.[44]

Nonetheless, on January 20, 2001, Susan Lisa Rosenberg walked out of the Federal Correctional Institution in Danbury, Connecticut with Clinton's pardon letter in her hand. She was a free woman.

Political cover was provided for the Rosenberg pardon decision one month earlier, courtesy of CBS News. The television news program *60 Minutes* broadcasted a journalistically flawed segment on its December 17, 2000, show. Cohost Morely Safer opened the segment with comments that were grossly misleading.

"Her name is Susan Lisa Rosenberg," said Safer. He added, "For the past 16 years, she's been in prison. If the government has its way, she could spend another 20 behind bars for a crime she says she did not commit and knew nothing about."[45]

Rosenberg had served *less* than *one-third* of her fifty-eight-year sentence for possessing one-third of a ton of guns and dynamite. She was not continuing to be incarcerated because of some trumped-up charge as Shafer had implied. She was serving out her sentence for one of the largest weapons cache seizures in American history. As with every other person sentenced to prison in the US, a presentence report is taken into consideration by the judge. Good deeds mitigate a sentence and bad conduct, including that for which someone is punished and that from which they escaped conviction, is also taken into consideration. Besides, there was no doubt regarding her involvement in the Brinks robbery. She cased the robbery location the day prior.

For her part in the in the Brinks robbery and slaying, Rosenberg remarked, "I really was a political person.... I supported the right of the oppressed people to armed struggle."[46] Clearly, Rosenberg was not repentant for her crimes.

In autumn 2004, Hamilton College in Clinton, New York, a progressive, liberal arts college with an enrollment of about eighteen hundred students overstepped the boundaries of decency. It offered an appointment to Rosenberg to teach a writing course at the college. A public outcry occurred, forcing Rosenberg to withdraw from the appointment.[47]

THE DYNAMITE

One of the elements that tied together various radicals not directly involved with the Family was the use of explosives from the same lot that was stolen in Texas.

A May 19th bombing campaign begun in early the 1980s used explosive material from one thousand pounds of dynamite stolen from a construction site in Austin, Texas in 1980. Austinite Elizabeth "Betty" Ann Duke, a 1960s leftist protestor turned radical criminal, was suspected of the theft as were Marilyn Jean Buck and Linda Sue Evans.[48]

As of this writing, Duke has been on the run for more than three decades. She was arrested in the mid-1980s on charges of harboring a Brinks robbery fugitive, illegal possession of firearms, and for illegally possessing more than two hundred pounds of explosives, including detonation cord, blasting caps, and fake identity documents of federal agents and employees. Duke had a pistol with a silencer in her possession when the police nabbed her. She was in the company of Dr. Alan Berkman, the doctor who treated Buck after she accidentally shot herself during the Brinks robbery shoot-out.

After Duke's arrest, authorities searched a garage she rented under a fake name and found 162 sticks of dynamite and bullet casings from weapons used in the Brinks robbery.[49] Duke fled from justice while awaiting trial in Philadelphia in 1985.

Among Duke's criminal activities was the November 1983 bombing of the US Capitol. A bomb placed near the Senate chamber that exploded left a gaping hole near the office of Senator Robert W. Byrd (Democrat, West Virginia) and caused more than a quarter of a million dollars of damage. In addition to the Capitol explosion, Duke, Buck, and Evans were believed to have been responsible for the 1983 bombings at the Washington Navy Yard and the National War College at Ft. McNair in Washington, DC.

A series of Wall Street explosions in February 1982 were attributed to the FALN, the violent Puerto Rican terror group (see Chapter 10). However, nearly all FALN members were arrested two years earlier. A carbon copy of a communiqué regarding the Wall Street bombings and purporting to be from the FALN was found in the apartment of May 19th member Sylvia Baraldini. This indicated that May 19th members likely carried out the bombings in the name of the FALN. The alleged FALN communiqué even expressed solidarity with the Brinks robbery defendants.

Several 1982 New Year's Eve bombings in New York City took place at police headquarters: at a federal courthouse and at two federal buildings that seriously wounded three police officers.[50] One had a leg blown off, one was blinded, and another was partially blinded.[51] The FALN was credited with bombings, however, forensics determined the bombs were built using explosive material from the Austin dynamite heist. Since the FALN terrorists were already in custody, it was likely the bombings were carried out by some or all the May 19th members who had not yet been apprehended: Susan Rosenberg, Timothy Blunk, Marilyn Jean Buck, and Betty Ann Duke.

LINDA SUE EVANS

It was after the arrest of Rosenberg that law enforcement officials had a clearer picture of the close ties between Rosenberg and Marilyn Jean Buck. This enabled authorities to trace Buck and accomplice Linda Sue Evans to a Bronx apartment and then to an apartment in Baltimore, Maryland. They missed capturing Buck in Baltimore but found weapons, including an Uzi submachine gun, and a treasure trove of important gang papers. The documents included detailed plans to bomb several Washington, DC federal offices including the Old Executive Office Building adjacent to the White House and a building at the US Naval Academy in Annapolis, Maryland.

Hot on Buck's trail, the FBI eventually tracked her to Dobbs Ferry, a small town north of New York City. The FBI captured Buck and Evans on May 11, 1985. Both were carrying pistols. Authorities wanted to apprehend Buck for more than her involvement in the Brinks robbery. She was already a fugitive for escaping from a federal prison in West Virginia in 1977 when she failed to return after a prison furlough to meet with her attorney. It was no surprise that Buck's attorney was Susan Tipograph. Evans was arrested for harboring Buck and three others who were involved in the Brinks robbery and murders.

Evans had her own criminal record. She received a three-year sentence in 1971 for aggravated assault, but she was released on probation after serving only ninety days. It was during her probation that Evans had a false death certificate submitted to the court claiming she had died.

Evans went to trial and was convicted in November 1985 of violating weapons laws by possessing a gun as a convicted felon. She was also convicted in three subsequent trials of illegally purchasing firearms in New Orleans, of harboring a fugitive, and of damaging government property by having set off the bomb in the US Capitol in November 1983. Evans was sentenced to a total of forty years' imprisonment.

While she was being tried for the bombing campaign of 1983 to 1985 in which bombs were detonated at three locations in Washington, DC and four in New York City, Evans joined Rosenberg, Buck, and four other defendants in issuing a statement. In part, the statement read, "The politically motivated indictment against us is part of a program of repression.... we will not allow ourselves to be part of a governmental show trial."[52]

After serving only fifteen years of her forty-year sentence, Linda Sue Evans was among the dozens of hardened criminals whose sentences Clinton commuted during the early morning hours of January 20, 2001.

THE REASON FOR THE COMMUTATIONS

The question is why would Clinton inflict such damage to his own legacy in the waning hours of his presidency by giving clemency to domestic terrorists who neither deserved it and who could offer no political or financial payback to him? Neither Susan Lisa Rosenberg nor Linda Sue Evans deserved to be released from prison. Neither one served anything close to a requisite sentence for their criminal acts. In Rosenberg's case, she was more than just a low-level soldier in the terrorist movement. In her memoir, she wrote she had taken the lead in "stockpiling arms for the distant revolution that...would soon come."[53] So what was the motive behind Clinton's commuting of the sentences of Rosenberg and Evans?

There were two factors behind the pardons. The least of the reasons was a political consideration in favor of Hillary. Two influential Upper West Side personalities, valuable for their support of Hillary's political career, were in favor of pardoning Rosenberg. Rabbi J. Rolando Matalon of the Temple B'nai Jeshurun included Rosenberg's parents in his congregation. Matalon was firm in his position that Rosenberg should be freed. The other New York City figure lobbying for Rosenberg's release was US Representative Jerrold Nadler. He was not only a firm Bill Clinton defender throughout Bill's many scandals, but he was also a political supporter of Hillary's 2000 Senate run.[54]

Yet there was still another, more insidious reason why Clinton pardoned both Rosenberg and Evans. He commuted their sentences as a gift to the extreme radical that still resides deep within the soul of Hillary Rodham Clinton.

Hillary has long had a fondness for the views and politics of extremists and radicals. Consider Saul Alinsky. He was so proud of his own reputation as a radical that he wrote two books on the topic: *Reveille for Radicals* and *Rules for Radicals*. Hillary was so enamored of the Chicago extremist that he was the subject of her ninety-two-page Wellesley College political science thesis. Yet in her autobiography, Hillary could only muster writing a single paragraph about someone who was such a big influence on her life. Perhaps this is because Hillary realized there is very little about Alinsky that would be viewed favorably by the typical, law-abiding American.

In *Living History*, what little Hillary wrote of Alinsky was delicately phrased. "His prescription for social change required grassroots organizing that taught people to help themselves by confronting government and corporations to obtain the resources and power to improve their lives."[55] Not surprisingly, Clinton failed to address any of Alinsky's countless shortcomings, including his flawed values and his repulsive tactics of confrontation. For example,

Alinsky bragged that as a young man, he directed college students on how to steal food from Chicago area restaurants.[56]

Alinsky enjoyed confrontation. He wrote, "The trouble is that to organize people, there's got to be action and all action on a minute-to-minute basis is rude and involves making a scene."[57] Alinsky preached that demonstrators should picket the homes of corporate executives or practice "fart ins" in office environments in order to achieve their goals.[58] He spoke admiringly of groups that tied up all of the restrooms at Chicago's O'Hare International Airport, piled rats on the steps of City Hall, dumped a truckload of garbage on a government official's lawn, and littered the sidewalks of a college campus with wads of chewing gum.[59] Radical organizers should not stop there, he argued. He urged "campus activists…[to] demand control of all the proxies in [a] university's investment portfolio"[60] in order to apply financial leverage.

Alinsky's dictum of pure attack was "Pick the target, freeze it, personalize it, and polarize it."[61] Alinsky further explained that criticizing an institution would not be as successful in achieving a desired outcome as if one were to instead attack an individual. "One of the criteria in picking your target is the target's vulnerability— where do you have the power to start?…. The other important point in the choosing of a target is that it must be a personification, not something general and abstract such as a community's segregated practices or a major corporation of City Hall."[62] Alinsky may have been the very first to advocate for the politics of personal destruction that the Clintons constantly complained they were the victim of, but were in fact very adept at using against those they opposed.

Huey P. Newton, cofounder of the Black Panther Party, agreed with Alinsky's tactics. Newton argued that the white oppressor "must be harassed until his doom. He must have no peace by day or night."[63] Hillary was quite fond of the Black Panthers, the progenitor of the Black Liberation Army.

Black Panther Party chief spokesman Eldridge Cleaver urged blacks to take private property by force. In *Soul on Ice*, Cleaver wrote, "The sanctity surrounding property is being called into question. The mystique of the deed of ownership is melting away. In other parts of the world, peasants rise up and expropriate the land from the former owners. Blacks in America see that the deed is not eternal, that it is not signed by God, and the new deeds, making blacks the owners, can be drawn up."[64]

Alinsky had little regard for corporate America, successful businessmen, government officials, organized religion—particularly Christianity—and law enforcement. He was also a bigot and a racist. There were certain activities and pursuits in which blacks should *not* be engaged. To Alinsky, a black intellectual has "joined the other side, moved away from his people."[65] A black police officer is "not only a pig but a black pig."[66]

Newton was more abrupt in identifying two types of blacks: "the field nigger and the house nigger."[67] To Newton's way of thinking, the "house nigger" was those blacks that were too close to whites. The Black Panthers' Cleaver singled out examples of blacks who apparently fell into Newton's category of blacks that were associated too closely with whites. They included "Roy Wilkins and the NAACP and all those bootlickers and Uncle Toms and black capitalists."[68] A segregation of the races was in order, argued Newton and Cleaver.

According to Alinsky, "all whites should get out of the black ghettos. It's a stage we have to go through. I'd like to see legislation enacted making it mandatory for all white businessmen and slum landlords in the ghettos to sell their stuff to blacks within an eighteen-month period. If they haven't done it by that time, then let the government come in—just like Urban Renewal—appraise their properties and businesses, condemn them, and then turn around and help blacks buy them with special funding of low-interest-rate loans."[69] Alinsky's agenda was not markedly different than the Black Liberation Army goal of segregating blacks from whites.

However, to Hillary's way of thinking, Alinsky was not radical enough. Alinsky "does not sound 'radical,'" wrote Clinton in her college thesis. Perhaps foreshadowing her own journey in elective politics, Hillary wrote, "[Alinsky] realizes that radical goals have to be achieved often by non-radical, even 'anti-radical' means. For Alinsky, the non-radical means involve the traditional quest for power to change existing situations."[70]

There were other extremists who influenced Hillary. She spent the summer of 1971 as an intern in the Oakland, California law firm of Treuhaft, Walker and Burstein, a fact she failed to mention in *Living History*. Robert Treuhaft, who would later invite Hillary to join the firm, said this of the firm's four partners, "Two were Communists, and others tolerated Communists."[71]

If not more radical than Alinsky and Treuhaft, then at least more violent and dangerous were the extremist gangs that Hillary admired. The relationship between Rosenberg and Evans and the Black Liberation Army, the successor organization of the Black Panther Party, likely explains why Rosenberg and Evans' fair and just sentences were commuted and drastically cut short as the Clintons left the White House.

Even today, Hillary cannot bring herself to admit that the Black Panther Party, an organization notorious for extreme violence and responsible for dozens of murders, was anything other than a peaceful group, in spite of decades of evidence to the contrary. In *Living History* Hillary described the Black Panthers of the late 1960s in very favorable terms even after their violence was well documented. She wrote, "The *non-violent*, largely black civil rights movement splintered into factions, and new voices emerged among urban blacks belonging to the Black Muslims and Black Panther Party [emphasis added]."[72]

The Black Panthers were nonviolent? The Black Panther Party, responsible for the deaths of dozens of Panthers, police officers, and others, was anything but nonviolent. According Eldridge Cleaver, the Black Panthers, a "Marxist-Leninist party,"[73] were dedicated "to fight a revolutionary struggle for the violent overthrow of the United States government and the total destruction of the racist, capitalist, imperialist, neo-colonialist power structure."[74] The US, Cleaver argued, "has to be totally obliterated"[75] and American society should undergo an "unequivocal destruction of capitalism and [install] in its place a socialist state."[76] According to Panthers cofounder Newton, "America is World-Enemy-Number-One."[77]

The only way to achieve these goals was through violence, according to Cleaver, an admitted serial rapist.[78] He said that peaceful methods were ineffective. Cleaver observed, "that many people in the black community were incensed at [Martin Luther King]" because of his adherence to nonviolence. Cleaver remarked, "I think that Martin Luther King performed a disservice to his people by carrying his policy of nonviolence to absurd lengths."[79]

Newton was more direct in stating that "the racist dog oppressors fear the armed people; they fear most of all Black people armed with weapons and the ideology of the Black Panther Party."[80]

Forty years before Hillary wrote *Living History*, her mentor Saul Alinsky argued that the Black Panthers "have more potential than most of the militants"[81] and they could be a "constructive force."[82] In contrast, the Weathermen, Alinsky wrote in *Rules for Radicals,* did not go far enough in order to achieve their goals and they instead "took the grand cop-out."[83] It is astonishing that Alinsky believed a group that was responsible for dozens of violent acts including robbery, bombings, and murder did not go far enough in order to achieve its goals.

Among the Black Panther Party's goals was the ultimate destruction of American society and American values and institutions. Newton offered to send Black Panther soldiers to join the Communist North Vietnamese and Viet Cong in fighting US troops. In an August 29, 1970, statement to Viet Cong leaders, Newton said, "In the spirit of international revolutionary solidarity the Black Panther Party hereby offers to the National Liberation Front and Provisional

Revolutionary Government of South Vietnam an undetermined number of troops to assist you in your fight against American imperialism."[84]

The Black Panther Party's support of "revolutionary" causes and leaders was common knowledge. According to Newton, leaders who were the most important inspiration to the Panthers included Fidel Castro, Che Guevara, Ho Chi Minh, Mao Tse-Tung, and North Korea's Kim Il-Sung, as well as Soviet-backed rebels in Mozambique and Angola.[85]

The violence of the Black Panthers was well known to the public at that time, including Yale Law School student Hillary Rodham, since she had a front row seat to their brutality and inhumanity. It was at Yale in 1970 that Hillary organized supporters of the several Black Panthers who were on trial in a downtown New Haven, Connecticut courtroom for a gruesome and grisly murder. Eight Black Panthers, including cofounder Bobby Seale, were on trial for the sadistic and brutal torture and murder of Alex Rackley, one of their own members.

Suspicious that Rackley may have been a police informant, the Black Panthers kidnapped him, tied him to a chair, and tortured him for two days, scalding him with boiling water, burning him with cigarettes, beating him with a blunt object, and stabbing him with an icepick. Seale gave the final order to "do away with him" that led to Rackley being shot twice in the head before his body was dumped.[86]

Hillary, having "gain[ed] prominence in the Yale protest movement,"[87] was among those who demonstrated deep concern for the "persecuted" Black Panthers but showed absolutely no sympathy or even concern for Alex Rackley, the man they had murdered. Thirty-four years later, in *Living History*, she could not bring herself to even acknowledge there was even a once-alive but now-dead victim that was the reason why the Panthers were on trial for murder in the first place. Alex Rackley's name was not worthy of even the slightest mention.

The Panthers were not guilty of murder, Hillary strongly implied in *Living History*. She claimed, "Thousands of angry protesters, convinced the Panthers had been set up by the FBI and government prosecutors, swarmed into the city [of New Haven]."[88] Even with the luxury of 20/20 hindsight, Hillary still romanticized about the poor, beleaguered Black Panthers for whom she apparently held great sympathy.

That the evidence against the Black Panthers was overwhelming did not seem to bother Hillary. Two of the Panthers admitted their guilt and testified against the others. The police had seized an incriminating audiotape of the Black Panthers' interrogation and "trial" of Rackley shortly before he was murdered. During the Panthers' trial, Hillary organized a vigil under the direction of Yale's left-wing Professor Thomas Emerson (known throughout campus as "Tommy the Commie") to ensure the "rights" of the Black Panthers were protected. Hillary and like-minded students routinely passed their observations to the American Civil Liberties Union.[89] At the same time Hillary was organizing Black Panther supporters, Huey Newton was claiming Seale and the other Panthers on trial were victims of "reactionary racist courts."[90]

Black Panther David Hilliard attended a campus rally in support of the defendants. He remarked, "[T]here ain't nothing wrong with taking the life of a motherf***ing pig." Hilliard then attacked and stomped all over a foreign exchange student who asked for time at the podium.[91] Years later, longtime Clinton friend and adviser Dick Morris wrote, "The Panther leaders who were on trial thought it was okay to torture and murder somebody. That's what Hillary Clinton was defending, people who thought it was okay to torture and murder somebody."[92]

The only ones guilty of lawlessness during this period, according to Hillary in *Living History*, was the Federal Bureau of Investigation, which, she claimed "broke the law in order to disrupt [the Black Panthers]."[93] In retrospect, Hillary may regret having been so forthright in her opinion by characterizing the Black Panthers as "non-violent" and the FBI as the true criminal element.

Hillary's radical Yale Law School days did not end with the Black Panthers' trial. Rather than join the centrist *Yale Law Journal*, Hillary instead served as an editor of the *Yale Review of Law and Social Action*. *Yale Review* was a far left-of-center publication that promoted repugnant views of the police. It is apparent that Hillary would prefer to keep quiet her involvement in the *Yale Review*. She made no mention of it in her autobiography, but she did mention the *Yale Law Journal*, the school journal in which she did *not* participate.

The *Yale Review* fall/winter of 1970 issue "included many cartoons depicting the police as hominid pigs, their snouts wet while they mutter 'niggers, niggers, niggers, niggers.' Another cartoon, under the caption 'What Is a Pig?' shows a wounded pig-man, bruised, bandaged, and on crutches from a severe beating. The answer to the question in the cartoon is 'A low natured beast that has no regard for law, justice, or the rights of the people; a creature that bites the hand that feeds it; a foul depraved traducer, usually found masquerading as the victim of an unprovoked attack.'"[94] To Hillary and her crowd, law enforcement officers were mere swine.

Hillary displayed extreme dislike and mistreatment of law enforcement officials throughout her years as the first lady of Arkansas and as first lady of the US. She required Arkansas state troopers to run personal errands for her, demanded Secret Service agents carry her luggage, once threw an object at a Secret Service limousine driver, and ordered Secret Service agents providing post-presidency protection to stand in the rain at her Chappaqua, New York home during a torrential downpour.[95]

Early during her years as First Lady, she wanted the Secret Service agents assigned to her protection to keep their distance. Hillary ordered members of her Secret Service detail to "Stay the f*** back, stay the f*** away from me! Don't come within ten yards of me, or else!"[96]

No president has ever questioned the loyalty of the Secret Service. Yet Hillary Rodham Clinton did. Early in her husband's first term, Hillary wanted to replace the entire White House Secret Service detail. She demanded a new crew of agents that she could be assured would be sympathetic to the Clintons. She ordered Deputy White House Counsel Vince Foster to find a way to fire the entire White House detail and replace them. Foster talked her out of it, noting that such action would likely lead to a public firestorm.[97]

Hillary's attitude toward law enforcement is not surprising. Huey P. Newton, cofounder of the Black Panther Party she admired, said this of the police: "the pigs are an agent of the ruling class."[98]

Hillary's disgust with law enforcement was mirrored by her disgust with the military. Throughout Bill's presidency Hillary, openly displayed contempt toward the troops. Hillary wanted the military to be neither seen nor heard. She preferred the military aides to the President not wear their uniforms while working in the White House.[99]

The US military was used on several occasions during Clinton's presidency including in Somalia, Bosnia and Herzegovina, Kosovo, Haiti, and Iraq bolstering his otherwise weak national security bona fides. Yet, in more than 550 pages, Hillary could not bring herself to write one kind word about America's servicemen and women in *Living History. Not one word.*

In sum, Hillary despised law enforcement and military service personnel as much as she apparently admired radical extremists such as the Black Panthers, the Black Liberation Army, and the Weather Underground.

It was the placating of the radical in Hillary Rodham Clinton that was the likely reason why Bill Clinton chose to commute the sentences of the undeserving, domestic terrorists Susan Lisa Rosenberg and Linda Sue Evans.

ENDNOTES

Preface

1. John Grisham, *The Broker*, (New York: Doubleday, 2005), 1.
2. Michael Daly, "Brother's Pal Can Cure Hil's Ills," *Daily News*, February 28, 2001.
3. George Rush and Joanna Molloy, "Hil's Brother Squeezed for Support," *Daily News*, June 10, 2002.
4. Todd S. Purdum, "The Clinton Pardons: The Brothers," *New York Times*, February 23, 2001.
5. Independent Inquiry Committee into the United Nations Oil-for-Food Programme, "Report on Programme Manipulation," October 27, 2005, 63.
6. Hillary Rodham Clinton, *Living History*, (New York: Simon & Schuster, 2003), 105.
7. Sumana Chatterjee, "Hillary Clinton Addresses Pardons Involving Brother, Campaign Aide," *Knight Ridder*, February 23, 2001.
8. Alex Massie, "How Hillary Brought Bill to Book," *Scotland on Sunday*, June 8, 2003.
9. "Sorting Out the Pardon Mess," *New York Times*, February 23, 2001. Editorial.
10. William J. Clinton, *My Life*, (New York: Alfred A. Knopf, 2004), 939.
11. Ibid., 940.
12. Ibid.
13. Ibid., 941.
14. Joan Walsh, "Unpardonable," *Salon*, February 21, 2001, accessed June 6, 2007, https://www.salon.com/2001/02/23/pardon_4/

Chapter 1

1. James Webb, "The Insult of Carter's Mass Pardon," *Wall Street Journal*, February 23, 2001.
2. W. H. Humbert, *The Pardoning Power of the President*, (Washington, DC: American Council on Public Affairs, 1941), 9.
3. Ibid., 10.
4. *United States v. Wilson*, 32 US (7 Pet.) 150. (1833).
5. *Biddle v. Perovich*, 274 US 480. (1927).
6. Testimony of Roger Adams, US Pardon Attorney, before US Senate Judiciary Committee, February 14, 2001.
7. Ibid.
8. Memo from Jack Quinn, White House counsel, to the president, addressed to Jamie S. Gorelick, deputy attorney general, Subject: Executive Clemency Policy, January 26, 1996.
9. W. H. Humbert, *The Pardoning Power of the President*, (Washington, DC: American Council on Public Affairs, 1941), 42.
10. "The Pardon That Brought No Peace," *Time*, September 16, 1974.
11. "The Failure of Mr. Ford," *New York Times*, September 9, 1974. Editorial.
12. James Webb, "The Insult of Carter's Mass Pardon," *Wall Street Journal*, February 23, 2001.

Chapter 2

1. Don Van Natta Jr. and Marc Lacey, "Access Proved Vital in Last-Minute Race for Clinton Pardons," *New York Times*, February 25, 2001.
2. Ibid.
3. Department of Justice clemency statistics, accessed March 7, 2007, https://www.justice.gov/pardon/clemency-statistics.
4. Rick Atkinson and Kevin Klose, "The Financial House Jackson Built With PUSH," *Washington Post*, January 27, 1984.
5. Marjorie Hunter, "Education Dept. Is Stopping Funds for a PUSH Program," *New York Times*, September 12, 1981.
6. Rick Atkinson, "Push Agency Asked to Return Funds," *The Washington Post*, April 10, 1984.

7. Jeff Gerth, "Questions Arise on Jackson Group's Finances," *New York Times*, January 29, 1984.

8. Michael Oreskes, "Jackson Rights Group Drowning in Debt," *New York Times*, July 4, 1987.

9. Stephen Lilly, "Creditors seek $676,000 from Call-Post Parent," *Business First-Columbus*, February 1, 1993.

10. Mark Rollenhagen, "Bustamante Pleads Guilty in Insurance Fraud Case," *Cleveland Plain-Dealer*, April 20, 1993.

11. Editorial, "Publisher's Four-Year Ordeal Ends with Probation," *Cincinnati Call & Post*, June 17, 1993.

12. Miriam Hill, "Bustamante Sentenced to Probation for 5 Years," *Cleveland Plain-Dealer*, June 12, 1993.

13. Clarence Page, "Racism, Prejudice and the Underuse of Economic Power," *Chicago Tribune*, May 16, 1990.

14. William E. Schmidt, "In Chicago, Renewed Uproar on Bigotry," *New York Times*, March 24, 1990.

15. John Camper, "Everything Falls in Place for Savage," *Chicago Tribune*, March 22, 1990.

16. John Camper and Andrew Fegelman, "Savage Overcomes Tough Challenge," *Chicago Tribune*, March 21, 1990.

17. Jason Meisner, "After Scramble, Mel Reynolds Finds 'One-Night Deal' to Avoid Jail Stay," *Chicago Tribune*, July 30, 2015.

18. Federal Election Commission database, accessed February 28, 2020, https://www.fec.gov/data/receipts/individual-contributions/?contributor_name=henry%20g.%20cisneros.

19. Central Intelligence Agency, "Improper Handling of Classified Information by John M. Deutch (1998-0028-IG), Report of Investigation," February 18, 2000.

20. General Counsel of the Department of Defense, Memorandum for the Secretary of Defense (Subject: Review of Allegations Regarding Dr. John Deutch), January 19, 2001.

21. Richard Green Jr., "Last Citadel Federal Defendant Sentenced," *Post and Courier*, March 26, 1997.

22. Jim Parker, "Knoth Gets 21-Month Sentence," *Post and Courier*, August 18, 2000.

23. Richard Green Jr., "'Pug' Ravenel Sentenced to 11 Months," *Post and Courier*, December 6, 1996.

24. Ibid.

25. Richard Green Jr., "Ravenel Sentencing Today," *Post and Courier*, December 5, 1996.

26. Ibid.

27. Richard Green Jr., "'Pug' Ravenel Sentenced to 11 Months," *Post and Courier*, December 6, 1996.

28. Barbara Olson, *Hell to Pay: The Unfolding Story of Hillary Rodham Clinton*, (Washington, DC: Regnery, 1999), 234.

29. Edward Klein, *The Truth About Hillary: What She Knew, When She Knew It, and How Far She'll Go to Become President*, (New York: Sentinel, 2005), 20.

30. Jamie Dettmer and Jennifer Hickey, "Not With a Bang but a Whimper," *Insight on the News*, February 10, 1997.

31. Joel Engelhardt, "Ex-Palm Beach Lawyer's Sentence Commuted A. Paul Prosperi Faced 8-Year Term," *Palm Beach Post*, January 21, 2001.

32. Federal Election Commission database, accessed March 1, 2016.

Chapter 3

1. Don Van Natta Jr. and Mark Lacey, "Access Proved Vital in Last-Minute Race for Clinton Pardons," *New York Times*, February 25, 2001.

2. Walter Goodman, "Television Review: A Prosecutor Goes on the Defensive," *New York Times*, May 19, 1998.

3. Ed Cafasso, "The Race for the White House; Poultry Firm Took Clinton Under Wing," *Boston Herald*, March 23, 1992.

4. David Maraniss and Michael Weisskopf, "In Arkansas, the Game is Chicken; Clinton's Critics Say His Ties to Poultry Industry Cost the State," *Washington Post*, March 22, 1992.

5. Ed Cafasso, "The Race for the White House; Poultry Firm Took Clinton Under Wing," *Boston Herald*, March 23, 1992.

6.   Sara Fritz, "Clinton Ties to Tyson Scion Still Drawing Critics' Fire," *Los Angeles Times*, June 12, 1994.

7.   David Stout, "2 Cleared in Gifts Tied to Ex-Cabinet Member," *New York Times*, February 14, 1997.

8.   Testimony of Donald C. Smaltz before the US House of Representatives Government Reform and Oversight Committee, December 10, 1997.

9.   Toni Locy, "Espy's Former Chief of Staff Indicted," *Washington Post*, April 23, 1997.

10.   Ibid.

11.   David Lightman, "Dodd Helped Friend Secure Presidential Pardon," *Hartford Courant*, February 24, 2001.

12.   David Lightman, "Clinton Eases through Highs, Lows; President's Personal History Filled with Tales of Survival," *Hartford Courant*, October 29, 1996.

13.   "Inside Those Clinton Pardons," *Daily News*, February 24, 2001.

14.   Associated Free Press, "Donor to Clinton Library Pressed for Pardon: Report," *The Irish Times*, March 4, 2001, accessed December 28, 2019, https://www.irishtimes.com/news/donor-to-clinton-library-pressed-for-pardon-report-1.376393.

15.   William Raspberry, "Pardoned but Still Disbarred," *Washington Post*, June 23, 2003.

16.   Victor F. Zonana, "SEC Files Big Insider Trading Suit," *Los Angeles Times*, June 5, 1992.

17.   Dennis Duggan, "Sealed with a Bow," *Newsday*, April 4, 1992.

18.   Don Van Natta Jr. and Marc Lacey, "Access Proved Vital in Last-Minute Race for Clinton Pardons," *New York Times*, February 25, 2001.

19.   Emily Smith, "Hard-Partying Finance Crook Pardoned by Clinton Facing New Accusations," *New York Post*, September 20, 2016, accessed December 28, 2019, https://nypost.com/2016/09/20/hard-partying-finance-crook-pardoned-by-clinton-facing-new-accusations/.

20.   Vera Haller, "Mulheren Convicted on Some Counts; Jury Deliberations Continue," *Associated Press*, July 10, 1990.

21. Don Van Natta Jr. and Marc Lacey, "Access Proved Vital in Last-Minute Race for Clinton Pardons," *New York Times*, February 25, 2001.

22. John Gorman, "Judge Took, Paid Bribes, Papers Say," *Chicago Tribune*, September 7, 1988.

23. "A Whitewater Chronology," *Wall Street Journal*, May 28, 2003.

24. Michael Isikoff, "Clinton Team Works to Deflect Allegations on Nominee's Private Life," *Washington Post*, July 26, 1992.

25. Dan Cooper, "United's Fall Raises Questions," *Austin Business Journal*, June 15, 1987.

26. Tim Green, "End of Opulence: The FDIC Will Try to Recover Cash by Selling Elegant Remnants of Failed United Bank," *Austin Business Journal*, November 2, 1987.

27. "Texas Digest," *Austin-American Statesman*, March 2, 1995.

28. Kirk Ladendorf, "Banker Had High Profile in Austin," *Austin American Statesman*, May 23, 2007.

29. Gaiutra Bahadur, "Ex-Banker Gets Pardon from Clinton; Austinite convicted of Bank Fraud," *Austin American Statesman*, January 21, 2001.

30. Wayne Slater, "New Land Office Official on Probation for Bank Fraud; Ruben Johnson Played Role in Commissioner Mauro's '82 Campaign," *Dallas Morning News*, July 2, 1997.

31. Ken Herman, "On Brink of His Dream, Mauro Suddenly Pauses," *Austin American Statesman*, July 6, 1997.

32. Greg Pierce, "Inside Politics," *Washington Times*, May 1, 2001.

33. Brian McGrory and Bob Hohler, "Records Show Generous Givers Treated to White House Events," *Boston Globe*, January 25, 1997.

34. Cosmo Macero Jr., "Fund-Raising Hub Lawyer Won Pardon for Client," *Boston Herald*, February 23, 2001.

35. Sally Jacobs, "When the Law Comes Calling, Beacon Hill Bigwigs Call on Thomas Dwyer—the Attorney Who Wins His Cases by Not Going to Court; The Master Fixer," *Boston Globe*, February 15, 1996.

36. Ted Bunker, "Ferber Under Scrutiny for Arkansas Deals," *Boston Herald*, May 13, 1996.

Chapter 4

1. "Pardons and M-O-N-E-Y," *Los Angeles Times*, February 23, 2001. Editorial.

2. Todd Purdum, "Politics: The Drug War," *New York Times*, April 30, 1996.

3. Joyce Milton, *The First Partner: Hillary Rodham Clinton*, (New York: William Morrow and Co., 1999), 165.

4. Barbara Olson, *Hell to Pay: The Unfolding Story of Hillary Rodham Clinton*, (Washington, DC: Regnery, 1999), 170.

5. Associated Press, "National Briefing; Mid-Atlantic: Pennsylvania: Hillary Clinton's Brother Testifies," *New York Times*, November 27, 2001.

6. David Brock, *The Seduction of Hillary Rodham Clinton*, (New York: The Free Press, 1996), 212-3.

7. William C. Rempel and Ralph Frammolino, "Clinton Lobbied to Help Rich Backer, Records Show," *Houston Chronicle*, March 24, 1992.

8. David Brock, *The Seduction of Hillary Rodham Clinton*, (New York: The Free Press, 1996), 213.

9. William C. Rempel and Ralph Frammolino, "Clinton Lobbied to Help Rich Backer, Records Show," *Houston Chronicle*, March 24, 1992.

10. Ibid.

11. David Brock, *The Seduction of Hillary Rodham Clinton*, (New York: The Free Press, 1996), 319.

12. Edward Klein, *The Truth About Hillary: What She Knew, When She Knew It, and How Far She'll Go to Become President*, (New York: Sentinel, 2005), 23.

13. Gary Aldrich, *Unlimited Access: An FBI Agent Inside the Clinton White House*, (New York: Regnery, 1996), 112.

14. Ibid., 118.

15. Joyce Milton, *The First Partner: Hillary Rodham Clinton*, (New York: William Morrow and Co., 1999), 273.

16. Gary Aldrich, *Unlimited Access: An FBI Agent Inside the Clinton White House*, (New York: Regnery, 1996), 155.

17. Joyce Milton, *The First Partner: Hillary Rodham Clinton*, (New York: William Morrow and Co., 1999), 273.

18. Michael Duffy, "Getting Out the Wrecking Ball," *Time*, December 19, 1994.

19. Memo from Jack Quinn, White House Counsel to the President, addressed to Jamie S. Gorelick, deputy attorney general, Subject: Executive Clemency Policy, January 26, 1996.

20. John J. Goldman, "'White Collar' Money Laundry is Smashed," *Los Angeles Times*, December 1, 1994.

21. Joseph B. Treaster, "US Says It Uncovered a $100 Million Drug-Money Laundry," *New York Times*, December 1, 1994.

22. John J. Goldman, "'White Collar' Money Laundry is Smashed," *Los Angeles Times*, December 1, 1994.

23. Joseph B. Treaster, "US Says It Uncovered a $100 Million Drug-Money Laundry," *New York Times*, December 1, 1994.

24. Justice Undone: Clemency Decisions in the Clinton White House (H. Rept. 107-454), US House of Representatives, May 14, 2002, 1724.

25. Andrew Selsky, "Outrage in Colombia over Clinton's Commutation of Drug-Money Launderer's Sentence," *Associated Press*, February 27, 2001.

26. Russell Crandall, "The Americas: In the War on Drugs, Colombians Die, Americans Are Pardoned," *Wall Street Journal*, April 20, 2001.

27. Andrew Selsky, "Outrage in Colombia over Clinton's Commutation of Drug-Money Launderer's Sentence," *Associated Press*, February 27, 2001.

28. Ibid.

29. Russell Crandall, "The Americas: In the War on Drugs, Colombians Die, Americans Are Pardoned," *Wall Street Journal*, April 20, 2001.

30. Ibid.

31. "Colombian General Hits Clinton Commutation," *Washington Times*, March 6, 2001.

32. "Former Colombian Drug Agent Blasts Clinton's Pardon of Trafficker," *Agence France Presse*, March 4, 2001.

33. Russell Crandall, "The Americas: In the War on Drugs, Colombians Die, Americans Are Pardoned," *Wall Street Journal*, April 20, 2001.

34. Charles C. Thompson II and Tony Hays, "Cash for Clemency? Drug Dealer's Reprieve Called 'Highly Suspicious,'" WorldNetDaily, March 13, 2001, accessed November 22, 2007, https://www.wnd.com/2001/03/8457/.

35. US District Court W.D. Tenn. Case 85-20120-G.

36. Charles C. Thompson II and Tony Hays, "Cash for Clemency? Drug Dealer's Reprieve Called 'Highly Suspicious,'" WorldNetDaily, March 13, 2001, accessed November 22, 2007, https://www.wnd.com/2001/03/8457/.

37. Carolyn Appelman, "County Sues 3rd Broker," *Albuquerque Journal*, January 18, 2001.

38. Carolyn Appelman, "Brokerage Denies Charges," *Albuquerque Journal*, February 6, 2001.

39. *Sandoval County, NM v. NBC Capital Markets and James T. Maness* was dismissed on May 20, 2002, according to Galen Bryant of Sandoval County government public affairs office on January 8, 2008.

40. Richard A. Serrano and Stephen Braun, "In Many Drug Cases, Normal Clemency Process Bypassed," *Los Angeles Times*, March 5, 2001.

41. Hans Camporreales, "Federal Drug-Sentencing Policy Draws Fire," *Deseret News*, July 7, 2000.

42. Richard A. Serrano and Stephen Braun, "In Many Drug Cases, Normal Clemency Process Bypassed," *Los Angeles Times*, March 5, 2001.

Chapter 5

1. Dale McFeatters, "The Pardon Game," Scripps Howard News Service, January 22, 2001.

2. 2000 Census: Arkansas population 2,810,872; US population 299,398,484; 34 of 239 December 2000 and January 2001 clemency recipients were from Arkansas.

3. Hillary Rodham Clinton, *Living History*, (New York: Simon & Schuster, 2003), 87.

4. Stephen Engelberg, "New Records Outline Favor for Hillary Clinton on Trades," *New York Times*, May 27, 1994.

5. Robert D. Hershey Jr., "Friend Did Futures Trades for Hillary Clinton," *New York Times*, April 11, 1994.

6.   John M. Berry, "Boom to Bust in Arkansas; Only Lawsuits Remain for First South S&L," *Washington Post*, August 30, 1987.

7.   "Kansas Firm Buys 49 Pct.," *Arkansas Democrat-Gazette*, September 1, 1989.

8.   John M. Berry, "Boom to Bust in Arkansas; Only Lawsuits Remain for First South S&L," *Washington Post*, August 30, 1987.

9.   George Wells, "Cox gets Fine, 4 Years in Thrift Case," *Arkansas Democrat-Gazette*, August 3, 1991.

10.   "FDIC Sues First South Auditors," *Arkansas Democrat-Gazette*, July 26, 1990.

11.   Larry Sullivan and George Wells, "Cox E.," *Arkansas Democrat-Gazette*, February 21, 1991.

12.   George Wells, "Cox Gets Fine, 4 Years in Thrift Case," *Arkansas Democrat-Gazette*, August 3, 1991.

13.   "Sen. Hillary Clinton Campaign Treasurer Gives Press Conference to Address Allegations of Corruption in Former Administration," CNN, February 23, 2001.

14.   Robert Patterson, "The Obama-Soros Connection," *Human Events*, September 9, 2010, accessed September 12, 2010, https://humanevents.com/2010/09/09/the-obamasoros-connection/.

15.   Barbara Olson, *The Final Days: The Last Desperate Abuses of Power by the Clinton White House*, (Washington, DC: Regnery, 2001), 156.

16.   David Johnson and Don Van Natta Jr., "The Clinton Pardons: The Lobbying; Clinton's Brother Pursued Clemency Bids for Friends," *New York Times*, February 23, 2001.

17.   "Sen. Hillary Clinton Campaign Treasurer Gives Press Conference to Address Allegations of Corruption in Former Administration," CNN, February 23, 2001.

18.   David Johnston, "Hollywood Friend Had Clinton's Ear for 2 Late Pardons," *New York Times*, February 24, 2001.

19.   "Sen. Clinton's Campaign Treasurer Denies Pardon Wrongdoing," CNN, February 23, 2001, accessed February 12, 2007, https://www.cnn.com/2001/ALLPOLITICS/02/23/clinton.pardons.01/.

20. Elizabeth Caldwell, "'93 Inquiry Focused on Legislator Ethics," *Arkansas Democrat-Gazette*, April 13, 1996.

21. Linda Friedlieb, "Lawmaker Admits Mail Fraud," *Arkansas Democrat-Gazette*, September 3, 1997.

22. "Inside Those Clinton Pardons," *Daily News*, February 24, 2001.

23. Ibid.

24. Andrea Harter, "Buy and Sell," *Arkansas Democrat-Gazette*, July 16, 1998.

25. Don Chaney, "LR Car Dealer Sues Financial Group over Financing," *Arkansas Democrat-Gazette*, April 3, 1997.

26. John Haman, "Fraud Alleged in Morgan Financial's Fall," *Arkansas Business*, September 22, 1997.

27. David Brock, *The Seduction of Hillary Rodham Clinton*, (New York: The Free Press, 1996), 86.

28. Ibid., 190.

29. Ibid., 230.

30. Ibid.

31. Barbara Olson, *Hell to Pay: The Unfolding Story of Hillary Rodham Clinton*, (Washington, DC: Regnery, 1999), 273-4.

32. Gary Aldrich, *Unlimited Access: An FBI Agent Inside the Clinton White House*, (Washington, DC: Regnery, 1996), 157.

33. John Haman, "Fraud Alleged in Morgan Financial's Fall," *Arkansas Business*, September 22, 1997.

34. William Green, "Extra Time for Daylight This Year," *Arkansas Democrat-Gazette*, March 30, 1987.

35. "Wilson Pleads Guilty to Using Loan Proceeds," *Arkansas Democrat-Gazette*, August 23, 1990.

36. Robert McCord, "Almost Everyone Ducks Issue of Seating Convicted Legislator," *Arkansas Democrat-Gazette*, January 15, 1991.

37. "2 Black Farmers Sue FmHA in LR," *Arkansas Democrat-Gazette*, March 11, 1985.

38. *Arkansas Democrat-Gazette*, March 21, 1985.

39. George Wells, "Court Orders Retrial, Finds Race Bias in Jury Selection," *Arkansas Democrat-Gazette*, September 14, 1989.

40. "Races Contested in 26 House Districts," *Arkansas Democrat-Gazette*, May 27, 1990.

41. Noel E. Oman, "McDougal Pardon Ends Long Whitewater Ordeal," *Arkansas Democrat-Gazette*, January 21, 2001.

42. James Scudder, *Arkansas Democrat-Gazette*, October 25, 1986.

43. Neil A. Lewis, "Swindle is Reported to Use the Name of Roger Clinton," *New York Times*, March 10, 2001.

44. Eric Pooley, "Meanwhile, Back in Arkansas…," *Time*, April 13, 1998.

45. Ibid.

46. Ibid.

47. Associated Press, "Statement by Independent Counsel on Conclusions in Whitewater Investigation," *New York Times*, September 21, 2000.

48. Ibid.

49. Ibid.

50. Ibid.

51. Ibid.

52. Byron York, "The McDougal Pardon: If You Knew Susan Like He Knows Susan," *National Review*, February 19, 2001.

53. Hugh Aynesworth, "Madison Appraiser Used Phony Values; Witness Tells of Questionable Loans," *Washington Times*, March 27, 1996.

54. Ibid.

55. Michael Haddigan, "Whitewater Loan Misuse Is Admitted," *Star-Ledger*, April 16, 1996.

56. Kelly P. Kissel, "Whitewater Broker Pleads Guilty to Fraud Charges," *Associated Press*, March 21, 1995.

Chapter 6

1. "Pardons on the Sly," *New York Times*, January 25, 2001. Editorial.

2. "The Real Rostenkowski Problem," *New York Times*, July 22, 1993. Editorial.

3. Glen Elsasser, "Rostenkowski Charges to Change," *Chicago Tribune*, February 29, 1996.

4.   Jan Crawford Greenburg, "Despite Plea, Rostenkowski Says He Really Wasn't Guilty," *Chicago Tribune*, April 10, 1996.

5.   Elaine S. Povich, "Rostenkowski Woes Could Hurt Clinton," *Chicago Tribune*, July 20, 1993.

6.   Maria Henson, "Manchester, N.H.," *Arkansas Democrat-Gazette*, April 27, 1987.

7.   Tom West, "Attorney for Nashua Addresses Conflict Issue," *Manchester Union-Leader*, September 1, 1989.

8.   Tom West, "Nashua Alderman Denies Conflict," *Manchester Union-Leader*, September 2, 1989.

9.   "Trash Suit," *Associated Press*, July 25, 1999.

10. Tammy Annis, "'Mystery Men' Deny Any Wrongdoing," *Manchester Union-Leader*, May 21, 1993.

11. Fran Riley, "Two from N.E. Get Presidential Pardons; Ex-N.H. Alderman WWII Hero Named," *Boston Globe*, December 23, 2000.

12. M. R. Kropko, "Jury Finds Hughes Guilty," *Associated Press*, August 1, 1987.

13. Richard M. Peery, "Martin Hughes, 85, Long Time Force in Labor Movement, Business, Politics," *Cleveland Plain Dealer*, March 11, 2006.

14. M. R. Kropko, "Jury Finds Hughes Guilty," *Associated Press*, August 1, 1987.

15. Sandra Livingston, "Ex-Labor Leader Finds Outlet for Political Expression," *Cleveland Plain Dealer*, November 5, 1994.

16. Sarah Treffinger, "Ex-Labor Leader Named in Bias Complaint," *Cleveland Plain Dealer*, February 8, 2002.

17. Allison Grant, "Credit Union Case Referred to Attorney General," *Cleveland Plain Dealer*, December 21, 2002.

18. Allison Grant, "State Review Prompts Change at Credit Union," *Cleveland Plain Dealer*, September 22, 2001.

19. Allison Grant, "United Credit Union Gets Conservator; Feds Remove Longtime Directors," *Cleveland Plain Dealer*, February 25, 2003.

20. Richard M. Peery, "Martin Hughes, 85, Long Time Force in Labor Movement, Business, Politics," *Cleveland Plain Dealer*, March 11, 2006.

21. Paul Nowell, "Auto Dealer Indicted on Charges of Conspiracy to Bribe Honda Execs," *Associated Press*, December 4, 1996.

22. Barry Meier, "Rick Hendrick's Days of Thunder," *New York Times*, July 10, 1994.

23. James Bennet, "Guilty Plea in Honda Bribery Case," *New York Times*, February 9, 1995.

24. Barry Meier, "Rick Hendrick's Days of Thunder," *New York Times*, July 10, 1994.

25. Melissa H. Maxman, "Indictment of Auto 'MegaDealer' Impacts the American Honda Multi-district Litigation," *Civil RICO Report*, January 22, 1997.

26. Hugh L. McColl Jr., "Education and the Economy," remarks by Hugh L. McColl Jr. at the Little Rock Regional Chamber of Commerce 2000 Annual Meeting, Little Rock, AR, December 7, 2000.

27. Associated Press, "Clinton Library Gets $8.4 Million in 2000," *New York Times*, August 23, 2001.

28. Maurice Possley, "2 Former Law Partners Plead Guilty in Greylord," *Chicago Tribune*, July 7, 1987.

29. Ken Armstrong and Steve Mills, "Inept Lawyers Still on List for Capital Cases; Reforms Fail to Weed Out Problems," *Chicago Tribune*, March 10, 2002.

30. Matt O'Connor and Carlos Sadovi, "Report: Cops Used Torture," *Chicago Tribune*, July 20, 2006.

31. Todd Lighty and Dan Mihalopoulos, "'We'll Keep Chasing Them': US Wins Round Against Graft, but Fight Isn't Over," *Chicago Tribune*, April 18, 2006.

32. Basil Talbott and Michael Briggs, "Daley Lobbyists Brace for US Transit Cuts," *Chicago Sun-Times*, February 6, 1995.

33. David Barboza, "John Tyson Kicked Drug Habit; Takes Leadership Challenge, Analysts Unsure of Don Tyson's Son, Look at Pending IBP Merger as Test," *Arkansas Democrat-Gazette*, March 11, 2001.

34. William J. Clinton, *My Life*, (New York: Alfred A. Knopf, 2004), 940.

35. Scott Van Laningham, "Searcy physician Exchanged Prescriptions for Purported Diamonds, Prosecutors Contend," *Arkansas Democrat-Gazette*, May 8, 1985.

36. George Wells, "Doctor Gets 20 Months, $40,000 Fine," *Arkansas Democrat-Gazette*, June 19, 1985.

37. "United States Attorney George W. Proctor Criticized the Medical Board," *Arkansas Democrat-Gazette*, April 26, 1986.

38. Jim Brooks, "Methadone a Growing Peril as State Sees Rise in Prescription-Drug Abuse," *Arkansas Democrat-Gazette*, September 25, 2006.

39. "Brooks Expected to Take Stand in House Own Defense," *Associated Press*, June 3, 1985.

40. Dan Even, "Brooks Denies Seeking Perks for Horse Racing Bill," *Associated Press*, June 3, 1985.

41. Dan Even, "Evidence on Tapes Hurt, Lawyer for Convicted State Lawmaker Says," *Associated Press*, June 5, 1985.

42. "County Reform; Lessons from the Past Still Unlearned," *Tulsa World*, January 13, 2001. Editorial.

43. Jay C. Grelen, "Presidential Pardon Clears Record of Former Commissioner," *Daily Oklahoman*, January 11, 2001.

44. Ibid.

45. Dawn Marks, "Former County Commissioner Received Presidential Pardon," *Daily Oklahoman*, February 2, 2001.

46. D. Lea Jacobs, *Friend of the Family: An Undercover Agent in the Mafia*, (Washington, DC: Howells House, 2002), 155-6.

47. "Former Sheriff Sentenced to 15-Year Prison Term," *Associated Press*, January 15, 1982.

48. Chris McCarter, "Ex-Sheriff Among 3 from State Pardoned by Clinton," *Greenville News*, January 15, 2001.

49. Howard Mintz, "After Turning His Life Around, Scotts Valley Man Gets Gift from Clinton; a Presidential Pardon," *San Jose Mercury News*, December 24, 2000.

50. Ibid.

51. Ibid.

52.   "No Hint of Scandal in S.C. Pardons," *Post and Courier*, March 4, 2001. Editorial.

53.   Maya Bell, "No Pattern to Pardons of Floridians," *Orlando Sentinel*, January 29, 2001.

54.   Debra Rosenberg, "Backstage at the Finale," *Newsweek*, February 26, 2001.

Chapter 7

1.   Note to White House Counsel Bruce Lindsey from his assistant, Dawn Woollen, after her conversation with Hugh Rodham regarding the Carlos Vignali executive clemency application.

2.   Richard A. Serrano, "Drug Kingpin's Release Adds to Clemency Uproar," *Los Angeles Times*, February 11, 2001.

3.   Richard A. Serrano, "Cover Story; Working the American System," *Los Angeles Times Magazine*, April 29, 2001.

4.   Jessica Reaves, "The Rumpled, Ragtag Career of Hugh Rodham," *Time.com*, February 22, 2001, accessed May 3, 2007, http://content.time.com/time/nation/article/0,8599,100329,00.html.

5.   Ted Rohrlich, "Convict's Father a Wealthy, Well-Liked Mediator on the L.A. Political Scene," *Los Angeles Times*, February 13, 2001.

6.   Ibid.

7.   Richard A. Serrano, "Cover Story; Working the American System," *Los Angeles Times Magazine*, April 29, 2001.

8.   Rene Sanchez, "Drug Felon's Powerful Supporters Retreat on Pardon," *Washington Post*, February 24, 2001.

9.   Linda Greenhouse, "Supreme Court Roundup," *New York Times*, May 14, 1996.

10.   Memo from Jack Quinn, White House counsel, to the president, addressed to Jamie S. Gorelick, deputy attorney general, Subject: Executive Clemency Policy, January 26, 1996.

11.   Ibid.

12.   Bob Von Sternberg, "Judge Who Sentenced Dealer in Minnesota Questions Clemency," *Star Tribune*, February 15, 2001.

13.   Trial Transcript, *US v. Vignali* (D. Minn. October 27, 1994) at 113-4.

14. Bob Von Sternberg, "Judge Who Sentenced Dealer in Minnesota Questions Clemency," *Star Tribune*, February 15, 2001.
15. Richard A. Serrano, "Drug Kingpin's Release Adds to Clemency Uproar," *Los Angeles Times*, February 11, 2001.
16. Matea Gold, "Vignali Case Casts Shadow over Mayor's Race," *Los Angeles Times*, February 20, 2001.
17. Matea Gold, "2 City Leaders Say They Regret Helping Dealer," *Los Angeles Times*, February 13, 2001.
18. Beth Shuster, "Baca Admits Call, Not Advocacy, on Felon's Clemency," *Los Angeles Times*, February 23, 2001.
19. Ted Rohrlich, "Convict's Father a Wealthy, Well-Liked Mediator on the L.A. Political Scene," *Los Angeles Times*, February 13, 2001.
20. Beth Shuster, "Baca Admits Call, Not Advocacy, on Felon's Clemency," *Los Angeles Times*, February 23, 2001.
21. Robin Fields, "A Quirky Sheriff Who's on the Move, out in Front and Feeling Some Heat," *Los Angeles Times*, May 7, 2006.
22. Matea Gold, "2 City Leaders Say They Regret Helping Dealer," *Los Angeles Times*, February 13, 2001.
23. "Los Angeles Cardinal Regrets Role in Pardon," *New York Times*, February 13, 2001.
24. Richard A. Serrano, "Cover Story; Working the American System," *Los Angeles Times Magazine*, April 29, 2001.
25. Todd S. Purdum, "A Convict in the Storm's Eye Had Plenty of Other Help," *New York Times*, February 22, 2001.
26. Dominic Berbeo, "Hertzberg Had Part in Pardon Flap," *The Daily News of Los Angeles*, February 16, 2001.
27. Matea Gold, "2 City Leaders Say They Regret Helping Dealer," *Los Angeles Times*, February 13, 2001.
28. Stephen Braun, "L.A. Politicians Urged Pardon of Cocaine Dealer," *Los Angeles Times*, February 12, 2001.
29. Matea Gold, "2 City Leaders Say They Regret Helping Dealer," *Los Angeles Times*, February 13, 2001.

30. Richard A. Serrano, "US Attorney Pursued Clemency Case," *Los Angeles Times*, February 13, 2001.

31. Ibid.

32. Richard A. Serrano, "Clinton Brother-in-Law Was Paid $400,000 to Help Win Clemencies," *Los Angeles Times*, February 22, 2001.

33. David Rosenzweig, "US Prosecutor to Step Down for GOP Successor," *Los Angeles Times*, March 16, 2001.

34. John Daniszewski, "Prosecutor Quits over Boss' Role in Pardon," *Los Angeles Times*, March 5, 2001.

35. Duncan DeVille, "Man Resigns from U.S. Justice Dept. Due to Clinton Quid Pro Quo," *The O'Reilly Factor*, Fox News, August 29, 2001.

36. Ted Rohrlich, "Molina, Hertzberg Wrote Letters for Convict's Pardon," *Los Angeles Times*, February 16, 2001.

37. Dominic Berbeo, "Hertzberg Had Part in Pardon Flap," *The Daily News of Los Angeles*, February 16, 2001.

38. Ted Rohrlich, "Molina, Hertzberg Wrote Letters for Convict's Pardon," *Los Angeles Times*, February 16, 2001.

39. Ibid.

40. Antonio Olivo, "Speculation Swirls Over Polanco Exit from Race," *Los Angeles Times*, March 11, 2001.

41. Stephen Braun, "Clinton Aides Say He Ignored Their Advice on Rich Pardon," *Los Angeles Times*, March 2, 2001.

42. Ibid.

43. Richard A. Serrano, "Clinton Brother-in-Law Was Paid $400,000 to Help Win Clemencies," *Los Angeles Times*, February 22, 2001.

44. Richard A. Serrano, "Drug Kingpin's Release Adds to Clemency Uproar," *Los Angeles Times*, February 11, 2001.

45. Ibid.

46. Richard A. Serrano, "Cover Story; Working the American System," *Los Angeles Times Magazine*, April 29, 2001.

47. Richard A. Serrano, "Clinton Brother-in-Law Was Paid $400,000 to Help Win Clemencies," *Los Angeles Times*, February 22, 2001.

48. Nancy Luque with ReedSmith, LLP, letter to House Committee on Government Reform, February 28, 2001.

49. Christopher Marquis, "A Clinton In-Law Received $400,000 in 2 Pardon Cases," *New York Times*, February 22, 2001.

50. Richard A. Serrano, "Clinton Brother-in-Law Was Paid $400,000 to Help Win Clemencies," *Los Angeles Times*, February 22, 2001.

51. James V. Grimaldi, "Hillary Clinton's Brother Was Paid for Role in 2 Pardons," *Washington Post*, February 22, 2001.

52. Peter Slevin, "Hillary Clinton Criticizes Brother; Husband's Brother Also Lobbied for Pardons but Failed," *Washington Post*, February 23, 2001.

53. James V. Grimaldi, "Hillary Clinton's Brother Was Paid for Role in 2 Pardons," *Washington Post*, February 22, 2001.

54. Margaret Carlson, "Life with Baby Hughie," *Time*, March 5, 2001.

55. Stephen Braun and Richard A. Serrano, "Clinton Pardons: Ego Fed A Numbers Game," *Los Angeles Times*, February 25, 2001.

56. Karen Tumulty, "The Ubiquitous Mr. Fix-It," *Time,* March 23, 1998, accessed March 12, 2001, https://www.cnn.com/ALLPOLITICS/1998/03/16/time/bruce.lindsey.html.

57. James V. Grimaldi, "Hillary Clinton's Brother Was Paid for Role in 2 Pardons," *Washington Post*, February 22, 2001.

58. Peter Slevin, "Hillary Clinton Criticizes Brother; Husband's Brother Also Lobbied for Pardons but Failed," *Washington Post*, February 23, 2001.

59. Nancy Luque with ReedSmith, LLP, letter to House Committee on Government Reform, February 28, 2001.

60. Stephen Braun, "Clinton Pardons: Ego Fed a Numbers Game," *Los Angeles Times*, February 25, 2001.

61. Greg Gittrich, "Hil's Brother Has Yet to Repay 134G," *Daily News*, March 2, 2001.

62. Jessica Reaves, "The Rumpled, Ragtag Career of Hugh Rodham," *Time.com*, February 22, 2001, accessed May 3, 2007, http://content.time.com/time/nation/article/0,8599,100329,00.html.

63. Richard A. Serrano, "Cover Story; Working the American System," *Los Angeles Times Magazine*, April 29, 2001.

64. Ted Rohrlich, "Convict's Father a Wealthy, Well-Liked Mediator on the L.A. Political Scene," *Los Angeles Times*, February 13, 2001.

65. "Justice Undone: Clemency Decisions in the Clinton White House (H. Rept. 107-454)," US House of Representatives, May 14, 2002, 1301.

66. Ibid., 1302.

67. Ted Rohrlich, "Informants Named Vignali's Father," *Los Angeles Times*, March 26, 2002.

68. Ibid.

69. Ibid.

70. "Justice Undone: Clemency Decisions in the Clinton White House (H. Rept. 107-454)," US House of Representatives, May 14, 2002, 1303.

71. Ibid., 1304.

72. Ibid., 1303-4.

73. Jeffrey Anderson, "Grocery King George Torres Fingered in Murders," *L.A. Weekly*, June 13, 2007.

74. Maureen Dowd, "With His Sister in the White House, Another Rodham Can Hear the Call," *New York Times*, February 18, 1994.

75. Margaret Carlson, "Life with Baby Hughie," *Time*, March 5, 2001.

76. Maureen Dowd, "With His Sister in the White House, Another Rodham Can Hear the Call," *New York Times*, February 18, 1994.

77. Keelin McDonell, "Oh Brother," *The New Republic*, July 23, 2007.

78. Maureen Dowd, "With His Sister in the White House, Another Rodham Can Hear the Call," *New York Times*, February 18, 1994.

79. Kurt Eichenwald, "Pardon for Subject of Inquiry Worries Prosecutors," *New York Times*, February 6, 2001.

80. Tony Pugh, "Experts Say Lax Rules on Supplements Helps Some Retailers Bilk Elderly," *Knight Ridder*, September 11, 2001.

81. Tracy Connor, "Pill-Push Whiz Was a Real Quackerjack at Marketing," *New York Post*, February 23, 2001.

82. Ibid.

83. "Nostrum Mogul Arrested for Tax Evasion," *National Council Against Health Fraud Newsletter*, January 1, 2003.

84.   Paul Brinkley-Rogers, "Rebuffed Donor Often in Conflict," *Miami Herald*, October 1, 2000.

85.   Ibid.

86.   Kurt Eichenwald, "Pardon for Subject of Inquiry Worries Prosecutors," *New York Times*, February 6, 2001.

87.   Ibid.

88.   Ibid.

89.   Statement by US Senator John Breaux before the Special Committee on Aging, September 10, 2001.

90.   "Owner Takes Fifth in Senate 'Miracles' Probe," CNN, September 10, 2001.

91.   Dennis Camire, "President of Dietary Supplement Firm Takes Fifth in Senate Questioning," *Gannett News Service*, September 11, 2001.

92.   *Federal Trade Commission v. Braswell*, CV 03-3700-DT (PJWx), 33.

93.   Federal Trade Commission (press release), "A. Glenn Braswell's Dietary Supplement Enterprise Targeted," May 27, 2003.

94.   "Potion Seller," *City News Service*, March 2, 2004.

95.   "Vitamin Magnate Pardoned by President Clinton Sentenced in Tax-Evasion Case," *City News Service*, September 13, 2004.

96.   James Ridgeway, "Reporters Looking for Kendall Coffey," *The Village Voice*, February 22, 2001.

97.   James V. Grimaldi, "Hillary Clinton's Brother Was Paid for Role in 2 Pardons," *Washington Post*, February 22, 2001.

98.   Michael Moss, "Officials Say Investigation Will Go On Despite Pardon," *New York Times*, February 8, 2001.

99.   Cynthia Tucker, "Posturing over Pardons Only Obscures Real Issue," *Palm Beach Post*, February 26, 2001.

100.   "Another Clinton Pardon; Mr. Braswell Gets His Ticket," *The Herald-Sun*, February 9, 2001. Editorial.

101.   David Ovalle, "Brother Says He Believes Businessman Found Dead Was Poisoned," *Miami Herald*, November 7, 2006.

Chapter 8

1. Keelin McDonell, "Oh Brother, the Return of the Rodhams," *The New Republic*, July 23, 2007.

2. "The US Connection in the Caucasus," *Intelligence Newsletter (N. 401)*, March 8, 2001.

3. Judi Hasson, "Panel Offers Evidence of China Link Beijing Bank Wired Funds to L.A. Man Prior to Donation," *USA Today*, July 11, 1997.

4. "The US Connection in the Caucasus," *Intelligence Newsletter (N. 401)*, March 8, 2001.

5. Ibid.

6. "Hillary Clinton's Brothers Go Nuts in Georgia," *Agence France Presse*, August 20, 1999.

7. David Ignatius, "Rambling Rodhams," *Washington Post*, September 16, 1999.

8. Ibid.

9. Viveca Novak and Jay Branegan, "Are Hillary's Brothers Driving Off Course?" *Time*, October 24, 1999.

10. Michael Daly, "Nuts! More Problems for Hil," *Daily News*, September 19, 1999.

11. "US President's Wife to Visit Georgian Province of Ajaria," *Kavkasia-Press News Agency*, September 11, 1999.

12. Al Kamen, "The Untied Nations," *Washington Post*, September 22, 1999.

13. Richard Sisk, "Hil Kin Bolt from Nut Deal," *Daily News*, September 18, 1999.

14. Ibid.

15. David Ignatius, "Rambling Rodhams," *Washington Post*, September 16, 1999.

16. "The Rodham Boys Cash In," *New York Post*, October 28, 1999. Editorial.

17. Viveca Novak and Jay Branegan, "Are Hillary's Brothers Driving Off Course?" *Time*, October 24, 1999.

18. Ibid.

19. Ibid.

20. Barbara J. Saffir, "Hillary's Brothers Halt Deal; White House Warns It Could Suggest Foreign Policy Shift," *Washington Times*, September 18, 1999.

21. Michael Daly, "Nuts! More Problems for Hil," *Daily News*, September 19, 1999.

22. Ibid.

23. Keelin McDonell, "Oh Brother, the Return of the Rodhams," *The New Republic*, July 23, 2007.

24. Charles Babington, "First Lady's Brothers Quit Export Venture in Republic of Georgia," *Washington Post*, September 17, 1999.

25. "Ajaria Unaware of US First Lady's Brothers' Pullout from Georgia Hazelnut Scheme," *BBC Worldwide Monitoring*, September 21, 1999.

26. John F. Harris, "Hazelnut Flap is Building; White House Disavows Clinton In-Law's Foreign Dealings," *Washington Post*, January 1, 2000.

27. David Ignatius, "As in the Hazelnut Caper, These Folks Don't Listen," *International Herald Tribune*, February 26, 2001.

28. John F. Harris, "Hazelnut Flap is Building; White House Disavows Clinton In-Law's Foreign Dealings," *Washington Post*, January 1, 2000.

29. David Ignatius, "As in the Hazelnut Caper, These Folks Don't Listen," *International Herald Tribune*, February 26, 2001.

30. Kevin Sack, "Pardoned Couple Say Access Has Served Them Well," *New York Times*, March 10, 2001.

31. Ibid.

32. Anthony D. Rodham, "What Was Tony Rodham's Role in Pardons Granted by the President?" *Larry King Live*, March 2, 2001.

33. Ibid.

34. "National Briefing; Mid-Atlantic: Pennsylvania: Hillary Clinton's Brother Testifies," *New York Times*, November 27, 2001.

35. George Rush and Joanna Molloy, "Hil's Brother Squeezed for Support," *Daily News*, June 10, 2002.

36. Dareh Gregorian, "Hill's Brother a Deadbeat," *New York Post*, December 20, 2007.

37. Remarks by Anthony D. Rodham on *Larry King Live*, March 2, 2001.

38. Keelin McDonell, "Oh Brother, the Return of the Rodhams," *The New Republic*, July 23, 2007.

39.   Philip Shenon, "Cambodia Trip by Brother of First Lady Alarms US Officials," *New York Times*, July 18, 1998.

40.   Lisa Getter, "Family Ties Put Rodham Brothers in Spotlight," *Los Angeles Times*, March 4, 2001.

41.   Joseph Farah, "Hillary's Brothers," WorldNetDaily.com, June 28, 2000, accessed December 9, 2007, https://www.wnd.com/2000/06/1630/.

42.   Lisa Getter, "Family Ties Put Rodham Brothers in Spotlight," *Los Angeles Times*, March 4, 2001.

43.   Kevin Sack, "Pardoned Couple Say Access Has Served Them Well," *New York Times*, March 10, 2001.

44.   Don Van Natta Jr., "Clinton Library Will Yield Details on Big Donations," *New York Times*, March 3, 2001.

45.   Mary Orndoff, "Sessions Asks Probe of Pardon of Ex-Banker," *Birmingham News*, March 3, 2001.

46.   Kevin Sack, "Pardoned Couple Say Access Has Served Them Well," *New York Times*, March 10, 2001.

47.   Judicial Watch, letter to Assistant US Attorney General Alice Fisher, October 6, 2006.

48.   Don Van Natta Jr., "Clinton Library Will Yield Details on Big Donations," *New York Times*, March 3, 2001.

49.   Keith Russell, "Autry's Widow Backs Gregory on Filing," *The Tennessean*, August 27, 2002.

50.   Ibid.

51.   Sheila Burke, "Clinton in-Law Fights Claim Filed in Federal Court," *The Tennessean*, February 28, 2007.

Chapter 9

1.   "Justice Undone: Clemency Decisions in the Clinton White House (H. Rept. 107-454)," US House of Representatives, May 14, 2002, 715.

2.   Associated Press, "Roger Clinton Faces Drunken Driving Inquiry," *New York Times*, February 19, 2001.

3.   Jean Merl, "Roger Clinton Gets Fine and Probation in Plea Bargain," *Los Angeles Times*, August 8, 2001.

4.	Roger Clinton, "Roger Clinton Speaks Out, *Larry King Live*, June 21, 2001.

5.	Phil Brennan, "Roger Clinton, Using President, Helped Gambino Crime Family," NewsMax.com, August 27, 2001, accessed July 9, 2007, https://www.newsmax.com/pre-2008/roger-clintonusing/2001/08/25/id/663328/.

6.	"Two Relatives of Carlo Gambino Charged in Heroin Smuggling Case," *Washington Post*, March 20, 1980.

7.	"Michele Sidona; Convicted," *The Economist*, April 5, 1980.

8.	Pamela Brownstein, "Court Papers Link Alleged Crime Figure with Sidona 'Kidnapping,'" *Associated Press*, December 6, 1984.

9.	Vera Haller, "Feds Charge Reputed Mobster with Supervising 'Joint Venture' Drug Conspiracy," *Associated Press*, January 5, 1990.

10.	"Justice Undone: Clemency Decisions in the Clinton White House (H. Rept. 107-454)," US House of Representatives, May 14, 2002, 739.

11.	Michael J. Gaines, memorandum, Subject: Rosario Gambino, January 30, 1996.

12.	Michael A. Stover, memorandum, Subject: Gambino, Rosario, Reg. No. 06235-0505, January 31, 1996.

13.	Ibid.

14.	Ibid.

15.	Marie Ragghianti, memorandum, Re: Roger Clinton Office Visit, December 23, 1997.

16.	Alison Leigh Cowan, "Roger Clinton's Dogged Effort for Drug Trafficker," *New York Times*, August 26, 2001.

17.	Federal Bureau of Investigation, "Report of Interview of Roger Clinton," (File #72-BA-96138), October 1, 1999.

18.	Ibid.

19.	Alison Leigh Cowan, "Roger Clinton's Dogged Effort for Drug Trafficker," *New York Times*, August 26, 2001.

20.	"Star Tanned in Pardon Plot," *New York Post*, August 29, 2001.

21.	Federal Bureau of Investigation, "Report of Interview of Roger Clinton," (File #72-BA-96138), October 1, 1999.

22. Christopher Newton, "Crime Family Paid Roger Clinton $50,000," *The Star-Ledger*, June 28, 2001.

23. Alison Leigh Cowan, "Pardon for Felon Considered After Kin Paid Roger Clinton," *New York Times*, June 28, 2001.

24. Peter Slevin and James V. Grimaldi, "Hillary Clinton Criticizes Brother," *Washington Post*, February 23, 2001.

25. Richard A. Serrano and Stephen Braun, "Roger Clinton Says He Promised Pardons," *Los Angeles Times*, February 24, 2001.

26. Ibid.

27. Alison Leigh Cowan, "House Committee Asks Roger Clinton to Explain Some Ties to Pardon Requests," *New York Times*, June 29, 2001.

28. Viveca Novak and Michael Weisskopf, "New Questions about Roger Clinton's Slippery Schemes," *Time*, June 30, 2001.

29. Alison Leigh Cowan, "House Committee Asks Roger Clinton to Explain Some Ties to Pardon Requests," *New York Times*, June 29, 2001.

30. Committee on Government Reform, "Justice Undone: Clemency Decisions in the Clinton White House (H. Rept. 107-454)," US House of Representatives, May 14, 2002, 800.

31. Alison Leigh Cowan, "Plea Mailed to Roger Clinton Was Flagged by President," *New York Times*, June 30, 2001.

32. Richard A. Serrano and Stephen Braun, "Alleged Pay-for-Pardon Bid by Roger Clinton is Probed," *Los Angeles Times*, March 8, 2001.

33. Neil A. Lewis, "Swindle Is Reported to Use the Name of Roger Clinton," *New York Times*, March 10, 2001.

34. Alison Leigh Cowan, "New Accusations Again Put Focus on Roger Clinton," *New York Times*, June 17, 2001.

35. Richard A. Serrano, "'Snookered' Out of a Pardon, Convict Says," *Los Angeles Times*, June 22, 2001.

36. Roger Clinton, "Roger Clinton Speaks Out," *Larry King Live*, June 21, 2001.

37. "Justice Undone: Clemency Decisions in the Clinton White House (H. Rept. 107-454)," US House of Representatives, May 14, 2002, 797.

38. Richard A. Serrano, "Roger Clinton Said to Be Deeply Tied to Pardons," *Los Angeles Times*, March 13, 2002, 1.

Chapter 10

1. Frank J. Prial, "Bombers Called Intent on Killing," *New York Times*, January 25, 1975.
2. *New York Times*, December 12, 1974.
3. Testimony of retired FBI special agent Donald R. Wofford before the Senate Judiciary Committee, September 15, 1999.
4. Fuerzas Armadas de Liberación Nacional, "Communiqué #2," December 11, 1974.
5. "The FALN and Macheteros Clemency: Misleading Explanation, Reckless Decisions, A Dangerous Message, Third Report by the [House] Committee on Government Reform," US House of Representatives, December 10, 1999, 8.
6. Ibid., 12.
7. Joanne Omang, "Puerto Rican Nationalists Don't Rule Out Violence," *Washington Post*, September 12, 1979.
8. Manuel Roig-Franzia, "A Terrorist in the House," *Washington Post Magazine*, February 22, 2004.
9. Testimony of Angel M. Cintron, Majority Leader of Puerto Rican House of Representatives, before the US Senate Judiciary Committee on September 15, 1999.
10. Frank J. Prial, "Bombers Called Intent on Killing," *New York Times*, January 25, 1975.
11. Malcolm N. Carter, *Associated Press*, August 4, 1977.
12. Testimony of retired FBI special agent Donald R. Wofford before the Senate Judiciary Committee, September 15, 1999.
13. Fuerzas Armadas de Liberación Nacional, "Communiqué #3," January 24, 1975.
14. Fuerzas Armadas de Liberación Nacional, "Communiqué #4," April 2, 1975.
15. Robert McFadden, "4 Killed, 44 Injured in Fraunces Tavern Explosion," *New York Times*, January 25, 1975.
16. Richard T. Pienciak, "Today's Focus: On the Trail of the Terrorists," *Associated Press*, July 14, 1978.

17. William Sater, *Puerto Rican Terrorists: A Possible Threat to US Energy Installations?* (Santa Monica, CA: Rand Corporation, 1981), 22.

18. *New York Times*, June 15, 1975.

19. William Schmidt, "PUERTO RICO: Slack Bootstraps," *Newsweek*, November 10, 1975.

20. William Sater, *Puerto Rican Terrorists: A Possible Threat to US Energy Installations?* (Santa Monica, CA: Rand Corporation, 1981), 22, 25.

21. Richard T. Pienciak, "Today's Focus: On the Trail of the Terrorists," *Associated Press*, July 14, 1978.

22. William Sater, *Puerto Rican Terrorists: A Possible Threat to US Energy Installations?* (Santa Monica, CA: Rand Corporation, 1981), 22-3.

23. Richard T. Pienciak, "Today's Focus: On the Trail of the Terrorists," *Associated Press*, July 14, 1978.

24. Charles Chamberlain, *Associated Press*, February 18, 1977.

25. Testimony of retired FBI special agent Donald R. Wofford before the Senate Judiciary Committee, September 15, 1999.

26. Paul Serafini, "Woman Convicted of Planting Bomb," *Associated Press*, May 22, 1980.

27. Richard T. Pienciak, *Associated Press*, July 13, 1978.

28. *Associated Press*, August 12, 1977.

29. William Sater, *Puerto Rican Terrorists: A Possible Threat to US Energy Installations?* (Santa Monica, CA: Rand Corporation, 1981), 22-3.

30. "Aviation Attacks," *Aviation Week & Space Technology*, May 29, 1978.

31. Stephen J. Lynton and Alfred E. Lewis, "Bomb Here Is Tied to 3 In N.Y. Area; Terrorists Claim Responsibility for Bomb Here; Terrorist Group Calls After Blast at Justice Dept.," *Washington Post*, May 23, 1978.

32. *Associated Press*, April 11, 1979.

33. Richard T. Pienciak, *Associated Press*, July 13, 1978.

34. Richard T. Pienciak, "Today's Focus: On the Trail of the Terrorists," *Associated Press*, July 14, 1978.

35. *Associated Press*, April 11, 1979.

36. "FALN Suspect Escapes in New York," *World News Digest*, June 8, 1979.

37. "Terrorists Bomb Chicago, Puerto Rico," *Facts on File World News Digest*, October 19, 1979.

38. "Puerto Ricans Blamed in Blasts," *Washington Post*, October 19, 1979.

39. "Puerto Rican Group Claims It Set Off Three Chicago Blasts," *Washington Post*, November 25, 1979.

40. Luis R. Matos, "Two US Sailors Dead, Eight Injured in Terrorist Ambush," *Associated Press*, December 3, 1979.

41. Susan J. Smith, "Ten Suspected Terrorists Get up to 90 Years in Prison," *Associated Press*, February 19, 1991.

42. Luis Feldstein Soto, "Puerto Rican Terrorists Taunt FBI, but Agency Is Closing In," *Houston Chronicle*, September 15, 1985.

43. William Sater, *Puerto Rican Terrorists: A Possible Threat to US Energy Installations?* (Santa Monica, CA: Rand Corporation, 1981), 27.

44. Lew Wheaton, "Saboteurs Blow Up Nine Nat'l Guard Planes," *Associated Press*, January 12, 1981.

45. John Rhodes, "FALN Bombs Rock Wall Street," *United Press International*, March 1, 1982.

46. John Castellucci, *The Big Dance: The Untold Story of Kathy Boudin and the Terrorist Family That Committed the Brinks Robbery Murders*, (New York: Dodd, Mead & Company, 1986), 282.

47. Robert D. McFadden, "F.A.L.N. Puerto Rican Terrorists Suspected in New Year Bombings," *New York Times*, January 2, 1983.

48. Richard L. Madden, "Wells Fargo Guard Accused of Stealing $7 Million in Cash," *New York Times*, September 14, 1983.

49. "14 Held in Wells Fargo Theft," *World News Digest*, September 20, 1985.

50. Luis R. Matos, "Two US Sailors Dead, Eight Injured in Terrorist Ambush," *Associated Press*, December 3, 1979.

51. Kenneth R. Bazinet, "FBI Claims Suspect Planned $7 Million Robbery," *United Press International*, October 7, 1985.

52. Ibid.

53. Brent Laymon, "Three Years After Arrests, Wells Fargo Trial Finally Gets Under Way," *Associated Press*, September 5, 1988.

54. Dean Golembeski, "Wells Fargo Defendant Pleads Guilty," *Associated Press*, September 6, 1988.

55. *United Press International*, October 14, 1988.

56. *United Press International*, December 6, 1988.

57. Mark A. Dupuis, "Four Convicted in Wells Fargo Heist," *United Press International*, April 10, 1989.

58. "The FALN and Macheteros Clemency: Misleading Explanation, Reckless Decisions, A Dangerous Message, Third Report by the [House] Committee on Government Reform," US House of Representatives, December 10, 1999, 3.

59. Ofensiva, '92, letter to Margaret Colgate Love, US pardon attorney, dated November 9, 1993.

60. "Thousands Demand Freedom for Jailed Puerto Rican Activist; Unconditional Support," *Hartford Courant*, August 30, 1999.

61. Transcript of Talk of the Nation, "President Clinton's Offer of Clemency to Members of the Militant Group FALN," National Public Radio, August 30, 1999.

62. Dick Morris, *Rewriting History*, (New York: Regan Books, 2004), 240.

63. Ibid., 241.

64. Mayra Martinez-Fernandez, memorandum to Jeffrey Farrow; Re: The Puerto Rican Political Prisoners, October 24, 1994.

65. Ibid.

66. Mayra Martinez-Fernandez, notes titled "Meeting at the WH Re: Puerto Rican Prisoners," June 21, 1995.

67. Jeffrey Farrow, email to Ricardo Gonzalez of the Office of the Vice President; Subject: Re: VP mtg w/ Hispanic Caucus on Friday 7/17, July 16, 1998.

68. Dan Morgan, "First Lady Opposes Puerto Rican Clemency Offer," *Washington Post*, September 5, 1999.

69. Dick Morris, *Rewriting History*, (New York: Regan Books, 2004), 243.

70. Roll Call Vote #398, House Concurrent Resolution 180, US House of Representatives (106th Congress), September 9, 1999.

71. Testimony of Gilbert G. Gallegos before the US Senate Judiciary Committee, September 15, 1999.

72. William J. Clinton, televised comments on evening of August 20, 1998, after ordering cruise missile strikes against Afghanistan and Sudan.

73. "Twelve Puerto Rican Prisoners Accept Clinton's Offer of Clemency," *Agence France Presse*, September 7, 1999.

74. Dirk Johnson, "Puerto Ricans Clinton Freed Leave Prisons," *New York Times*, September 11, 1999.

75. David Johnston, "The Nation; Pardons: Having to Say You're Sorry," *New York Times*, September 12, 1999.

76. William Sater, *Puerto Rican Terrorists: A Possible Threat to US Energy Installations?* (Santa Monica, CA: Rand Corporation, 1981), 25.

77. "F.A.L.N. Tied to 49 Blasts Since Aug, '74," *New York Times*, February 20, 1977.

78. William Sater, *Puerto Rican Terrorists: A Possible Threat to US Energy Installations?* (Santa Monica, CA: Rand Corporation, 1981), 21.

79. Ibid., 25.

80. Ibid., 21.

81. Fuerzas Armadas de Liberación Nacional, "Communiqué #3", January 24, 1975.

82. Documents and Communiqués from the Revolutionary Public Independence Movement and the Armed Clandestine Movement, *Toward People's War for Independence and Socialism in Puerto Rico: In Defense of Armed Struggle*, January 1979, 45.

83. William Sater, *Puerto Rican Terrorists: A Possible Threat to US Energy Installations?* (Santa Monica, CA: Rand Corporation, 1981), 22.

84. New York Times, June 15, 1975, 37.

85. William Sater, *Puerto Rican Terrorists: A Possible Threat to US Energy Installations?* (Santa Monica, CA: Rand Corporation, 1981), 25.

86. William Schmidt, "PUERTO RICO: Slack Bootstraps," *Newsweek*, November 10, 1975.

87. William Sater, *Puerto Rican Terrorists: A Possible Threat to US Energy Installations?* (Santa Monica, CA: Rand Corporation, 1981), 22, 25.

88. Ibid., 22.
89. Sandra Salmans and Phyllis Malamud, "Everything Blew," *Newsweek*, January 12, 1976.
90. William Sater, *Puerto Rican Terrorists: A Possible Threat to US Energy Installations?* (Santa Monica, CA: Rand Corporation, 1981), 22, 25.
91. Ibid., 22.
92. Ibid.
93. Documents and Communiqués from the Revolutionary Public Independence Movement and the Armed Clandestine Movement, *Toward People's War for Independence and Socialism in Puerto Rico: In Defense of Armed Struggle*, January 1979, 45.
94. Richard T. Pienciak, "Today's Focus: On the Trail of The Terrorists," *Associated Press*, July 14, 1978.
95. William Sater, *Puerto Rican Terrorists: A Possible Threat to US Energy Installations?* (Santa Monica, CA: Rand Corporation, 1981), 22-3.
96. Ibid., 23.
97. Ibid.
98. *New York Times*, September 23, 1976.
99. Charles Chamberlain, *Associated Press*, February 18, 1977.
100. Bernard Cohen, *Associated Press*, February 19, 1977.
101. "FALN Linked to New Bombings," *World News Digest*, April 9, 1977.
102. Peter Kihss, *New York Times*, April 12, 1977.
103. "Three Die in Chicago Riots," *World News Digest*, June 18, 1977.
104. Paul Serafini, "Woman Convicted of Planting Bomb," *Associated Press*, May 22, 1980.
105. Richard T. Pienciak, *Associated Press*, July 13, 1978.
106. William Sater, *Puerto Rican Terrorists: A Possible Threat to US Energy Installations?* (Santa Monica, CA: Rand Corporation, 1981), 26.
107. Ibid., 23.
108. *Associated Press*, August 12, 1977.
109. William Sater, *Puerto Rican Terrorists: A Possible Threat to US Energy Installations?* (Santa Monica, CA: Rand Corporation, 1981), 23.
110. Ibid., 26.

111. "Bomb Explodes Outside N.Y.C. Public Library," *Washington Post*, October 12, 1977.

112. William Sater, *Puerto Rican Terrorists: A Possible Threat to US Energy Installations?* (Santa Monica, CA: Rand Corporation, 1981), 23.

113. Ibid., 26.

114. *Associated Press*, October 19, 1977.

115. William Sater, *Puerto Rican Terrorists: A Possible Threat to US Energy Installations?* (Santa Monica, CA: Rand Corporation, 1981), 23.

116. *Associated Press*, January 13, 1978.

117. *New York Times*, January 31, 1978.

118. William Sater, *Puerto Rican Terrorists: A Possible Threat to US Energy Installations?* (Santa Monica, CA: Rand Corporation, 1981), 24.

119. Ibid.

120. *Associated Press*, March 13, 1978.

121. "Around the Nation," *Washington Post*, March 25, 1978.

122. "Aviation Attacks," *Aviation Week & Space Technology*, May 29, 1978.

123. Stephen J. Lynton and Alfred E. Lewis, "Bomb Here Is Tied to 3 In N.Y. Area; Terrorists Claim Responsibility for Bomb Here; Terrorist Group Calls After Blast at Justice Dept.," *Washington Post*, May 23, 1978.

124. William Sater, *Puerto Rican Terrorists: A Possible Threat to US Energy Installations?* (Santa Monica, CA: Rand Corporation, 1981), 24.

125. Ibid.

126. Luis Feldstein Soto, "Puerto Rican Terrorists Taunt FBI, but Agency Is Closing In," *Houston Chronicle*, September 15, 1985.

127. William Sater, *Puerto Rican Terrorists: A Possible Threat to US Energy Installations?* (Santa Monica, CA: Rand Corporation, 1981), 24.

128. "Terrorists Bomb Chicago, Puerto Rico," *World News Digest*, October 19, 1979.

129. Charles Chamberlain, *Associated Press*, October 18, 1979.

130. "Puerto Rican Group Claims It Set Off Three Chicago Blasts," *Washington Post*, November 25, 1979.

131. Luis R. Matos, "Two US Sailors Dead, Eight Injured in Terrorist Ambush," *Associated Press*, December 3, 1979.

132. "Gun-Hunting Raiders May Have Had Inside Knowledge," *Associated Press*, January 15, 1980.

133. William Sater, *Puerto Rican Terrorists: A Possible Threat to US Energy Installations?* (Santa Monica, CA: Rand Corporation, 1981), 27.

134. Kathy Sawyer and Edward Walsh, "Terrorists Invade Offices of Carter, Bush Campaigns," *Washington Post*, March 16, 1980.

135. Testimony of retired FBI special agent Richard S. Hahn before the US Senate Judiciary Committee on September 15, 1999.

136. Connie Arena, "Power Returning to Puerto Rico," *Associated Press*, April 12, 1980.

137. "Five Groups Claim They Bombed Statue of Liberty," *Associated Press*, June 4, 1980.

138. Paul Raeburn, "Demonstrators Storm Reagan Campaign Headquarters," *Associated Press*, November 3, 1980.

139. "Police Investigate Pipe Bomb Explosions," *Associated Press*, December 22, 1980.

140. Luis Feldstein Soto, "Puerto Rican Terrorists Taunt FBI, but Agency Is Closing in," *Houston Chronicle*, September 15, 1985.

141. William Sater, *Puerto Rican Terrorists: A Possible Threat to US Energy Installations?* (Santa Monica, CA: Rand Corporation, 1981), 27.

142. Robert D. McFadden, "F.A.L.N. Puerto Rican Terrorists Suspected in New Year Bombings," *New York Times*, January 2, 1983.

143. Ibid.

Chapter 11

1. Dick Morris, *Rewriting History*, (New York: Regan Books, 2004), 241.

2. Agence France Presse, "Hillary Clinton Supports a Palestinian State," *New York Times*, May 7, 1998.

3. Larry Cohler-Esses, "Israel Foe Gives Hil 50G; Muslim Group Backs Palestinian Use of Force," *Daily News*, October 25, 2000.

4. Ibid.

5. Jonathan Wells, "Radical Islam; Outspoken Cleric, Jailed Activist Tied to New Hub Mosque," *Boston Herald*, October 28, 2002.

6. Larry Cohler-Esses, "Israel Foe Gives Hil 50G; Muslim Group Backs Palestinian Use of Force," *Daily News*, October 25, 2000.

7. Steven Emerson, "Friends of Hamas in the White House," *Wall Street Journal*, March 13, 1996.

8. Larry Cohler-Esses, "Terror Backer Works for U.S.," *Daily News*, October 31, 2000.

9. Federal Election Commission, "Financial Disclosure for Hillary Rodham Clinton for Senate, Inc.," (FEC #C00346544) for period 4/01/00 through 6/30/00.

10. Jonathan Wells, "RADICAL ISLAM; Outspoken Cleric, Jailed Activist Tied to New Hub Mosque," *Boston Herald*, October 28, 2003.

11. Michael Isikoff, "Lobbying for Libya—and Bush," *Newsweek*, October 28, 2004.

12. Beth J. Harpaz, "Clinton Campaign to Return $50,000 from Muslim Fund-Raiser," *Associated Press*, October 25, 2000.

13. Ibid.

14. Larry Cohler-Esses, "Israel Foe Gives Hil 50G; Muslim Group Backs Palestinian Use of Force," *Daily News*, October 25, 2000.

15. Federal Election Commission, "Financial Disclosure for Hillary Rodham Clinton for Senate, Inc.," (FEC #C00346544) for period 10/19/00 through 11/27/00.

16. Christopher Andersen, *American Evita*, (New York: William Morrow, 2004), 187-8.

17. Barbara Olson, *The Final Days: The Last, Desperate Abuses of Power by the Clinton White House*, (Washington, DC: Regnery, 2001), 175.

18. William A. Orme Jr., "While Mrs. Clinton Looks On, Palestinian Officials Criticize Israel," *New York Times*, November 12, 1999.

19. Eric J. Greenberg, "Anatomy of a Pardon," *Jewish Week*, January 26, 2001.

20. Steve Lieberman, "Many in Rockland Think Deal Was Made for New Square Men's Commutations," *The Journal News*, March 4, 2001.

21. Suzan Clarke, "New Square Leader Dies at 79," *The Journal News*, March 10, 2004.

22. Eric J. Greenberg, "Charges Rock New Square: Questions about Chasidic Leadership Emerge as Feds Indict Six in Alleged Scam of Federal Programs; Community Claims Gov't Vendetta," *Jewish Week*, June 6, 1997.

23. Edward Helmore, "Word Is Made Flesh as God Reveals Himself...As a Fish," *The Guardian*, March 16, 2003.

24. Randal C. Archibold, "4 Who Got Leniency Defrauded US for Religion," *New York Times*, January 26, 2001.

25. US Department of Education, "Semiannual Report to Congress (No. 35), April 1, 1997-September 30, 1997," Office of Inspector General, 21.

26. Eric J. Greenberg, "Witness: Yeshiva Faked Documents for Grants," *Jewish Week*, December 4, 1998.

27. Benjamin Weiser, "6 Indicted in Fraud Over Use of Grants for Hasidic Groups," *New York Times*, May 29, 1997.

28. Eric J. Greenberg, "Charges Rock New Square: Questions about Chasidic Leadership Emerge as Feds Indict Six in Alleged Scam of Federal Programs; Community Claims Gov't Vendetta," *Jewish Week*, June 6, 1997.

29. Greg B. Smith, "Religious Bigs Are Indicted," *New York Daily News*, May 29, 1997.

30. Greg B. Smith, "Religious Bigs Are Indicted," *New York Daily News*, May 29, 1997.

31. Steve Lieberman, "County," *The Journal News*, May 8, 2002.

32. Randal C. Archibold, "4 Who Got Leniency Defrauded US for Religion," *New York Times*, January 26, 2001.

33. Eric J. Greenberg, "Charges Rock New Square: Questions about Chasidic Leadership Emerge as Feds Indict Six in Alleged Scam of Federal Programs; Community Claims Gov't Vendetta," *Jewish Week*, June 6, 1997.

34. "New Square Assembles Its Own Legal Dream Team: Chasidic Village Is Anything but 'Otherworldly'," *Forward*, June 20, 1997.

35. Eric J. Greenberg, "Pardon Plan Raised in Sept.," *Jewish Week*, March 2, 2001.

36. Eric J. Greenberg, "Charges Rock New Square: Questions about Chasidic Leadership Emerge as Feds Indict Six in Alleged Scam of Federal Programs; Community Claims Gov't Vendetta," *Jewish Week*, June 6, 1997.

37. Debra Nussbaum Cohen, "Focus on Issues: Should religious Jews be held to a higher ethical standard?" *Jewish Telegraph Agency*, June 12, 1995.

38. Government Accounting Office, Student Financial Aid Programs; Pell Grant Program Abuse (GAO/T-OSI-94-8), October 27, 1993.

39. Russ Buettner, "It Takes A Lot of Taxpayers to Fund Village," *Daily News*, February 12, 2001.

40. Eric J. Greenberg, "Feds, Chasidim Reach Pact: First Government Takeover of Religious School to End as Rockland Community Agrees to Pay 1 Million Fine," *Jewish Week*, May 31, 1996.

41. Ibid.

42. Eric J. Greenberg, "Charges Rock New Square: Questions about Chasidic Leadership Emerge as Feds Indict Six in Alleged Scam of Federal Programs; Community Claims Gov't Vendetta," *Jewish Week*, June 6, 1997.

43. Greg B. Smith, "Religious Bigs Are Indicted," *New York Daily News*, May 29, 1997.

44. Benjamin Weiser, "6 Indicted in Fraud Over Use of Grants for Hasidic Groups," *New York Times*, May 29, 1997.

45. Ibid.

46. Steve Lieberman, "New Square Founder Faces Federal Prison," *The Journal News*, May 6, 2002.

47. Eric J. Greenberg, "Anatomy of a Pardon," *The Jewish Week*, January 26, 2001.

48. "Knesset Blocks Sanctuary Bid for New Square Man," *Forward*, July 6, 2001.

49. "Fugitive Cannot Do Time in Israel," *The Journal News*, August 6, 2001.

50. Eric J. Greenberg, "Skverer Deal: Fugitive from Upstate Chasidic Village Pleads Guilty to Defrauding Federal Government," *The Jewish Week*, February 1, 2002.

51. Steve Lieberman, "Ex-New Square Trustee Gets 6 Years," *The Journal News*, May 23, 2002.

52. Larry Neumeister, "Prosecutor Closes Probe into Clinton New Square Clemency Grants," *Associated Press*, June 21, 2002.

53. Steve Lieberman, "Ex-New Square Trustee Gets 6 Years," *The Journal News*, May 23, 2002.

54. Patricia Hurtado, "5 Years in Fraud Case; Hasidic Community Founder Bilked Gov't," *Newsday*, May 23, 2002.

Chapter 12

1.   John F. Harris, "For the Clintons' Last Act, Reviews Don't Look Good," *Washington Post*, January 27, 2001.

2.   Department of Treasury, Office of Foreign Assets Control, memorandum (COMPL 94253) dated September 16, 1994.

3.   Michael Dobbs, "Rich Made His Fortune by Breaking the Rules," *Washington Post*, March 13, 2001.

4.   Marcia Vickers, "The Rich Boys; An Ultra-Secretive Network Rules Independent Oil Trading. Its Mentor: Marc Rich," *Business Week*, July 18, 2005.

5.   Gordon Pitts, "'King of Zug' Reigns over Trading Network; Controversial Marc Rich Has Long Been a Part of the Buying and Selling of the World's Mineral Wealth," *The Globe and Mail*, August 16, 2005.

6.   Jim Hougan, "King of the World; Marc Rich," *Playboy*, February 1994.

7.   A. Craig Copetas, *Metal Men: How Marc Rich Defrauded the Country, Evaded the Law, and Became the World's Most Sought-After Corporate Criminal*, (New York: Perennial, 2001), 119.

8.   Shawn Tully and Ford S. Worthy, "Secrets of Marc Rich," *Fortune*, January 23, 1984.

9.   Jim Hougan, "King of the World; Marc Rich," *Playboy*, February 1994.

10. Ibid.

11. Matthew McAllester, "Rich's Suspect Ties; Sources: Clinton Could Have Learned Russian Mob Links," *Newsday*, March 1, 2001.

12.   Maureen Dowd, "In Marc Rich's Case, Bill and Hill Were Manipulated,"
      Hamilton Spectator, February 12, 2001.

13.   Marcia Vickers, "The Rich Boys; An Ultra-Secretive Network Rules
      Independent Oil Trading. Its Mentor: Marc Rich," *Business Week*, July 18,
      2005.

14.   Subcommittee on Terrorism, Narcotics, and International Operations,
      Hearing Report 102-350, Pt. 3, US Senate, 790-1.

15.   Subcommittee on Terrorism, Narcotics, and International Operations,
      Hearing Report 102-350, Pt. 1, US Senate, 61.

16.   "The US Connection in the Caucasus," *Intelligence Newsletter (N. 401)*,
      March 8, 2001.

17.   Judi Hasson, "Panel Offers Evidence of China Link Beijing Bank Wired
      Funds to L.A. Man Prior to Donation," *USA Today*, July 11, 1997.

18.   "The US Connection in the Caucasus," *Intelligence Newsletter (N. 401)*,
      March 8, 2001.

19.   Richard Sisk, "Hil Kin Bolt from Nut Deal," *Daily News*, September 18,
      1999.

20.   Alison Leigh Cowan, "Plotting a Pardon; Rich Cashed in a World of Chits
      to Win Pardon," *New York Times*, April 11, 2001.

21.   David Ignatius, "Rambling Rodhams," *Washington Post*, September 16,
      1999.

22.   A. Craig Copetas, *Metal Men: How Marc Rich Defrauded the Country,
      Evaded the Law, and Became the World's Most Sought-After Corporate
      Criminal*, (New York: Perennial, 2001), 119.

23.   Ibid., 122.

24.   Marcia Vickers, "The Rich Boys; An Ultra-Secretive Network Rules
      Independent Oil Trading. Its Mentor: Marc Rich," *Business Week*, July 18,
      2005.

25.   A. Craig Copetas, *Metal Men: How Marc Rich Defrauded the Country,
      Evaded the Law, and Became the World's Most Sought-After Corporate
      Criminal*, (New York: Perennial, 2001), 141.

26.   Michael Dobbs, "Rich Made His Fortune by Breaking the Rules," *Wash-
      ington Post*, March 13, 2001.

27. Associated Press, "State Seeks Rich's Account," *New York Times*, May 3, 2001.

28. Independent Inquiry Committee into the United Nations Oil-for-Food Programme, "Report on Programme Manipulation," October 27, 2005, 63.

29. Ibid.

30. Ibid., 65-7.

31. Hearing of the House International Relations Committee, Subject: The Oil-for-Food Program: Tracking the Funds, February 17, 2004.

32. Jerry Seper, "Grand Jury Probes Rich-Saddam Link," *Washington Times*, December 17, 2004.

33. Marcia Vickers, "The Rich Boys; An Ultra-Secretive Network Rules Independent Oil Trading. Its Mentor: Marc Rich," *Business Week*, July 18, 2005.

34. A. Craig Copetas, *Metal Men: How Marc Rich Defrauded the Country, Evaded the Law, and Became the World's Most Sought-After Corporate Criminal*, (New York: Perennial, 2001), 176.

35. Ibid., 177.

36. Michael Dobbs, "Rich Made His Fortune by Breaking the Rules," *Washington Post*, March 13, 2001.

37. A. Craig Copetas, *Metal Men: How Marc Rich Defrauded the Country, Evaded the Law, and Became the World's Most Sought-After Corporate Criminal*, (New York: Perennial, 2001), 179.

38. Ibid., 177.

39. Ibid., 188.

40. Ibid., 193.

41. Ibid., 195.

42. *U.S. v. Marc Rich, et al. 83 Cr. 579 (SWK) (8.D.N.Y.)*

43. A. Craig Copetas, *Metal Men: How Marc Rich Defrauded the Country, Evaded the Law, and Became the World's Most Sought-After Corporate Criminal*, (New York: Perennial, 2001), 196.

44. Bo'az Ga'on, "Rich as Korach, Ma'ariv," *Weekend Magazine*, October 1, 1999.

45. Jim Hougan, "King of the World; Marc Rich," *Playboy*, February 1994.

46.   Ibid.

47.   Marc Rich, letter to Ruth H. Van Heuven, US consul general, Zurich, Switzerland, dated October 27, 1992.

48.   Eran Tiffenbraun and Mody Kreitman, "Exposé: Using Pollard to Get Rich," *Yediot Achronot*, February 23, 2001.

49.   Minister of Interior, Immigration and Justice, Republic of Bolivia, letter to US Consul General, dated September 9, 1983.

50.   Bo'az Ga'on, "Rich as Korach, Ma'ariv," *Weekend Magazine*, October 1, 1999.

51.   Ibid.

52.   Alison Leigh Cowan, "Plotting a Pardon; Rich Cashed in a World of Chits to Win Pardon," *New York Times*, April 11, 2001.

53.   Kathleen A. Behan with Arnold & Porter, letter to Marc Rich, dated July 21, 1999.

54.   John Mintz, "Clinton Reverses 5-Year Ban on Lobbying by Appointees," *Washington Post*, December 29, 2000.

55.   Executive Clemency, Code of Federal Regulations, 28 C.F.R. §§ 1.1 to 1.11.

56.   Morris Weinberg, testimony before the House Committee on Government Reform and Oversight, February 8, 2001.

57.   US Pardon Attorney, letter addressed to Lonnie Anne Pera, Esq., in the case of Fernando Fuentes Coba.

58.   Roger C. Adams, prepared remarks before the Committee on the Judiciary, US Senate, February 14, 2001.

59.   Michael Dobbs, "Rich Made His Fortune by Breaking the Rules," *Washington Post*, March 13, 2001.

60.   Ibid.

61.   Marcia Vickers, "The Rich Boys; An Ultra-Secretive Network Rules Independent Oil Trading. Its Mentor: Marc Rich," *Business Week*, July 18, 2005.

62.   Gordon Pitts, "'King of Zug' Reigns over Trading Network; Controversial Marc Rich Has Long Been a Part of the Buying and Selling of the World's Mineral Wealth," *The Globe and Mail*, August 16, 2005.

63. Barbara Olson, *The Final Days: The Last, Desperate Abuses of Power by the Clinton White House*, (Washington, DC: Regnery, 2001), 141.

64. Kenneth R. Bazinet, "Bill: Those I Pardoned 'Paid in Full'," *Daily News*, January 22, 2001.

65. Marc Rich letter to Ruth H. Van Heuven, US consul general, Zurich, Switzerland, dated October 27, 1992.

66. Ed McCullough, "War Protester Yearns to Come Home," *Los Angeles Times*, March 18, 2001.

67. Ibid.

68. William J. Clinton, *My Life*, (New York: Alfred A. Knopf, 2004), 941.

69. Aaron Tonken, *King of Cons*, (Nashville, TN: Nelson Current, 2004), 327.

70. R. Emmett Tyrrell Jr., *The Clinton Crack-Up: The Boy President's Life After the White House*, (Nashville, TN: Thomas Nelson, 2007), 84.

71. Aaron Tonken, *King of Cons*, (Nashville, TN: Nelson Current, 2004), 251.

72. Maureen Dowd, "In Marc Rich's Case, Bill and Hill Were Manipulated," *Hamilton Spectator*, February 12, 2001.

73. Bob Franken, "Marc Rich Pardon: Congressional Hearings on Controversial Clinton Decision Continue," CNN, February 8, 2001, accessed May 3, 2007, http://transcripts.cnn.com/TRANSCRIPTS/0102/08/se.13.html.

74. July 15, 1998, check in the amount $250,000; August 7, 1999, check in the amount $100,000; and May 11, 2000, check in the amount $100,000.

75. Kenneth R. Bazinet, "Bill: Those I Pardoned 'Paid in Full'," *Daily News*, January 22, 2001.

76. Barbara Olson, *The Final Days: The Last, Desperate Abuses of Power by the Clinton White House*, (Washington, DC: Regnery, 2001), 138.

77. Timothy P. Carney, "The Story of Clinton's Marc Rich Pardon," WorldNetDaily.com, February 5, 2001.

78. Dick Morris, *Rewriting History*, (New York: Regan Books, 2004), 179.

79. Aaron Tonken, *King of Cons*, (Nashville, TN: Nelson Current, 2004), 250-3.

80. Alison Leigh Cowan, "Plotting a Pardon; Rich Cashed in a World of Chits to Win Pardon," *New York Times*, April 11, 2001.

81. Alison Leigh Cowan, "Documents Show a Complex Campaign to Win a Pardon," *New York Times*, February 10, 2001.

82. Alison Leigh Cowan, "Rich Pardon Reportedly Followed Pledge to Charity of Former Wife," *New York Times*, May 1, 2001.

83. Aaron Tonken, *King of Cons*, (Nashville, TN: Nelson Current, 2004), 258.

84. "Being Rich; Denise Rich Denying Her Contributions to the Clintons Bought Her Fugitive Ex-Husband's Pardon," *20/20*, ABC, April 27, 2001.

85. Morris Weinberg, testimony before the House Committee on Government Reform and Oversight, February 8, 2001.

86. Barbara Olson, *The Final Days: The Last, Desperate Abuses of Power by the Clinton White House*, (Washington, DC: Regnery, 2001), 65.

87. Carl Bernstein, *A Woman in Charge: The Life of Hillary Rodham Clinton*, (New York: Alfred A. Knopf, 2007), 546.

88. Dick Morris, *Rewriting History*, (New York: Regan Books, 2004), 178.

89. "Clinton Library Gets $8.4 Million in 2000," *New York Times*, August 23, 2001.

90. William J. Clinton, "My Reason for the Pardon," *New York Times*, February 18, 2001.

91. Morris Weinberg, testimony before the House Committee on Government Reform and Oversight, February 8, 2001.

92. William J. Clinton, *My Life*, (New York: Alfred A. Knopf, 2004), 941.

93. Ibid.

94. Alison Leigh Cowan, "Panel Says Top Justice Dept. Aide Held Information on Rich's Pardon," *New York Times*, March 13, 2002.

95. Eran Tiffenbraun and Mody Kreitman, "Exposé: Using Pollard to Get Rich," *Yediot Achronot*, February 23, 2001.

96. Jake Tapper, "Anatomy of a Pardon," Salon.com, February 13, 2001, accessed May 12, 2007, https://www.salon.com/2001/02/14/email_2/.

97. Jonathan S. Tobin, "A Matter of Opinion: Did the Jews Make Him Do It? Clinton's Pardon of Marc Rich Puts Israeli and American Jewish Leaders on the Spot," *Jewish Exponent*, February 22, 2001.

98. Zev Chafets, "Jewish Leaders Unpardonable Role," *Daily News*, February 15, 2001.

99. Beth J. Harpaz, "Jews Divided over Rich Pardon," *Associated Press*, March 29, 2001.

100. Michael Isikoff, "'I Made a Mistake'; The ADL's Abe Foxman Admits the Jewish Organization Received a $100,000 Grant from Marc Rich but Maintains He Wasn't 'Bought,'" *Newsweek*, March 23, 2001.

101. Julie Wiener and Matthew E. Berger, "Charity at a Price," *The Jerusalem Post*, February 16, 2001.

102. Delinda C. Hanley, "From the Jewish Press: Jewish Pressure on Clinton Moves Fugitive Marc Rich from 'Most Wanted' to 'Most Want to Forget' List," *Washington Report on Middle East Affairs*, April 30, 2001.

103. Alison Leigh Cowan, "Some Used in Pardon Effort Were Unaware of the Purpose," *New York Times*, January 26, 2001.

104. Beth J. Harpaz, "Jewish Group Says Rich Representatives Sought Pardon Help for Money," *Associated Press*, March 28, 2001.

105. Alison Leigh Cowan, "Some Used in Pardon Effort Were Unaware of the Purpose," *New York Times*, January 26, 2001.

106. Alison Leigh Cowan, "Plotting a Pardon; Rich Cashed in a World of Chits to Win Pardon," *New York Times*, April 11, 2001.

107. R. Emmett Tyrrell Jr., *The Clinton Crack-Up: The Boy President's Life After the White House*, (Nashville, TN: Thomas Nelson, 2007), 47.

Chapter 13

1. Patrice O'Shaughnessy, "Pardon of Radical Enrages 2 Families," *Daily News*, February 18, 2001.

2. Telephone interview of Edward O'Grady Jr. by Mark Hyman, 24 January 2008.

3. Ron Jacobs, *The Way the Wind Blew: A History of the Weather Underground*, (New York: Verso, 1997), 13.

4. Federal Bureau of Investigation (Chicago Field Office), "Foreign Influence—Weather Underground Organization," (WUO) CG 100-40903, classified Top Secret, August 20, 1976, 3.

5.   "Terrorism: Review of 1988 and the Prospects for 1989," press briefing at George Washington University, The Elliott School of International Affairs, December 19, 1988.

6.   Federal Bureau of Investigation (Chicago Field Office), "Foreign Influence—Weather Underground Organization," (WUO) CG 100-40903, classified Top Secret, August 20, 1976, 284.

7.   Sarah Anderson, "Blast from the Past: The UW in the Riotous 1960s and '70s," *The Daily*, January 18, 2007.

8.   "And Now for the Rest of the Story," *Washington Post*, March 17, 1990. Editorial.

9.   Douglas Robinson, "Townhouse Razed by Blast and Fire; Man's Body Found," *New York Times*, March 7, 1970.

10.   Ibid.

11.   Peter McGrath et al, "Return of the Weatherman," *Newsweek*, November 2, 1981.

12.   Huey P. Newton, *To Die for the People: The Writings of Huey P. Newton*, (New York: Random House, 1972), 25.

13.   Lee Lockwood, *Conversation with Eldridge Cleaver: Algiers*, (New York: Delta, 1970), 54.

14.   Ruth-Marion Baruch and Pirkle Jones, *The Vanguard: A Photographic Essay on the Black Panthers*, (Boston: Beacon Press, 1970), 17.

15.   John Castellucci, *The Big Dance: The Untold Story of Kathy Boudin and the Terrorist Family That Committed the Brinks Robbery Murders*, (New York: Dodd, Mead & Company, 1986), 220.

16.   Ibid., 154.

17.   Claudia Wallis, "Bullets from the Underground," *Time*, November 2, 1981.

18.   John Castellucci, *The Big Dance: The Untold Story of Kathy Boudin and the Terrorist Family That Committed the Brinks Robbery Murders*, (New York: Dodd, Mead & Company, 1986), 253.

19.   Ibid., 41.

20.   "Agents Search for Four Men in Fatal Robbery," *Associated Press*, June 3, 1981.

21. John Castellucci, *The Big Dance: The Untold Story of Kathy Boudin and the Terrorist Family That Committed the Brinks Robbery Murders*, (New York: Dodd, Mead & Company, 1986), 162.

22. "Brinks Offers a Reward Of $100,000 in Killing," *New York Times*, June 4, 1981.

23. John Castellucci, *The Big Dance: The Untold Story of Kathy Boudin and the Terrorist Family That Committed the Brinks Robbery Murders*, (New York: Dodd, Mead & Company, 1986), 297.

24. Steve Lieberman, "Brinks Radical Seeks Clemency," *Westchester County Journal News*, October 19, 2000.

25. John Castellucci, *The Big Dance: The Untold Story of Kathy Boudin and the Terrorist Family That Committed the Brinks Robbery Murders*, (New York: Dodd, Mead & Company, 1986), 296.

26. Robert D. McFadden, "FBI Asserts Fugitives Had a Network of 'Safe Houses,'" *New York Times*, May 13, 1985.

27. "The Rosenberg Case; Susan Rosenberg Believes She Is Being Kept in Prison for a Crime She Was Never Tried For," *60 Minutes*, December 17, 2000.

28. John Castellucci, *The Big Dance: The Untold Story of Kathy Boudin and the Terrorist Family That Committed the Brinks Robbery Murders*, (New York: Dodd, Mead & Company, 1986), 261.

29. Paul Moses, "Insider Testifies at Radicals' Trial," *Associated Press*, June 19, 1983.

30. John Castellucci, *The Big Dance: The Untold Story of Kathy Boudin and the Terrorist Family That Committed the Brinks Robbery Murders*, (New York: Dodd, Mead & Company, 1986), 274.

31. "New Indictment Broadens Charges Against Brink's Suspects," *Associated Press*, September 21, 1982.

32. Aidan Conway et al, *Upping the Anti, a Journal of Theory and Action, Number Five*, (Ontario: Thistle Printing, 2007), 165.

33. John Castellucci, *The Big Dance: The Untold Story of Kathy Boudin and the Terrorist Family That Committed the Brinks Robbery Murders*, (New York: Dodd, Mead & Company, 1986), 281.

34. Ibid., 142.

35. Peter J. Sampson, *United Press International*, December 12, 1984.

36. John Castellucci, *The Big Dance: The Untold Story of Kathy Boudin and the Terrorist Family That Committed the Brinks Robbery Murders*, (New York: Dodd, Mead & Company, 1986), 295.

37. Ibid., 296.

38. Benjamin Weiser, "Former Terrorist Now Fights for Parole," *New York Times*, November 5, 1999.

39. Mike McIntyre, "Inmates of Danbury's Federal Prison Draw International Support," *Hartford Courant*, January 22, 1997.

40. Steve Lieberman, "Brinks Radical Seeks Clemency," *Westchester County Journal News*, October 19, 2000.

41. Steve Lieberman, "Police, Residents Remember Two Officers Who Were Slain During '81 Brinks Robbery," *Westchester County Journal News*, October 21, 2000.

42. Ibid.

43. "The Rosenberg Case; Susan Rosenberg Believes She Is Being Kept in Prison for a Crime She Was Never Tried For," *60 Minutes*, December 17, 2000.

44. John Castellucci, "Suspect in Brinks Robbery Seeks Clemency from Clinton," *Providence Journal-Bulletin*, December 26, 2000.

45. "The Rosenberg Case; Susan Rosenberg Believes She Is Being Kept in Prison for a Crime She Was Never Tried For," *60 Minutes*, December 17, 2000.

46. Ibid.

47. Kathleen McGrory, "Artist-in-Residence Withdraws from Teaching Course at Hamilton College," *University Wire*, December 23, 2004.

48. James Pinkerton, "Still on the Run; Now 54 and a Grandmother, '60s Radical from Austin Remains on FBI's Wanted List," *Houston Chronicle*, October 29, 1995.

49. Ibid.

50. Robert D. McFadden, "F.A.L.N. Puerto Rican Terrorists Suspected in New Year Bombings," *New York Times*, January 2, 1983.

51. James Pinkerton, "Still on the Run; Now 54 and a Grandmother, '60s Radical from Austin Remains on FBI's Wanted List," *Houston Chronicle*, October 29, 1995.

52. James Rowley, "Kunstler Says Case Is Political Effort to Silence Dissent," *Associated Press*, June 24, 1988.

53. Susan Rosenberg, *An American Radical: Political Prisoner in My Own Country*, (New York: Citadel Press Books, 2011), 19.

54. Deborah Orin et al, "Nadler, Rabbi Behind Pardon for '81 Brink's Slaying Suspect," *New York Post*, January 23, 2001.

55. Hillary Rodham Clinton, *Living History*, (New York: Simon & Schuster, 2003), 38.

56. Marion K. Sanders, *The Professional Radical: Conversations with Saul Alinsky*, (New York: Harper & Row, 1970), 18.

57. Ibid., 89.

58. Joyce Milton, *The First Partner: Hillary Rodham Clinton*, (New York: William Morrow and Company, 1999), 22.

59. Marion K. Sanders, *The Professional Radical: Conversations with Saul Alinsky*, (New York: Harper & Row, 1970), 74-6.

60. Ibid., 79.

61. Saul D. Alinsky, *Rules for Radicals*, (New York: Vintage, 1971), 130.

62. Ibid., 133.

63. Huey P. Newton, *To Die for the People: The Writings of Huey P. Newton*, (New York: Random House, 1972), 84.

64. Eldridge Cleaver, *Soul on Ice*, (New York: Ramparts Books, 1992), 127.

65. Marion K. Sanders, *The Professional Radical: Conversations with Saul Alinsky*, (New York: Harper & Row, 1970), 82.

66. Ibid., 82.

67. Huey P. Newton, *To Die for the People: The Writings of Huey P. Newton*, (New York: Random House, 1972), 93-4.

68. Lee Lockwood, *Conversation with Eldridge Cleaver: Algiers*, (New York: Delta, 1970), 45.

69. Marion K. Sanders, *The Professional Radical: Conversations with Saul Alinsky*, (New York: Harper & Row, 1970), 83-4.

70.   Hillary D. Rodham, "There Is Only the Fight…An Analysis of the Alinsky Model," (Thesis Paper), May 2, 1969.

71.   Carl Bernstein, *A Woman in Charge: The Life of Hillary Rodham Clinton*, (New York: Alfred A. Knopf, 2007), 83.

72.   Hillary Rodham Clinton, *Living History*, (New York: Simon & Schuster, 2003), 44.

73.   Huey P. Newton, *To Die for the People: The Writings of Huey P. Newton*, (New York: Random House, 1972), 25.

74.   Lee Lockwood, *Conversation with Eldridge Cleaver: Algiers*, (New York: Delta, 1970), 54.

75.   Ibid., 56.

76.   Ibid., 65.

77.   Huey P. Newton, *To Die for the People: The Writings of Huey P. Newton*, (New York: Random House, 1972), 190.

78.   Eldridge Cleaver, *Soul on Ice*, (New York: Ramparts Books, 1992), 26.

79.   Lee Lockwood, *Conversation with Eldridge Cleaver: Algiers*, (New York: Delta, 1970), 115.

80.   Huey P. Newton, *To Die for the People: The Writings of Huey P. Newton*, (New York: Random House, 1972), 85.

81.   Marion K. Sanders, *The Professional Radical: Conversations with Saul Alinsky*, (New York: Harper & Row, 1970), 85

82.   Ibid., 86

83.   Saul D. Alinsky, *Rules for Radicals*, (New York: Vintage, 1971), xvii.

84.   Huey P. Newton, *To Die for the People: The Writings of Huey P. Newton*, (New York: Random House, 1972), 178.

85.   Ibid., 201.

86.   Joyce Milton, *The First Partner: Hillary Rodham Clinton*, (New York: William Morrow and Company, 1999), 35.

87.   Barbara Olson, *Hell to Pay*, (Washington, DC: Regnery, 1999), 54.

88.   Hillary Rodham Clinton, *Living History*, (New York: Simon & Schuster, 2003), 45.

89.   Joyce Milton, *The First Partner: Hillary Rodham Clinton*, (New York: William Morrow and Company, 1999), 37.

90. Huey P. Newton, *To Die for the People: The Writings of Huey P. Newton*, (New York: Random House, 1972), 226.

91. Joyce Milton, *The First Partner: Hillary Rodham Clinton*, (New York: William Morrow and Company, 1999), 38.

92. Dick Morris, *Rewriting History*, (New York: Regan Books, 2004), 107.

93. Hillary Rodham Clinton, *Living History*, (New York: Simon & Schuster, 2003), 44.

94. Barbara Olson, *Hell to Pay*, (Washington, DC: Regnery, 1999), 59-60.

95. R. Emmett Tyrrell Jr., *The Clinton Crack-Up: The Boy President After the White House*, (Nashville, TN: Thomas Nelson, 2007), 62-4.

96. Gary Aldrich, *Unlimited Access: An FBI Agent Inside the Clinton White House*, (Washington, DC: Regnery, 1996), 139.

97. Carl Bernstein, *A Woman in Charge: The Life of Hillary Rodham Clinton*, (New York: Alfred A. Knopf, 2007), 280.

98. Huey P. Newton, *To Die for the People: The Writings of Huey P. Newton*, (New York: Random House, 1972), 173.

99. Robert "Buzz" Patterson, *Dereliction of Duty: The Eyewitness Account of How Bill Clinton Compromised America's National Security*, (New York: Regnery, 2003), 85.

ACKNOWLEDGMENTS

THE PUBLISHING OF *Pardongate* occurred very quickly considering I will have two books published in less than a year. This is not what normally happens. My previous book, *Washington Babylon*, went on sale fourteen months after I signed the contract with the publisher and many thought that was a quick turnaround. Those fourteen months included all the research, writing, editing, proofreading, publishing, and distribution.

Pardongate will go on sale a mere four months after I signed the book contract. This is because the research and writing of this book was completed long before I signed the contract in early 2020. I had written the manuscript thirteen years earlier in 2007. My agent at the time shopped the book to countless publishers, including the biggest in the business. No one was interested. A publishing industry insider told me I would not get the book published because it was assumed Hillary Clinton would run for and be elected president the following year. "They only want books that genuflect to Hillary," he told me. Obviously, he was right.

In early 2020, I figuratively dusted off the manuscript and literally dusted off several bankers boxes of research material and updated the entire book. The rest is in the hands of the public.

I am thankful to Anthony Ziccardi, publisher of Post Hill Press, who offered to publish this book even though sales of *Washington Babylon* did not meet our expectations. The good news is *Washington Babylon* is still available for purchase!

I sincerely appreciate the work of my managing editor Madeline "Maddie" Sturgeon who steered this process magnificently and had the right touch at all times. I would also like to thank editor Kate Post for making appropriate suggestions and challenging details, when warranted. Of course, I must thank R. Emmett "Bob" Tyrrell, Jr. whose friendship I value and who agreed for a second time in less than a year to write a foreword for me even though he was in the middle of writing his own book.

The folks I thanked in *Washington Babylon* for encouraging me to write truly deserve thanks for *Pardongate*. This was my first effort after their prodding, encouraging, cajoling, and lecturing me to write. My sincerest thanks to John Bilotta, Richard Miniter, and Thomas Lipscomb.

I must give a shout out to Nimitz Library at the US Naval Academy and the Anne Arundel County Public Library system. They had or were able to get on loan every single book I needed. The Library of Congress was another valuable resource.

Each day I think of the Johns Hopkins three and I say a little prayer for them.

I will end these acknowledgements in the same manner in which I have ended hundreds of live TV news specials. I give thanks and share my gratitude to our military, law enforcement, firefighters, EMTs, and other emergency personnel for their service to our communities and our nation.

ABOUT THE AUTHOR

Author photo by Monumental Arts

MARK HYMAN IS an Emmy Award-winning, investigative journalist who knows how to get the critical details of a story. In more than forty years, his life experiences include naval officer, veteran, intelligence officer, weapons inspector, Congressional Fellow, lobbyist, business executive, writer, radio personality, television host, and investigative journalist.

Whether it was inspecting Soviet-made weapons systems, reporting from a war zone, walking the halls of Congress, or one of his other many life experiences, Mark has gained keen insight into what constitutes a great story that must be told. What sets his storytelling apart from others is that he adds context, when appropriate, so the readers not only learn the who, what, when, and where, but also the why.